LAW FOR GCSE

FOURTH EDITION

Peter She... ...B, LLM

Director of Legal Studie...

Advisory editor
Paulene Coll...

Barrister, formerly Head...
at Staffordshire Univers...

Former chief examiner... ...ard and
the University of Lond...

LONGMAN

Addison Wesley Longman Limited
Edinburgh Gate, Harlow
Essex CM20 2JE, England
and Associated Companies around the World

First published in 1987
Second edition 1990
Third edition 1994
Fourth edition 1998
Second impression 1999

ISBN 0582 318920

20 00001 855

Typeset by Longman Malaysia Limited
Printed in Singapore (COS)

The Publishers' policy is to use paper manufactured from sustainable forests

CONTENTS

PREFACE

It is always a mistake to take your eye off the ball. In the years since the last
edition of this book, much has changed. In just about every area covered by
this text, the law has been developed by the courts and by Parliament. The
party in government has changed—after the best part of two decades. In this
new edition I have tried to track the changes we have seen and spot the key
developments to come.

The examination questions for GCSE Law tend to be compilations of
short questions and interpretative exercises drawn upon statements of one
kind or another. In this new edition I have included a number of 'indicative'
questions which represent the kind of thing students might expect as
'shorter' questions, together with examples of the questions that were set by
the major Examining Boards in 1996 and 1997.

I owe debts of gratitude to Paulene Collins for her encouragement and
support, to Bill Cole, Steven Hudson and Michael Prout for lending me their
expertise, and to the publishers for their patience.

I have stated the law as I believe it to be on a surprisingly sunny autumn
afternoon in 1997.

Saltash
Cornwall   Peter Shears

Acknowledgements

The author and publisher would also like to thank the following examination
boards for permission to use questions from their examination papers:
LEAG/Edexcel
NEAB/SEG/Assessment & Qualification Alliance
Welsh Joint Eduction Committee

TABLE OF CASES

v

TABLE OF STATUTES

CHAPTER 1

What is Law?

DEFINING THE LAW

It's a bit like defining an elephant. You may have trouble constructing an acceptable definition of law, but you would recognise a law if you saw one.

The law is a civilising influence within a society. Some writers have argued that the progress of a society towards a civilisation can be measured by the sophistication of its legal systems. As the society becomes more complex then the system of rules develops, along with the machinery for enforcing those rules effectively.

This is not to say that the rules necessarily reflect the developed wisdom or morality within society. Law and morality are not necessarily linked. Obviously, if there were little or no reflection of the popular view within the law, then respect for the law would be lost, but the great moral debates within a society do not necessarily result in legal reform.

One such issue centres on the 'sanctity of life'. This is reflected in debates on capital punishment and abortion, on suicide, euthanasia, on so-called mercy killings and on nuclear arms, chemical weapons and so on. Another emphasis lies on the 'quality of life'; in discussions about family relationships, the ease and availability of divorce, adultery, 'latch-key' children, pornography, the spread of vile video cassettes, the mysteries of the Internet, and so on.

While a single debate might stimulate a reform of the law, the dynamic of discussion and debate within a society, continually developing, and re-evaluating moral standpoints, has no essential link with law and law reform. A definition of law ought to assist understanding of law. It ought to be an aid to elucidation. But there is no generally accepted definition. It could be described as a set of rules we live by that prescribes rights and duties, responsibilities and obligations for every member of the society we live in. These rules not only provide limits to what we can and cannot do, but they also prescribe the manner in which various ends can be achieved, for example, making a will.

Tighter definitions abound. Each reflects the attitude of its author towards the function of the law. Examples include: 'a coercive order of human behaviour' (Kelsen), 'a body of principles' (Salmond), 'rules of action' (Blackstone), 'prophesies of what the courts will do' (Holmes), 'what officials do about disputes' (Llewellyn).

The law must have something to do with rules and their enforcement. Some of these rules rely for their effectiveness upon the individual involved. For instance, if a toaster does not work properly the buyer should assert his rights within the contract by means of which he acquired it. Thus if the person trying to make toast for breakfast was the recipient of the toaster as a birthday present the buyer should complain. Only the parties to a contract can enforce it. Other rules will be enforced no matter what the individual wants. The victim of incest will not have the final say as to whether the offender is prosecuted. The client after a successful, hygienic, but unlawful abortion may be the last person to wish the offender punished—but the decision rests elsewhere. These differing aspects of the nature and purpose of the law must each be appreciated clearly.

This book is about English law. The Scots are a law unto themselves, and the Scottish legal system is also different. So too, although to a lesser extent, is the legal system in Northern Ireland. There are considerable and increasing overlaps between these legal systems within the United Kingdom as a whole. But for the purposes of this book no rule should be assumed to extend beyond England and Wales.

CLASSIFYING THE LAW

To understand how the legal system fits together, it may be useful to examine a variety of ways in which it can be taken apart and each part examined. That is, there are several possible ways to classify the law.

Civil and Criminal law

This is the most basic of classifications. Very broadly, criminal law is concerned with the general well being and civil law with individual rights and duties. It might be wrong, however, to classify an individual act as being either a civil or a criminal wrong. Many acts are both. For example, if you take your coat to be cleaned and the cleaner steals it then, clearly, the crime of theft has been committed. Furthermore there is a breach of the contract to clean and a tort of conversion (denial of your right to your property) has also been committed. It is not in the act itself that the distinction lies, but in the consequences which may follow from it. After you have been run over in a road accident the driver could be arrested and charged with the crime of dangerous driving and he could be sued by you, the victim, in the tort of negligence. The act of driving so as to injure you was therefore a criminal offence and a civil wrong. This is sometimes called 'dual liability'.

There have been attempts made at defining crime generally, but the criminal law really comprises nothing more than the total of those activities which those responsible for creating and developing the criminal law have seen fit to include. Lord Atkin said (in *Proprietary Articles v. Attorney-General for Canada* (1931)):

The domain of criminal jurisprudence can only be ascertained by examining what acts at any particular period are declared by the State to be crimes and the only common nature they will be found to possess is that they are prohibited by the State and that those who commit them are punished.

The nature of criminal liability will be considered in more detail later (Chapter 15), but the activities embraced by the criminal law extend from treason, murder and rape at one end to exporting antiques without a licence, flying a kite near an airfield, 'feeding' parking meters, failing to sign your driving licence, sounding the car horn while the car is at rest and conversing with a bus driver at the other.

Similarly, various aspects of civil law will be drawn out in more detail in subsequent chapters, but it should be understood that while the criminal law comprises most of what the average citizen imagines as the law (at least at first), the civil law is a vast thing—a thousand years old and still growing The more important areas within its scope include contract law, which in its applied aspects includes the sale of goods and services, credit, hire-purchase, agency, contracts of employment and landlord and tenant agreements—to name but a few. The civil law also includes the law of tort—an umbrella term for actions in negligence, nuisance, defamation, trespass and others. Further, it includes property law, the law of succession, most of family law and the law of trusts.

Later (Chapters 6 and 7) attention will be drawn to the nature of proceedings in civil and criminal law. They are easily distinguished: the procedure is different; the point of the proceedings is different; the outcome is different. These distinctions are marked with differences in the terminology used. It is an elementary error to confuse the terminology and say, for example, 'trespassers will be prosecuted' for they cannot be (except in rare instances such as squatting or where byelaws have made trespass criminal, e.g. on the railways). Trespass is (generally) a tort. Tort is civil law. In civil proceedings the plaintiff sues the defendant. If he succeeds he obtains judgment in his favour and he will be awarded a remedy, the point of which is to compensate him for the civil wrong which the defendant has been shown on a balance of probabilities to have done him. This remedy may take the form of an order that the defendant pay the plaintiff money (damages) or perform a contractual obligation (decree of specific performance) or desist from infringing the plaintiff's civil law rights (injunction) or transfer property to him. There are other civil remedies too.

Criminal proceedings, on the other hand, involve the prosecutor prosecuting the accused (or the defendant) so as to prove him guilty beyond reasonable doubt (so that the bench of magistrates or the jury, if there is one, are sure) and thus secure a conviction and a sentence, the point of which is to punish the convicted person and to deter him and others from such activity in the future. The range of punishment is wide. It extends from conditional discharges and even absolute discharges at the one end to life imprisonment at the other. (It might be an interesting exercise to check whether capital punishment has been completely abolished.) The power of the court varies from offence to offence and indeed from court to court within the hierarchy of the court system. This range of possible sentences will be examined more closely later (Chapter 7).

Private and Public law

Civil law is sometimes called private law for the obvious reason of its content. It is the law concerned with private individuals and their rights and duties, voluntarily assumed or otherwise, towards other private individuals. In contrast is sometimes taken public law. This is a wider concept than criminal law, but it includes criminal law. Also included are constitutional, administrative and social welfare law. Together these four elements comprise that law which has a public, overall, character.

Constitutional law

Constitutional law, the law of the British constitution, is often said to be unwritten in the sense that there is no single document in Britain called 'The Constitution'. However, every British protectorate and colony has one, and so does nearly every country in the world. The reasons for this state of affairs are historical. There has been no fresh start after a revolution or other landmark in our history, unlike in the United States or Malaysia. Nevertheless, there are many documents from which the British constitutional law can be collected. There are Acts of Parliament, like the Bill of Rights 1689, the Act of Settlement 1701, the Act of Union with Scotland 1707 and the European Communities Act of 1972, all of which contain major rules of constitutional law. Rules of more detailed importance are to be found in such statutes as the Representation of the People Acts 1983 and 1985, the Peerage Act 1963, the Parliament Acts of 1911 and 1949 and the Local Government Act 1988, among many others. It seems that every year statutes are made which add to the constitutional law. Indeed, after the referendum votes in September 1997 it seems likely that fundamental changes may be made in the near future.

Further to this the law is found in common law rules such as the fundamental rule which pronounces that Parliament is sovereign, a rule now affected by the European Communities Act 1972. Furthermore there is a collection of conventions which applies to the constitution and there are the residual powers within the royal prerogative. Finally there exists the law and custom of Parliament itself, concerning its functions, procedures, privileges and immunities. This, then, is the subject matter of constitutional law.

Administrative law

Administrative law is concerned with public authorities. It comprises the law relating to the formation, powers and duties of such authorities and the procedures involved when they are formed or where their powers are exercised, or duties fulfilled. It is also concerned with the relationships between such public authorities, between the authorities and their employers and between them and the public at large.

Administrative law can be seen as a network of controls over the use of public powers, but it also provides the means by which the workload of public authorities can be successfully achieved. It provides the means for getting things done.

The public authorities in question extend from the Crown through the nationalised industries, the Commission for Racial Equality, ACAS (the Advisory, Conciliation and Arbitration Service), the BBC and Independent Television Commission local government, the Equal Opportunities Commission, and many others, including the maze of administrative tribunals set up, among other things, to settle disputes about the use of public power.

Social welfare law

Social welfare law is a relatively recent arrival on the scene of public law. Lord Scarman has written:

> Social security is now the subject of rights and duties. Inevitably, therefore, it is a legal subject.

In 1942 the famous Beveridge Report on social insurance and allied services was published. It described the aims of the social security system as the fulfilment of need and the purpose of payments made within its stunningly detailed rules and regulations as being:

> . . . to abolish want by ensuring that every citizen willing to serve according to his powers has at all times an income sufficient to meet his responsibilities.

The McCarthy Report in 1972 in New Zealand stated a slightly different aim for their social welfare law:

> . . . to ensure that everyone is able to enjoy a standard of living much like that of the rest of the community, and thus is able to feel a sense of participation in and belonging to the community.

Whatever the aims, and whether or not it is successful as a means of achieving them, social welfare law is concerned with the nature of contributory and non-contributory benefits (i.e. whether or not the claimant is paid according to a record of input into the system), unemployment benefit and benefits for sickness, disability, invalidity, maternity, children, and death. It covers compensation for industrial injuries, pensions on retirement and for war service. Finally, it is concerned, increasingly these days, with the 'topping up' of income by means of benefits such as income support and family credit. Details of these will be examined later (Chapter 19).

Municipal and public international law

Another way of classifying the law is to split it between municipal and public international law. Municipal law is the law of one state—in our case the United Kingdom. Thus municipal law for this purpose would comprise the law of England and Wales taken together with that of Scotland and that of Northern Ireland. The distinction is drawn between this, the law of a single state, and public international law which regulates dealings between different states and which is largely made up of treaties, conventions and international agreements.

COMMON LAW AND STATUTES

The whole of the law of England and Wales can be split according to where it arose, that is, classified by source. The law is either made by the judges—developing principles case by case, by analogy with earlier cases, along fairly settled lines, as will be examined later (Chapter 3) or it is made in a broad sweep by Parliament by means of statutes (Acts of Parliament). There is, as will be seen (Chapter 3), a prescribed method for the creation of a statute.

Judge-made law is called common law. In theory it is comprised of rules which already exist and simply require pronouncement by the judge. In fact, of course, judicial creativity does exist, although it varies between judges. Acts of Parliament (statutes) sometimes enable others (e.g. ministers, local authorities) to make laws on a very restricted basis. These laws appear as 'rules' or 'regulations' or 'byelaws' and while they are made by others they possess the delegated authority of Parliament. All this law made by or on behalf of Parliament, taken together, is called legislation. Contract law and the law of tort are almost entirely common law while company law and the law of employment have been created almost entirely by means of legislation.

COMMON LAW AND EQUITY

'Common law' is a slippery phrase. It is used to distinguish judge-made law from law made by Parliament. It is also used to distinguish that law originating from the English system as exported to other nations and law made along the lines of Roman law, called civil or civilian law. It is essential to be careful with terminology, not just with the terms used but also with their context. This classification takes the phrase 'common law' yet again and uses it to distinguish the law developed by the judges (as opposed to legislation) and to pick out the law which dates back across the centuries to the old common law courts and that law which (although developed by the judges) dates back to the Court of Chancery (the court from which the modern Chancery Division was developed: see Chapters 2 and 4). This is a body of law called 'equity'. It is important to be able to spot equitable rules and principles and to be able to distinguish them from common law rules and principles. To do this requires some grasp of the history which gave rise to these two systems or strains of law within the English law taken as a whole. This brief look at English legal history will be taken next.

CHAPTER 2

How the Law has Grown

LAW BEFORE THE NORMAN CONQUEST

English law in any overall sense dates back to the Norman Conquest. Before then no unified system of law existed over the country. Indeed the country itself was unrecognisable as the unified whole, with a central government, as is so familiar today.

The picture before the Conquest was one of a country split into shires. The shires were split into hundreds and the hundreds into vills or townships. Life was local. Law was local. It was based on local custom. It was administered in local courts. These were at the hundred level and at the shire level. There were also at about this time courts organised by the local landowners called manorial or seignorial courts.

There were broad laws initiated by the Anglo-Saxon Kings. These were called dooms, but they were not often made. There was a council of advisers around the king, called the Witan, but in as much as it had any judicial function, it served only to settle disputes between the larger landowners. It was a political forum for the few.

LAW AFTER THE CONQUEST

I have persecuted the natives of England beyond all reason. Whether gentle or simple I have cruelly oppresed them; many I have unjustly disinherited; innumerable multitudes perished through me by famine or the sword . . . I fell on the English of the northern shires like a ravening lion. I commanded their houses and corn, with all their implements and chattels, to be burnt without distinction, and great herds of cattle and beasts of burden to be butchered wherever they are found. In this way I took revenge on multitudes of both sexes by subjecting them to the calamity of a cruel famine, and so became the barbarous murderer of many thousands, both young and old, of that fine race of people. Having gained the throne of that kingdom by so many crimes I dare not leave it to anyone but God
William's death-bed confession according to Ordericus Vitalis, c. AD 1130

Some of the effects of the Norman Conquest were to centralise the focus of the legal system, to unify the disparate local customs into one law common to the whole country (common law), and to create the basic structure of the court system which lasted until the late nineteenth century and beyond—but all that took hundreds of years.

It would have been impossible, for example, for the Norman king to abolish the local courts run by the lords of the manor and assume their jurisdiction. There was no legal obstacle, but these courts were an important source of income to the lords and no diminution escaped resistance from them. The central system of courts gradually took over and the manorial courts wasted away—over about 300 years.

An interesting factor in this fading away was the Statute of Gloucester 1278, which provided that no personal action for less than £2 could be commenced in the royal courts. This was an attempt to maintain the jurisdiction and existence of the local courts. However, the common law judges in the royal courts took it to mean that no action for more than £2 could be dealt with by the local courts. So, with the fall in the value of money which would seem inevitable over time, the jurisdiction wasted away.

Another important factor in the centralisation of judicial activity was the emergence and evolution of the writ system.

THE WRIT SYSTEM

A writ was the document necessary to start an action in a royal court. It was a sealed letter, sent in the name of the king, containing instructions for the recipient. For example, if the plaintiff, (the party doing the suing) wanted to obtain redress for injuries to himself or his property, he would pay for the issue of a writ of trespass. The letter would be addressed to the sheriff of the county where the cause of action arose and would command the officer to see to it that the defendant be brought before the royal justices to answer for his actions.

Writs were obtained from the Chancery Writ Office, a department of state. If there was no writ on the register of writs (in stock, as it were) to cover the particular claim the plaintiff wished to bring, then, for an extra fee, the clerks would produce one to fit. However, this rather haphazard manner of law making was largely brought to an end in the thirteenth century. The combined effect of the Provisions of Oxford 1258 and the Statute of Westminster II 1285 was to allow the creation of new writs only where they were very similar to existing ones. Nevertheless, this gradual method of development did provide the basis of much of the common law we have today.

THE CURIA REGIS

In as much as the Anglo–Saxon kings had gathered around their close advisers and friends (the Witan), the Norman kings had a far more formal institution called the Curia Regis or 'King's Court'. The Curia formed the central administration. It comprised the king and his most powerful underlings, the great land barons, and a host of lesser members who gradually became specialised in various areas of administration. The full Curia met several times each year, a scene of great pomp and ceremony, but the administrators met more often. Parliament can be traced back to the larger meetings, the court system to the lesser.

THE ROYAL COURTS AND JUDGES; THE EMERGENCE OF THE COMMON LAW

The royal courts, before which the parties named in the various writs were ordered to appear, were presided over by officials sent from the Curia called itinerant justices. They acquired this name because their journeys were regular and fairly predictable. Unless they were killed by dissatisfied litigants (far from unknown), they would follow the circuits traced most clearly under the reign of Henry II (1159–1189), to whom we owe a great debt for the structure of the legal system. Indeed the circuits survive today, and were in regular use until the early 1970s.

Royal officials had visited locally and extensively for the first time in 1085 and 1086 during the compilation of the 'Domesday Book'—an amazing achievement, without parallel in European history, and only possible in a conquered country. It shows the activity of William I as an administrator and systematiser rather than as a legislator. The original two volumes, and the chest constructed for their preservation, are still to be found in London. In the Middle Ages it was so respected that it was referred to simply as 'The Record'. Every county, every village is described; all the owners and servants were noted; even the livestock was counted. The objects were to establish the rights of the Crown, owner of everything by conquest, and, more importantly, to establish the potential for taxation. The reverence for 'The Record' is thought to underlie the respect still paid to official records kept by the administration and by the courts. Indeed it is not too much of a leap in imagination to see these royal officials, representatives of the king, the apex of the feudal structure of the country, becoming judicial officials, royal justices. They called on a regular basis for administrative and, later, judicial purposes.

The idea of a judge on circuit is very familiar. Even in the worst 'western' films an accused is thrown into jail until the judge visits town. It was much the same with the itinerant justices. While it was a reliable and attractive, although expensive, proposition to have a dispute settled in the royal courts at Westminster, it was a more realistic proposition to have it settled locally and avoid the bother, expense and danger of travel. Thus the royal courts sitting locally became increasingly popular.

The law applied in these local courts was, obviously, the local customary law. Gradually, however, by a process of sifting and choosing between varying local customs found while on circuit, the justices, when meeting together at Westminster (where they were based), gently moulded together the common law, the law common to the whole country.

The process was neither simple nor swift, but it seems largely to have been completed by about 1250 when Henry of Bratton, or Bracton as he is commonly called, the first great writer of English law wrote his *Treatise on the Law of England*. This very important work created the impression of English law as a whole body of connected principles. He cites more than 500 cases of the king's judges. He was a judge himself, working mostly in Devonshire. From his work it is clear to see the emergence of the use of past cases as authority for the result of the case in hand. This is broadly called the doctrine of precedent and is vital to the development of our law today. By this time the king's courts were the arenas for most cases of importance (except those involving ecclesiastical disputes). There were few statutes to hamper the judges and little of the pressure of Parliament (so familiar today) against the orderly development of the law. There are few local customs which deviate from the common law. As the royal courts supplanted the local courts so the common law replaced local customs. Their procedure was better. Trial by jury was developed.

There are few landmark dates, but 1215 is one: the Lateran Council then forbade the involvement of the clergy in the awful trials by ordeal. Since no representative of the Almighty to whom the settlement of the question had been submitted was available, trial by ordeal vanished, to be replaced with trial by jury. The importance of the local courts was further eroded.

The central royal courts at Westminster developed gradually from the administrative functions of the Curia Regis. The first was the Court of Exchequer, which emerged from the tax department of the Curia as the arena for the settlement of revenue disputes although this jurisdiction was widened by various methods. For example, the court obtained jurisdiction to try cases brought over debts by use of a trick (properly called a legal fiction) called *quominus*. It worked like this: A cannot pay money he owes the Exchequer because he has none. However, B owes A money and it is for this reason that A is less able to pay (*quominus* means 'by which the less'). Therefore if the court were to reconcile the dispute over the debt it would be able to enforce the issue of revenue collection, its proper function. The jurisdictional distinctions between the common law courts grew very cloudy.

The next to appear was the Court of Common Pleas, which was basically a court for the adjudication of civil disputes between individuals. This was created by Henry II in answer to a promise in Magna Carta (1215) to have a fixed place for the settlement of 'common pleas'.

The third court was called the Court of King's Bench. It developed from hearings of both civil and criminal matters within the Curia at meetings 'coram rege' ('in the presence of the king'). Apart from civil and criminal work the Court of King's Bench, presumably because of its royal origin, possessed a supervisory jurisdiction over the procedures used (although not strictly the decisions taken) in the other courts.

THE DEVELOPMENT OF EQUITY

By the thirteenth century there were problems in these common law courts. The judges were professional lawyers, whereas before they had been clerics. As lawyers they seemed more devoted to procedural matters than the development of the law and its use to achieve justice in individual cases. So much so that litigants who made procedural errors had their cases dismissed—whatever the depth of injustice they had suffered.

More specifically, many potential litigants were unable to bring actions before the courts because there was no writ on the Register of Writs to match the claim they wished to bring. The creation of entirely new writs had been stopped, so novel actions went unheard. Obviously, to bring an action on the writ closest to the claim amounted to a procedural error, and a waste of time and, importantly, money. Furthermore, even if a suitable writ could be found the only remedy available to the successful plaintiff was damages. The basic common law remedy was, and is, damages. There were plaintiffs for whom damages, a financial award, were inadequate or unsuitable. The plaintiff wanted his property back, not its monetary value. He wanted a persistent infringement of his legal rights stopped, not an award of money to compensate for the interference. In modern terms if your neighbour is playing his Oasis CD as if he were in the middle of a desert, you will not want just damages to compensate you for the noise and inconvenience; you will be looking for an injunction to stop him! For these procedural and substantive reasons there grew a need for an alternative approach.

In a feudal system with a strong centralised administration, the logical avenue of complaint at the shortcomings of the mechanisms provided is towards the centre, to the king. Dissatisfied claimants petitioned the king in person. At first these petitions were dealt with individually by the king and justice was administered by him as the 'fountain of justice', despite the rules and procedures of the courts. Naturally the pressures grew. Equally naturally the work was delegated.

A central figure in the administration, the Curia Regis, was the Chancellor. He was responsible for the Chancery where his clerks issued writs to prospective litigants. He was the logical choice of official to deal with petitions about injustice on behalf of the king.

At first these were dealt with at formal meetings within the Curia. By the mid-fourteenth century petitions were addressed to the Chancellor alone rather than to the king or the Curia. In 1474 there is recorded the first case where the Chancellor issued a decree in his own name rather than in the name of the king. The Court of Chancery had emerged.

Over the years a body of principles developed within this court. This became known as Equity. It was (and is) not a systematic body of law. It was never intended to be so. It was only developed as and when the procedure or the substance or the remedy offered within the common law courts was seen to be inadequate.

As Lord Cowper explained (in *Dudley* v. *Dudley* (1705)):

> Now equity is no part of the law, but a moral virtue, which qualifies, moderates, and reforms the rigour, hardness, and edge of the law, and is a universal truth; it does also assist the law where it is defective and weak in the constitution (which is the life of the law) and defends the law from crafty evasions, delusions, and new subtleties, invented and contrived to evade and delude the common law, whereby such as have undoubted right are made remediless; and this is the office of equity, to support and protect the common law from shifts and crafty contrivances against the justice of the law. Equity therefore does not destroy the law, nor create it, but assist it.

So it is today: there is a supplementary system of law called equity. The most important part of it is the law of trusts. It is no longer necessary to go to a different kind of court to bring an action on, for example, a trust. The court system was radically restructured by the Judicature Acts of 1873–1875. It is true that the work of the courts is split amongst them for administrative convenience, but the necessity to go to court twice for, say, damages as compensation for an infringement of legal rights in the past (common law court) and then an injunction to prevent repetition in the future (court of equity) has gone. The administration of the two systems—the mainstream common law and the supplementary tributary equity—has been merged, although the systems themselves remain separate.

It follows that if a plaintiff is seeking a remedy which lies in the traditional jurisdiction of equity—say an injunction to prevent unlawful behaviour in future, or a decree of specific performance whereby the court will instruct an uncooperative party to a contract to perform his side of the bargain—then that plaintiff must satisfy the same standards which were required by the Chancellor back in the fourteenth century. The award of an equitable remedy lies in the discretion of the court. On the other hand the award of damages in an action based on principles of common law is automatic. The successful plaintiff must get damages if he proves his case (although the amount of money, called the 'quantum' is for the court to decide).

These standards required by the Chancellor included, for example, that the petitioner must have come 'with clean hands'. This means that a petition based on unfairness and injustice by the defendant could not be brought by a plaintiff who himself had acted unfairly or unjustly. Consider, for example, the plaintiff in the case *Overton* v. *Bannister* (1844). Here a minor was entitled to benefit from a trust on attaining full age. She masqueraded herself as having done so, and the trustees paid up. Later when she really did come of age she sued them, asking to be paid again. She could prove her real age. The strict construction of the trust documents might have indicated that she had a right to be paid. However the case concerned the law of trusts, a part of the law of equity developed by the Court of Chancery over the centuries on the basis of justice, fairness and good conscience. Naturally the plaintiff lost.

Another centrally important feature, or maxim, of equity is 'delay defeats equity'. The complaint is of unfairness and injustice and the petition is for a remedy. It is not surprising, then, that the court would (and will) refuse to award an equitable remedy if the plaintiff has delayed making his application. As Lord Camden said (in *Smith* v. *Clay* (1767)):

> A court of equity has always refused its aid to stale demands when a party has slept upon his rights and acquiesced for a great length of time. Nothing can call forth this court into activity but conscience, good faith and reasonable diligence.

In the early days the Court of Chancery acted in inconsistent ways, case by case, each on its merits. Indeed the Chancellor's judgment of fairness and justice varied as between successive holders of the office. So much so that one of the greatest English historical scholars, John Selden (who lived from 1584 to 1654), wrote:

> Equity is a roguish thing, for it varies with the length of the Chancellor's foot.

It would be a mistake to regard equity today as being anything haphazard. It is rooted in a sense of natural justice, but it is staked and tied by the doctrine of precedent and by the laws of evidence and procedure to the same extent as the common law. It is, however, still true to say that whereas the occasion upon which an equitable remedy can be sought is settled, its actual award is still at the discretion of the court.

CHAPTER 3

How the Law is Made: the Sources of Law

HISTORICAL SOURCES

Looking back over English legal history (as we did a little in Chapter 2) it is plain to see that the old local customs found in England at and around the time of the Norman Conquest are the historical source of our common law. They were moulded together, over a period of many years, by the itinerant justices so as to form a recognisable body of law common to the whole country. We also saw (in Chapter 2) that the methods and rulings of the old Court of Chancery can be regarded as the historical source of the supplementary system of law which is called Equity. One of the difficulties in discussing 'sources' of law is that much depends on what you mean by 'sources'—and it is here that we note what Humpty Dumpty said.

These are broad, long-range ideas of historical sources of law. Views can be shorter and more specific. For example, the Criminal Cases Review Commission (CCRC) has been operating since 31 March 1997. This non-departmental public body was set up under the terms of the Criminal Appeal Act 1995 to consider cases referred by the Home Office where there is a question of miscarriage of justice. The creation of the CCRC had been recommended in the 1993 Report of the Royal Commission on Criminal Justice which had been set up on 14 March 1991 by the then Home Secretary in the light of public concern about notorious miscarriages of justice such as that involving the 'Birmingham Six'. So here the 1993 Report was a historical source of the 1995 Act.

LITERARY SOURCES

These are sometimes called information sources. The literary source of any law is where we go to find it written down. It might be within an Act of Parliament. Old Acts are published in the Statutes of the Realm (1235–1713), the Statutes Revised (1235–1948) and in other works. New statutes are published by Her Majesty's Stationery Office (HMSO) as and when they are passed. It is important to look over a few Acts, to become familiar with the layout and (sometimes strange) terminology which is used. An example is shown on p. 16.

If the law is not within an Act, then it might be traceable to the judgment in a particular case. It will be necessary to look up the decision in the law reports. There are a number of such reports published. The most authoritative are those produced under the auspices of the Incorporated Council of Law Reporting, called the 'Law Reports', and the 'Weekly Law Reports', although there are also many reliable reports published by others. The best known are the 'All England Law Reports'. Law reports are a record of what the judge actually said in the case. They make interesting reading.

LEGAL SOURCES

The phrase 'legal sources of law' seems a little circular. The legal source of law is that characteristic of it which makes it more than just a rule which can be followed or not. It is the source which gives the law its legal validity and quality. It makes the rule binding as law. R. J. Walker described the legal sources as 'the gates through which new principles can find entrance into the law'. The big 'gates' are legislation and case law. There are some smaller 'gates' too.

LEGISLATION

Legislation comprises Acts of Parliament, often called statutes, together with various rules, regulations and byelaws which are made by others with the authority of Parliament delegated to them by Act of Parliament. Collectively, this law is called delegated legislation.

An Act of Parliament always begins with the same words:

> Be it enacted by the Queen's most Excellent Majesty, by and with the advice and consent of the Lords Spiritual and Temporal, and Commons, in this present Parliament assembled, and by the authority of the same as follows:

What follows is law.

The Protection from Harassment Act 1997, shown on page 16, is an example. It was introduced to deal with the notorious practice of 'stalking' but it also contains the potential to cover a range of other matters, including the kind of intrusive journalism that was so widely discussed after the tragic death of Diana, Princess of Wales in September 1997.

An Act might have been created for any of several purposes. Some Acts openly create new law. For example, the Transport Act 1981 lowered the maximum engine size which a provisional licence holding motor cyclist can ride to 125 cc from 250 cc. It also introduced the compulsory wearing of seat belts in cars. Incidentally, these changes were brought about by this 1981 Act amending an earlier Act, the Road Traffic Act 1972, which contained most of the law about road traffic matters. It is common for statutes to contain sections which have this amending effect on earlier Acts. All this material was consolidated into the Road Traffic Act 1988, then fairly extensively

Protection from Harassment Act 1997

CHAPTER 40

ARRANGEMENT OF SECTIONS

Protection from Harrassment Act 1997 Crown copyright; reproduced by kind permission of HMSO

amended by the Road Traffic Act 1991. Legislation is a dynamic subject.

If the Act was not designed to create new law, it might be a repealing measure. For example, the Trade Union and Labour Relations Act 1974 was designed, among other things, to repeal the controversial Industrial Relations Act 1971.

Alternatively the Act might be a measure designed to tidy up the law, such as a consolidating statute, which draws together existing statute law on one subject under one heading; one example of this is the Sale of Goods Act 1979 which gathered together the old Sale of Goods Act 1893 and the four intervening amending statutes. In a sense, then, the 1979 Act was a republication of the 1893 Act in its then current form. Another tidying up measure is a codifying Act. This gathers together all the existing law on a given topic—statutes, cases, regulations and all. The old Sale of Goods Act 1893 was a good example of such a measure. Sir Mackenzie Chalmers drew together all the existing laws, from all sources, into a codified whole.

It has now been further amended by two Acts passed in 1994.

Once a statute is made it must be repealed for it to lose its validity as law. It does not fade away like old soldiers—although many statutes do become obsolete. Also, a new Act may obviously change the wording of a previous Act and therefore, by implication may repeal the old Act or part of it. We have the Law Commission now, to spot them and recommend their repeal. Parliament can make or unmake any law it chooses. This is called parliamentary sovereignty. It was lucidly defined in 1885 by A. V. Dicey, one of our greatest writers on constitutional law:

> The principle of parliamentary sovereignty means neither more nor less than this, namely, that Parliament thus defined has, under the English constitution, the right to make or unmake any law whatever; and, further, that no person or body is recognised by the law of England as having a right to override or set aside the legislation of Parliament.

It has been argued, however, that since the Treaty of Accession was signed on 22 January 1972, we parted with a little of this sovereignty in joining the European Community. Not that the treaty is law here, but the statute implementing it is—as Lord Denning said (in *Blackburn* v. *Attorney-General* (1971)):

> It is elementary that these courts take no notice of treaties until they are embodied in laws enacted by Parliament, and then only to the extent that Parliament tells us.

We will return to check the extent to which Europe can make law for us, but first it is important to see just how Parliament creates a statute. It is the most powerful form of law. Law can be made in the form of regulations, and so on, by those delegated sufficient authority by Parliament; it can be made, or at least developed, by judges in individual cases but Parliament can sweep away acres of case law, custom, rules and regulations and earlier statutes too, by a single Act. We must see how it is done.

Creating a statute

A government with a working majority will dominate law-making by Parliament. Manifesto promises appear as discussion documents (called green or white papers) and later as debating documents for the Houses of Parliament called Bills. It would be wrong, however, to assume that all government backed Bills are the result of manifesto promises. Of the Bills introduced by the 1970–74 Conservative Government only 8 per cent were attributable to their election manifesto. The 1974–79 Labour Government figure was 13 per cent.

It is possible for any of the 659 members of the House of Commons to introduce a private member's Bill. Unless the government supports the idea (whether actively or passively by not opposing it) then the Bill has little chance of enactment. Each year, on the second Thursday of the parliamentary session, there is a ballot of those members who wish to introduce Bills privately. The top twenty names are guaranteed time to introduce a Bill. There are thirteen Fridays, from 9.30 a.m. to 2.30 p.m. set aside where private members' Bills have precedence over government business. The top six in the ballot generally have a good chance of success. Pressure groups like the Consumers' Association, Justice, the Howard League for Penal Reform and many others hang like wasps round a jam jar, awaiting the result of the ballot, prepared to bombard the successful few with many new ideas and free lunches! Some of this legislation reflects great public concern, such as The Activity Centres (Young Person's Safety) Act 1995 which was piloted through Parliament by Plymouth Devonport's MP, Derek Jamieson, with the intention of preventing a repetition of the tragic accident in Lyme Bay.

At the ballot in 1997 the winner was Michael Foster, the Labour MP for Worcester. He decided to promote the Wild Mammals (Hunting with Dogs) Bill. This attracted massive public reaction. An estimated 100 000 people opposed the purpose behind the Bill at a countryside rally in London in July 1997. It was reported in October 1997 that the Government was seeking ways to kill off the Bill to prevent it wrecking Labour's heavy legislative programme, in that, when it reached the Lords, pro-hunting peers would launch a series of damaging delaying tactics, and, in the process, would prevent early implementation of Government measures on education, crime and devolution.

It is also possible for a private member to introduce a Bill under the 'ten minute' rule. If given prior leave, a member may speak in favour of the introduction of a Bill for ten minutes. This ensures publicity, and this is the general idea. For example, Michael Fabricant proposed legislation in 1992 to outlaw the practice of adding service charges to restaurant bills. It caused a great deal of heat and smoke, but no fire resulted. Very few such speeches result in statutes, although the Murder (Abolition of the Death Penalty) Act 1965 started in this way. It is often claimed that the ability of private members to introduce Bills is of great constitutional significance. The truth is that approximately 86 per cent of such Bills which find their way onto the statute book do so with considerable government backing.

The central point of government power lies within the Cabinet. This is a committee of about twenty members, personally selected by the Prime Minister. Within the Cabinet there are many sub-groups called Cabinet committees. One such group is chaired by the Leader of the House of Commons. It is responsible for considering proposals for new legislation brought by government departments. It is also responsible for the preparation of the Queen's Speech. This is read by the monarch at the beginning of each session of Parliament (which runs from November to October) and lays out the proposals for legislation that year. There is a second Cabinet committee called the Legislation Committee. It is chaired by the Lord Chancellor, and it is responsible for the implementation of the timetabled programme. The Bills, the debating documents, are drafted by specialists called parliamentary counsel. The most important Bills are public Bills, designed to change the general law throughout England and Wales. If Scotland is to be included it must be expressly included, and sometimes a parallel Bill for Scottish law will be enacted.

Parliament also debates private Bills. These are sponsored by local authorities, public corporations and a few by large public companies. Obviously, they are designed to affect only the legal position of the private sponsor. For example, The Henry Johnson, Sons & Co. Limited Act 1996 which provides for this company, an international transportation agent, to become registered under the laws of the Republic of France and to be removed from the register in England. A local Act may affect the public. For example, The City of Westminster Act 1996. This Act provides power for the Westminster City Council to serve closure notices on unlicensed 'sex establishments' within the City boundaries.

Bills can be presented in either of the Houses of Parliament, but they must pass through both. As a general rule, the less controversial Bills (e.g. consolidation measures) are introduced into the Lords first and the ones likely to cause more fuss are read first in the Commons. Money bills must start in the Commons.

The enactment of a Bill	There are a number of formal stages through which a Bill must pass before it becomes an Act and therefore law. Each is a kind of hurdle. There is debate and discussion at all but the initial stage. The process enables government back-benchers to participate, and it also gives the opposition a chance to impress the electorate. Furthermore, it provides a number of occasions upon which the government can reconsider its proposals and perhaps modify them, if necessary. There is, therefore, a tangled web of politics woven into what might otherwise appear to be a rather dry procedure for lawmaking.

We will consider the enactment of a public Bill which is introduced first in the House of Commons. The vast majority of such introductions are made by written notice. Every day in Parliament there is an order paper, a kind of agenda for the meeting. On the order paper for the chosen day there appears the title of the Bill and the names of those promoting it. At the beginning of public business the Speaker (the chairman) calls upon the member who formally hands a document made to look like a Bill to the clerk. If the introduction is made by a minister then a short speech will be made to move the

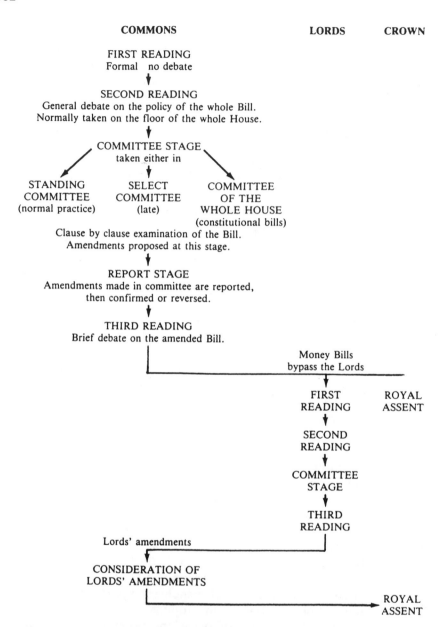

COMMONS	LORDS	CROWN

The passage of a Bill through Parliament

presentation of the Bill. The clerk will then read out the title of the Bill. No questions are put. This is called the first reading. A day is chosen for the second reading and an order is made for the Bill to be copied and distributed.

When the day for the second reading arrives there are two possible methods of handling it. If the Bill is not very controversial then it can be referred to a second reading committee which reports back to the House and recommends a formal acceptance of the Bill without debate. This saves the time of the rest of the House. However, if twenty members object then this cannot be done so there does not have to be much controversy among the 659 members to mean that a second reading debate must take place. This debate is, in theory, as Erskine May (a famous writer about parliamentary procedures) puts it:

> the most important stage through which the Bill is required to pass; for its whole principle is then at issue, and is affirmed or denied by a vote of the House.

In fact, with a working majority for the government, the result is not in doubt and the debate (on the outlines and principles of the Bill rather than the fine details) loses its edge. If the Bill requires expenditure then the House must pass a financial resolution at this stage. This has the effect of limiting the possibilities of expansion, and increased expenditure, at later stages.

While the first reading is very brief and formal, the second is a debate only in outline. It is the next stage at which the details of the Bill are examined: this is the committee stage.

Most Bills are dealt with by standing committees of fifteen to fifty MPs. There are usually about ten working on Bills at any one time. This obviously saves time on the floor of the House, although where a Bill is particularly important (e.g. the Bill for the European Communities Act 1972) or particularly controversial (such as the Bill which led to the Sunday Trading Act 1994), then this stage is taken on the floor in Committee of the Whole House. The members of these committees are chosen for their qualifications and interests and the party balance generally reflects that in the House. Therefore, if the government has a large majority there it will control the committees too, and it is likely that the Bill going into committee will emerge with very few changes apart, perhaps, from those inserted by the appropriate minister, reflecting his second thoughts.

Once the committee has finished with the Bill it goes back to the House for the report stage at which the committee chairman produces the refined product for the scrutiny of the House. Amendments can be made (or unmade if the government was defeated in committee). This is the symbolic gesture of the whole House assuming responsibility for the Bill. Even if no amendment has been made, the Bill must be reported and only if the Bill has been considered by Committee of the Whole House is this stage dispensed with.

The last stage in the Commons is the third reading. This usually follows immediately on the report stage and is taken without debate unless six or more members object. Where the Bill is debated here only verbal changes can be made. The principles of the Bill are now settled. This is the last opportunity for the House to reject the Bill before it passes on to the Lords for their consideration. If the vote is carried the Bill is said to have 'passed through the House'.

In the Lords the Bill goes through substantially the same stages again. Often the committee stage of the Bill is taken by the whole House rather than by a small group of members as happens in the House of Commons. The atmosphere is more informal: the vitriolic exchanges in the other House are rarely heard.

When the Bill emerges from the Lords it may well have been altered. Sometimes this is a reflection of the inbuilt Conservative majority there. The Bill now returns to the Commons for reconsideration in its amended form. If the changes are not acceptable they are unmade and the Bill is sent back to the Lords. Usually a compromise is reached. If it cannot be, then the Commons have the last word.

The Parliament Acts 1911 and 1949 have curtailed the power of the Lords to use their power to delay. This allows them to hold up a money Bill (certified as such by the Speaker) for a month and any other Bill for a year. The Lords can no longer stop a Bill becoming law if the elected chamber wishes it to be enacted. The Welsh Church Act 1914, the Government of Ireland Act 1914 and the Parliament Act 1949 were passed without the Lords' assent. The War Crimes Act 1991 was sent for Royal Assent even though the Bill had been defeated twice in the House of Lords. The procedure was threatened in the Trade Union and Labour Relations (Amendment) Bills 1975, 1976 and the Aircraft and Shipbuilding Industries Bills in 1976 and 1977—but a compromise was reached in these instances.

The final stage of enactment is the royal assent—a pure formality today, last being refused in 1707. It may be given by the sovereign in person—this was last done in 1854 or it may be signified on her behalf by specially appointed officers called commissioners. The usual procedure (under the Royal Assent Act 1967) is that the chairman in each House (the Speaker and the Lord Chancellor) simply notifies the assent to both Houses. The words of the royal assent are '*la reyne le veult*' for public Bills and '*la reyne remercie ses bons sujets, accepte leur benevolence et ainsi le veult*' for financial Bills.

Once the assent has been given, personally, by the commissioners or (as is usual) by notification, the Bill becomes law. In other words, it has been enacted.

Another procedure which is largely untried is called the 'fast track' or Jellicoe Committee (the Special Public Bill Committee of the House of Lords) procedure. This is designed to facilitate the codification and/or consolidation of particularly complex areas of law where 'normal' parliamentary time would probably not be made available.

Changes to come?   The Government's manifesto promised to set up a committee to consider ways to make Parliament more relevant and more effective and help address what they perceived to be a national crisis of confidence in the UK political system.

In June 1997 the Select Committee on the Modernisation of the House of Commons was set up to examine ways in which the procedure for examining legislative proposals could be improved. Their first report was published on 29 July 1997 and entitled 'Towards a Modern House of Commons'. The Committee makes a number of recommendations designed to improve the legislative process itself. (Later reports will deal with such issues as the scrutiny of European legislation, voting arrangements, the parliamentary calendar and the conduct of debate.)

The main recommendations within the first Report include:

- the programming of legislation to enable better consideration of Bills. At present, there is no room for compromise. Either the parties agree on how a measure is discussed or the Government imposes a guillotine;
- a new Daily Agenda to replace the current Order Paper. The current document has been widely criticised as difficult to understand and a mystery to all but the initiated. The new agenda would set out the expected times for the day's business and make it easy to find required pages in the document;
- increased opportunity for pre-legislative scrutiny and better consultation. The Government has already promised to publish seven Bills in draft. The Report recommends the use of *ad hoc* or Select Committees to consider such proposals;
- a number of other detailed changes designed to improve the way the House works. These include allowing all Committees to sit in recess; better explanatory material published with Bills in order to make the legislative process more transparent; thrashing out differences on the principle of a clause first to encourage more constructive amendments on the line-by-line stage later;
- more flexibility in certain circumstances to allow Bills to carry over to the next parliamentary session so that vital work to date is not wasted.

Delegated legislation

Not all our law is made by our Parliament. Some is made by others who are authorised to do so by Parliament. These laws are just as effective as sources of rights and duties as Acts of Parliament. The law made by means of delegated authority is called delegated legislation. This lawmaking power is always delegated within very strict limits. It is not a new idea, nor a reflection of the march of technological progress, although this has had an effect on the amount of rules, regulations, orders and so on, which are now made in this way. The practice of delegating authority was seen in 1832, in the Cholera Prevention Act (2 & 3 Will. 4, c.10—the way statutes used to be named), which was designed to resist the spread of the dreadful disease of cholera. See how the power is delegated so that urgent requirements can be met without constant referral to Parliament:

> Whereas it has pleased Almighty God to visit the United Kingdom with the disease called the cholera . . . and whereas with a view to prevent as far as may be possible, by the Divine Blessing the spreading of the said disease, it may be necessary that rules and regulations may from time to time be established within cities, towns or districts affected with or which may be threatened by the said disease, but it may be impossible to establish such rules and regulations by the authority of Parliament with sufficient promptitude to meet the exigency of any such case as may occur.

This power to cater for emergencies is one of the main reasons for Parliament delegating authority.

Another reason for delegating authority is the need for fine detail in law making – much more than Parliament would have time (or perhaps expertise) to meet. For example, building works must comply with building regulations. These are detailed and serve various purposes. It had been observed by the Government's Construction Minister, Nick Raynsford, that:

> a building could comply with Building Regulations on completion, but could then require alteration before it is used in order to comply with the Health and Safety Regulations. This is not good for business and not good regulation.

Accordingly, the Building Regulations (Amendment) Regulations 1997 (S.I. 1997 No. 1904) were made on 31 July 1997. They will come into force on 1 January 1998, substituting modified Parts in Schedule 1 to the Building Regulations 1991 (S.I. 1991 No. 2768), as follows:

> in place of the current Part K (Stairs, Ramps and Guards) there will be a new Part K — Protection from Falling, Collision and Impact; and
> in place of the current Part N (Glazing: Materials and Protection) there will be a new Part N – Glazing: Safety in Relation to Impact, Opening and Cleaning.

The minister explained that:

> from 1 January 1998, a building that complies with the Building Regulations will automatically comply with the corresponding Health and Safety Regulations. This is a good example of what we mean by better regulation.

It is also pretty complicated stuff!

More accessible perhaps is The Supply of Beer (Tied Estate) (Amendment) Order 1997 which was made on 22 July 1997 and, following approval by both Houses of Parliament, came into force on 27 August. This Order amends the Tied Estate Order 1989 under the powers contained in S. 56 of the Fair Trading Act 1973. It requires that the UK's national brewers and large brewery groups change their agreements before 1 April 1998 to allow their tenants and loan tie recipients to buy at least one battle-conditioned beer from whomever they choose.

The laws which are made using authority delegated by such statutes appear in one of three main forms.

The first, and most dignified, is the Order in Council. This is used to implement matters of major importance. For example, during the Second World War the government acted by Order in Council in the exercise of powers delegated by the Emergency Powers (Defence) Acts 1939 and 1940. These orders are drafted by the appropriate government department and rubber stamped by the Queen in Council—an echo of the Queen and her court of advisers.

The second form is the byelaw. These are rules made by an authority subordinate to Parliament (e.g. local authorities) for the regulation, administration or management of their district or property or undertaking. In the Local Government Act 1972, for example, it says:

> 235 (1) The council of a district and the council of a London borough may make byelaws for the good rule and government of the whole or any part of the district or borough, as the case may be, and for the prevention and suppression of nuisances therein.

It is usual to find posters containing the local byelaws on signs at the corners of commons or on lamp posts.

The third form that delegated legislation takes is the detailed variety of regulations, orders, rules, schemes, warrants and directions and so on, whatever the term used in the enabling Act.

There is substantial criticism of the increased delegation of lawmaking power. It is said to be given to those who are not answerable at the ballot box, since, in reality, the instrument containing the law is drafted by the civil service, not the minister. Furthermore it is said that the old maxim *ignorantia juris non excusat* (ignorance of the law is no excuse) can hardly be appropriate these days when there are more than 2000 statutory instruments made each year—over 5000 pages of them. (In 1974 there were 8669 pages!) It is added that Parliament does not scrutinise the exercise of its delegated power sufficiently. There is often some distance between the grant and use of such power; the Emergency Powers (Defence) Act 1939, for example, conferred power to make regulations, orders under the regulations, directions under the orders and licences under the directions.

To answer these criticisms there must be convincing reasons for delegating authority. Obviously, a great deal of parliamentary time is saved. Only about 100 working days of each parliamentary session are used for the legislative programme, and the government simply could not keep to its timetable without delegating the detailed lawmaking to others. Secondly, as we saw above, there may be emergencies to be met. There is a need for the power to make law quickly. Parliament is not always sitting, and rarely acts quickly even when it is. Thirdly, the increased technicality of life requires increasingly technical law (such as building regulations), beyond the expertise of most members of Parliament. Ministers are given power and the duty to consult experts while using it. Similarly, local knowledge is required to make useful byelaws for any particular district. It is obviously necessary to delegate power to the locally elected representatives.

These are the reasons for delegating power. It is argued that adequate controls do exist over its use. Parliament can revoke the grant of power. It retains the right to legislate in the same areas. There is a Joint Scrutiny Committee which has responsibility for keeping an eye on the use of the delegated authority, and drawing the attention of Parliament to any controversial measures. Sometimes (rarely) the enabling Act requires that Parliament itself must approve an instrument. The courts can be asked to examine whether an instrument has been drafted outside the limits of the delegated power (*ultra vires*). One example of this can be seen in *R.* v. *Secretary of State for Health ex parte United States Tobacco International Inc.* (1991) where regulations banning the sale of oral snuff were struck down as being disproportionate to the health danger and having been made without adequate consultation. Parliament itself calls to account the responsible minister at Question Time. This is an effective quality control. The minister must answer for his department's activities.

LAW FROM THE EUROPEAN COMMUNITY

Since the United Kingdom agreed to join the European Community in 1972 there has been a new source of law. The Treaty of Accession was implemented by the European Communities Act 1972. Under this Act the institutions of the community have legislative power over the UK:

> 2 (1) All such rights, powers, liabilities, obligations and restrictions from time to time created or arising by or under the Treaties, and all such remedies and procedures from time to time provided for by or under the Treaties are without further enactment to be given legal effect or used in the United Kingdom shall be recognised and available in law, and be enforced, allowed and followed accordingly.

The importance of community law cannot be overstated. Lord Denning said (in *Bulmer* v. *Bollinger* (1974)):

> . . . when we come to matters with a European element the Treaty is like an incoming tide. It flows into the estuaries and up the rivers. It cannot be held back.

On the other hand, Community law does not affect the whole of our law. When it exists it is so important as to outweigh our law. It is increasingly found in such areas as agriculture, consumer protection, the free movement of workers, social security, competition and some aspects of company law. Nevertheless, it would be a mistake to underestimate its importance. There have been many cases where the supremacy of Community law over national laws has been clearly illustrated. As examples: *Marleasing SA* v. *La Commercial International de Alimentacion SA* (1990), where matters of Spanish law were overruled and *Francovich* v. *Republic of Italy, Bonifaci* v. *Republic of Italy* (1991), where a similar fate befell the Italians. (These cases turn upon the failure of member states to implement Directives.)

The foundation stones of Community law are the treaties. These are the Treaty of Paris (1951) which established the European Coal and Steel Community and the two Treaties of Rome (1957) which established the European Atomic Energy Community and the European Economic Community. The member states of the Community have several broad aims, including economic integration in the short term and political integration later. It is suspected that the United Kingdom is more in favour of the former than the latter. In any event, following upon the ratification of the Single European Act by means of the European Communities (Amendment) Act 1986 a 'single market' was formed within the member states at the end of 1992. This brought a lifting of tariff barriers, common passports and many similar blessings.

The debate about the nature and consequences of EC membership centred upon the Maastricht Treaty, and its ratification by member states. This treaty is intended to expand further the scope of Community activity and move the member states closer to economic and political integration.

It created the European Union on 1 January 1993. (At one point the word 'federal' was used.) This Union is based upon the European

Community, and supplemented by the other provisions of the Maastricht Treaty. A common foreign and security policy is envisaged, as is a common interior and justice policy. The Union has these objectives:

1 to promote balanced and sustainable economic progress by means of an area without internal frontiers, and movement towards economic and monetary union, and ultimately a single currency;
2 to assert itself internationally through common foreign, security and defence policies;
3 to strengthen the protection of the rights and interests of its nationals through the introduction of Union citizenship, developing close cooperation on justice and home affairs;
4 to maintian and develop existing EC law, and build upon it.

However, this treaty also incorporates the principle of 'subsidiarity' which is designed to put a brake upon what Professor Lasok has called 'the adventurism of the Community institutions and the ambitions of their bureaucracy'. The treaty provides that 'any action of the Community shall not go beyond what is necessary to achieve the objectives of the Treaty'. It adds that the Community will act 'only if and in so far as the objectives of the proposed action cannot be sufficiently achieved by member states'.

Within the EU, basic Community policies are implemented and developed by means of various instruments which are usually drawn up by the European Commission and sent for agreement to the Council of Ministers. The Commission works closely with the governments and civil servants of member states. Indeed, it has been argued that the United Kingdom government is now free to act (if other member states agree) as a legislative authority, avoiding the scrutiny and control of Parliament, by initiating changes in Community law which then have direct effects on English law. The European Commission is a committee of twenty, drawn though not equally, from the fifteen member states. This Commission is supposed to have a European point of view and in some areas, such as the fine details of law about agriculture, it has legislative power itself, delegated to it by the Council of Ministers. The Council, which is composed of a senior minister from each of the fifteen member states, is overtly nationalist in viewpoint. Each member speaks for his own state. There is also a European Parliament which has 626 directly elected members and little practical power, although its opinion is usually sought about legislative proposals. It has the power to remove the Commission from office if it can muster a two-thirds majority to do so. Recently a 'cooperative procedure' has been developed by means of which these three Community institutions can make joint decisions. The powers of the Parliament were increased by the Single European Act and the Maastricht Treaty.

The instruments which implement Community law and which emanate from these institutions appear in various forms. Regulations are made, directives issued, decisions made, recommendations made and opinions delivered. Of these, recommendations and opinions have no binding force upon those towards whom they are directed and so are not strictly part of Community legislation, although they are technically part of the 'instruments' referred to in the 1972 Act (above) and could therefore be the basis of rule-making in the United Kingdom. Regulations, directives and decisions comprise community legislation. Of these, regulations are the most important. They are binding and directly applicable in all member states. They confer rights and duties which must be recognised by the national courts within member states. They pass straight into our law, with no need for parliamentary approval. Directives are not generally self-executing but instructions to make law rather than laws in themselves. So member states are given a period of time, perhaps two or three years, within which certain prescribed laws must be made within each state, in accordance with the directive, and using the state's own legislative machinery. As an example, Part 1 of The Consumer Protection Act 1987, is designed to implement the European Directive on Products Liability, which was adopted in the summer of 1985 and had to be implemented by member states by the summer of 1988. Interestingly, the European Court has sometimes been prepared to overlook this distinction and hold that a directive is capable of providing legal rights for an individual despite the fact that the member state has not implemented it fully (e.g. *Van Duyn* v. *Home Office* (1975), *Becker* v. *Finanzamt Munster-Innenstadt* (1982) and see *Marleasing* and *Francovich* above, p. 26).

Finally, decisions: under Art. 189 of the EEC Treaty a decision is 'binding in its entirety upon those to whom it is addressed'. So a member state might be bound, or just a single company within a state. They are usually administrative decisions implementing Community law, like granting authorisations or exceptions.

There is a select committee in each of our Houses of Parliament which scrutinises Community policies and legislative proposals, so that our Parliament is kept aware of what is happening in the area of Community law.

STATUTORY INTERPRETATION

Acts of Parliament lay down general rules. Sooner or later an individual will be charged that he has infringed such a rule and a court will be called upon to decide whether a general rule has been broken in a particular case. Usually there is little trouble with the words of the rule as used in the Act; the meaning is usually clear. Sometimes, however, it is not and the court, still required to decide, must interpret the words.

Over the years a clumsy collection of so-called 'rules' of statutory interpretation has been developed.

The first, and perhaps most obvious approach, is known as the 'literal rule'. This reflects the traditionally narrow view which the courts have taken of statutory interpretation. The words in the Act are applied strictly and literally. The ordinary and natural meaning of the words used is regarded as being the meaning intended by Parliament. Lord Reid said (in *Black-Clawson* v. *Papierwerke* (1975)):

> We often say that we are looking for the intention of Parliament, but that is not quite accurate. We are seeking the meaning of the words which Parliament used. We are seeking not what Parliament meant but the true meaning of what they said. In the comparatively few cases where the words of a statutory provision are only capable of having one meaning, that is the end of the matter and no further enquiry is permissible.

This rule was employed in *Whiteley* v. *Chappell* (1868) where the statute in question made it a criminal offence to pretend to be 'any person entitled to vote' at an election. The accused had masqueraded himself as someone whose name was still on the list but who had died. The 'literal rule' applied here disclosed no offence, because the dead person was no longer 'entitled to vote' (*see* also *Fisher* v. *Bell* (1960), below, p. 198).

Glanville Williams wrote:

> The literal rule is a rule against using intelligence in understanding language. Anyone who in ordinary life interpreted words literally, being indifferent to what the speaker or writer meant, would be regarded as a pedant, a mischief-maker or an idiot.

The Law Commission published a report in 1969 suggesting legislation to reform statutory interpretation. They too were critical of the literal rule:

> . . . to place undue emphasis on the literal meaning of the words of a provision is to assume an unattainable perfection in draftsmanship.

Where the literal rule in action leads to arrant nonsense (rather than a result which is clearly not what Parliament intended) then modification of approach is permitted.

So we have the 'golden rule'. Parke B said (in *Becke* v. *Smith* (1836)):

> It is a very useful rule in the construction of a statute to adhere to the ordinary meaning of the words used, and to the grammatical construction, unless that is at variance with the intention of the Legislature to be collected from the statute itself, or leads to any manifest absurdity or repugnance, in which case the language may be varied or modified so as to avoid such inconvenience, but no further.

So it was that when in *R.* v. *Allen* (1872) the accused was charged with bigamy, contrary to the Offences against the Person Act 1861:

> 57. Whosoever, being married, shall marry any other person during the life of the former husband or wife, whether the second marriage shall have taken place in England, or Ireland or elsewhere . . . shall be liable to (imprisonment) for any term not exceeding seven years.

In the case the point was made that, marriage being a change of legal status, a person cannot 'marry' while married because he is already married. Think about it! The court felt able to interpret the phrase 'shall marry' in the Act as meaning 'go through a ceremony of marriage'. The accused was convicted. The 'golden rule' had been applied.

The third rule—quite inconsistent with the other two—is called the 'mischief rule', or the rule in *Heydon's Case* (1584). In that case the use of the rule was explained:

Four things are to be discussed and considered: (i) What was the common law before the making of the Act? (ii) What was the mischief and defect for which the common law did not provide? (iii) What remedy hath Parliament resolved and appointed to cure the disease of the commonwealth? (iv) What is the true reason for the remedy? Judges shall make such construction as shall suppress the mischief and advance the remedy.

So when the mischief rule is used, the courts seek out what Parliament intended to stop and they see to it that it gets stopped—whatever the words might, taken literally, mean.

The case *Smith* v. *Hughes* (1960) concerned the interpretation of a section of the Street Offences Act 1959. This Act makes it a criminal offence for a common prostitute to loiter or solicit in a street or public place for her professional purposes. The ladies accused here had been attracting customers by tapping on the glass upstairs at a first floor window. Obviously, they were not 'in the street', as the Act said it required, yet Parker CJ said:

Everybody knows that this was an Act intended to clean up the streets, to enable people to walk along the streets without being molested or solicited by common prostitutes. Viewed in that way, it can matter little whether the prostitute is soliciting while in the street or is standing in a doorway or on a balcony, or at a window, or whether the window is shut or open or half open. In each case her solicitation is projected to and addressed to somebody walking in the street.

The 1969 Law Commission Report recommended a move away from the 'literal rule' towards the 'mischief' approach. It must be admitted that there is a danger in allowing the judges too much freedom to elaborate the expressed wishes of Parliament. It could tempt people towards litigation where they 'gamble' on the outcome of a case. Nevertheless a move away from the bald 'literal' interpretation of statutes must be welcome.

Apart from, and in addition to, these three rules there are other approaches, rules, guidelines and presumptions which the courts use when interpreting statutes. Incidentally, several of them have Latin names. Lawyers use Latin as a shorthand. (Some say they use it as a smokescreen too!)

1 *Ut res magis valeat quam pereat*—let the thing stand rather than fall. Assume that the draftsman is not repeating himself.
2 *Expressio unius, exclusio alterius*—what is included excludes that which is not. So that if particular words like 'house' and 'office' are not followed by general words like 'other buildings', then the generalities are excluded.
3 *Ejusdem generis*—of the same kind. So, if general words do follow particular ones, they must be interpreted so as to include only things 'of the same kind'. For example, 'dogs, cats (particular) and other animals (general)' would exclude lions, tigers and camels but it might include budgies and ornamental fish.
4 Presume that unless the Act specifically states that it does so, it does not oust the jurisdiction of the courts, alter the settled common law, infringe international obligations, repeal earlier Acts, deprive an owner of his property, extend its effect beyond the United

Kingdom, nor create 'strict liability' offences (i.e. those for which no intention need be proved, like parking on a double yellow line and other more serious offences—*see* Chapter 15).

Further to these rules and presumptions, statutes usually contain interpretation sections (e.g. the Sale of Goods Act 1979, s. 61) which define words used in the Act. There is also the Interpretation Act 1978 which assists in an overall way (e.g. singular includes plural, masculine includes feminine). The judges also take into account the long title of an Act but not the margin notes. Generally, external documents like discussion papers and Hansard are not used. Hansard is the verbatim record of what is said in Parliamentary debates. Until the tax case of *Pepper* v. *Hart* (1993) it seemed to be settled that Hansard would not be referred to by the courts. However, the House of Lords in that case has held that, subject to parliamentary privilege, such materials as Hansard can be taken into account where:

1 the legislation is ambiguous or obscure or the literal meaning leads to an absurdity,
2 the material relied on consists of statements made by a minister or other promoter of the Bill together, if necessary, with such other parliamentary material as is necessary to understand such statements and their effect and
3 the statements relied on are clear.

Since that case we have seen in *Massmould* v. *Payne* (1993) and, similarly, in *Sheppard* v. *IRC* (1993) that where the legislation was declared to be clear enough, reference to Hansard is not permitted, even where the meaning that could be found there differed from that gathered from the legislation itself. In *Van Dyck* v. *Secretary of State for the Environment* (1993) the legislation was unclear and so was Hansard! On the other hand, in *Three Rivers District Council* v. *Bank of England (No. 2)* (1996), a case following the collapse of the Bank of Commerce and Credit International (BCCI), the general purposes of the Banking Acts 1979 and 1987 were gathered from Hansard on an assertion that they should comply with a European Directive (77/780), imposing supervisory duties on the Bank of England.

If an Act follows on a particular formal report then it seems to have been established in *Black-Clawson* v. *Papierwerke* (1975) that reference can be made to it while identifying the mischief the Act sought to correct.

CASE LAW

Having considered legislation and its related topics, we now need to observe the other main source of law in action—case law—or law from decided cases, developed over the years by the judges, case by case, by analogy with earlier cases. The idea is simple. If the facts of a case are similar to an earlier one, particularly one decided by a superior court, then the rule laid down ought to be followed.

Of course, the consistency of decision-making extends back for centuries across English legal history, but the formal structure of binding authority which exists today required two foundations: first, a clear hierarchy within the court system; after all, if the decisions of superior courts are to be binding on inferior ones, it is as well to be able to distinguish between them The present hierarchy was achieved by the Judicature Acts 1873–1875. They created the framework of courts we have today, although some details have been modified. Second, a reliable system of law reports was required. If the court is to follow an earlier decision, then the report of that earlier case must be authoritative. This was finally achieved in 1865 when the General Council of Law Reporting was established: it was incorporated in 1870. The Law Reports and Weekly Law Reports are published under the auspices of the Incorporated Council. They are of great authority and are checked by the judges before publication. There are still private reports published, as there have been over the centuries. Probably the most famous are the All England Law Reports.

So the formal rule whereby one court is bound to follow the decision of another court taken earlier in a similar case is only about a hundred years old.

This formality is sometimes called the doctrine of precedent or *stare decisis*. Case law is the source of law. The doctrine of precedent is the mechanism by which it develops.

The doctrine of precedent: who binds whom?

The binding nature of a decision works down the court system (see also pp. 43–44):

The Court of the European Communities

Where the case turns upon a point of Community law then the European Court has the last word. The European Communities Act 1972 says:

> 3 (1) For the purpose of all legal proceedings any question as to the meaning or effect of any of the treaties, or as to the validity, meaning or effect of any community instrument, shall be treated as a question of law and, if not referred to the European Court, be for determination as such in accordance with the principles laid down by and any relevant decision of the European Court.

So the court in Luxembourg has the last word on matters of Community law. Under the EC Treaty the English courts obtain rulings on points of Community law (which commonly take a year or more to obtain) which they then apply to the case at hand. It is a method of centralising and stabilising the interpretation of Community law.

The House of Lords

Apart from matters of Community law, the House of Lords is the final court of appeal within the English legal system. Its decisions on civil and criminal matters bind all inferior courts. Until 1966 it even bound itself! On 26 July 1966 the then Lord Chancellor, Lord Gardiner, issued the famous Practice Statement. It has been regarded as binding, although it was not made as part of the judgment in a case.

Their Lordships regard the use of precedent as an indispensable foundation upon which to decide what is the law and its application to individual cases. It provides at least some degree of certainty upon which individuals can rely in the conduct of their affairs, as well as a basis for orderly development of legal rules. Their Lordships nevertheless recognise that too rigid adherence to precedent may lead to injustice in a particular case and also unduly restrict the proper development of the law. They propose therefore to modify their present practice and, while treating former decisions of this House as normally binding, to depart from a previous decision when it appears right to do so. In this connection they will bear in mind the danger of disturbing retrospectively the basis on which contracts, settlements of property and fiscal arrangements have been entered into and also the especial need for certainty as to the criminal law. This announcement is not intended to affect the use of precedent elsewhere than in this House.

This is a lucid explanation of the present position in the House. The power to over-rule has been used only very sparingly since 1966. Indeed, if one party to a case wishes to ask the House to exercise this power it must state so clearly in the documents of the case (Procedure Direction (1971)). One example is *Murphy* v. *Brentwood District Council* (1990) where the House expressly overruled its earlier decision in *Anns* v. *London Borough of Merton* (1977).

The Court of Appeal In simple terms, this court is always bound by decisions of the House of Lords and it is generally bound by its own decisions. The court is split into a civil and criminal division.

The civil division can only depart from its own decisions in the three instances set out in 1944 by the then Master of the Rolls, Lord Greene (in *Young* v. *Bristol Aeroplane Co Ltd* (1944)), who said that:

1 the court is entitled and bound to decide which of two conflicting decisions of its own it will follow;
2 the court is bound to refuse to follow a decision of its own which conflicts with a House of Lords decision;
3 the court is not bound to follow a decision which was taken *per incuriam* (i.e. in ignorance of a relevant authority such as an Act or previous decision).

Further to these, it was held in *Boys* v. *Chaplin* (1968) that interlocutory (i.e. preliminary to actually dealing with the case) decisions are not binding.

In the criminal division it is thought that since the liberty of the individual concerned may be at stake then a slightly less rigid approach is appropriate. *R.* v. *Gould* (1968) is a notable example, where the earlier decision in *R.* v. *Wheat and Stocks* (1921) was expressly over-ruled. The cases concern whether a reasonable belief that a previous marriage has been dissolved is a defence to a bigamy charge. From the later case it appears that it is. The present position was set out very clearly in the judgment of the Court of Appeal itself in *R.* v. *McIlkenny and others* (1991)—popularly referred to as the case of the 'Birmingham Six'. Here the court stated that its function is limited to a power of review rather than that of a full appeal. It has no power to upset the verdict of a jury on a question of fact unless it considers a conviction to be unsafe or unsatisfactory under all the circumstances of the case. It has no power to state whether it regards the appellant as innocent. The only issue for them is whether or not the verdict of the jury can stand.

The High Court

Where civil cases are tried at first instance the decisions do not bind other High Court judges. The divisional courts do follow their own rulings, except occasionally in the Queen's Bench Division. Otherwise the High Court is bound by the Court of Appeal and the House of Lords.

The Crown Court and the courts of inferior jurisdiction

No precedents are set by the decisions of these courts (which include county courts and magistrates' courts) and all the courts above are binding. When a High Court judge sits in the Crown Court, however, it seems probable that the usual High Court position would apply, although this is, as yet, unclear.

To what extent are the decisions binding?

The court bound by settled authority is bound by the essence of the earlier case, the precedent.

The judgment of a court can be divided into two. Each part has a Latin name: the *ratio decidendi* and the *obiter dicta*.

The ratio decidendi

This translates as 'the reason for the decision', but the meaning is less clear. No judge actually says 'now, this is the reason for my decision'; the *ratio* of any case has to be sifted from the words of the judgment. Methods vary. Thus definitions of precisely what the *ratio decidendi* of any case is also vary.

Professor Cross:

> Any rule of law treated by the judge as a necessary step in reaching his conclusion.

Professor Goodhart:

> The *ratio decidendi* of a case can be defined as the material facts of the case plus the decision thereon.

Professor Wambaugh:

> When a case turns on only one point, the proposition of the case, the reason of the decision, the *ratio decidendi*, must be a general rule without which the case must have been decided otherwise.

So in general terms, the *ratio* of a case is the rule of law which dictated the outcome of the case. In *Donoghue* v. *Stevenson* (below) the plaintiff won because there was a rule of law which required the defendant to take care.

The obiter dicta

The ratio is the essence of the case. Everything else belongs to the *obiter dicta* (which translates as 'words spoken by the way'). While it may be a matter of conjecture what precisely constitutes the *ratio*, it is agreed that everything which does not is *obiter*.

Only the *ratio* of a case is binding. *Obiter dicta* may be persuasive, particularly where, for example, a judge has explained hypothetical situations and stated what the law would be and one of these sets of circumstances actually appears. For the doctrine of precedent to work it is not necessary to await the recurrence of precisely the same facts; only the essential relationships need reappear.

Consider these two cases which concern the tort of negligence.

Donoghue v. *Stevenson* (1932). Here the plaintiff suffered through finding the remnants of a decomposed snail in ginger beer which she was drinking. She sued the manufacturer. It was held that he owed his consumers a duty to take care since he and they were 'neighbours' in law. Lord Atkin said:

> You must take reasonable care to avoid acts or omissions which you can reasonably foresee would be likely to injure your neighbour. Who then, in law, is my neighbour? The answer seems to be persons who are so closely and directly affected by my act that I ought reasonably to have them in contemplation as being so affected when I am directing my mind to the acts or omissions which are called in question.

Ross v. *Caunters* (1979). A solicitor drew up a will. There was a gift in it to the wife of one of the witnesses. The Wills Act 1837, s.15, prevented her taking it simply because she was his wife and such people cannot benefit in this way. She sued the solicitor for negligence. It was argued that there could be no negligence because the solicitor owed the plaintiff no duty of care. They were not 'neighbours' in law. Sir Robert Megarry V-C said:

> The solicitors owed a duty of care to the plaintiff since she was someone within their direct contemplation as a person so closely and directly affected by their acts and omissions in carrying out their client's instructions to provide her with a share of his residue that they could reasonably foresee that she would be likely to be injured by those acts or omissions . . . a direct application of the principle of *Donoghue* v. *Stevenson*.

These two cases may appear quite different. However, the judge felt that they were close enough for the first to be a binding authority on the second. The essence was the same, even though the circumstances were radically different. The basic principle appears again in a very different factual situation in *Murphy* v. *Brentwood District Council* (1990).

However, it is not as simple as that. It was not simple in these cases cases (why would they have been dragged through the courts?), and it is never as simple as it might appear here. Judges vary in their preparedness to extend established principles. It has to do with the personality of the judge, the circumstances of the case and the current state of public policy. These are delicate and tangled threads. Julius Stone, a brilliant Australian professor of law, wrote in 1959 (*22 Modern Law Review*):

> In short a 'rule' or 'principle' as it emerges from a precedent case is subject in its further elaboration to continual review, in the light of analogies and differences, not merely in the logical relations between legal concepts and propositions, not merely in the relations between fact situations, and the problems springing from these; but also in the light of the import of these analogies and differences for

what is thought by the latter court to yield a tolerably acceptable result in terms of 'policy,' 'ethics,' 'expediency' or whatever other norm of desirability the law may be thought to subserve. No 'ineluctable logic,' but a composite of the logical relations seen between legal propositions of observations of facts and consequences, and of value judgments about the acceptability of these consequences, is what finally comes to bear upon the alternatives with which 'the rule of *stare decisis*' confronts the courts, and especially appellate courts. And this, it may be supposed, is why finally we cannot assess the product of their work in terms of any less complex quality than that of wisdom.

On the other hand, Lord McCluskey, a Scottish Judge, in the 1986 Reith Lectures stressed that, in his opinion, Parliament should make the law and that judges should confine themselves to administering it. He warned against judges substituting their own notions of justice for the requirements of the law. It is not the function of judges to advance social or moral aims, he argued: 'justice itself is not a legal concept, but an extra-legal or pre-legal one. In so far as he builds a just society the judge's role is to be not an architect but a bricklayer.' He went on to comment on the very 'neighbour principle' which we have considered. He pointed out that it was disputed by two Law Lords at the time, and had been previously described by an Appeal Court judge as 'little short of outrageous'—this despite the fact that no layman would dispute the soundness of the proposition which Lord Atkin described.

The advantages and disadvantages of having a 'doctrine of precedent' are set out neatly in the *Practice Statement* quoted earlier. In list form the advantages are said to be:

1 certainty, in that where a point has been settled then lawyers are enabled to advise their clients accordingly;
2 the possibility of growth, which is provided by the system having been, as it were, opened at the apex in 1966;
3 the wealth of detailed rules which has been assembled over many years of steady growth and the practical nature of the law thus developed, since it is based upon cases that actually happened rather than the hypothetical situations envisaged by statutes.

The disadvantages are said to be:

1 the rigidity which is inevitable within a system which is open only at the apex; a bad decision taken at a high level could remain for many years until a litigant has the time and the money and a closely similar case comes along;
2 the practice of distinguishing where some judges avoid the binding nature of precedents by seizing upon some artificial distinction between the case before them and the precedent and thereby creating illogicality;
3 the wealth of detail brings with it enormous bulk and complexity, making the law difficult and expensive to discover; and
4 the system itself is an unsatisfactory way of developing the law in that it relies upon suitable cases coming up (the 'accidents of litigation'). It is said that the advantages outweigh the disadvantages.

CUSTOM

If the legal system is traced back far enough it will lead to ancient local customs. Today local customs are not very important as a source of law, but they are occasionally recognised as having binding force. Such a local custom is described as being a usage or rule which has gathered the force of law and is binding within a defined area upon the persons affected by it. It is for the person who alleges that the custom exists to prove that it does. This is often the resort of those about to be affected by, for example, a building project. In order to obtain judicial recognition there are various hurdles to leap.

1 The custom must be reasonable. In *Wolstanton* v. *Newcastle-under-Lyme Corporation* (1940) it was alleged that the descendant of the lord of the manor had inherited the right to undermine land without having to compensate for subsidence thereby caused. This was unreasonable.

2 It must be certain as to the subject matter of the persons benefiting and of the locality. In *Wilson* v. *Willes* (1806) the tenants of a manor claimed the right to cut turf for their lawns. This was too uncertain.

3 The locality must be recognisable, e.g. a manor or a parish or a field. In *Mercer* v. *Denne* (1905) the right alleged was to dry fishing nets upon a particular stretch of beach. This was upheld.

4 The custom must be, apparently, ancient. That means that it must have existed as Sir Edward Coke wrote:

   since a time when the memory of man runneth not to the contrary.

   A date of 1189 has been set, but in practice the oldest local people testify, and then those opposing the right are put to it to show that at some time between the earliest date established by this testimony and 1189 the right did not exist. In *Simpson* v. *Wells* (1872) the right alleged was to obstruct the footway with a refreshment stall on 'fair days'. Sadly the fair in that place dated only from 1327.

   The right must have been continuously available since 'time immemorial'. It need not have actually been used continuously. This was confirmed in *New Windsor Corporation* v. *Mellor* (1975), where the right of the local people to 'indulge in sports and pastimes' upon the village green, called Bachelors' Acre, was upheld.

5 The alleged right must have been peaceably used, *nec per vim*, *nec clam*, *nec precario* (neither through force, nor stealth, or the need to obtain permission).

6 Fairly obviously, it must not be contrary to any statute, since these local customs are only recognised as exceptions to common law.

7 It must be consistent with other recognised customs in that area. Sir William Blackstone wrote:

   If one man prescribed that by custom he has a right to have windows looking into another's garden, the other cannot claim a right by custom to stop up or obstruct those windows; for those contradictory customs cannot both be good, nor both stand together.

MINOR SOURCES

It is worth considering briefly a collection of other sources and influences which have helped to shape the law despite being of lesser importance.

The Law Merchant

Lex mercatoria, as it is sometimes known, was the body of customary rules drawn from the practices of merchants, partly based in international law, and dating back to the Middle Ages. The merchants had their own courts called 'pie poudre' and 'staple', using swift and simple procedures and using their own rules.

The debts we owe to the law merchant include the concept of negotiability (which allows a document containing an order to pay money to be transferred from one person to another), and thus bills of exchange, and many aspects of the law of partnerships, agency and insurance. In addition, much of maritime law stems from this source. Mercantile and maritime law have always been close relatives.

Canon law

Church law developed apart from the common law, and was administered in separate ecclesiastical courts. The debts owed here are of two kinds. First there are rules of canon law which passed into the general areas, such as most of family law and probate together with particular offences, like blasphemy and blasphemous libel. It is interesting that these offences are preserved whereas others, like adultery and usury, were never generally adopted. The second debt is more one of general approach. This is clearly seen in the doctrines and practices of equity (considered in Chapter 2). This is so because the early Lord Chancellors were churchmen.

Roman law

This is the whole basis of most continental legal systems, but it has had very little effect in English law. This effect itself is only indirect. Canon law is based to some extent on Roman law (the clerics were highly trained in it) and canon law has influenced English law. Further to this, there is an international aspect to mercantile and maritime law which is Roman in origin. Interestingly, the law in Scotland, which of course, differs in important ways from English law, is much more 'Roman' in character. However, in this book we deal only with English law (which may be just as well).

Textbooks

Before law reports became as totally reliable as they are today, that is, before 1865, textbooks were often cited as authority for law. Nowadays they are used when there is little or nothing in the way of precedents from which the court can take guidance. For example, in the extraordinary case of *R. v. Collins* [1972] two of the leading textbooks on the law of theft were consulted when the court was dealing with a fine point about burglary, ladders and a predominantly naked man ([1972] 2 All ER 1105).

LAW REFORM

The law, through the operation of the doctrine of judicial precedent, may become out of date and in need of reform. Or there may be a need for a more general reform of a complete area of law. In 1965 the Law Commissions Act created a committee of five full-time lawyers, 'to take and keep under review all the law . . . with a view to its systematic development and reform, including in particular the codification of such law, elimination of anomolies, the repeal of obsolete and unnecessary enactments, the reduction of the number of separate enactments and generally the simplification and modernisation of the law'. The Law Commissioners produce reports, recommendations and draft bills, the majority of which are adopted and become law. There is a separate Commission for Scotland.

If a branch of the law has evolved piecemeal then a 'consolidating' statute may be passed which brings together all the existing statute law in a consolidated form with the aim of clarifying the law. A 'codifying' statute differs from consolidation in that it brings together the existing statute and common law in a given area, again to clarify and simplify the law. Examples of codifying statutes are the Offences against the Person Act 1861 and the Sale of Goods Act 1893 (now repealed and replaced by the Sale of Goods Act 1979). In all cases one of the main problems is in finding the necessary parliamentary time for such legislation since it often lacks popular appeal and is unlikely to win votes from the electorate.

A Criminal Law Revision Committee also exists to keep under review areas of the criminal law which need reform.

If there is a question of considerable public importance which requires investigation and a report then a Committee to review or a Royal Commission may be established; for example the Royal Commission on Criminal Justice which was established in March 1991 by Kenneth Baker, then the Home Secretary, after the release of the 'Birmingham Six'. The Report was published in July 1993, containing 352 recommendations for change. These cover virtually every aspect of the criminal justice system. Many of these have been adopted. For example, the Criminal Cases Review Authority has been 'up and running' since 31 March 1997. But nothing is static in current law. In February 1997 the Prison Reform Trust published a paper calling for another Royal Commission to review all current aspects of crime and responses to crime.

Indicative questions

1 (a) Describe the way in which European Community law affects the passing of legislation in the United Kingdom. *(10 marks)*

(b) Assess the impact of membership of the European Community on the sovereignty of the United Kingdom Parliament. *(10 marks)*

2 **'The amount of delegated legislation has increased dramatically in recent years. There are arguments for and against this system of law-making.'**

Below is a list of these arguments.
  (i) It is undemocratic.
  (ii) It saves parliamentary time.
  (iii) There may be sub-delegation.
  (iv) Parliament does not have the necessary expertise.

  (a) Explain how **one** of these arguments can be seen as an advantage of delegated legislation. *(2 marks)*

  (b) Explain how **one** of these arguments can be seen as a disadvantage of delegated legislation. *(2 marks)*

  SEG

3 (a) Name *three* of the stages of a statute (an Act of Parliament). *(3 marks)*

  (b) Name *two* of the institutions which must approve the statute, before it becomes law. *(2 marks)*

  (c) Explain how the making of delegated legislation differs from the making of a statute. *(3 marks)*

  (d) Explain *two* possible advantages which delegated legislation may have over statute law. *(4 marks)*

  (e) Delegated legislation has been the subject of some criticism. Explain what *two* of these criticisms are. *(4 marks)*

  (f) In the light of these criticisms, explain what has been done both to control and to improve the system of delegated legislation. *(4 marks)*

  SEG

4 Study the extract below and then answer **all** parts of the question which follows.

Their Lordships regard the use of precedent as a vital foundation upon which to decide what is the law and how to apply it to individual cases. It provides at least some degree of certainty upon which individuals can rely in the conduct of their affairs, as well as a basis for the orderly development of legal rules.

Their Lordships nevertheless recognise that keeping too rigidly to precedent may lead to injustice in a particular case, and may also unduly restrict the proper development of the law.

They propose therefore to change their present practice. Whilst still treating their former decisions as normally binding, they propose to depart from a previous decision when it appears right to do so.

In this connection, they will bear in mind the special need for certainty as to the criminal law.

Source: adapted from *The Lord Chancellor's Practice Statement*, 1966

  (a) Name
    (i) the Court **and**
    (ii) the judges
       to which the Practice Statement applies. *(2 marks)*

(b) The Practice Statement makes a number of references to the doctrine of precedent. Explain how the system of binding operates through the hierarchy of courts in England and Wales. *(8 marks)*

(c) A precedent can be either binding or persuasive. Explain and illustrate the difference between these two different types of precedent. *(6 marks)*

(d) Explain why the Lord Chancellor saw the 'special need for certainty in the criminal law'. Do you think he was right? *(6 marks)*

(e) Explain why 'keeping too rigidly to precedent' could be seen as a disadvantage of the doctrine of precedent. *(6 marks)*

(f) Taking into account
   (i) any other advantages or disadvantages of precedent, **and**
   (ii) the change introduced by the 1966 Practice Statement, explain whether or not you consider precedent to be a good system. *(12 marks)*

SEG

5 Study the extracts below and then answer **all** parts of the question which follows.

Extract 1
In the 1966 Practice Statement, Lord Gardiner, on behalf of himself and his fellow Law Lords, stated that:
Their Lordships regard the use of precedent as an indispensable foundation upon which to decide what is the law . . . . It provides at least some degree of certainty upon which individuals can rely . . . .
Their Lordships nevertheless recognise that too rigid adherence to precedent may lead to injustice . . . and also . . . restrict the proper development of the law. They propose therefore to modify their present practice and, while treating former decisions of this House as normally binding, to depart from a previous decision when it appears right to do so. In this connection they will bear in mind . . . the special need for certainty as to the criminal law.

Extract 2
LORDS CRITICISE LAW ON AGE OF CRIMINAL KNOWLEDGE
The House of Lords called on Parliament yesterday to reform the "serious shortcomings" of the law that children between the ages of 10 and 13 cannot be convicted of a crime unless they are proved to know right from wrong. In a test ruling . . . five Law Lords said that the present law gave rise to anomalies and absurdities. Lord Lowry said, "This is a classic case for Parliamentary investigation, deliberation and legislation . . . . The time has come to examine further a doctrine . . . which is capable of producing inconsistent results."
Despite their misgivings, the five Law Lords upheld the presumption against criminal liability for those aged 10–13 and agreed that the presumption was still part of the Common Law, even though the time was ripe to review it.

Source: adapted from *The Times*, 17 March 1995, with reference to the case of *Curry* v. *DPP* (1995)

(a) With regard to the doctrine of precedent, explain the significance of the following:
   (i) *ratio decidendi;* *(3 marks)*
   (ii) *obiter dicta;* *(2 marks)*
   (iii) Law Reports. *(2 marks)*

(b) Explain why the major advantage of precedent referred to by Lord Gardiner, i.e. certainty, would be especially significant to the following people:

    (i) a solicitor; *(2 marks)*

    (ii) an officer of the Legal Aid Board when deciding whether or not to grant civil Legal Aid; *(3 marks)*

    (iii) a newly appointed judge; *(2 marks)*

    (iv) a law student answering a problem question. *(2 marks)*

(c) Precedent relies on a system by which courts are organised into a strict hierarchy.

    Explain and illustrate this statement. *(6 marks)*

(d) Briefly explain what Lord Gardiner meant by the following:

    (i) ". . . to depart from a previous decision when it appears right to do so"; *(2 marks)*

    (ii) ". . . the special need for certainty as to the criminal law". *(2 marks)*

(e) Despite the new powers available to the House of Lords from 1966, their Lordships were clearly reluctant to overrule the presumption against criminal liability for those aged 10–13 which, therefore, remains part of the Common Law.

    (i) What is the Common Law? *(2 marks)*

    (ii) Why do you think the House of Lords was reluctant to overrule this law and called upon Parliament to reform the Law? *(4 marks)*

(f) If Parliament were to change the law, new legislation would be required. In the context of legislation, explain what is meant by the following:

    (i) a Green Paper; *(2 marks)*

    (ii) a White Paper; *(2 marks)*

    (iii) the Committee Stage; *(2 marks)*

    (iv) the Royal Assent. *(2 marks)*

SEG Summer 1997 (Higher)

CHAPTER 4

Where the Law is Administered

The law is administered where anyone makes a judicial decision. So courts are, obviously, included. So too are tribunals. Policemen and ministers of the crown also administer the law. In this chapter we shall examine the court system of England and Wales and then consider tribunals at work.

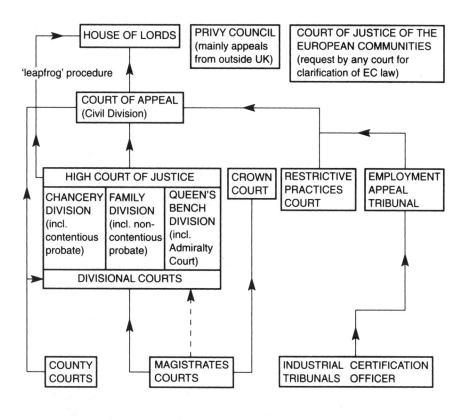

Appeals are indicated thus ——————

Appeals by way of case stated, thus – – –

System of courts exercising civil jurisdiction; reproduced with permission from *Smith and Keenan's English Law*, 10th edition, by Denis Keenan, Pitman Publishing

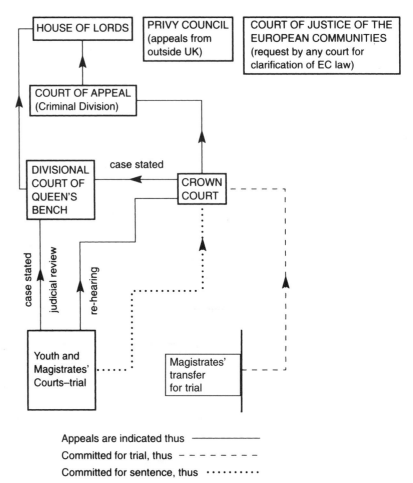

System of courts exercising criminal jurisdiction; reproduced with permission from *Smith and Keenan's English Law*, 10th edition, by Denis Keenan, Pitman Publishing

CLASSIFYING THE COURTS

The court system today reflects the massive reorganisation carried out by the Judicature Acts 1873–75. Before that there was a mild form of chaos both within the courts and between them. The Judicature Acts set up the Supreme Court of Judicature. There is no such place: the term is a collective one for the Court of Appeal, the High Court and the Crown Court. Interestingly, the House of Lords is not part of the Supreme Court, despite being the final court of appeal in most matters. This reflects a political accident. The Liberal government, with Lord Selbourne, drafted and passed the 1873 Act which, among other things, abolished the House of Lords as a final court of appeal (not as the second chamber of Parliament) in line with their policy against inherited power. The Act did not come into force until 1875. Meanwhile the Conservatives took power under Disraeli in February

1874. They reinstated the House in its judicial capacity, but neglected to place it within the Supreme Court.

There are various ways in which the present courts could be classified. First, courts might be 'inferior' or 'superior'. This shows how some are limited both in the cases they can try and the geographical area over which they have jurisdiction, whereas others have no such limits placed upon them.

Second, courts might be 'first instance' or 'appeal' courts. A court of first instance is a court which tries cases for the first time, e.g. the county court in a civil dispute, or the magistrates' court in a criminal action. Because courts can make mistakes when arriving at decisions, opportunities exist for having the mistakes rectified. Hence there is an appeal procedure, whereby the aggrieved party can take his case to a higher court and have the matter reviewed. In such cases, the matter will come before an appeal court, e.g. the Court of Appeal which, if it finds that the decision of the lower court was wrong, will reverse it and substitute its own decision.

Third, courts might be 'courts of record' or not. A court of record keeps its records on a permanent basis and has the power to fine and imprison for contempt of its authority and orders.

Fourth, courts might be 'civil' or 'criminal' according to the nature of the matters dealt with. This, with only a couple of exceptions, is not a clear line since many courts deal with both.

The civil/criminal classification is the one most used, but the fact that it is neither clear nor particularly logical should be noted.

CIVIL COURTS

It is important to realise that there are courts which do not fit easily into a classification scheme. It is important to understand at least broadly how the courts fit together. The structure is, of course, largely designed for appeal routes. It is also important to know a little of the work of each court which deals with civil cases.

The Court of Justice of the European Communities

This is not strictly an English court. It does, however, have a certain authority within the English legal system. Where a point in any case concerns the interpretation of Community law, any court may, and the final court of appeal in a member state must (under Art. 177 of the EEC Treaty), refer the case to the European Court for a ruling. This is binding authority on the point of law. The national court must then decide the case in the light of the interpretation dictated to it. Naturally, the court has jurisdiction within the Community to deal with Community disputes.

There are fifteen judges in the European Court. They are appointed for six years and they can be reappointed; most have been, some three times. They appoint a president from among their number, who serves for three years at a time. There is an emphasis on written submissions rather than oral argument. The court is assisted by nine Advocates-General. They are independent advisers, one of whom is assigned to

The Court of Justice of the European Communities; reproduced with permission from the Court

each case by the President of the Court. It is provided by the EEC Treaty, Art. 166:

It shall be the duty of the Advocate-General, acting with complete impartiality and independence, to make, in open court, reasoned submissions on cases brought before the Court of Justice, in order to assist the Court.

This is done by giving an 'opinion' about a case after it has been heard and before the court gives judgment. The Advocate-General sits on the bench, but not with the judges. It is a very important job. Judges have transferred to it. The European Court gives a single judgment, with no reference being made to dissenting opinions. The judgment is enforced through the national courts of member states. The judgment tends to be rather dry. The opinion of the Advocate-General, however, is likely to be full and reasoned and thus of more use as an explanation of the relevant Community law.

On 31 October 1989 the Court of First Instance opened for business. It was immediately given 151 cases which had been pending before the European Court. This new court has two functions: to reduce the workload of the European Court (and thus to speed the disposal of cases) and second to handle cases which fall within its jurisdiction as set out in the Decision under which it was created (Dec. 88/591), such as staff cases, between the Community and its servants. It is intended that the Court of First Instance should develop into a specialised fact-finding tribunal with particular expertise in the economic effects of complex cases. There is a right of appeal to the European court, but only on points of law.

The House of Lords For most cases this is the final court of appeal within the English court system. It may no longer have the last word in Community law, but otherwise, and in both civil and criminal cases, there is nowhere else to go to have a decision reconsidered. The law as settled in the case can be changed by legislation, or even (in rare circumstances, as has been noted in Chapter 3) over-ruled in a later, similar case by the court itself. Otherwise, this is where the last cards are played.

The Law Lords usually sit in groups of three or five, or sometimes seven (as in *Cassell* v. *Broome* (1972), *DPP* v. *Majewski* (1977) and *Pepper* v. *Hart* (1993). They do so unrobed in the Palace of Westminster, in a committee room. The court sat for the first time as a committee on 26 May 1948. Before then, the hearings were regarded as ordinary sittings of the House of Lords as the second chamber of Parliament. This committee procedure was intended as a temporary measure: the House of Commons Chamber had been destroyed by enemy action on 10 May 1941. The Commons moved into the Lords' Chamber and the Lords into the King's Robing Room in the Royal Gallery. When rebuilding was in progress in 1945 the builders installed a heating system below the Robing Room which made it impossible to hear what was being said. The pile-drivers downstairs drowned even the loudest of advocates. As a result the Law Lords moved to a committee room, from where they have yet to emerge. The Law Lords themselves are the senior members of the English judiciary. They are, in practice, appointed from the Court of Appeal from time to time as the need arises. In theory they could come from the High Court or even directly from the practising Bar. There can be between seven and twelve judges. Usually they include Scottish and Irish judges. This reflects the fact that the House serves as final court of appeal for the Court of Session in Scotland and the Court of Appeal in Northern Ireland. The House is not the final appeal court for Scottish Criminal cases. When the Appellate Jurisdiction Act 1876 was passed, the Court was to be composed of just two judges. At that time they were Lord Blackburn and Lord Gordon of Drumearn.

The Lord Chancellor (a government appointment) is responsible for the work of the court, and sometimes presides in person. On the rare occasions when the Appellate Committee sits in the Lords' Chamber he usually presides, robed and bewigged.

The jurisdiction is almost entirely appellate. The court hears appeals from the Court of Appeal (and its equivalent in Scotland and Northern Ireland). There is no right to appeal: permission must be granted, either from the Court of Appeal or the House itself. The case must be one of public importance. In criminal cases the issues must be based on a point of law. In practice virtually all final appeals are on such points and ninety per cent of them are on the interpretation of statutes.

The House also entertains appeals direct from the High Court in civil cases according to the 'leap-frog' procedure provided by the Administration of Justice Act 1969. Here, the trial judge must issue a certificate that the case is one of public importance and, either that it concerns statutory interpretation, or that the outcome is bound by a previous decision of the House itself (which would, obviously, also bind the Court of Appeal). Further to this certificate, the House itself must give leave to appeal. In this way the case 'leap-frogs' the Court of Appeal. (An interesting illustration here is *Vestey* v. *Inland Revenue Commissioners* (1979), which is a case showing both the 'leap-frog' procedure and the House using its power to overrule its own previous decisions, assumed in the Practice Statement in 1966, which was noted in Chapter 3.)

As will be noted below, the Queen's Bench Division of the High Court has a certain criminal jurisdiction. Appeals lie directly to the House in such cases, again with leave and only in really important cases. This is provided by the Administration of Justice Act 1960. The House also hears cases from the Courts-Martial Appeal Court.

The Court of Appeal (Civil Division)

The Judicature Acts 1873–75 created the Court of Appeal, although its present form dates only from 1966. On 1 October of that year the Criminal Appeal Act 1966 came into force; it split the court into two divisions, civil and criminal. The civil division deals with cases from the High Court, the county courts, the Restrictive Practices Court and also from various tribunals such as the Employment Appeal Tribunal and the Lands Tribunal.

The court consists of a maximum of 32 Lord Justices of Appeal. In rare cases a sole judge may sit to hear an appeal but the usual number is two or three. They are generally appointed from the High Court, although it is possible for a practising barrister to be appointed. The Master of the Rolls presides in the civil division. Further to these the Lord Chancellor, former Lord Chancellors, the Law Lords and the President of the Family Division of the High Court all have the right to sit. More often, and particularly in the criminal division, High Court judges sit with the Lord Justices of Appeal.

The court has the power to uphold or reverse the decision of the lower court. It can, but very rarely does, order a new trial. This might happen, for example, where new evidence has come to light which could, had it been available at the time the case was tried, have affected the lower court's decision. It can also reassess damage awards, as it did in October 1989 in the famous libel case *Sutcliffe* v. *Pressdram* (1989).

In November 1997 the Report of a Review of the Court of Appeal (Civil Division) was published. The Chairman, sir Jeffrey Bowman, said:

> Our report contains important recommendations to the Lord Chancellor for reducing the number of cases coming to the Court of Appeal and for improving practice and procedures in the Civil Appeals Office and in the Court itself. We believe that the quality of justice will be improved by these changes. The elimination of delays in the Court of Appeal and the facility for simpler appeals to be heard more locally should yield substantial benefits to all litigants and will allow the Lords Justices of Appeal to devote their valuable time and skills to the most important issues.

The Review's major recommendations include that: certain appeals which now reach the Court of Appeal (Civil Division) should be heard at a lower level — the largest category of such cases being appeals against decisions in fast track cases; the requirement for leave to appeal should be extended to nearly all cases; there should be also an increasing role for appropriate judicial case management; there is a need for more focused procedures. Cases should also be better prepared at a much earlier stage in the process and realistic timetables should be set which must be strictly observed; the Court should impose appropriate time limits on oral argument on appeals; the balance of judicial time should lean more towards reading and less towards sitting in court; there is a need to develop the use of information technology to support the other recommendations of this Review, and information for litigants in person about the appeal process and what it can deliver must be available at an early stage (the information must be easily understandable and delivered in a range of different ways).

The High Court of Justice

The High Court was created by the Judicature Acts 1873–75, but in its present form it dates only from 1971, when the Administration of Justice Act 1970 was implemented. The court generally sits in the Royal Courts of Justice, an elegant building at the Aldwych end of the Strand in London. The building was designed in a thirteenth-century style in 1874 by G E Street. It also houses the Court of Appeal, but, unlike that court (except in the rarest of circumstances), the High Court also sits at other centres around the country. Indeed, wherever a High Court judge (called a 'puisne' judge, pronounced 'puny') sits, there sits the High Court. The Lord Chancellor bears the ultimate responsibility for such matters. Puisne judges are appointed from among barristers or solicitors of long standing and are usually appointed from the ranks of Queen's Counsel. The maximum number of puisne judges is currently 98. In theory circuit judges can be promoted, but this is not common.

The High Court is split into three basic divisions, each of which is further divided. In theory, any puisne judge can deal with any High Court matter; in practice they specialise. Often this specialisation reflects their professional expertise when they were barristers. This is especially true in the Chancery Division. There is no jurisdictional limit to the High Court's civil work, although the smaller cases are dealt with by the county courts (*see* below). Each of the three divisions has an appellate jurisdiction. This work is mostly done in separate courts, confusingly called divisional courts. The Courts and Legal Services Act 1990 has made significant changes in the jurisdictional division of work between the High Court and the County Court.

The Chancery Division

Here the first-instance jurisdiction covers the administration of the estates of the dead, trusts, mortgages, rectification of deeds, partnerships, the winding-up of companies, bankruptcy, revenue, planning and landlord and tenant disputes. Sometimes these and other cases are dealt with within the division by particular courts.

There are, for example, the Companies Court, the Patents Court and the Court of Protection which deals with managing the affairs of mental patients.

The appellate jurisdiction covers appeals from decisions of the Inland Revenue Commissioners, and appeals on bankruptcy and land registration cases from county courts. This division is presided over by the Lord Chancellor in theory and the Vice-Chancellor in practice.

The Family Division

This division was created by the Administration of Justice Act 1970. There used to be a division called Probate, Divorce and Admiralty—a strange mixture, once called by Sir Alan Herbert (whose entertaining writings are highly recommended), the Divison of 'Wills, Wives and Wrecks'. The Family Division took over the wives, the wrecks went to the Queen's Bench Division, and the Family and Chancery Divisions divided the wills: the contentious cases go to Chancery.

Obviously, the first-instance jurisdiction covers family matters, such as all cases concerning marriage including its validity and termination (except undefended divorces, which are county court material), legitimacy, wardship, adoption, guardianship, custodianship, domestic violence and disputes over family property. The court also deals with matters arising under the Human Fertilisation and Embryology Act 1990, such as ordering that a child carried by another woman is to be regarded as the child within a marriage.

The appellate jurisdiction reflects the fact that minor domestic matters can be dealt with at first instance elsewhere, and the appropriate appeal route would lie here. Thus, cases from the county, magistrates' and Crown Courts in such matters are dealt with by a divisional court of two or three puisne judges. This division is presided over by the President of the Family Division.

For many years it has been argued that we ought to have a 'Family Court' within our court system. In November 1986, in a report called *Family Justice: A Structure for a Family Court*, the British Agencies for Adoption and Fostering put forward a proposal that a court be set up which would take over all family jurisdiction except juvenile crime. It should have two tiers, roughly equivalent to the county court and the Family Division of the High Court. They go on to suggest the removal of jurisdiction from magistrates, but that laymen be incorporated into the new court. They also stress the role of conciliation. Brenda Hogget drew a fine picture of the complexity of family law jurisdiction in 1986 (6 *Legal Studies*), in her article: 'Family Courts or family law reform— which should come first?'. Her hypothetical example involves four kinds of court: Juvenile (three times), the High Court (twice), the Crown Court and the County Court (three times). A governmental consultative document on reforming family law jurisdiction was published in 1986. The idea of family courts was once again dismissed by the government during debate on the Children Act 1989, although an interdepartmental working party was set up to review the area. The main opposition to reform from the Lord Chancellor's Department seems to be based on cost.

The Queen's Bench Division

This is the largest and the most over-worked of the three. It is presided over by the Lord Chief Justice.

The first-instance jurisdiction covers mainly contract and tort actions. These are cases involving claims for huge awards of damages (lesser matters are dealt with by county courts).

The division also includes the Admiralty Court, which deals with such matters as claims for injury or loss through collisions at sea, the ownership and loss of and from ships, towage and salvage. It is common to find experienced laymen (called lay assessors) who assist the judge in the Admiralty Court.

Also included here is the Commercial Court which provides, in addition to open-court hearings of commercial claims, an arbitration service for businessmen. These claims might include insurance, banking, agency and negotiable instruments. Such alternative means of dispute resolution as arbitration, conciliation and mediation are particularly useful where the costs of litigation far outweigh the amount of money at stake.

Within the division there is also an Election Court composed of two puisne judges, which deals with disputes over the validity of elections and reports to the Speaker of the House of Lords (under the Representation of the People Act 1983). A recent illustration is the setting aside of the general election result of May 1997 in Winchester, upon the application of Gerry Malone.

The appellate jurisdiction is complicated. A single judge can hear appeals from certain tribunals (e.g. the Pensions Appeals Tribunal) and from commercial arbitrations, particularly on points of law (under the Arbitration Acts 1950 and 1979). The divisional court, of two (usually) or three judges, has a certain civil appeal function, for example, from the Solicitors' Disciplinary Tribunal.

However, the divisional court has two other important functions. First it hears the appeals from magistrates' courts and the Crown Court (where the case has been tried in a magistrates' court and has been to the Crown Court for appeal or sentence) by way of 'case stated'. This strange phrase means simply an appeal on the basis, not that the facts found were wrong, but that either the decision as to the law relating to those facts was wrong or the decision-makers were acting beyond their jurisdiction.

Second, it exercises the supervisory jurisdiction which this division has inherited from the ancient Court of King's Bench, at which the monarch himself originally presided. This power is one to scrutinise the activities of all the inferior courts, tribunals and other arenas in which decisions affecting the rights of individuals are made (including decisions by ministers) and to see that these decisions are taken in a proper manner. The court does not usurp the decision-making power itself; it merely checks the manner of its exercise. The court has four main weapons. They are three prerogative orders and one prerogative writ (these very names indicate their royal ancestry).

The first order is called *mandamus* ('we order') and it used to compel the execution of a legal duty. It must be a duty and not a discretionary power. Thus in *R.* v. *Bedwelty UDC* (1934), *mandamus* was issued at the request of a ratepayer who insisted that the local authority should allow an examination of its accounts, whereas in *Re Fletcher's Application* (1970) the order was refused to an applicant who insisted that the Parliamentary Commissioner (the Ombudsman) should investigate his complaint. This was because the relevant statute provides that he 'may' investigate. He has a discretion. It is not a legal duty.

The second order is prohibition; the third is called certiorari. Lord Atkin explained (in *R. v. Electricity Commissioners* (1924)):

> Both writs are of great antiquity, forming part of the process by which the King's Courts restrained courts of inferior jurisdiction from exceeding their powers. Prohibition restrains the tribunal from proceeding further in excess of jurisdiction; certiorari requires the record or the order of the court to be sent up to the King's Bench Division, to have its legality inquired into, and, if necessary, to have the order quashed . . . Doubtless in their origin (they) dealt almost exclusively with the jurisdiction of what is described in ordinary parlance as a court of justice. But (their) operation has extended to control the proceedings of bodies which do not claim to be, and would not be recognised as, courts of justice. Wherever any body of persons having legal authority to determine questions affecting the rights of subjects, and having the duty to act judicially, act in excess of their legal authority they are subject to the controlling jurisdiction of the King's Bench Division.

Prohibition, then, is available to prevent such a body as Lord Atkin was referring to from acting without jurisdiction or contrary to the rules of natural justice. It is applicable before the event.

After the decision has been taken, certiorari may be appropriate. This order lies to correct the decision taken without jurisdiction, or contrary to natural justice or where there is an error of law actually in the written record of the case. The phrase 'natural justice' is used here. Maugham J explained (in *Maclean* v. *Workers' Union* (1929)):

> The phrase is, of course, used only in a popular sense and must not be taken to mean that there is any justice natural among men. Among most savages there is no such thing as justice in the modern sense. The phrase 'the principles of fair natural justice' can only mean, in this connection, the principles of fair play so deeply rooted in the minds of modern Englishmen that a provision for an inquiry necessarily imparts that the accused should be given his chance of defence and explanation.

This requirement of 'fair play' is usually explained by means of two rules with Latin names. The first is *audi alteram partem*, which means 'let the other side be heard'. Allegations that this rule has been broken usually involve lack of time allowed to prepare a defence or indeed lack of notice of the hearing itself, whether an oral hearing is necessary, whether the right to cross examine witnesses exists, the right to be represented by a lawyer, and so on. The other rule is *nemo judex in causa sua*, which means 'no-one should be a judge in his own cause'. It is sometimes called the rule against bias. A very famous instance of this rule being broken concerned a Lord Chancellor, Lord Cottenham, who had decided a case in favour of a canal company in which he held shares, although it is said that he had forgotten about them. The case is called *Dimes* v. *Grand Junction Canal Proprietors* (1852). Lord Campbell said:

No-one can suppose that Lord Cottenham could be, in the remotest degree, influenced by the interest that he had in this concern; but, my Lords, it is of the last importance that the maxim that no man is to be a judge in his own cause be held sacred. And that is not to be confined to a cause in which he is a party but applies to a cause in which he has an interest . . . This will be a lesson to all inferior tribunals to take care not only that in their decrees they are not influenced by their personal interest but to avoid the appearance of labouring under such an influence.

There are two other orders available from the divisional court, the injunction and the declaration. Often an injunction is applied for via the office of the Attorney-General in a relator action. This means, in theory, that the Attorney-General, on behalf of the public, seeks to have an activity stopped. This is commonly done to stop the activity pending a full hearing by a court. The declaration is not so much a remedy as a means of clarifying what the law is. Once the position has been made clear, the parties abide by it. Thus it may have the same effect as a remedy.

As a point of procedure the applicant is able to apply for judicial review rather than ask for any one order. This procedure follows the recommendations of the Law Commission in their 1976 Report No. 73 and is contained within the Rules of the Supreme Court (R.S.C. ord.53) and also partly in statute form by the Supreme Court Act 1981, s.31.

Finally on the divisional court, a brief glance at *habeas corpus*. When somebody is imprisoned or restrained illegally, no matter by whom, his release can be obtained by means of this writ. The court will require the imprisoner to justify the restraint. If he cannot, the individual is freed. In *R. v. Jackson* (1891) a man would not let his wife leave the house. In *ex parte* Daisy Hopkins (1891) the Vice-Chancellor of the University of Cambridge locked up a woman for 'walking with a member of the University'. There are few modern instances. These tend to come from those in detention awaiting extradition or deportation or where an immigrant has been refused entry and is awaiting his return. For example, *R. v. Governor of Brixton Prison ex parte Osman (No. 4)* (1992) where the applicant had made four applications for the writ in order to escape extradition to Hong Kong where he was to face criminal charges. This was his fifth application. It failed too. The writ has, however, a long and valiant history. It dates at least from Magna Carta (signed on 15 June 1215: 'To no one will we sell, to none will we deny, to none will we delay, right or justice'). It was on an application for *habeas corpus* that slavery was declared illegal in England (*Sommersett* v. *Stewart* (1772)) when a negro was released even though slavery was legal in his home territory.

County courts

The county courts were established in 1846 by the County Courts Act 1846 to provide quick and inexpensive relief in the case of small civil disputes. The general jurisdiction and procedures are governed by the County Courts Act 1984 and the Courts and Legal Services Act 1990, and rule and orders made under them. The courts are staffed by a circuit judge, appointed on the advice of the Lord Chancellor. There are approximately 260 county courts. They are local courts in districts throughout England and Wales. The judge normally sits alone, though on very rare occasions trial may be by a jury of eight persons (e.g. in cases of fraud). In addition to there being a judge, each court has a District Judge. There is also a permanent official called the chief clerk who runs the office and is in charge of the office staff. The District Judge is empowered to try cases where the amount of money involved does not exceed £3000 (soon to be raised to £5000). If both parties agree, however, the jurisdiction of the District Judge extends to any matter within the jurisdiction of the court. About 90 per cent of all civil cases are brought in county courts. The vast majority are for small (e.g. £500–£750) money debts.

Cases are normally brought within the district where the defendant lives or carries on business, or, if land is involved, where the land is situated. A 'default' action can be started in any county court. Appeals from the county court generally lie to the Court of Appeal (Civil Division). The jurisdiction of the county courts is very wide. It covers:

1 actions in contract and tort. In the case of certain torts (e.g. defamation) the court has no jurisdiction unless both parties agree;
2 equity matters, such as trusts, mortgages and dissolution of partnerships;
3 actions involving title to land;
4 actions concerning probate and letters of administration;
5 winding-up of companies;
6 matrimonial causes. Under the Matrimonial and Family Proceedings Act 1984 a county court may be designated a divorce county court, and has jurisdiction in the case of undefended divorces. In fact, all matrimonial causes (e.g. a divorce and nullity) must begin in a divorce court, though defended cases will be transferred to the High Court. All county courts are able to hear applications brought under the Domestic Violence and Matrimonial Proceedings Act 1976;
7 adoption and custodianship of children;
8 landlord and tenant disputes;
9 race-relations;
10 consumer credit;
11 some county courts, such as those in large ports, have Admiralty jurisdiction;
12 arbitration.

This last point—arbitration—is of great and increasing importance within the county courts. Since the Administration of Justice Act 1973 virtually any county court matter can be dealt with in a relatively informal way. The arbitrator (usually the District Judge) sits unrobed and the proceedings are heard in private. The strict rules of evidence do not necessarily apply. Arbitration can be requested by either party. If a case concerns a claim of up to £3000 (or £1000 in personal injury claims) then arbitration is automatic unless the circumstances are exceptional, as they were in *Pepper* v. *Headley* (1982), where an automatic reference to arbitration was rescinded when the case became very complicated and the costs increased. Lawyers' fees are not recoverable in these arbitration hearings (*see* below). So it is that small claims, particularly consumer disputes, are usually handled in this way. There are around 90 000 such claims each year.

Typical examples are:

1 claims arising out of the purchase, hire or repair of consumer goods;
2 claims against persons providing consumer services, e.g. garages, plumbers, electrical appliance repairs;
3 claims for arrears of rent;
4 claims arising out of negligence, e.g. a road accident. Normally this is covered by insurance, but if the amount claimed is less than the excess on the policy, or if the driver wants to retain his no claims bonus, the injured driver or pedestrian can sue the driver who was allegedly negligent.

Small claims are normally initiated and dealt with by the plaintiff acting on his own behalf. Indeed the cost of employing a solicitor to speak for the plaintiff is not recoverable even if the action succeeds. An action is started by filling in a 'request' form and a 'particulars of claim' form (sometimes a combined form is used). These are available at the office in the local county court. If the plaintiff succeeds he will be entitled to recover some of the expenses incurred in bringing the claim. These include:

1 costs of bringing the action. (This is roughly 10 per cent of the size of the claim. It is paid by the plaintiff when the forms are completed and handed in at the court);
2 out of pocket expenses (e.g. police reports, company searches);
3 witnesses' expenses.

In February 1985 the Lord Chancellor set in hand a major review of the system of civil justice in England and Wales in order to find ways to 'cut the delays, the cost and the complexity of civil litigation'. As part of this work a consultation paper was issued on 23 September 1986, which was based on the findings of a special survey of the small claims service within the county courts carried out by a firm of management consultants. This survey makes interesting reading. The small claims service was created in 1973. Nowadays most claims for money or damages in the county courts are dealt with in this way. In 1985, 44 700 small claims were disposed of, as against 28 900 claims tried in the ordinary way. The study shows general satisfaction with the service, although a great variation of practice between courts. Some take only sixteen weeks to dispose of small claims, others up to a year.

Many of the recommendations contained within the resulting Report have been put into effect by the Courts and Legal Services Act 1990. One important aspect was the distribution of the workload between the High Court and the County courts.

There are now certain 'criteria' that are to be taken into account:

1 the financial substance of the action;
2 the importance of the action (to outsiders and/or the general public);
3 the complexity of the facts;

County Court Summons

Case Number	*Always quote this*	

In the

County Court

The court office is open from 10am to 4pm Monday to Friday

Telephone:

Seal

This summons is only valid if sealed by the court
If it is not sealed it should be reported to the court

Keep this summons. You may need to refer to it

(1)
Plaintiff's full name address

(2)
Address for sending documents and payments
(if not as above)
Ref/Tel no.

(3)
Defendant's full name
(eg Mr, Mrs or Miss where known)
and address
Company no.
(where known)

What the plaintiff claims from you

Brief description of type of claim

Particulars of the plaintiff's claim against you

Amount claimed	
Court fee	
Solicitor's costs	
Total amount	
Summons issued on	

Signed
Plaintiff or plaintiff's solicitor
(or see enclosed particulars of claim)

N1 Default summons (fixed amount) (Order 3, rule 3(2)(b)) (11.95)   *Printed by Satellite Press Limited*

What to do about this summons

You have 21 days from the date of the postmark to reply to this summons
(A limited company served at its registered office has 16 days to reply)
If this summons was delivered by hand, you have 14 days from the date it was delivered to reply

You can

• dispute the claim

• make a claim against the plaintiff

• admit the claim and costs in full and offer to pay

• admit only part of the claim

• pay the total amount shown above

You must read the information on the back of this form. It will tell you more about what to do.

Small claims form; Crown copyright; reproduced by kind permission of the Controller of Her Majesty's Stationery Office

If you do nothing	**Judgment may be entered against you without further notice. This will make it difficult for you to get credit.**
If you dispute the claim	Complete the white defence form (N9B) and return it to the court office within the time allowed. The notes on the form explain what you should do. It is not enough to contact the plaintiff by telephone or letter.
If you want to make a claim against the plaintiff (counterclaim)	Complete boxes 5 and 6 on the white defence form (N9B) and return the form to the court office. The notes at box 5 explain what you should do.
If you admit all of the claim and you are asking for time to pay	Fill in the blue admission form (N9A). The notes on the form explain what you should do and where you should send the completed form. You must reply within the time allowed.
If you admit all of the claim and you wish to pay now	**Take or send the money including any interest and costs to the person named at box (2) on the front of the summons.** If there is no address in box (2), send the money to the address in box (1). You should ensure the plaintiff receives the money within the period given for reply. Read 'How to Pay' below.
If you admit only part of the claim	Fill in the white defence form (N9B) saying how much you admit, and why you dispute the balance. Then **either:** Pay the amount admitted as explained in the box above; **or** If you need time to pay fill in the blue admission form (N9A) and return the forms to the court office within the time allowed.

Costs

In addition to the solicitor's costs for issuing the summons, a plaintiff's solicitor is entitled to add further costs if the court enters judgment against you.

Interest on judgments

If judgment is entered against you and is for £5,000 or more the plaintiff may be entitled to interest on the total amount.

Registration of judgments

If the summons results in a judgment against you, your name and address may be entered in the Register of County Court Judgments. **This will make it difficult for you to get credit.** A leaflet giving further information can be obtained from the court.

Further advice

Court staff cannot give you advice on points of law, but you can get help to complete the reply forms and information about court procedures at any county court office or Citizens Advice Bureau. The address and telephone number of your local court is listed under 'Courts' in the phone book. When corresponding with the court, please address forms or letters to the Chief Clerk. Always quote the whole of the case number which appears at the top right corner on the front of this form; the court is unable to trace your case without it.

How to Pay	**Certificate of service** To be completed on the court copy only
• **PAYMENT(S) MUST BE MADE to the person named at the address for payment** quoting their reference and the court case number.	Served on
• **DO NOT bring or send payments to the court. THEY WILL NOT BE ACCEPTED.**	By posting on
• You should allow **at least** 4 days for your payments to reach the plaintiff or his representative.	Officer
• Make sure that you keep records and can account for all payments made. Proof may be required if there is any disagreement. It is not safe to send cash unless you use registered post.	
• A leaflet giving further advice about payment can be obtained from the court.	Not served on (reasons)
• If you need more information you should contact the plaintiff or his representative.	

N1 Default summons (fixed amount) (Order 3, rule 3(2)(b)) (11.95)

Printed by Satellite Press Limited

Notes on filling in a Default Summons (fixed amount)

- Complete form N1 using a typewriter or word processor if possible
- If you need to fill it in by hand, write in **black ink** using block capitals. Do not write outside the boxes
- Supply the court with 1 original and a copy for **each defendant**

1   Plaintiff   *the person making the claim*

Fill in the full name and address or place of business of the person making the claim. If you are:

- **a company registered under the Companies Act 1985,** give the address of the registered office and describe it as such
- **a person trading in a name other than your own,** give your own name followed by the words 'trading as' and the name under which you trade
- **two or more co-partners suing in the name of their firm,** 'A Firm' an assignee, say so and give the name, address and occupation of the assignor
- **a minor under 18 required to sue by next friend,** state this and give full names, address or place of business, and occupation of next friend. You will also need to complete and send in Form N235 (which you can get from the court office)
- **suing in a representative capacity,** say in what capacity

2   Address for service and payment

If the summons is completed by a solicitor or by your legal department, the name, address and reference of the solicitor or legal department must be in box 2. The court will use this address for sending documents to you (service). (If the address is the same as shown at box 1, please write 'as above' in box 2.)

- **a plaintiff who is not represented by a solicitor or legal department must not use box 2** except for an address to which payment may be made. In this case you must delete the word 'service' in the title to box 2.

3   Defendant   *the person against whom the claim is made*

Fill in the defendant's surname and (where known) his or her initials or names in full. You must identify the defendant as fully and accurately as possible. Also give the defendant's address or place of business (if the owner of a business). If the company is a limited company, give the company number if you can the number should be on any invoice or letter from the company). Say whether the defendant is male or female and, if under 18, state 'minor'. If the defendant is:

- **a company registered under the Companies Act 1985,** the address given must be the registered office of the company (you must describe it as such) or its place of business. If the summons is not sent to the registered office, there is a risk that it will not come to the notice of an appropriate person in the company. As a result, the court may be asked to set aside any judgment or order that has been made. If the registered office and place of business are not in the same court area, you may decide to choose the address which is most convenient to you. However remember that if the company you are suing defends the case, the case will automatically be transferred to the company's local court
- **a person trading in a name other than his own** who is sued under that name, add 'A Trading Name'
- **two or more co-partners** sued in the name of their firm, add 'A Firm'
- **suing in a representative capacity,** say in what capacity

4   Where to send the summons

Fill in the name and full address of the court where you are sending the summons. You can ask any county court in England and Wales to issue it. You will usually choose your local court or the court for the area where the defendant lives or carries on business. Bear in mind that if the person you are suing defends the case, the case will automatically be transferred to the defendant's local court.

5   What the claim is for

Put a brief description of your claim in the box (eg price of goods sold and delivered, work done, money due under an agreement).

6   Particulars of your claim

Give a brief statement of the facts of your claim and its value. Include any relevant dates and sufficient details so that the defendant understands what your claim is for. He is entitled to ask for further details. If there is not enough space, enclose a separate sheet for the court and a copy for each defendant. The court can help you in setting out your particulars of claim.

If you wish to claim interest you must include it in your particulars of claim. You must word your claim as follows: 'The plaintiff claims interest under section 69 of the County Courts Act 1984 at the rate of 8% a year, from [date from which you are claiming interest] to [date you are issuing summons] of £ [enter amount] and also interest at the same rate up to the date of judgment or earlier payment, at a daily rate of £ .' For more information on interest see leaflet 2 (How do I make a small claim in the County Court).

7   Amount claimed

Fill in the total amount you are claiming, including any interest. The court fee and solicitor's costs are based on this and you should enter these too. A leaflet setting out the current fees is available from the court.

8   Signature

The person filling in the form should sign and date it, unless enclosing separate details of claim (in which case the enclosed sheets should be signed).

9   How the claim will be dealt with if defended

If the total you are claiming is for £3,000 or less and/or your claim for damages for personal injury is worth £1,000 or less, it will be dealt with by arbitration (small claims procedure) unless the court decides the case is too difficult to be dealt with in this informal way. If the claim is not dealt with by arbitration, costs, including the costs of help from a legal representative, may be allowed.

If the total you are claiming is more than £3,000 and/or you are claiming more than £1,000 for damages for personal injury, it can still be dealt with by arbitration if you or the defendant ask for it and the court approves. If your claim is dealt with by arbitration in these circumstances, costs may be allowed.

Costs and the grounds for setting aside an arbitration award are strictly limited.

Further information on how to issue a default summons and what happens after issue can be obtained from any county court office

N443 Notes on filling in a default summons (fixed amount) (12.95)   *Printed by Satelline Press Limited*

4 the legal issues;

5 the remedies or the procedures involved in the matter;

6 whether a transfer of the case to the county court is likely to speed up the handling of the case.

Now subject to these criteria:

1 the county court should try any action worth less than £25 000, all personal injury claims under £50 000 and all probate and equity matters under £30 000;

2 the High Court should handle all matters above £50 000, all applications for judicial review and all applications for *Anton Piller* and *Mareva*-type injunctions;

3 cases involving claims between £25 000 and £50 000 should be allocated according to the criteria, and if the High Court thinks that a case should have been brought before the lower court, then a costs penalty can be imposed.

Magistrates' courts The jurisdiction of the magistrates' court is predominantly criminal but it does have some civil jurisdiction. The civil jurisdiction of the magistrates includes the following:

1 affiliation orders;

2 matrimonial relief (e.g. protection against violence, maintenance orders);

3 custody, adoption and guardianship of children;

4 orders committing children to the care of the local authority;

5 granting and renewing licences for licensed premises;

6 enforcement of rate demands, taxes and certain debts owed to the gas, electricity and water undertakings and local authorities;

7 granting and renewing licences under the betting and gaming legislation.

When dealing with family law matters such as **1–3** above the magistrates are specially trained and at least one woman justice must sit. The public are excluded and the press restricted. Appeals lie to the Family Division of the High Court in groups **1–4**. Under the Children Act 1989 the court is empowered to issue a 'child assessment order' which will last seven days and permits social services to report on whether children should be removed from home.

CRIMINAL COURTS

The Court of Justice of the European Communities/The House of Lords We saw these in the last section. The vast majority of their work lies in civil and administrative matters, but they do handle criminal cases too.

The Court of Appeal (Criminal Division) We saw the broad composition of the Court of Appeal in the last section. The Criminal Division was created by the Criminal Appeal Act of 1966. The division replaced the Court of Criminal Appeal (which had itself replaced the Courts for Crown Cases Reserved under the Criminal Appeal Act 1907). Much of its jurisdiction is now defined by the 1966 Act as amended in January 1996 by the Criminal Appeal Act 1995. The court is presided over by the Lord Chief Justice. In addition to the composition described above, since January 1995, by virtue of the Criminal Justice and Public Order Act 1994, it has been possible for Circuit Judges to sit in the Criminal Division. There are defined limits to this capacity and the judges must be approved by the Lord Chancellor.

This division deals with appeals from the Crown Court against conviction or sentence. The Attorney-General can refer cases to the court (under the Criminal Justice Act 1972, s.36(1)) for consideration of points of law after an acquittal. The court's judgment will not affect the acquitted person, but it may affect future cases. The Criminal Justice Act 1988, ss. 35 and 36, provides that the Attorney-General can refer a case to the Court of Appeal where he feels that the sentence imposed was either unduly lenient or unduly severe. A recent illustration is *R. v. Harnett* (Attorney-General's Reference No. 60 of 1996) (1997).

Section 1 of the Criminal Appeal Act 1995 provides that all appeals against conviction and sentence must either have leave of the Court of Appeal or a certificate of fitness for appeal from the trial judge. Section 3 of the 1995 Act repeals section 17 of the Criminal Appeal Act 1968 which permitted the Home Secretary to make a reference to the Court of Appeal following a conviction on indictment or on a finding of not guilty by reason of insanity. Much of this function has (since 31 March 1997) now been assumed by the Criminal Cases Review Commission.

The Crown Court

The Crown Court was created by means of the Courts Act 1971, implementing the Beeching Commission Report. Three main kinds of judges preside, depending upon the seriousness of the case: High Court judges, circuit judges and part-time judges called recorders.

The sittings of the court are held in first-, second- and third-tier centres, based on six circuits in England and Wales. The first-tier courts are the most important, and deal with the most serious cases. The circuits are the Northern, the North-Eastern, the Midland and Oxford, the Wales and Chester, the Western and the South-Eastern. Each has a Circuit Administrator. They are based in Manchester, Leeds, Birmingham, Cardiff, Bristol and London, and are managerial rather than judicial officers. Each circuit has a presiding judge to carry the judicial responsibility (there are three in the South-Eastern Circuit, including the Lord Chief Justice).

The Crown Court has exclusive jurisdiction over all serious criminal trials, called trials on indictment (pronounced 'inditement'). These are the cases that are too serious to be tried by magistrates, but they are not of equal seriousness. They are divided into four classes. The three types of judge are attached to the classification.

Class 1

These include any offences where the death penalty survives, plus murder, genocide, offences under the Official Secrets Act 1911, s.1,

Crown court scene (from *Rumpole of the Bailey*; © Thames Television)

and incitement, conspiracy or attempts at any of these. Being the most serious offences, these cases are always tried by High Court judges.

Class 2

These include manslaughter, infanticide, child destruction, rape, unlawful abortion, incest or intercourse with a girl under thirteen, sedition, mutiny, piracy, offences under the Geneva Conventions Act 1957, s.1, and incitement, conspiracy or attempts at these. Here, the judge is usually of the High Court rank, but if the presiding judge of the circuit so authorises, any such trial could be dealt with by a circuit judge or a recorder.

Class 3

This is the residual category: any offence triable solely on indictment not classified elsewhere is a Class 3 offence. Any of the three types of judge can try them.

Class 4

These are triable by any of the judges, and mostly include the offences where the accused could have been tried by magistrates, but given the choice, elected to be tried by judge and jury in the Crown Court.

The court also deals with appeals from magistrates' courts and juvenile courts and committals for sentence from magistrates' courts. On these occasions it is normal for two, three or four magistrates to sit with the judge, the decision being a majority one. Appeal cases involve a rehearing of the evidence when the appeal relates to disputed facts.

Divisional Court of QBD

We met this court in the last section. It was noted there that there lies an appeal from the magistrates' court and the Crown Court by way of case stated on the application of the law to decided facts.

Magistrates' courts Magistrates are also known as justices of the peace. Magistrates may bind over persons to keep the peace and be of good behaviour—a useful and cheap way of dealing with trouble between neighbours, *inter alia*. This office is very ancient. It dates from the end of the twelfth century when, as 'keepers' rather than 'justices' of the peace, their task was administrative rather than judicial. By the mid-fourteenth century the judicial aspect had developed. It was enacted in 1344:

> . . . that two or three of the best people of each county should be assigned as guardians of the peace by the King's Commission (18 Edw. III stat. 2, 1344).

Their precise powers and duties varied from time to time, but by 1368 they were exercising judicial powers regularly and alone. The title of 'justice of the peace' appeared officially for the first time in 1361. As Professor Plucknett wrote (in 1929):

> For the rest of the Middle Ages, and indeed ever since, hardly a Parliament passed without adding some new duty to the work of the justices of the peace.

Over 97 per cent of criminal trials take place in magistrates' courts. Over 50 per cent of people imprisoned are sent there by magistrates.

Magistrates' courts are local. They have a geographical jurisdiction as well as a legal one. That is, they deal with particular matters that arise within their prescribed area. There are no juries in magistrates' courts. Justices are appointed to a particular commission area. Each county, all the London commission areas and the City of London have separate commissions. Justices are appointed by the Lord Chancellor on behalf of the Queen, although in the counties of Greater Manchester, Merseyside and Lancashire appointments are made on her behalf by the Chancellor of the Duchy of Lancaster. These appointments are made upon the recommendations of local and regional advisory committees. There are 30 000 lay magistrates. (On

Magistrates court; reproduced by kind permission of David Sparrow

1 January 1997 there were 30 374 in England and Wales, of whom 14 516 were women and 15 858 were men.)

They are appointed from applicants aged 27 or above, but they were not normally appointed from people aged older than 55. This generally accepted limit was extended to 65 in the summer of 1997. They are not salaried, but expenses are paid. There is no legal qualification, but training courses are compulsory. A new training scheme will come into effect in September 1998. The Lord Chancellor has said:

> This will mean that, instead of a list of topics and a required number of hours, training will be organised and delivered around magistrates being able to demonstrate that they have acquired the necessary areas of knowledge and skills required at different stages in their magisterial career . . . While attendance at courses will still play a part in the training process, I hope more can be done by way of learning through the experience of sitting as a magistrate, supported and assisted by more experienced colleagues, specially selected and trained to act as monitors, particularly for newly appointed magistrates.

There are 90 stipendiary magistrates who are full-time salaried justices who are legally qualified (barristers or solicitors of at least seven years' experience) and who possess the full powers of a bench of lay magistrates (who most often sit in groups of three). They sit alone, usually in large cities and towns where the pressure of work is greatest. There are over forty in London, where they are called 'metropolitan stipendiary magistrates'. There are about half as many again spread around the rest of the country.

There are also some ex-officio magistrates who hold the office because they hold or have held another office. For example, High Court judges and the Lord Mayor and aldermen of the City of London are ex-officio magistrates.

Each bench of magistrates is assisted by a legally qualified and specially trained justices' clerk. The clerk also runs the court, helps to train new magistrates and administers the legal aid system in his court. The clerks have assistants who are similarly legally qualified.

The magistrates have the jurisdiction to conduct summary trials and the responsibility to screen the evidence before committing an accused for trial at the Crown Court.

Summary trial

This is the trial of summary offences and of those more serious offences where the accused had the choice and chose summary trial. Summary offences are minor, often regulatory offences carrying up to the magistrates' limits as to punishment (generally six months and/or a £5000 fine). The vast majority are motoring offences. Under the Magistrates' Courts Act 1980 s.12, it is often possible to plead guilty by post to these offences. There are over 1 500 000 people convicted each year of summary offences in England and Wales. About 90 per cent of those accused of summary offences plead guilty.

The Magistrates' Courts Act 1980, ss.17 *et seq.*, detail the offences where the accused is able to choose the mode of trial: these offences are said to be triable either way. If the accused is to be given the choice, the clerk will always warn him that if he elects summary trial (which he usually does), the magistrates reserve the right to commit him to the Crown Court for sentence if they feel he deserves punishment beyond their powers. These powers, apart from fines and imprisonment, include the power to make compensation orders in favour of the victim of crime, restitution orders where appropriate, supervision orders and community service orders.

Committal proceedings

Where the alleged offence is too serious for summary trial it is called 'indictable' or 'triable on indictment only'. The indictment itself is the written accusation against the accused. Technically, the bench is one of examining magistrates here and not a court properly so called.

The Royal Commission on Criminal Justice, chaired by Runciman (thus, the 'Runciman Commission'), recommended in 1993 that all committal hearings should be abolished but Part V of the Criminal Procedure and Investigations Act 1996 provides a modified procedure so that only written statements, depositions and other documents and exhibits may be brought into evidence by the prosecution. A s.6(1) committal (what used to be called an 'old style' or 'full' committal) will now involve the reading aloud of written statements and (at the court's direction) a summary of statements not read out. A s.6(2) committal (or what used to be called a 'new style' or 'paper' committal) will involve no consideration of prosecution evidence on the basis that all evidence is in writing, the defendant is legally represented and that he does not wish to submit that the evidence is insufficient to try the defendant.

Youth courts

Some magistrates are specially trained to sit in youth courts. These exist under the authority of the Children and Young Persons' Act 1933. This statute contains, in s.44(1), a statement of fundamental importance. It was quite a step away from tradition in the 1930s although it seems pretty unremarkable today:

> Every court in dealing with a child or young person who is brought before it, either as an offender or otherwise, shall have regard to the welfare of the child or young person and shall in a proper case take steps for removing him from undesirable surroundings and for securing that proper provision is made for his education and training.

Youth courts try children (those who are at least ten and under fourteen years old) and young persons (those who are at least fourteen but under eighteen). The modern basis of much of this work is the Children Act 1989. Incidentally, criminal proceedings cannot be brought against a child under ten. The Criminal Justice Act 1991 has made formal provision for the increased involvement of parents in their children's appearances before the court. Generally they must attend if the child is 16 or less (for 17 year olds they may be required). There is provision for the court to meet at extraordinary times such as in the evening or at weekends, so that parents can attend without the need for time off work. The court can order the parents to pay any fine imposed. If the child is younger than 16, the parent can be asked to 'enter into a recognisance', that is, be bound over to take proper care of the child. This is limited to £1000. If the request is unreasonably refused, a fine of up to that amount can be imposed instead.

The policy considerations seem to be clear. Parents are not to be allowed to abrogate their responsibilities to bring up their children in a proper manner. It remains to be seen whether this is the right club for the shot! The court must meet in a different room or at a different time from (at least one hour before or after) the adult hearings. The public are excluded, but not the press. However, there are press restrictions; for example, they are not allowed to publish the offender's name without specific authority from the court or the Home Secretary. There are three justices, usually including at least one woman.

Some cases are too serious to be tried in a Youth Court. One of the most appalling and recent cases involving children was the trial of two ten-year-old boys, Thompson and Venables, for the murder of the toddler James Bulger. At their trial in the Crown Court both boys were sentenced to be detained at Her Majesty's pleasure with a recommendation that each serve a minimum of eight years. The Lord Chief Justice then increased this to ten years and the Home Secretary then increased the term further to fifteen years. His decision was challenged by way of judicial review under Order 53 of the Rules of the Supreme Court. The Court of Appeal held in *R.* v. *Secretary of State for the Home Department ex parte Venables and Thompson* (1996) that although the Home Secretary has power to decide the tariff, on the facts of this case he had taken into account extraneous factors, including public opinion, and must now reconsider the process by which he made his decision. In June 1997 the House of Lords held by a majority of three to two that he had acted unfairly when he treated the two youngsters in the same way as he might have treated adult murderers, raising the minimum term to fifteen years. They ruled that the Home Secretary had the power to set a provisional tariff but that it must be flexible enough to allow regular reviews.

They also ruled that Mr Howard acted improperly in taking into account public petitions such as that signed by some 278 000 people and reacting to coupons from readers of *The Sun*. He should have ignored the 'high-voltage atmosphere of a newspaper campaign'. Lord Steyn added that such material was 'worthless' and incapable of telling him in a meaningful way the true state of informed public opinion based on all the material facts of the case.

Lord Browne-Wilkinson said the murder was a 'cruel and sadistic crime' which had given rise to much public concern and outrage. He backed the right of a Home Secretary to set a tariff to be served but said it had to be flexible in order to allow him to reconsider the position in the light of the child's development and progress while in detention. He said Mr Howard had adopted a policy which totally excluded such factors from consideration during the tariff period.

> The unlawfulness lies in adopting a policy which totally excludes from consideration during the tariff period . . . their progress and development, necessary to determine whether release from detention would be in the interests of the welfare of the applicants.

Any policy based on a tariff had to be flexible and should take into account retribution, deterrence and the welfare of the child.

COURTS WITH SPECIAL JURISDICTIONS

Employment Appeal Tribunal

Sir John Donaldson, when he was the Master of the Rolls, said:

a superior court of record presided over by a judge of the Court of Appeal, the Court of Session or the High Court, is a court and not a tribunal, whatever it may be called. (*Law Society's Gazette*)

This court was created by the Employment Protection Act 1975 which has now been taken into the Employment Protection (Consolidation) Act 1978, but the provisions are the same:

135(1) The Employment Appeal Tribunal established under section 87 of the Employment Protection Act 1975 shall continue in existence by that name for the purpose of hearing appeals under section 136.

(2) The Employment Appeal Tribunal . . . shall consist of:—

(*a*) such number of judges as may be nominated from time to time by the Lord Chancellor from among the judges (other than the Lord Chancellor) of the High Court and the Court of Appeal;

(*b*) at least one judge of the Court of Session nominated from time to time by the Lord President of that Court; and

(*c*) such number of other members as may be appointed from time to time by Her Majesty on the joint recommendation of the Lord Chancellor and the Secretary of State.

(3) The members of the Appeal Tribunal appointed under section (2)(b) shall be persons who appear to the Lord Chancellor and the Secretary of State to have special knowledge or experience of industrial relations, either as representatives of employers or as representatives of workers . . .

136 (1) An appeal shall lie to the Appeal Tribunal on a question of law arising from any decision of, or arising in any proceedings before, an industrial tribunal under, or by virtue of, the following Acts—

(*a*) the Equal Pay Act 1970;

(*b*) the Sex Discrimination Act 1975;

(*c*) the Employment Protection Act 1975;

(*d*) the Race Relations Act 1976;

(*e*) this Act.

The EAT also deals with appeals on law or fact from decision of the Certification Officer under various statutes. This officer decides, for instance, whether a union is genuinely independent of an employer's control for the purpose of genuine representative activity.

There is an appeal route from this court to the Court of Appeal, or the Court of Session in Scotland. It has a central office in London, but it can sit anywhere in the country. It is properly constituted with a judge and two or four laymen, although one layman will do, if the parties agree to this. If there is more than one layman they must equally represent employers' and workers' points of view. Hearings are public, except where national interests or important points, such as vital trade secrets, are at stake. Legal aid is available. Witnesses can be summoned, the production of documents can be ordered and all its judgments can be enforced.

However, the procedure is relatively informal. Robes are not worn, there is no bench or witness box and the court can be addressed without standing up. Costs are not generally awarded against the losing party, unless the proceedings are regarded as having been unnecessary and/or vexatious.

Coroners' courts Coroners are appointed by the county councils from barristers, solicitors or medical practitioners of at least five years' standing. They can be dismissed by the Lord Chancellor for inability or misconduct. The office of coroner dates from the twelfth century. Today, the appointment and jurisdiction of coroners is governed by the Coroners Act 1988, which consolidates the earlier legislation.

This court has a geographical jurisdiction—like the magistrates' and county courts. It is a local court, the main function of which is to inquire into deaths in its districts where there is reasonable cause to suspect:

1 that the deceased died a violent or unnatural death; or
2 the death was sudden and the cause unknown; or
3 the death occurred in prison.

If the coroner so decides, (and in defined circumstances under the Coroners Act 1988, s.8(3) there is no choice) a jury of seven, nine or eleven will be appointed to assist in deciding the identity of the deceased, the cause of death and where the death took place. Majority verdicts of the jury are acceptable, provided that there are not more than two dissentients. The procedure is inquisitorial, the coroner himself questioning witnesses who can be compelled to attend. Other interested persons can be represented, and, with the coroner's permission, they can question the witnesses. There are no speeches to the coroner, nor to the jury.

The other area of coroners' jurisdiction concerns treasure trove, of which Sir William Blackstone wrote (in 1765):

> Where any money or coin, gold, silver, plate or bullion, is found hidden in the earth, or other private place, the owner thereof being unknown . . . the treasure belongs to the King: but if he that hid it be known, or afterwards found out, the owner and not the King is entitled to it.

The coroner used to decide whether the articles in question were hidden, in which case they want to the Exchequer (and as a matter of custom the owner of the land and especially the finder were compensated), as with the Roman silver found in Mildenhall, Suffolk in 1946 (now in the British Museum), or just lost, in which case the finder was allowed to keep them, unless the true owner could be traced.

Now, under the Treasure Act 1996 (which came into force on 24 September 1997) things have changed. The old law of treasure trove has been abolished and replaced with new definitions and a criminal offence of failure to report a find. The definitions are complex and subject to expansion should the Secretary of State so choose but, in general terms, any hidden object (except a single coin) that contains at least 10 per cent silver or gold and is at least 300 years old is treasure. Broadly, unless the true owner can be found, it belongs to the Crown. The new provisions will be elaborated by means of a Code of Practice. One of the key policy issues behind this change in the law is the increasing popularity of the use of metal detectors. It has been estimated that they find more than 400 000 objects each year. Obviously, those who regard the 'hobby' as a business (called 'nighthawks') do not pay much attention to the law, old or new, but it is hoped that the 'normal' enthusiast will co-operate, for at least a share in the value of what is found.

Restrictive Practices Court

This court was set up originally by the Restrictive Trade Practices Act 1956 (now consolidated into the Restrictive Practices Court Act 1976 and the Restrictive Trade Practices Act 1976) to inspect agreements relating to the supply of goods and services to see that they are not contrary to statute nor unfair to consumers. The Fair Trading Act 1973 and the Resale Prices Act 1964 added to the workload. The Director General of Fair Trading makes most of the referrals to the court. The court is composed of five judges and ten laymen with appropriate experience appointed by the Lord Chancellor on behalf of the Queen. Three of the judges come from the High Court, one from the Court of Session in Scotland and one from the Supreme Court of Northern Ireland. Usually the court comprises one judge and two laymen, although if the matter is only one of law a judge may sit alone. In any case his is the only verdict on points of law. Appeals lie to the Court of Appeal, the Court of Session or the Court of Appeal of Northern Ireland.

In recent years there has been considerable discussion about this whole area of the law. Broadly, the suggestions are: to introduce a general ban on anti-competitive agreements between companies, scrapping the current registration scheme. Further, professional bodies will be added to the regulation and fines for breaking the new laws will be raised to a maximum of 10 per cent of turnover. It is clear that our membership of the European Community, bringing with it a new emphasis on preserving competition, will mean that this area of our law will be restructured.

Courts-martial

These are concerned only with the armed forces. They are governed by statute, mainly the Army and Air Force Acts 1955 and the Naval Discipline Act 1957. Minor disciplinary offences are dealt with by superior officers. Very serious cases, such as murder or rape, are handed over to the civilian courts. Otherwise, serious offences are dealt with by courts-martial.

The procedure in courts-martial is similar to that of the civilian courts. The accused can be represented. The court has a legally qualified adviser on the relevant points of the law. The decision is taken by three or five superior officers. There is a preliminary inquiry to see that there is a case to answer. There is no jury. An acquittal is final, but a finding of guilt is subject to confirmation by a superior officer. This is seen as a check against injustice.

There has been, since 1951, a Courts-Martial Appeal Court. This is now governed by the Courts-Martial (Appeals) Act 1968. It is very similar to the Court of Appeal (Criminal Division) both in procedure and in the fact that the Lords Justices of Appeal preside, with High Court judges and various others appointed by the Lord Chancellor.

Naval Courts

The Merchant Shipping Act 1894 provides that the commander of any of Her Majesty's ships while abroad can convene a Naval Court to deal with any matter of immediate importance, such as the wrecking, abandonment or loss of a ship. Naval officers preside. The procedure is formal. The powers are considerable (including fines and imprisonment). An appeal route lies to the divisional court of the Queen's Bench Division and thereafter to the Court of Appeal.

Ecclesiastical courts

There is an ancient and complex hierarchy of courts within the Church of England. They no longer have jurisdiction over laymen.

Court of Chivalry

In *Manchester Corporation* v. *Manchester Palace of Varieties* (1955) this court was convened to decide whether a theatre could display the coat of arms of the City of Manchester. It had not been convened since 1737. Its jurisdiction is to adjudicate upon the right to use armorial bearings and ensigns. In theory it is presided over by the Earl Marshal. The Lord Chief Justice sat on his behalf in 1955. It seems to have no power to enforce its judgments.

Judicial Committee of the Privy Council

Under the terms of the Judicial Committee Act 1833, the Committee consists, in theory, of the Lord President of the Council, ex-Lords President, the Lord Chancellor, the Law Lords, the senior judges of the overseas jurisdictions (who sit on cases from their own countries from time to time), and other members of the Privy Council who hold or who have held high judicial office. In practice the Lord Chancellor and four of the Law Lords sit unrobed, using a procedure similar to that used in the House of Lords when sitting as a court. Because of its composition, decisions of this court carry highly persuasive authority, although, because of its jurisdiction, its authority cannot be binding within the UK court system.

The jurisdiction falls into five broad categories:

1 final appeals from the Isle of Man, the Channel Islands, British Colonies and Protectorates and from those Commonwealth countries who have not decided to handle their final appeals internally;

2 appeals from the Admiralty Court when sitting as a 'prize court' (dealing with the ownership of ships and cargo in connection with capture by enemy warships), and from the Colonial Courts of Admiralty and the Court of Admiralty of the Cinque Ports;

3 appeals from the ecclesiastical courts;

4 medical appeals from those struck off by the Professional Conduct Committee of the General Medical Council (under the Medical Act 1983);

5 special references from the sovereign concerning, for example, the powers of colonial judges and legislation in Jersey.

TRIBUNALS

In addition to the ordinary courts there has grown up in post-war years a network of over 50 statutory tribunals dealing with various areas of law: employment, welfare, and so on. Examples include: the Industrial Tribunals, Social Security Appeals Tribunal, Medical Appeals Tribunal, Mental Health Review Tribunals, Pensions Appeal Tribunal, Immigration Appeals Tribunal, Agriculture Land Tribunal, the Lands Tribunal, Plant Varieties and Seeds Tribunal, Commissioners of Income Tax, VAT Tribunals, Rent Tribunals and Data Protection Tribunal. These tribunals differ from the courts in that they are staffed by specialists in particular fields rather than by judges. For example, an industrial tribunal hearing an unfair dismissal case will be staffed by persons who have had considerable experience in industry, one from or representing an employers' organisation, the other representing a trade union or workers' organisation. Similarly, where a person applies for industrial injury benefit, his application will not be successful unless it can be shown that the injury or disease arose out of the employment; this matter will be decided by a medical appeals tribunal, consisting of two doctors and a lawyer.

The purpose of such tribunals is to provide cheap and quick justice. Procedure is informal with the members of the tribunal asking questions of appellant and respondent. The advantages of tribunals are said to be:

- specialist knowledge which can be brought to bear on particular issues;
- the procedure is informal and not accusatorial;
- there are no court fees and costs are not normally awarded;
- decisions are normally arrived at quickly;
- they reduce the pressure of work on the ordinary courts;
- they are not bound to follow their own previous decisions.

They thus have wide discretionary power.

On the other hand, the disadvantages are that:

- tribunal decisions are not so well publicised as court decisions;
- tribunal hearings are sometimes held in private and this can arouse public suspicion;
- reasons for decisions are not always given;
- lack of insistence on the strict rules of evidence can lead to injustice;
- representation is not always allowed, and legal representation is rare;

- technical expertise does not always provide judicial impartiality and tribunal chairmen are not always lawyers;
- rights of appeal are limited;
- wide discretionary power can lead to inconsistency and unpredictability.

These tribunals, although numerous, have very limited and specific jurisdiction, granted by statute. Their decisions often reflect policy as much as law. They have had fairly uniform standards imposed upon them by a statute of 1958, consolidated into the Tribunals and Inquiries Act 1971, and now replaced by the Tribunals and Inquiries Act 1992. The 1958 Act implemented most of the recommendations of the Franks Committee, which reported in 1958. These standards include the giving of reasons for decisions, the appointing of chairmen by the Lord Chancellor, allowing clear appeal routes on points of law to the High Court and allowing representation (although this is not often by lawyers). There is a Council on Tribunals which meets once a month to scrutinise the workings of the major tribunals, and reports on them annually. The Council deals with complaints about tribunals from the public. There are very few of these; about 40 a year from the 200 000 cases heard. Presumably, either there is very little wrong with the tribunals—or very few people have heard of the Council. The Council has published a Report 'Model Rules of Procedure for Tribunals', with the aim of providing a comprehensive set of procedural rules, and reducing the alleged unevenness of tribunal practice.

Industrial tribunals   An example: the Royal Commission on Trade Unions and Employers' Associations described the purpose of industrial tribunals as being to provide:

> an easily accessible, speedy, informal and inexpensive procedure for the settlement of disputes between employers and workers.

Professor Rideout describes them as:

> among the greatest and most successful inventions of administrative law.

Industrial tribunals were first set up in 1964 under the Industrial Training Act to decide matters concerning levies which employers had to pay, for having their workforce trained, to industrial training boards. Since then their jurisdiction has increased and extends to matters relating to:

- contracts of employment;
- unfair dismissal;
- health and safety at work;
- sex discrimination;
- race discrimination;
- equal pay;
- redundancy.
- and a variety of other claims relating to maternity pay, trade union membership and activity, contract claims upon termination of employment and so on.

It is worth noting here that while there are various limits to the award-making powers of the tribunal, there is no such limit (although there are guidelines) with regard to sex or race discrimination. The former is as a result of the Sex Discrimination and Equal Pay (Remedies) Regulations 1993 (following the European Court decision in *Marshall* v. *South West Hampshire Area Health Authority (No. 2)* (1993)) and the latter follows the Race Relations (Remedies) Act 1994.

The chairman of each tribunal is a barrister or solicitor of at least seven years' standing who sits with two lay members, one representing an employers' organisation or the self-employed, the other an employees' organisation. Tribunals sit at about ninety-five centres throughout the country. The decision is by majority and is normally given at the hearing, though in more difficult cases it will be sent to the parties at a later date. Hearings are normally in public but can be in private where an issue involving national security arises. Appeal lies to the Employment Appeal Tribunal on a question of law, except in the case of certain appeals concerning the enforcement of health and safety at work procedures in which case appeal is to the High Court, Queen's Bench Division.

Domestic tribunals These tribunals are rather different. They are concerned with the internal regulation of an organisation rather than with the implementation of broad governmental policy. They can be divided into two types. First, there are those based on contract, so that if you join an organisation you thereby subject yourself to the jurisdiction of its internal regulation. Trade unions, social clubs and some professional organisations have such tribunals. Second, there are those domestic tribunals created by statute such as the Professional Conduct Committee of the General Medical Council (Medical Act 1983) and the Solicitors' Disciplinary Tribunal (Solicitors Act 1974). Tribunals like these have appeal routes into the court system. Those which rest in contract law do not, although their procedures are under the supervision of the divisional court of the Queen's Bench Division.

INQUIRIES

These hearings are different from courts and from tribunals in that they tend to be set up to do a particular job rather than to perform a continuing function. There are several different kinds of inquiries:

1 Tribunals of Inquiry which are set up, as and when needed, by Parliament in order to discover all the facts surrounding a particular event. The appropriate Secretary of State is responsible. Powers given are usually equivalent to those of the High Court to summon witnesses and order the production of documents. Such inquiries followed the Profumo scandal (1963), the Aberfan disaster (1966), 'Bloody Sunday' in Londonderry (1968), the fire at Bradford City's football ground (1986) and the freeing of the 'Guildford Four' (1989). Such inquiries are often demanded, but rarely conducted.

For example there was a loud call for such a review after the deaths of four children from Plymouth on a school canoeing training session in the early summer of 1993, but no inquiry followed.

2 Inquiries into objections; for example, public local inquiries into the compulsory acquisition of land for hospitals, roads, new towns, or local inquiries into alternative proposals, for example, various routes for a new road.

3 Inquiries into accidents, such as railway and aircraft crashes, to establish causes (rather than place the blame). A recent example is the Health and Safety Executive announcing a full public inquiry to run parallel with the Railways Inspectorate's own inquiry after the train crash in Southhall on Friday 19 September 1997. Six people died, thirteen were seriously injured and a further 150 were described as 'walking wounded'.

4 Investigations of companies under the Companies Acts.

5 Planning inquiries under the town and country planning legislation which are held in order to compile county 'structure plans' and 'local plans' regarding medium and long-term developments of land use.

Local inspectors conduct inquiries and report to the appropriate minister. The minister makes the decision, and must answer for it in Parliament. Reasons must be given (since the passing of the Tribunals and Inquiries Act 1958), and despite the fairly common absence of an appeal route, the rules of natural justice must be observed.

The Council on Tribunals supervises inquiries as well. The Lord Chancellor can make procedural rules for inquiries (under the Tribunals and Inquiries Act 1971), but only after consultation with the Council.

Indicative questions

1 (a) What are 'committal proceedings' in the Magistrates' Courts? (*2 marks*)

(b) Explain what is meant by 'a summary trial'. (*2 marks*)

(c) What is the difference between an appeal against conviction and an appeal against sentence? (*2 marks*)

(d) Trials in a civil court and a criminal court are different. Describe two important differences. (*2 marks*)

LEAG

2 The County Court can offer a 'small claims' procedure, which operates by the process of arbitration.

(a) Explain what type of case can be dealt with using the 'small claims' procedure in the County Court. (*2 marks*)

(b) Describe the steps that the plaintiff would need to follow in order to sue someone through the small claims procedure up to, but not including, the hearing of the case. (*6 marks*)

(c) Describe one situation, other than in the County Court, where arbitration can be used to resolve disputes. Explain who would act as arbitrator in this situation. (*4 marks*)

(d) Explain two advantages and two disadvantages of arbitration over an ordinary action in court. (*8 marks*)

SEG 1989

3 Cases which require a hearing can be tried in a variety of different courts, including: the Magistrates or Youth Court; Crown Court; County Court or High Court. Disputes can also be settled in one of a range of specialist tribunals.

In **each** of the following cases, state which court or tribunal would **try** the case, and **briefly** explain why you have chosen this particular venue.

(a) Gregory, aged 16, has been charged with the murder of his younger brother. (*2 marks*)

(b) Jameila claims that she has been ignored at work for promotion, either because she is black or because she is a woman. (*2 marks*)

(c) Nazir is involved in a car accident caused by Donald's negligent driving. Nazir has been told that he should be seeking damages of around £35 000. (*2 marks*)

(d) Justin and his next-door neighbour, Benedict, are involved in a heated argument where blows are exchanged. Neither has a criminal record, and the prosecution is suggesting that both should be bound over to keep the peace. (*2 marks*)

SEG Summer 1997 (Foundation)

CHAPTER 5

The Personnel of the Law

THE LEGAL PROFESSION

The legal profession in England and Wales is divided into barristers, solicitors, legal executives and licensed conveyancers. The general term lawyer can be taken to mean any of these or indeed just to indicate that someone knows some law The main division, into barristers and solicitors, dates back to about 1340, although the title of 'solicitor' only dates from the fifteenth century. Before then, their work was done by three groups—solicitors, attorneys and proctors. They fused in 1831 when the Law Society was created, and all the remaining distinctions were removed by the Judicature Act 1873. Legal executives, as a separate branch, date only from 1963 when their Institute was set up.

Barristers

There are about 9000 'barristers-at-law'. They conduct cases in court. Their main role is one of advocacy. They once had an exclusive 'right of audience' in the higher courts. This formed one of the central points of debate about the future of the legal profession in the United Kingdom which resulted, in part, in the Courts and Legal Services Act 1990 in accordance with the provisions of which, in December 1993, the Lord Chancellor and four senior judges approved an application by the solicitors' governing body, the Law Society, for solicitors in private practice to be granted rights of audience in both civil and criminal proceedings in the House of Lords, the Court of Appeal, the High Court and the Crown Court. This was effected under ss. 27–33 of the 1990 Act and alters the traditional divide between solicitors and barristers. Barristers now have to compete with solicitors. The change was much welcomed by the Law Society, although it is uncertain how many of the 50 000 solicitors in private practice will undergo the necessary training to obtain advocacy certificates.

By the spring of 1997, around 450 solicitors in private practice had acquired rights of audience in the higher courts. A further 170 applications were in the system. It seems that those in criminal law practices reliant on legal aid funding and commercial and financial city practices are the most likely to apply for extended rights of audience but, clearly, an extremely small proportion of the 55 000 solicitors in private practice have expressed an interest. Those who claimed that the tradition of centuries was doomed seem to have overstated the position.

Barristers belong to one of the four Inns of Court, i.e. Lincoln's Inn, Gray's Inn, the Inner Temple and the Middle Temple. These Inns are unincorporated societies governed by the Masters of the Bench, who themselves are judges or senior barristers. A person wishing to become a barrister must apply first to become a student at one of the Inns. He must keep terms, i.e. dine at his Inn a certain number of times (usually twenty-four) and pass the necessary professional examinations before being called to the Bar. In September 1997 these professional examinations (the 'Bar Vocational Course') were offered outside of London for the first time. Several 'provincial' centres have had their courses validated. The question of cost and the inconvenience of having students travelling to London to 'dine' was resolved in March when it was announced that, with effect from October 1997, this would be replaced by an educational programme involving lecture evenings, residential weekends or one-day lectures, with the aim of making travelling to London more worthwhile. The Lord Chancellor's Advisory Committee on Legal Education had questioned the need for the dining requirement. Traditionally, the Inn was not only a place of work but where barristers lived (rather like colleges at Oxford and Cambridge) and the continuation of dining is advocated in order to ensure the perpetuation of the customs and traditions of the Bar. On a more practical point, the requirement at least to sit and eat with other barristers may well clarify both the career plans of the aspirant barristers ('I couldn't possibly/my ambition is to work with people like this') and the observation by practitioners of likely candidates to fill future vacancies in chambers. The trainee barrister must then become a pupil in chambers with a qualified barrister (a 'pupil master') for one year. After six months he is allowed to present minor cases on his own in court, provided that he has completed an approved practical training course. A barrister's work also consists of paper-work, e.g. advising solicitors on legal problems (called 'giving counsel's opinion') and drafting pleadings for use in litigation. Some barristers spend little time in court. Those at the Chancery Bar, for example, work in the office ('chambers') handling work ('receiving instructions') from solicitors and offering advice on points of law concerning such matters as disputed wills or rights on intestacy, transfers of property or rights under trusts and settlements. The simple distinction between the two main branches of the legal profession, one in the office and the other in court, is inaccurate, and has become more so. However, it is true to say that barristers, unlike solicitors, are generally more detached from direct contact with clients and from the day-to-day worries of running a firm.

The principal governing body of the Bar is the General Council of the Bar. This body lays down general policies and is concerned to promote and uphold the standards, honour and independence of the Bar. It has certain disciplinary powers. Training and education matters are shared between the Senate and the Inns of Court.

Traditionally, barristers did not make contracts with their clients. However fictional it may appear, they were paid as an 'honorarium'. It followed that unpaid barristers could not sue for their fees. However, more as a reaction to the notoriously slow handing over of payments to barristers by their instructing solicitors than out of a desire to break with tradition, s.61 of the Courts and Legal Services Act 1990 permits barristers to make contracts for their services. You cannot sue him for negligence in the conduct of your case, except for work done in chambers (his office).

This exception was seen in *Saif Ali* v. *Sydney Mitchell and Co* (1978) which was about a car crash. A barrister advised suing only one defendant. By the time his error was noticed it was too late to sue another one. (There is a statutory limitation period of three years during which personal injury claims must be brought.) This common law immunity now appears in the Courts and Legal Services Act 1990, s.62.

The barrister gets paid when your solicitor pays him on your behalf, and adds the fee to your bill. A barrister cannot, in theory, refuse to represent a client. The barrister has a duty to respect the confidence of his client. He cannot take instructions directly; you must brief him via your solicitor, although some barristers have special permission to work in law centres directly with the public. Your solicitor is likely to have chosen counsel for you. This is said to be a good quality control of the Bar, since without a good reputation, a barrister is unlikely to get much work. In these days of citizen's charters and the like we find the Bar Council amending its code of conduct with regard to the acceptance of work. Before taking a case on, counsel must consider their own competence in the area concerned and whether the matter could be dealt with more appropriately or economically by another barrister or by a solicitor. The only criterion to be applied is the best interests of the client. Barristers cannot form partnerships or share profits. They usually share chambers and the services of a clerk with whom solicitors usually negotiate fees, etc.

Barristers have a divided loyalty. They must do their best for their clients, but they owe duties to the court as well. The proper development of the law requires that all relevant material is drawn to the attention of the court in all cases. The barristers have a duty to do this, even if such materials may sometimes adversely affect their client's cause.

If a barrister is successful over a number of years he might apply to the Lord Chancellor to be appointed Queen's Counsel. Sometimes QCs are referred to as 'silks' because the gowns they wear in court are made of silk whereas 'junior' barristers' gowns are made of 'stuff'. Becoming a QC is often referred to as taking silk. Incidentally, a junior barrister is one in practice but not a QC. During the year of practical experience required before becoming a junior, barristers are 'pupils'.

Having risen to the dizzy heights of the rank of QC a barrister is less likely to do anything but appear as an advocate and give opinions, although changes in the relevant rules enabled QCs to draft documents and removed the strictness of the old two counsel rule which meant that if one briefed (employed) a QC then a junior had to be employed too. Although the rule is no longer strict, QCs still commonly appear in court with juniors.

Solicitors

There were 72 258 practising solicitors in England and Wales in 1997. A 'Solicitor of the Supreme Court' is a general practitioner in law. His main function is to advise clients on legal and financial matters. His work consists chiefly in conveying land and houses, checking title to land, drawing up wills, forming companies and advising on matrimonial matters and criminal law. This conveyancing work used to be a professional monopoly for solicitors; however, now, under the Courts and Legal Services Act 1990, building societies and banks offer conveyancing services. They are provided by 'authorised practitioners' who can be solicitors, barristers, licensed conveyancers or notaries. There is a danger here that many smaller firms of solicitors may disappear, close or merge, as this traditional mainstay is removed, and that this will reduce proper access to legal services generally outside large cities and towns. Solicitors in larger firms tend to specialise, e.g. one may specialise in taxation, whilst another may specialise in company law. Neither solicitors nor barristers can form themselves into limited liability companies. Solicitors practise either alone or in partnership. Many solicitors are employed in industry and local government jobs.

As far as court work or litigation is concerned, the solicitor prepares the case and ascertains the facts. He also arranges for witnesses to be present and documents to be submitted. We saw above that some solicitors now have rights of audience in the higher courts. If these have not been acquired an individual practitioner has only a limited right of advocacy. He can appear in the county court and magistrates' court. He can also appear in the Crown Court on an appeal from the magistrates' court and where the accused has been sent by the magistrates for sentence to the Crown Court. In bankruptcy matters he can appear in the High Court. In addition, he may appear before an industrial tribunal. It seemed clear that he could not appear in the High Court, even to read out a formal and unchallenged statement. This was settled in *Abse* v. *Smith* (1986), where an apology was read to a court in part-settlement of a defamation action. It had been suggested that a solicitor should act in order to save costs. In accordance with a Practice Direction issued in May 1986, solicitors are allowed to perform functions just like this. Such is the pressure exerted by cases involving famous people!

In order to become a solicitor it is necessary to pass the appropriate professional examinations. The papers taken will vary with the applicant's initial qualifications. It is usual for an applicant to have a degree. Naturally, greater exemptions are available to those who have degrees in law. It is also necessary to serve a period of apprenticeship (popularly called 'articles' but properly called 'a training contract') working in a solicitor's office. The usual period is two years. Having qualified in this way the candidate has his name entered onto the Roll (by the Master of the Rolls). It is not possible for a newly admitted solicitor to practise alone straightaway since for his first three years he must have an experienced supervising solicitor to oversee and vouch for his accounts. As a result, three years are normally served working in another practice. In fact few solicitors in general practice do not work within partnerships. Sometimes such firms can become very large.

The governing body of solicitors is the Law Society. Eighty-five per cent of solicitors belong to it, but it has power, notably disciplinary, over all practising solicitors. It organises the admission, education and training of prospective solicitors. It represents solicitors in dealing with the public. It maintains a Compensation Fund to which all solicitors contribute annually and from which clients can be repaid losses caused by the default or neglect of solicitors. Discipline is regulated by the Solicitors Disciplinary Tribunal. It stands apart from the Law Society. In 1974 in response to complaints that claims against solicitors were dealt with by other solicitors this body took over the work earlier undertaken by a Disciplinary Committee which had been set up in 1919. The Tribunal sits with two solicitor members and one lay person. It has the power to fine solicitors (up to £5000 on each allegation), to suspend from practice (usually for between 6 months and 5 years), or to strike a solicitor from the Roll. That is to remove a solicitor from practice.

The activities of such a powerful body will inevitably be tested from time to time. For example, in *Re A Solicitor* (1992) it was held that it had the power to admit evidence that might not be admissible in court, because it can regulate its own procedure.

In September 1986 a Solicitors' Complaints Bureau was opened for business. It described itself as 'a separate organisation set up by the Law Society to investigate complaints against solicitors'. Olé Hansen commented: 'This is rather like saying the rear wheel is a separate part of a bicycle.' The bureau adopted a formal 'mission statement': to strengthen and maintain the confidence of the public and the profession in the conduct and service of solicitors.

None the less, in September 1996 the Solicitors' Complaints Bureau was replaced by the Office for the Supervision of Solicitors which aims to improve the complaints handling system so as to ensure the speedy handling of other than the most difficult of cases. The then Legal Services Ombudsman, Michael Barnes, in his 1995 Report (published in June 1996) continued to monitor the progress of the profession (both barristers and solicitors) in dealing with complaints. He issued a warning that if significant improvement was not made then the Law Society would lose its complaint-handling functions.

Solicitors are contractually bound to their clients. They can sue for their fees, and be sued for negligence. For example, in *Dickinson* v. *Jones, Alexander & Co* (1989), solicitors who made an inept bargain in a woman's divorce negotiations were told to pay £425 071 in damages and interest, and in *Corfield* v. *D S Bosher & Co* (1992) it was held that negligent failure by a solicitor to advise a client of the time limit for appeal following arbitration will entitle the client to recover damages for his lost chance of success. The solicitor/client relationship is basically one of principal and agent. Thus, the solicitor has the agent's right to indemnity for acts done and liabilities incurred within his authority as agent. Further to this, the relationship is regarded by equity as 'fiduciary'; that is, both sides must show the utmost good faith. Each must disclose everything to do with the case: you must tell your solicitor everything, and he must respect your confidence. Indeed, he cannot be forced, even by a court, to reveal what you have told him. This is called privilege. Much of the law relating to solicitors, their status, discipline, remuneration, etc., is contained in the Solicitors Act 1974 (as amended by the Administration of Justice Act 1985 and the Courts and Legal Services Act 1990). With regard to remuneration, you can always have your bill checked by the Law Society if you regard it as excessive.

Legal executives

The Institute of Legal Executives was established in 1963 in order to give professional status to those people who work in solicitors' offices but who, for one reason or another, have not been admitted as solicitors. There are examinations to pass and a period of apprenticeship to serve in order to become a legal executive. This period can be as long as eight years before Fellowship of the Institute can be granted. Legal executives perform a variety of functions side by side with solicitors. Obviously, if a solicitor must be employed for a particular task then legal executives are excluded, but otherwise they have wide areas of experience and knowledge. Some specialise and achieve high levels of expertise.

The Lord Chancellor, using a power conferred by the Administration of Justice Act 1977, has granted a limited right of audience to legal executives. Thus, since the County Courts (Right of Audience) Order 1978 came into force, legal executives have been able to speak in the county courts for unopposed adjournments and applications for judgment by consent. Under the Courts and Legal Services Act 1990 legal executives will be able to acquire wider rights of audience in court and be able to engage in more pre-trial work.

In November 1997 the Lord Chancellor wrote to the President of the Institute of Legal Executives, Mrs Patricia Dilley, informing her that the Institute's application to be allowed to grant rights of audience to its members has been approved by the Lord Chancellor and the senior judges designated to adjudicate on applications under the Courts and Legal Services Act 1990.

This approval marks an important stage in the formal procedure laid down in the 1990 Act although it then remained for the application to be considered by both Houses of Parliament before an Order in Council could be made. The application would allow ILEX to grant limited extended Rights of Audience to suitably qualified Fellows. Rights of audience certificates will be granted for civil proceedings, matrimonial proceedings and coroner's courts proceedings.

THE JUDGES

Professor Griffith (in his book, *The Politics of the Judiciary*) has written:

The most remarkable fact about the appointment of judges is that it is wholly in the hands of politicians. High Court and circuit judges, recorders, stipendiary and lay magistrates are appointed by or on the advice of the Lord Chancellor who is a member of the Cabinet. Appointments to the Court of Appeal, to the Judicial Committee of the House of Lords, and to the offices of Lord Chief Justice and President of the Family Division are made on the advice of the Prime Minister after consultation with the Lord Chancellor, who himself consults senior members of the judiciary before making his choice or consulting with the Prime Minister.

It is interesting that the power to choose is vested in the politicians, but it is also important to observe that there are minimum qualifications which must be possessed by those from whom such choices can be made.

Law Lords

Properly called Lords of Appeal in Ordinary or members of the Judicial Committee of the House of Lords, they are usually chosen from the judges in the Court of Appeal but the minimum qualification is that the candidate should have been qualified as a barrister for fifteen years. On appointment they are created life peers. They also sit in the court called the Judicial Committee of the Privy Council (*see* Chapter 4).

Lords Justices of Appeal

They sit in the Court of Appeal, and are usually promoted from the High Court, although the minimum requirement is qualification as a barrister for fifteen years.

High Court judges

Also called puisne judges, they are usually appointed direct from practising barristers, of at least ten years' standing. It is possible, but rarely done, for a circuit judge to be promoted to the High Court. In July 1993 the first solicitor, Michael Sachs, was appointed a High Court Judge. In April 1997 two solicitors were appointed as Queen's Counsel (Lawrence Collins and Arthur Marriott). This was described as a 'symbolic breakthrough'. In September 1997 both were authorised by the Lord Chancellor to sit as Deputy High Court Judges. He said:

> I intend to recognise the talents of all parts of the legal profession and to reward the ablest practitioners. I want to open up the ranks of the higher judiciary.

Circuit judges

These are the judges who preside in county courts and the Crown Court and they are appointed from barristers or solicitors of long standing or from recorders of three years' experience.

Recorders

These are the part-time judges of the Crown Court and they are chosen from solicitors or barristers who have been professionally qualified for at least ten years and who are prepared to sit for at least one month each year.

District judges

These work in the county courts. They act as clerk to the court, and have the power to try certain cases—broadly, those involving matters worth up to £5000 (more if the parties consent). As the need and workload requires, assistant and deputy district judges can also be taken on. All these can be appointed from amongst those who have held advocacy qualifications for seven years.

THE JUDICIAL OFFICERS

The Lord Chancellor The Lord Chancellor is the head of the legal profession and judiciary and nominal head of the House of Lords sitting as a court. The office involves a political as well as a legal appointment, in that he is a member of the government and Speaker of the House of Lords. Appointment is by the Prime Minister and the Lord Chancellor is a Cabinet minister. In addition to being head of the judiciary, he is Chairman of the Judicial Committee of the Privy Council. He advises the Queen on the appointment of High Court and circuit judges, justices of the peace, stipendiary magistrates and recorders. He is the keeper of the Great Seal of the Realm—which is the signature of the Crown in its corporate capacity. The Lord Chancellor changes with a change of government. The Lord Chancellor is also actively concerned with law reform. The Law Commission, which was set up in 1965 to promote law reform, has its members appointed by the Lord Chancellor.

There is a theory called the separation of powers which holds it to be a sound organisation for a state where the judiciary, the legislature and the executive are kept apart. In Britain this is seen to some extent, but nothing like completely. Here, for instance, is the Lord Chancellor with a place in the judiciary (a judge), the legislature (a speaker in the House of Lords in Parliament) and the executive (a member of the Cabinet).

The Attorney-General He is a legal adviser to the government. As such he is a practising barrister and head of the English Bar; points of professional etiquette are referred to him. He is also a Member of Parliament (usually in the House of Commons) and the appointment changes with change of government. His role in advocacy is to prosecute in important criminal cases and represent the Crown in civil matters. In addition he brings cases on behalf of the general public, e.g. cases of public nuisance.

The Solicitor-General He is the deputy of the Attorney-General and assists him in his work. He is a practising barrister and normally a Member of Parliament. The appointment changes with a change of government. Both the Attorney-General and the Solicitor-General are called the Law Officers of the Crown and as such both are barred from private practice.

Director of Public Prosecutions The Director of Public Prosecutions is a senior civil servant and therefore remains when governments depart. Appointment is by the Attorney-General and, in order to qualify, the DPP must be a barrister or solicitor of at least ten years' standing. The DPP is concerned only with criminal matters. The DPP's functions are set out in the Prosecution of Offences Act 1985, s.3, as including the conduct of virtually all criminal proceedings. This is done by using the Crown Prosecution Service, unless the case is particularly important or difficult, when the DPP's own Treasury Counsel will act. The DPP has overall responsibility for the operation of the Crown Prosecution Service.

Sometimes the consent of the Attorney-General is necessary before prosecutions can be initiated by the DPP, e.g. under the Official Secrets Acts 1911 to 1989.

Masters

There are various matters which must be dealt with between the commencement of a legal action (the serving of documents etc.) and the actual hearing. They are sometimes called interlocutory matters, and include the production of documents and decisions on the best place and date for the hearing.

In the High Court there are Queen's Bench Masters (appointed from barristers of at least ten years' standing) and Chancery Masters (appointed from solicitors of at least ten years' standing). There are also officers called Taxing Masters who deal with the assessment of costs in court actions. They too are appointed from solicitors of at least ten years' standing.

The Official Solicitor

This is an officer of the court who appears on behalf of those unable to help themselves namely:

- the mentally ill;
- children being adopted;
- people in prison for contempt of court.

Official Referees

These are specialist circuit judges who deal with cases requiring detailed scrutiny of books and documentation, like alleged accounting frauds.

Circuit administrators

When the circuit system was last considered, when the Crown Court network was devised in 1971, officers called circuit administrators were appointed to each of the six circuits (*see* Chapter 4). They deal with the efficient management of the circuit for which they are responsible. All administrative difficulties are referred to them.

On each circuit there are also presiding judges, of High Court rank, who are responsible for the efficient use and availability of judges. They liaise with the circuit administrator.

LAYMEN AMONGST THE PERSONNEL OF THE LAW

Lay magistrates

These were considered in the last chapter when we dealt with magistrates' courts. There are over 30 000 lay justices—paid only expenses. About 95 per cent of criminal trials are dealt with by them. The judicial system, at least at the petty end of criminal justice, could not be run without them.

Tribunal panel members

These too were considered in Chapter 4. The tribunal network is large and developing. The use of laymen in the administration of justice there is essential. Their expertise and practical experience is of central importance in the handling of the matters referred to tribunals.

Lay assessors

In the same way as lay panel members assist tribunals with expertise, lay assessors assist certain courts and mainly tribunals. They are professional or scientific experts who provide their knowledge and experience to assist the judge. They are most often found in the Admiralty Court, which is technically part of the Queen's Bench Division of the High Court. Here they advise the judge in cases concerning collision at sea, poor seamanship, navigational error and so on. They can also be found in other courts within the QBD, when matters involving detailed scientific investigation are being dealt with.

Juries

Anyone between 18 and 70 years old can be summoned to sit as a juror, unless he is among those excluded—such as lawyers, judges, policemen, the mentally ill and certain convicted criminals. There is also a category of people who can be excused jury service—like MPs, medical practitioners, people remanded on bail, members of the armed forces and those aged 65 or over. If a good enough reason can be given to the officer of the court who (representing the Lord Chancellor) summons a panel of jurors, then they might avoid serving. The most common excuse is a long-standing holiday booking. Many of the detailed rules here are set out on the Jury summons. There was a Practice Declaration on excusal from jury service published in late 1988. It makes plain sense: 'jury service is an important public duty which individual members of the public are chosen at random to undertake. The normal presumption is that, unless a person is excusable as of right for jury service . . . he or she will be required to serve when summoned to do so.' The direction goes on to envisage excusal on grounds such as personal hardship, conscientious objection and so on and adds. 'Each such application should be dealt with sensitively and sympathetically.' Patricia Wynn Davies wrote: 'Trial by jury is one of the few instances in which ordinary people are called upon to make truly momentous decisions about their fellow citizens. But for far too many, including large numbers of people with wise heads on middle-aged shoulders, the first instinct is to figure out a way of avoiding that responsibility.' Nevertheless, as ordinary people, juries are sometimes inclined towards making extraordinary decisions. For example, the trial of Clive Ponting in 1985 involved charges of offences under s.2 of the Official Secrets Act 1911 arising out of disclosures in the press on the sinking of the *Belgrano* during the Falklands war. The judge directed the jury to convict but they ignored him and acquitted. Similarly, consider the acquittal of Cynthia Payne in 1987 on charges of controlling prostitutes under the Sexual Offences Act 1956. Further, there is the case of Stephen Owen in 1992. He was charged with the attempted murder of the lorry driver who had killed his twelve-year-old son. The driver was sentenced to eighteen months' imprisonment but served only twelve. This, together with certain features of the running down, seemingly resulted in Owen shooting the driver. Despite overwhelming evidence the jury acquitted him. In *R.* v. *Kronlid and Others* (1996) three women allegedly broke into a British Aerospace factory and caused damage to a jet fighter estimated at £1.5 million. The jury acquitted the defendants of

In the Crown Court at
Plymouth

Jury Service

Your juror's number

You must go to

The Crown Court
The Law Courts
Armada Way
PLYMOUTH

on

at 9.30   am/pm

You have been chosen for jury service. Your name was chosen, at random, from the list of people who are registered to vote in elections.

This form is your jury summons. It tells you when and where to start your jury service.

During your jury service you may be asked to go to another court nearby.

Warning

You may have to pay a fine if

you do not attend for jury service without a good reason

or you are not available to be a juror when your name is called

or you are not fit to be a juror because of drink or drugs.

✉ **To contact the jury summoning officer please get in touch with**

There are rules about who may be a juror. Some people whose names have been chosen cannot be jurors. These rules are explained on pages 2 and 3. When you have read them, you **must** fill in the Reply to the Jury Summons on pages 4 and 5, and send it to the court **within 7 days** of the day you received it.

If you need more advice about the rules, the jury summoning officer will be pleased to help you. But before you contact the officer, please read all of the summons. You may find your question is answered.

The jury summoning officer
(with the authority of the Lord Chancellor)

Issued on

The Jury Summoning Officer
Crown Court Office
Armada Way South
PLYMOUTH PL1 2ER

☎ Telephone 01752 674808

When you write or telephone **please give your juror's number** which is at the top of this page.

5221   5221 296

page 1

Please turn to page 2>

Jury summons; Crown copyright; reproduced by kind permission of the Controller of Her Majesty's Stationery Office

Rules about jury service

Some people cannot be jurors by law. These people are **not qualified** for jury service.
Other people may, by law, **have the right to be excused** from jury service.

Are you qualified for jury service?

> **Warning**
> You may have to pay a fine if you serve on a jury knowing that you are not qualified for jury service.

You are qualified for jury service if
> you will be at least 18 years old
> and under 70 years old
> on the day you start your jury service

and your name is on the Register of Electors for Parliamentary or Local Government elections

and you have lived in
> the United Kingdom
> **or** the Channel Islands
> **or** the Isle of Man
> for a period of at least 5 years
> since you were 13 years old.

But you are not qualified for jury service if
> you are someone listed in
> Box A
> **or** Box B
> **or** Box C (on page 3)
> **or** Box D (on page 3).

Do you have the right to be excused from jury service?

The law gives some people the right to be excused from jury service if they want to be excused.
You may ask the jury summoning officer to excuse you from jury service if

> you are more than 65 years old

or you have been on jury service during the past 2 years. **This does not apply if you were a juror at a coroner's court.**

or you have been a juror and the court excused you for a period that has not yet ended.

or you are someone listed in Box E (on page 3).

Please turn to page 4>

Box A   Convictions

You are not qualified for jury service
- if you have **ever been** sentenced
    to imprisonment for life
    or to imprisonment, or youth custody for 5 years or more
    or to be detained during Her Majesty's Pleasure or during the pleasure of the Secretary of State for Northern Ireland
- if you have in the **last 10 years** served any part of a sentence of imprisonment, youth custody or detention
    or received a suspended sentence of imprisonment or an order for detention
    or been subject to a community service order
- if you have in the **past 5 years** been placed on probation
- if you are currently on bail in criminal proceedings

This list relates to sentences passed in the United Kingdom, the Channel Islands or the Isle of Man.

Box B   Mental disorders

You are not qualified for jury service
- if you suffer, or have suffered, from a mental disorder and, because of that condition,
    you are resident in a hospital or other similar institution
    or you regularly attend for treatment by a medical practitioner
- if you are in guardianship under section 37 of the Mental Health Act 1983
- if a judge has decided that you are not capable of managing and administering your property or affairs because of mental disorder.

If you are in any doubt whether this list applies to you, please talk to your doctor or ask someone to explain it to you.

page 2

86

Box C   The Judiciary and other people concerned with the Administration of Justice

The Judiciary

You are not qualified for jury service if you are, or ever have been

- a judge
- a stipendiary magistrate
- a justice of the peace
- the Chairman or President; the Vice-Chairman or Vice-President; the registrar or assistant registrar of any tribunal.

Others concerned with the Administration of Justice

You are not qualified for jury service if you have been, **at any time within the last 10 years**

- an authorised advocate, or authorised litigator
- a barrister, a barrister's clerk or assistant
- a solicitor or articled clerk
- a legal executive employed by solicitors
- a Public Notary
- a member of the staff of the Director of Public Prosecutions
- an officer employed under the Lord Chancellor and concerned with the day to day administration of the legal system
- an officer, or member of the staff, of any court whose work is concerned with the day to day administration of the court
- a coroner, deputy coroner or assistant coroner
- a justices' clerk, deputy clerk or assistant clerk
- one of the Active Elder Brethren of the Corporation of Trinity House of Deptford Strond
- a shorthand writer in any court
- a court security officer
- a governor, chaplain, medical officer or other officer of a penal establishment
- a member of the board of visitors of a penal establishment
- a prisoner custody officer
- the warden, or a member of the staff, of a probation home, probation hostel or bail hostel
- a probation officer or someone appointed to help them
- a member of a Parole Board, or of a local review committee
- a member of any police force (this includes a person on central service, a special constable, or anyone with the powers and privileges of a constable)
- a member of a police authority or of any body with responsibility for appointing members of a constabulary
- an Inspector or Assistant Inspector of Constabulary
- a civilian employed for police purposes or a member of the metropolitan civil staffs
- someone employed in a forensic science laboratory

Box D   The Clergy

You are not qualified for jury service if you are

- in holy orders
- a regular minister of any religious denomination
- a vowed member of any religious order living in a monastery, convent or other religious community.

Box E   People who have the right to be excused

You have the right to be excused if you are one of the following people

Parliament

- a Peer or Peeress who is entitled to receive a writ of summons to attend the House of Lords
- a Member of the House of Commons
- an Officer of the House of Lords
- an Officer of the House of Commons

European Assembly

A representative to the assembly of the European Communities.

Medical and other Professions

- a dentist
- a nurse
- a medical practitioner
- a Veterinary surgeon or a Veterinary practitioner
- a midwife
- a pharmaceutical chemist

if you are practising the profession and you are registered, enrolled or certificated under the law which relates to your profession

The Forces

You may be excused if you are a full-time member of

- the army, navy or air force
- the Queen Alexandra's Royal Naval Nursing Service
- any Voluntary Aid Detachment serving with the Royal Navy

and your commanding officer certifies to the jury summoning officer that your absence would be 'prejudicial to the efficiency of the service'.

others concerned

- A practising member of a religious society or order whose tenets or beliefs are incompatible with jury service.

page 3

Reply to the Jury Summons

- Read pages 1, 2 and 3 of this summons
- Fill in this Reply and send it to the court within **7 days** of the day you received it.

Warning

You may have to pay a fine if
   you refuse to give the information which is necessary
   to decide if you are qualified to be a juror

or   you deliberately give false information, or cause or
   permit, someone to give false information.

Part 1   About you

Your jury number
*This number is given
on page 1*

Title   Mr ☐   Mrs ☐   Miss ☐   Ms ☐   Other *(please say)*

Surname or family name

Other names
Please put all your names

Day	Month	Year

Date of birth

Address

Telephone number
Please give a daytime number

Part 2   Are you qualified for jury service?

- Have you lived in the United Kingdom, the Channel Islands or the Isle of Man for a period of at least 5 years, **since you were 13 years old?**

   No ☐ Go to Part 5   Yes ☐

- Read the list in Box A on page 2.
  Have you been convicted of an offence, and been given a sentence which is in this list?

   No ☐   Yes ☐ Go to Part 5

- Read the list in Box B on page 2.
  Do you suffer from a mental disorder in this list?

   No ☐   Yes ☐ Go to Part 5

- Read the lists in Boxes C and D on page 3.
  Are you involved in the administration of justice or a member of the clergy?

   No ☐   Yes ☐ Go to Part 5

page 4   *Please turn to page 5>*

Part 3   Deferral and Excusal   *Please read Note 1 on page 6* ➤ ➤

A   Do you want your jury service **deferred**?   No ☐ Go to **B**   Yes ☐ Please say why in **Box A**

Box A   I would like my jury service deferred because

Say **when** you will **not** be available for jury service and **why** not.

Go to Part 4

B   Do you want to be **excused** from jury service?   No ☐ Go to Part 4   Yes ☐ Please say why in **Box B**

Box B   I would like to be excused because

Go to Part 5

Part 4   Disability   *Please read Note 2 on page 6* ➤ ➤

Do you have a disability for which the court will need to make special arrangements?   No ☐ Go to Part 5   Yes ☐ Please say what special arrangements in the box

The special arrangements are

Go to Part 5

Part 5   Declaration   *Please read the Warning on page 6* ➤

I have read the jury summons and the warnings on pages 1, 2, 4 and 6.
The information I have given is true to the best of my knowledge.
I understand that the answers I have given may be checked and that I may be prosecuted if I have deliberately given false information.

Signed

Date

What to do next

Tear off this sheet. Send it to the court in the envelope which was sent with this summons.

Keep the other pages carefully and take them with you when you go to the court.

Note 1 About deferral and excusal

A list of those who have the right to be excused is given in Box E on page 3. Please read the list carefully before you fill in Part 3.

Jury service may be inconvenient for many people, but some people have special problems which make it very difficult for them to do jury service.
If this applies to you, you may ask the jury summoning officer to

- **Put your service off to a later date.**
  This is called 'deferral'. Jury service may only be deferred once.

or - **Excuse you from jury service on this occasion.**
  You will only be excused if the jury summoning officer is satisfied that it would not be reasonable to expect you to do jury service during the next year.

How long will jury service last?
You may be concerned about the length of jury service.
It usually lasts for 10 working days. If a trial is likely to last longer you will be asked **at the court** if this would be difficult for you.

Note 2 About disability

There is a local information leaflet with this summons. This leaflet will tell you about the court's facilities for disabled people.

The court will try to meet your special needs but you may be discharged if there is doubt about your capacity to be a juror.

Warning

You may be discharged from jury service if there is doubt about your capacity to be a juror because of insufficient understanding of English.

charges of criminal damage under the Criminal Damage Act 1971. They were members of a peace group and wished to disarm the jet so as to prevent its use by the Indonesian Government who, they believed, were suppressing the people of East Timor.

Deliberation techniques vary. In October 1994 Stephen Young won a retrial after conviction for two murders when it emerged that four wavering jurors used a ouija board to call up the spirits of the victims in an attempt to elicit from them who had killed them. This took place in a hotel room, not the jury room, but it nevertheless amounted to a 'material irregularity' in jury deliberations as jurors must confine themselves to consideration of the evidence presented in court and not include elaboration obtained elsewhere. Individuals can be called to serve more than once. It is an offence not to attend. At the trial the jurors are sworn in. The defendant can no longer challenge potential jurors without giving reasons (Criminal Justice Act 1987). The whole panel can be challenged (very rare), for example, on the basis that a proper selection has not been made from the electoral roll. This is called challenging the array. In the rare instance of insufficient jurors having been summoned, any eligible person passing by the court can be required to attend. Such activity is called praying the tales, and the unlucky stroller is called a 'talesman'. The theory is that jurors are randomly selected. However this has been challenged. Baldwin and McConville demonstrated in 1979 that immigrants are under-represented. Twenty-eight out of 3912 jurors selected for 326 juries in Birmingham were of Asian or West Indian origin, whereas the census figures indicated then that ten times that number ought to have been present.

The function of a jury is to decide upon matters of fact. Juries are found every day in the Crown Court, where life can become interesting. In *R. v. Schot* and *R. v. Barclay* (1997), in the Court Appeal, it was doubted whether a trial judge should have sought clarification of a note he received from the jury stating that they were unable to come to a decision owing to their 'conscious beliefs' and asking his advice. Following receipt of a second note the judge asked for the names of the jurors involved, which he should not have done. On being informed that two jurors (including the foreman) were involved, the judge discharged the whole jury. He then held both jurors to be in contempt of court and sentenced them to 30 days' imprisonment. In fact they only served one day but the Court of Appeal held that each appellant should have been dealt with differently and that the judge had made an error of judgement. There was a real danger of bias and the judge could have discharged the appellants and sought a majority verdict. The court held that s.8(1) of the Juries Act 1974 provides that conscientious objection to jury service was not an exemption but came within s.9(4), permitting discretionary excusal, and a properly empanelled juror was not accountable for anything said or done in discharge of the office, nor punishable for contempt for returning a perverse verdict, nor indictable for breaking the oath. A juror who 'wilfully would not find for either side' should be fined. The key authority is Bushell's Case

(1670). Juries are also found in coroners' courts. It is possible, but very rare to find them in county courts and the High Court (e.g. 1 per cent of QBD cases). Here, they deal with defamation, malicious prosecution, false imprisonment and some fraud cases.

Verdicts are usually unanimous. However, majority verdicts are acceptable to the judge after two hours and ten minutes of jury deliberation. The majority must be at least ten where the jury consists of twelve. Only 6 or 7 per cent of jury verdicts are by majority in criminal cases. There are more in civil cases, but civil juries are very rare. Most of the law about juries has been consolidated into the Juries Act 1974. The crime of threatening or bribing jurors is called embracery.

The Criminal Justice and Public Order Act 1994 provides for a new offence of witness and juror intimidation.

The senior judiciary have clear views about the value of the jury system: Lord Taylor CJ, speaking in March 1996, strongly supported the jury system which Lord Devlin had described as 'the lamp that shows that freedom lives'. It was, he said, no exaggeration to say that the jury system was as old as Parliament and as fundamental to our democracy: a form of it was clearly referred to in Magna Carta. There were difficulties with very long trials, but no acceptable alternatives. He said:

> I view with considerable anxiety suggestions that guilt or innocence should be determined by panels of 'experts'.

Indicative question

1 Read the following passage carefully, and then answer the questions which are based upon it.

Tony and Tessa are twins, aged sixteen years. They both have good GCSE results and are studying for their A-levels. They would both like to have careers in law. Tony would like to be a solicitor, and Tessa a barrister. They do not live in a univeristy town, and Tony does not want to leave home to study in a university or polytechnic. Tessa would like to study away from home.

(a) Explain how Tony may become a solicitor. *(5 marks)*

(b) Describe how Tessa may become a barrister. *(5 marks)*

(c) State, with reasons, which of the twins, once qualified, is more likely to become a judge. *(4 marks)*

(d) What effect will proposed changes in the structure of the legal profession have upon the future careers of Tony and Tessa? *(6 marks)*

WJEC

CHAPTER 6

Bringing a Case in the Civil Courts

CIVIL ACTIONS

Where one party sues another for an alleged breach of the civil law then a civil action takes place. The parties are plaintiff and defendant. Should an appeal against the decision be lodged later, they would be called appellant and respondent. The parties might be individuals, or companies or partnership firms. The purpose of the action is to obtain a civil remedy. There is a variety of remedies, but the most common is damages—money—assessed as compensation.

AN ACTION IN THE HIGH COURT

The jurisdiction of the civil courts was considered in Chapter 4. Obviously, the case would be brought initially in a court of first instance. The best-known first instance civil courts are the county courts—which deal with small cases, and the High Court—which deals with larger ones. This is a very broad generalisation; for details see Chapter 4.

We will consider the procedures followed in the High Court. As an example we will follow an action for alleged negligence, resulting in serious personal injuries to the plaintiff. We will assume that the plaintiff can afford to bring the action—i.e. that he can pay his costs. If he wins he may recover them from the defendant. If he loses he may have to cover his and the defendant's costs. It is a risky and expensive business and whether the plaintiff wins or loses his case he may still have to pay some of his own legal costs. If he has insufficient resources, but a good case, then he may qualify for legal aid. He will get 'legal assistance' anyway. We will consider these topics later. Even if the plaintiff can afford to sue, he ought to do his best, through his solicitor if need be, to settle without litigation. A famous cartoon called 'Litigation' portrays a farmer pulling on the horns of a cow, with another pulling on the tail. Underneath there is a barrister milking the cow. It is as well to remember this when trying to find enough common ground to settle an action. However, if the plaintiff cannot settle, and he can afford to sue, the following is the usual procedure.

IN THE PLYMOUTH COUNTY COURT   Case no:

B E T W E E N :

Plaintiff

and

Defendant

PARTICULARS OF CLAIM

1.   On the [date of accident], the Plaintiff was lawfully driving a motor vehicle along [name of road/direction/site of accident] when he/she was involved in a [collision - insert type of accident] with a [make of Defendant's vehicle] registration number   driven by the Defendant.

2.   The motor vehicle driven by the Defendant drove into the rear of the Plaintiff's stationary vehicle. [give details of the accident].

3.   The accident described at paragraph 1 hereof was caused by the negligence of the Defendant.

PARTICULARS OF NEGLIGENCE

The Defendant was negligent in that he/she:

Statement of claim

(i)   Failed to keep any proper look out;

(ii)   Drove at a speed which was in all the circumstances excessive.

(iii) Failed to heed the presence of the Plaintiff's motor vehicle along the highway.

(iv)   Drove into the rear of the Plaintiff's motor vehicle.

(v)   Failed to stop, swerve, slow down or otherwise control his/her motor vehicle so as to avoid a collision.

(vi)   Further the Plaintiff says res ipsa loquitur.

[a] The Plaintiff was convicted of   at Magistrates Court on   199 and the Plaintiff intends to rely upon the said conviction as evidence of liability in this Action.

4.   In consequence of the matters aforesaid, the Plaintiff has suffered injury, loss and damage.

PARTICULARS OF INJURY

[b] The Plaintiff was born on [date of birth]. Please see medical reports attached hereto.

PARTICULARS OF LOSS

Full particulars are contained within the Schedule of Special Damages served herewith.

AND the Plaintiff claims:

[c] 1.   Damages [limited to/exceeding £5,000.00].

     2.   Interest pursuant to Section 69 of the County Courts Act 1984 at such rates as the Court may seem just:

          (i)   upon general damages at the rate of 2% per annum from the date herein until judgment or sooner payment, and;

         (ii) upon special damages at the Full Special Investment Account Rate from the date such losses were incurred until judgment or sooner payment.

     3.   Costs.

Dated this   **day of**

. . . .

Solicitors for the Plaintiff

The plaintiff serves the writ

A writ is obtainable from the Central Office of the Supreme Court in London or from the district registry (*see* p. 94). The plaintiff briefly outlines his claim in the writ (i.e. negligence) and the remedy sought (i.e. unliquidated damages). Next the writ is served on the defendant, i.e. he is given a sealed copy, or, alternatively (and more usually) his solicitor accepts service of the writ on his behalf.

The defendant acknowledges service of writ

Acknowledgment is made by the defendant returning an acknowledgement form to the court office from which the writ was issued.

Pleadings

Pleadings are then delivered by one party to another; this can take a very long time. Pleadings are drafted by counsel and cover all material facts. They consist of the following:

The statement of claim

This is sent by the plaintiff to the defendant and sets out his cause of action (e.g. negligence), losses incurred and injuries suffered. It is important that this be drafted with care, since at the trial the plaintiff will not be able to make any allegation of which the defendant has no knowledge. If the statement lacks detail the defendant can ask for 'further and better particulars'.

The defence

This is sent by the defendant to the plaintiff. In the defence the defendant's version of the events is set down and any specific denials of allegations made by the plaintiff. If the defendant does not specifically deny an allegation, he will be taken to have admitted it by the court. The plaintiff can require 'further and better particulars' of the defence. If the defendant feels that he has an action against the plaintiff he can issue a counterclaim.

The reply

This is not always used but enables the plaintiff to answer any new point raised by the defendant in his defence document.

Preparing the evidence

Once the pleadings have been exchanged (often only a statement of claim and a defence will appear), the parties are in a position to build their cases. Evidence will be crucial. Any relevant documents held by either party must be disclosed to the opponent. It is called discovery of documents and it can be ordered by the court if necessary. The idea is to confine the trial, when it happens, to clearly disputed issues. Surprise documents are not encouraged.

If one side has knowledge which is essential evidence to the other then, and again in the interests of clarifying the issues, questions are formally asked (and replies can be ordered). Such questions are called interrogatories. A simpler exercise is the notice to admit. If our negligence action concerned a faulty repair on a vehicle, then the defendant might be required to admit that the signature on a repair bill was his. This reduces the mass of evidence which the plaintiff has to take into court to prove his case. If he intends to refer to a document which is in the possession of the defendant he might issue a notice to produce a document. This will put the defendant on notice to have the paper with him in court, where the plaintiff intends to refer to it in the contested evidence.

Once the 'paper-chase' is complete, the case is 'set down' for trial.

The trial

When the day of the trial arrives the parties may be kept waiting. A list of cases is prepared in advance and backlogs are common. This might provide a last chance to settle out of court.

When the case is eventually 'called on' the plaintiff's counsel speaks first. The disputed issues are outlined to the judge (and in the rare event of one having been sworn in for a civil trial, the jury). Then the plaintiff's witnesses are called and examined, cross-examined (by the counsel acting for the defendant) and, if cross-examination has weakened any of the original answers, the witness is re-examined.

Incidentally, although witnesses usually attend willingly (their expenses are paid) if they are reluctant to do so they can be forced to by a 'subpoena'. Ignoring this amounts to contempt of court: a fine—or even imprisonment—could follow. The evidence is given on oath or affirmation. If a witness produces a story remarkably different from what the plaintiff expected, then the judge can give permission for him to be treated as a 'hostile witness', and questions can be put to destroy the credibility of the evidence brought out by the party who called the witness. Naturally, cross-examination by the defence counsel is always designed to do this. Technology marches on. In *Garcin* v. *Amerindo* (1991) it was held that evidence can be given by means of television linkage. This was a case where the required evidence could, so it was held, be given more effectively by video link from New York than by the witnesses in person, in the UK.

Once the plaintiff's counsel has finished presenting his case it is the turn of the defence to seek to refute it. If the case seems extremely thin, then the defence might submit that there 'is no case to answer', and if the judge agrees, then the case is dismissed.

If the defence calls witnesses then the plaintiff's counsel will cross-examine, seeking to undermine the evidence they give. Once both sides have presented their evidence each will sum up to the judge; first the defence, then the plaintiff. Naturally, the burden of proving the case usually lies on the party who brought it, the plaintiff. He must prove his case 'on a balance of probabilities'—he must show that his evidence is more likely than not to be correct. As there is usually no jury, the judge will decide both matters of fact and of law and deliver his judgment. If he decides to take time to consider, and delivers it later, it is referred to as a 'reserved' judgment. He always gives the legal reasoning behind his decision. This is called the '*ratio decidendi*' and it forms the essence of the case for the purpose of the doctrine of precedent (*see* Chapter 3).

The losing party may wish to appeal. If it is the defendant who has lost, an application for a 'stay of execution' might be made to delay the implementation of the judgment pending the appeal.

The appeal route would, of course, be to the Court of Appeal (Civil Division). If there are grounds to appeal against the final decision (as opposed to a decision on an intermediate, perhaps procedural, matter) then there is generally a right to appeal. No leave to appeal need be sought. These grounds for appeal must be more than just disappointment at the result of the case. The loser might feel that the trial judge was mistaken in the view he took of the law in question, or in his understanding of the weight and nature of the evidence or in that he refused to admit admissible evidence or refused to exclude inadmissible evidence. If there was a jury, the ground for appeal might be that the judge misdirected it.

This action was brought in order to obtain monetary compensation for injuries caused by negligence—called damages. The idea of damages is to compensate the party who has suffered financial loss or physical injury. That is, to restore him financially to the position he would have been in were it not for the defendant's wrongful conduct. Damages can be general and special, liquidated and unliquidated. Incidentally, under the Courts and Legal Services Act 1990, the Court of Appeal can subsitute an award of damages where a civil jury has awarded an excessive or inadequate sum.

We have considered the procedure in the High Court. However, personal injury cases where the claim is for less than £50 000, as most claims are, will be brought in the County Court.

General and special damages

Suppose that David, while on his way to work, is knocked down by a bus driven negligently by Charlie, a bus driver employed by Greenminster County Council. If David can show that Charlie was negligent, David is entitled as of right to:

1 general damages in respect of the injury (to cover pain and suffering); and
2 special damages to compensate him for loss of earnings, if the injury has prevented him from going to work.

Liquidated and unliquidated damages

Liquidated damages are ascertainable or fixed damages and are most common in the event of a breach of contract. Here both parties agree that, if a certain eventuality takes place or does not take place, one shall pay to the other an agreed sum of money, e.g. a builder might agree with a building owner that if a certain section of work is not handed over by a certain date, damages will become payable to reimburse the building owner for his loss. If the fixed sum is greatly in excess of the loss which was or might have been suffered as a result of the breach of contract, then it might be seen as a 'penalty' clause. The court ignores penalty clauses and awards the loss sustained.

Unliquidated damages are damages whose amount is not agreed upon in advance, i.e. unquantified damages. This is the normal remedy in tort where the judge determines how much a defendant should pay to a plaintiff.

On very rare occasions a court might award 'exemplary' damages, if they have been applied for, and if the wrong done to the plaintiff is sufficiently outrageous. In *Sutcliffe* v. *Pressdram* (1989), however, the Court of Appeal reduced an award of £600 000 because exemplary damages had not been claimed and the award far exceeded the amount needed to compensate the plaintiff.

ENFORCEMENT

If the plaintiff is successful and is awarded damages he becomes a judgment creditor and the defendant a judgment debtor. If the money is not paid, then the judgment debtor must return to court to have the judgment enforced. The civil courts do not do so unless asked. The possible ways of enforcement include sending the bailiffs to take goods belonging to the judgment debtor, selling them at public auction and giving the amount due to the judgment creditor and any balance back to the judgment debtor. In the High Court this is done by means of a writ called *'fieri facias'*—commonly called 'fi.fa.' Another way is to have an 'attachment of earnings order' made. Then the defendant's employers will deduct instalments at source. A 'garnishee' order could be made, instructing someone who owes the judgment debtor money to pay it direct to the judgment creditor. A charging order could be made over the judgment debtor's property, which, if pressed, could result in it being sold. There are other possibilities too, but each has its limitations.

The initial step in civil litigation is for the prospective plaintiff to ask himself 'if I win could he pay me?' If he could not it will be an elaborate waste of a lot of time. Such an impecunious defendant is called 'a man of straw'. Never sue a man of straw.

Apart from damages there are various other remedies available where appropriate from civil courts, such as injunctions and decrees of specific performance. They are considered elsewhere in this book—with discussions on equity (Chapter 2), tort (Chapter 12) and contract (Chapter 13).

Reform of the civil justice system

There had been pronounced and prolonged criticism of the civil justice system, so, in 1994, the then Lord Chancellor appointed Lord Woolf, the Master of the Rolls, to review the rules and procedures of the civil courts in England and Wales with a view to improving access and to create one set of procedural rules. He published an interim Report in July 1995, and his Final Report in July 1996. This contains the basis of the most radical overhall of the civil justice system this century. Lord Woolf said that it would create 'a new landscape for civil justice'.

A draft of new Civil Proceedings Rules was also published with the Final Report. These are intended to harmonise and simplify procedures for all High Court and county court cases and replace the two separate rule books for the Supreme Court and the county courts.

Lord Woolf's proposals include a new system of case management by the courts to reduce costs and delay in civil litigation. There would be fast track procedure for cases up to £10 000, with a maximum timetable of 30 weeks, a guideline for maximum legal costs at the top of the fast track of £2500, excluding VAT and disbursements, and pre-action protocols would be used to encourage a more co-operative approach to dispute resolution and promote fair settlements, avoiding litigation wherever possible. The Report also contains detailed proposals to increase access to justice in key areas of litigation (medical negligence, housing, multi-party actions and judicial review).

Commenting on the work of his inquiry, Lord Woolf said:

> My primary concern has been to improve access to justice, in particular for individuals and small businesses. I believe the key to this is enabling people to resolve their disputes in a more co-operative and less confrontational way than our traditional litigation system allows.

Some of the changes advocated in the Interim Report have been implemented:

- the value limit for automatic reference into the small claims procedure has been increased from £1000 to £3000 for all claims, except those for personal injury.
- the Vice-Chancellor, Sir Richard Scott, was appointed to take on additional civil justice responsibilities in order that the needs of the civil justice system be promoted and to provide judicial leadership in the field of first instance civil cases;
- the Civil Procedure Act 1997 came into force in April 1997, providing for a unified rule committee (the Civil Procedure Rule Committee) in order to make rules of procedure applying to the Supreme Court and county courts alike;
- a research grant of £65 000 was awarded to the Royal Courts of Justice branch of the Citizens' Advice Bureau in order to fund an experimental extension of their current advice service to litigants in person.

Following the general election in 1997, with a new Lord Chancellor in office, it became uncertain when or if the more radical proposals would ever become law.

In June 1997 The Lord Chancellor, Lord Irvine of Lairg, opened the whole matter again by appointing Sir Peter Middleton (currently Deputy Chairman of Barclays Bank and the Chairman of BZW, and Permanent Secretary to the Treasury between 1983 and 1991) to undertake a review of civil justice and legal aid reforms. Regarding civil justice reforms, his terms of reference were to consider whether existing proposals for reform are the right way to meet the objective to reduce the cost, delay and complexity of civil litigation and to make recommendations on whether the current proposals are workable, whether they are likely to be cost-effective, what the priorities should be for their implementation (where appropriate), and whether there are alternative approaches that ought to be examined further. In particular, the review was to consider whether the civil justice reforms can be implemented without imposing costs which outweigh savings both for potential litigants and the courts. Having received the report, the Lord Chancellor said in October 1997 (at the Solicitors' Annual Conference in Cardiff) "we will expand the small claims procedure", proposing that the small claims limit should be raised to £5000 except for Personal Injury claims which would initially stay at £1000.

> We will adopt Lord Woolf's proposals for more hands-on management of cases by judges. I intend to oversee the creation of two new routes through civil justice to replace the complexities of the present: a fast-track and a multi-track to be up and running in April 1999.

Further, he announced consultation on whether the fast-track limit should be set at £15 000 instead £10 000 as Lord Woolf suggested. He proposed that the fast-track should be accompanied by an associated fixed-costs regime and undertook to consult the professions.

He said that he had his sights set on a longer-term goal of a Community Legal Service which was a Manifesto pledge

The principal aim of a Community Legal Service will be to help people decide if their problem is really a legal one and, if it is not, to point them in the right direction for appropriate help. There are many existing information and advice sources: the CABs, the Law Centres, the Advice Centres, and mediation bodies.

We intend to co-ordinate these services under a coherent scheme which will provide a service to the whole public which is both easy to access and to understand. We have now launched the first Regional Legal Services Committee – a network covering the whole of England and Wales to follow. These Committees will be providing key information and advice to the Legal Aid Board and Government about the needs and priorities of the regions they serve. Local communities should have a strong say in the development of information and advice services which meet their needs.

I want, as Lord Chancellor, to preside over a legal system that is so highly respected for its speed, its economy and efficiency, that lawyers can begin to compete in public esteem with teachers and doctors and nurses in what they put into society.

Indicative question

1 Simon is suing Jill for failing to pay him £250, which is owed for work he did for her. He does not believe that it is worth consulting a solicitor for a case this small, but he needs some help on the stages he must go through to bring this case to court.

For *each* of the following stages, write in the space provided the correct answer from the list given below. You may use an answer more than once if you think it is appropriate.

Stages

(a) Summons issued by

(b) Pre-trial review before

(c) Arbitration proceedings before

(d) If it is possible to appeal against the award made in the arbitration, where will it go?

List of answers
The police   The Registrar No appeal possible   A High Court judge
A magistrate An arbitrator   The Court of Appeal The county court office

(*4 marks*)

SEG

CHAPTER 7

Bringing a Case in the Criminal Courts

CRIMINAL TRIALS

The parties to a criminal trial are usually the Queen and the individual accused. The prosecution is brought by the Crown on behalf of us all, so whereas a civil action would be named in reports after the parties involved (e.g. *Donoghue* v. *Stevenson*), most criminal cases are referred to like this: *R.* v. *accused*, where 'R.' stands for 'Rex' if there is a king on the throne and 'Regina' if we have a queen. So the case might be called *R.* v. *Jones*.

The prosecution is actually brought by a barrister in the Crown Court or a barrister or solicitor in the magistrates' court. It is possible, although rare, for a private individual to initiate criminal proceedings. In some particular areas of the criminal law, for example, the Trade Descriptions Act 1968, alternative agencies initiate prosecutions (in the case of the 1968 Act it will be the trading standards departments of local authorities). The Director of Public Prosecutions is often involved in the prosecution of really serious crimes (*see* Chapter 5).

Under the Prosecution of Offences Act 1985 a system involving 1591 lawyers and 2133 support staff was created. Thirty-one Chief Prosecuting Officers cover the forty-three police forces in England and Wales. Each office is divided into districts headed by Branch Crown Prosecutors and staffed by Crown Prosecutors (solicitors or barristers) who have a general advocacy qualification under the Courts and Legal Services Act 1990. The prosecutors are independent of the police. They decide whether to prosecute (except in the rare and serious cases where the DPP must act)—and they conduct these prosecutions. This frees the police to go about the business of solving crime. The overall control and responsibility for the Crown Prosecution Service lies with the DPP.

The accused will attend the trial either because he has been summoned to attend by the court (if it is a relatively minor charge) or because he has been arrested (for a more serious matter) by the police and produced from custody for the trial.

All criminal cases are heard initially by magistrates. We considered in Chapter 4 how the court deals with the trial of summary offences and the preliminary inspection of the evidence to be brought in the trial of a more serious—indictable—offence.

It may well be that the accused has been committed for trial but released on bail to wait his turn in the overworked courts. The questions involved in the granting of bail will be examined later (Chapter 15). The place of trial will depend upon the seriousness of the charge. The accused is presumed innocent until the prosecution has established their case 'beyond reasonable doubt'—so that the magistrates or the jury, as the case may be—are sure of his guilt.

SUMMARY TRIAL PROCEDURE

This is the procedure used by the magistrates when dealing with the trial of summary offences and of those offences 'triable either way' when summary trial has been selected. Incidentally, where a summary offence is alleged the prosecution must normally be brought within six months of the commission of the offence (unless a statute creating an offence states otherwise (Magistrates' Courts Act 1980, s.127)).

Most summary trials are for motoring offences. These are mostly to be found in the Road Traffic Act 1988 (as substantially amended by the Road Traffic Act 1991) which provides that where an offence such as speeding, careless or dangerous driving is alleged then the accused must be warned at the time of the offence that prosecution will be considered. If this is not done (unless the driver did not stop, or he or the registered keeper of the vehicle could not be traced in time), then the driver or keeper must be presented with a summons or a notice of intended prosecution within fourteen days of the offence.

As to the procedure at the trial, the accused appears at court to answer the summons. The justices' clerk will read out the offence with which he is charged and ask if the defendant is pleading guilty or not guilty. For example, it might be a charge of theft contrary to the Theft Act 1968, s.1. The prosecutor will then go on to outline the events to which the charge relates, summarising the events of the particular morning when the accused was observed to have left a supermarket without paying for the seven packs of Angel Delight in his pockets, and so on.

For any offence which is triable only summarily and not punishable by more than three months' imprisonment, the accused will often be offered the opportunity to plead guilty by post, and therefore not have to turn up at court (Magistrates' Courts Act 1980, s.12). However, from the example above, our accused, charged with a minor case of theft, intends to plead not guilty and so is required to attend.

This offence is 'triable either way', a point that has been criticised. Shoplifting takes up 14 per cent of Crown Court time in London. The James Committee recommended (in 1975) that theft of property valued at up to £20 should be triable only summarily, but the proposal was not enacted. It is thought that a conviction for theft is particularly damaging to the reputation. John Spencer wrote: 'Quite why a conviction for petty theft should be so much more damaging than one for the purely summary offences of minor vandalising, fare-dodging or indecent exposure nobody can ever explain; but some legal matters are so emotional that rational argument becomes impossible.' Given that this offence is triable either way, a choice of mode of trial must be made. The prosecution can insist on trial on indictment in the Crown Court. They very rarely do. The magistrates form a view, having heard the opinion of first the prosecution, then the defence. If they decide on Crown Court trial that is the end of the matter. If they decide on summary trial, the accused must consent. The Royal Commission on Criminal Justice which reported in July 1993 recommended that this choice be removed from the accused. Eighty per cent of offences which are triable either way are tried by magistrates. Section 49 of the Criminal Procedure and Investigations Act 1996 amends the mode of trial procedure. A defendant is able to plead guilty or not guilty to 'triable either way' offences immediately before the magistrates decide on mode of trial. If the defendant pleads guilty, the court goes on either to sentence or commit him to the Crown Court for sentence. If he pleads not guilty, or fails to enter a plea, the court decides on mode of trial. The idea here is to increase the proportion of cases dealt with by the magistrates' court rather than the Crown Court but it has been criticised for putting defendants under undue pressure to plead guilty without knowing the strength of the prosecution's case. In order to elect jury trial, defendants will have to enter no plea or a not guilty plea.

Because our accused wishes to plead not guilty and trial by the magistrates has been settled upon, the prosecutor now presents the case against him, calling witnesses as desired. Obviously the policeman who observed the events in question will be called. The accused's defence solicitor can cross-examine the witnesses after they have given their evidence for the prosecution.

If the evidence appears very thin, particularly after the cross-examination of the prosecution witnesses, then the defence may submit that there is no case to answer. If the magistrates agree, the case is dismissed.

Otherwise the defence then presents evidence and calls witnesses. It may be that the accused is the only one.

A speech can be made by or on behalf of the accused, before or after or instead of his sworn evidence. (The procedure of making an 'unsworn statement from the dock', however, has been abolished.)

After both sides have presented their cases the magistrates deliver their verdict. They often retire to a nearby room to discuss it first. They can call on the clerk for advice on matters of law, but not about the facts.

If they find that the (prosecution) case has been proved the court will pronounce sentence. The chairman of the bench does so. Usually the defence makes a speech in mitigation first. In our case, for instance, it might be that the accused can show a pattern of absentmindedness. Both sides can address the court about his character. His previous convictions, if any, are brought to the court's attention. The sentence, if the man is convicted, in such a case as this, would probably be a fine.

Apart from this case, summary trial by magistrates could lead to any of a variety of sentences. The list includes absolute discharge, conditional discharge, binding over, fines, probation, community service orders, imprisonment (generally five days to six months for any single offence), suspended sentences of imprisonment, and others. One sentence which is of increasing importance is the Compensation Order. These can be made instead of or in addition to any other order. The maximum is £5000 per offence, and, of course, such an order relieves the victim of the crime from the need to bring civil proceedings for compensation. Sentence can be deferred until a report on the convicted person's mental, physical, social or personal circumstances has been obtained. The sentence could also be increased to 'take into consideration' other offences which have been admitted by the prisoner despite his not having been convicted of them.

The court could also order restitution (e.g. of stolen goods still in his possession) and/or any necessary revision of the required contribution towards legal aid, if he had been in receipt of it, and/or forfeiture of any property used for criminal purposes. There are certain limited circumstances where the prisoner could be committed to the Crown Court for sentence for a summary offence; for example where a fresh offence has been committed during the operational period of a suspended sentence imposed by the Magistrates' Court. The sentence for this later offence can now be added to the punishment for the earlier offence (for which the sentence had been suspended). Alternatively, it might be that the accused has been convicted of an offence which was triable either way and his record of previous convictions indicates that a heavy punishment would be in order.

There is an appeal route to the Crown Court against conviction or sentence on grounds relating to matters of fact and/or matters of law. The whole case is reviewed. There is also an appeal route to the Divisional Court of the Queen's Bench Division of the High Court by way of case stated (*see* Chapter 4).

PROCEDURE FOR TRIAL ON INDICTMENT

The trial of these more serious—indictable—offences, and of those offences triable either way where trial on indictment has been selected, takes place in the Crown Court before a judge and jury. The nature and structure of the Crown Court system was examined in Chapter 4. The jury as an institution involving laymen in the administration of justice was considered in Chapter 5. Before appearing in the Crown Court for trial, these cases would have been considered by a magistrates' court conducting 'committal proceedings' (*see* Chapter 4). The accused may have been remanded in custody or (more likely) remanded on bail; the system of bail will be considered later (*see* Chapter 15).

Part I of the Criminal Procedure and Investigations Act 1996 introduced a new requirement of disclosure of evidence by both the prosecution and the defence. This is the first time that the defence in a Crown Court has been subjected to such a requirement.

The prosecution must disclose all relevant unused material which might undermine its case. This is called 'primary prosecution disclosure'. The court can allow non-disclosure of material where it would not be 'in the public interest'. Any material which is not sensitive nor disclosed should be referred to in a document supplied to the defence.

In Crown Court proceedings the defence must provide a defence statement disclosing in general terms the nature of their defence and particulars of any alibi which is to be relied upon. The prosecution must then make 'secondary disclosure' to the defence of any additional unused material which might reasonably be expected to assist the defence as disclosed in the defence statement.

An indictment is a formal document containing the accusation of crime which is read out to the accused in court. There will be a statement of the alleged offence and the particulars of where and when it is alleged to have been committed by the accused. This is the start of his trial. It is called the 'arraignment'. He will then be asked to plead guilty or not guilty. If he pleads guilty the evidence and the accused's background and previous convictions (if any) will be presented. Then he will be sentenced. If he pleads not guilty, or if he refuses to plead (which is taken as a not guilty plea), the trial proceeds. The jury is sworn in, each unchallenged (*see* Chapter 5) member saying:

> I swear by almighty God that I will faithfully try the defendant and give a true verdict according to the evidence.

Anyone who prefers not to take the oath (which has religious overtones) can affirm.

The prosecution barrister puts forward his case first. His is the burden of proof. He gives his opening speech to the jury and he tells them what to expect. Then he calls his witnesses and, on oath, each gives his 'evidence in chief' in response to the questions put. 'Leading questions'—putting words into the witness's mouth—should not be asked. Hearsay evidence is not usually allowed; the witness can only say what he saw or heard—first- not second-hand evidence is required. Then the accused's barrister can cross-examine the witness, obviously, to check the value of the evidence given, to expose any shortcomings or weaknesses of what has been said, or to cloud or weaken the evidence in the minds of the jury. The prosecution barrister can re-examine if he feels he can restore the quality of the evidence.

After all the prosecution witnesses have been examined, defence counsel opens his case. The accused can give evidence, if he wishes but he cannot be forced to. He can no longer make an unsworn statement from the dock. Then the defence witnesses are called, examined, cross-examined and re-examined as necessary.

Next prosecuting counsel sums up his case to the jury, after which defence counsel does likewise. Then the judge sums up the whole case—drawing the attention of the jury to the relevant points of law and the burden of proof, the value of corroboration, the dangers of evidence which is largely based on visual identification alone. The judge must do all he can to clarify the issues for the jury, but he must not assume the task of the jury himself. He cannot order the jury to convict, no matter how inevitable a conviction might be on the evidence (*R*. v. *Gordon* (1991)).

The jury must be left to decide matters of fact in accordance with the judge's directions on matters of law. The jury then retires to consider its verdict.

This usual procedure is varied sometimes, for example, where the jury is taken to the scene of the crime so as to understand the evidence better: if a view of this kind is arranged it comes as early in the trial as possible.

If the verdict is not guilty, the accused is freed. If guilty, he must be sentenced. The judge hears evidence of background and any previous convictions. The defence will usually make a plea in mitigation, stressing the essential good character and worthiness of the prisoner, the isolated nature of this criminal act, and so on. Reports on the prisoner's condition can be ordered. Other admitted offences can be taken into consideration.

The sentence will be taken from a list including:

- death (only for treason and for piracy with violence);
- imprisonment (which may come fully into operation, or be fully or partly suspended (the Criminal Justice Act 1991 has made very complicated rules controlling the powers to impose or suspend custodial sentences));
- youth custody (for those between fifteen and twenty-one);
- fines (the 1991 Act introduced a system of unit fines with the idea of measuring the penalty against means, but this was abolished by the Criminal Justice Act 1993);
- and a variety of non-punitive orders like hospitalisation, community service, probation (and other 'community orders' like a curfew), absolute or conditional discharge, binding over, deportation (for those with no right of abode), disqualification from driving, compensation, restitution, forfeiture and contribution towards costs.

The prisoner can appeal against conviction and/or sentence, on matters of fact and/or law to the Court of Appeal (Criminal Division). The appeal must usually be lodged within twenty-eight days of conviction. If the appeal is only on a matter of law then it can be lodged as of right. On a matter of fact or mixed fact and law, leave to appeal must be given by the Court of Appeal or the trial judge. The most common basis for appeals is misdirection of the jury in the trial judge's summing up.

In rare cases, with leave of the Court of Appeal or the House of Lords, a further appeal can be made to the House of Lords. In this instance the case must be of general public importance.

Reform of the criminal justice system

The Royal Commission on Criminal Justice (chaired by Lord Runciman) reported in July 1993 and made 352 recommendations for improvements in the criminal justice system. The Commission took two years to report and followed some notable miscarriages of justice, including the 'Guildford Four', the 'Birmingham Six', the 'Maguire Seven', Judith Ward, the 'Tottenham Three' and Stefan Kiszko. These cases illustrated features of the criminal justice system which people would prefer to believe do not exist, such as the fabrication of evidence, exploitation of vulnerable suspects and the great difficulty of unpicking the results of such activities. A judge and jury can only be as good as the evidence they hear. Many of the recommendations for change that the Runciman Commission made have now seen the light of day within such statutes as the Criminal Justice and Public Order Act 1994, Police and Magistrates' Court Act 1994 (already consolidated into the Justices of the Peace Act 1997), the Criminal Appeal Act 1995 and the Criminal Procedure and Investigations Act 1996.

Some changes have attracted severe criticism, such as the removal of a suspect's right to silence during police questioning and at trial by the Criminal Justice Order Act 1994, ss. 34–37.

Indicative question

1 Mark and Susan, who are business partners, collect original oil paintings. They buy most of their pictures from second-hand shops and each hopes that one day they will discover a painting by a famous artist.

Mark has acquired a picture of some sunflowers, which he believes is an original and very valuable. He goes away on holiday and leaves the picture in his bedroom.

While he is away, Susan, who has a key to Mark's house, takes the painting without Mark's knowledge, so that she can have it looked at by an expert. Before Susan can return the painting, Mark returns home. On discovering that the painting is missing he informs the police.

Susan is later arrested with the painting in her possession and charged with theft.

(a) Explain what will happen to Susan following her arrest, before she is put on trial. (*4 marks*)

(b) Susan's trial could take place in one of two courts. Name them both. What is the main difference in the trial conducted in these two courts? (*4 marks*)

(c) What will the prosecution need to prove if she is to be found guilty of theft? Give details of all aspects of the proof needed. (*8 marks*)

(d) Is Susan likely to be found guilty or not guilty of theft? Give reasons for your answer. (*4 marks*)

SEG

CHAPTER 8

Legal Aid and Assistance

INTRODUCTION

Lord Denning summed up the impact of the various forms of financial assistance on the availability of legal advice when he said:

> I have often said that since the Second World War the greatest revolution in the law has been the system of legal aid. It means that in many cases the lawyers' fees and expenses are paid for by the state: and not by the party concerned.

The key to understanding here is to spot the different ways in which the poor and rather poor can (in theory at least) get the help of a solicitor at a low price or at no cost at all, namely:

- legal advice and assistance—the 'Green Form' scheme;
- legal advice and assistance—'assistance by way of representation';
- legal aid for civil court proceedings;
- legal aid for criminal court proceedings.

Until quite recently there was a formal system of 'fixed fee' interviews where for £5 a solicitor would provide only advice for half an hour. The practice, however, is to give a potential client an initial interview for free anyway. The 'fixed fee' scheme died a natural death. It may be worth noting that free advice on legal problems is available at Citizens' Advice Bureaux (many have a rota of solicitors who give their time and effort free), neighbourhood law centres and similar places.

The provision of legal aid was once entrusted to the Law Society. However, the Legal Aid Act 1988 transferred the function to the Legal Aid Board, an incorporated body. Since 1994 the Board has delegated some of its functions and restructured the payments structure for both civil and criminal legal aid by setting up a franchising operation. This involves making contracts for specified work with firms of solicitors for providing specific services at or above defined standards.

LEGAL ADVICE AND ASSISTANCE

The 'Green Form' scheme

This scheme covers practical help from a solicitor: advice, writing letters, negotiating on a client's behalf, obtaining the specialist opinion

Green Form

To be used ONLY by solicitors with a franchise contract which covers the category of work into which this green form falls

GF 7 [Key Card]

LEGAL AID BOARD LEGAL AID ACT 1988

Legal aid account no: _____

Ref: _____

(Copy from extension / authority before sending claim)

➤ If you do not have a franchise contract covering the category of work into which this claim falls, complete form GF1.

➤ If you give advice and assistance about making a will you must submit form GF4 with your claim.

➤ You should keep a copy of the entire green form.

Client's details
Please use block capitals *Delete the one which does not apply*   [Male/Female*]

Surname: _____   First names: _____

Address: _____

Postcode: _____

National Insurance No: [ ][ ][ ][ ][ ]   Date of Birth: _____

Capital details
(give these details even if the client gets income support, income-based Jobseeker's Allowance, family credit or disability working allowance)   [A]

How many dependants (partner, children or other relatives of his/her household) does the client have? _____

Give the total savings and other capital which the client has (and if relevant his or her partner)

Client: £ _____

Spouse (or person living as if a spouse of the client): £ _____

Total: £ _____

Income details
[B]

Does the client get Income Support, any income-based Jobseeker's Allowance, Family Credit or Disability Working Allowance?

[ ] Yes: ignore the rest of this section   [ ] No: give the total gross weekly income of

The client: £ _____

The client's spouse (or person living as if a spouse of the client): £ _____

Total: £ _____

Calculate the total allowable deductions: Income tax: £ _____   [C]

National Insurance contributions: £ _____   [D]

Spouse (or person living as if a spouse of the client): £ _____   [E]

Attendance allowance, disability living allowance, constant   [F]

attendance allowance and any payment made out of the Social Fund: £ _____

Dependent children and other dependants: *Age*   *Number*

Under 11 _____ £ _____

11 to 15 _____ £ _____

16 to 17 _____ £ _____

18 and over _____ £ _____   [G]

Less total deductions: £ _____

Total weekly disposable income: £ _____

Client's declaration

I confirm that:

➤ I am over the compulsory school-leaving age (or, if not, the solicitor is advising me under Regulation 14(2A) Legal Advice & Assistance Regulations 1989);

➤ I have/have not (delete whichever one is not correct) previously received help from a solicitor on this matter under the green form; and

➤ I understand that I might have to pay my solicitor's costs out of any property or money which is recovered or preserved for me.

As far as I am aware, the information on this page is correct. I understand that if I give false information I could be prosecuted.

Signed: _____   Date: ____ / ____ / ____

96/11/12

'Green Form'; reproduced by kind permission of the Legal Aid Board

Attach a completed Form GF3 as proof of every financial extension (including any granted under devolved powers)

Category of problem *Please tick the relevant box*

☐ Personal injury ☐ Debt ☐ Housing ☐ Welfare benefits ☐ Crime ☐ Immigration ☐ Employment

☐ Consumer/general contract ☐ Matrimonial/family: *please also tick one of the following boxes:*

☐ Other *specify in the summary*

☐ Petitioner in divorce or judicial separation ☐ Child support assessment
☐ Respondent in divorce or judicial separation ☐ Other family matters
(please specify in the summary)

Solicitor charge

Has any money or property been recovered for the client? ☐ No: go on to the next section ☐ Yes: please give details:

Devolved powers

Was an extension granted under devolved powers?
☐ No: go on to the next section
☐ Yes: please give date devolved powers were first exercised and complete and attach from GF3 with this form ___/___/___

Have you exercised devolved powers by accepting an application from a child/patient? ☐ No ☐ Yes: please give details in the summary below

Have you exercised devolved powers by accepting an application from a client resident outside England or Wales? ☐ No ☐ Yes: please give details in the summary below

Have you exercised devolved powers by accepting an application where advice has been given by a previous solicitor? ☐ No ☐ Yes: please give details in the summary below

Was telephone advice given before the Green Form was signed? ☐ No ☐ Yes: please explain why in the summary below & include the amount claimed in the attendances time

Did you attend the client away from the office before the Green Form was signed *(you can claim outward travel costs but not time)*? ☐ No ☐ Yes: please explain why in the summary below & include your outward travel costs in the disbursements section

Was this a postal application? ☐ No ☐ Yes: please explain why in the summary below

Summary of work

Has a legal aid certificate or order been granted or applied for? ☐ No ☐ Yes: give the reference: _____

Please give below a brief summary of the work done *(if necessary continue on a separate piece of paper and attach it to this claim):*

	Preparation	Attendance	Travel
Total time			
old rate:			
current rate:			
Total costs			
old rate:	£	£	£
current rate:	£	£	£

Details of disbursements	£	VAT
Counsel's fees:		
Mileage:		
Other disbursements:		
Totals		

Letters and Telephone Calls *(not telephone advice calls)*

		Number	£
Letters written	old rate:		
	current rate:		
Telephone calls	old rate:		
	current rate:		
	Total		

	Claimed	Area office use only Assessed
Profit costs: £		£
VAT on profit costs: £		£
Total disbursements: £		£
VAT on disbursements: £		£
Total claim: £		£

➤ I certify that all the information given in this claim is correct: I have not claimed and will not otherwise claim for the same items from the Legal Aid Fund and I have held a valid practising certificate throughout the conduct of this matter.

Solicitor's personal signature: _____ Date: ___/___/___ Sol ref: _____

Name & address of firm/office: _____

October 1996

of a barrister, preparing a case, for example, if his client has been called to an industrial tribunal hearing where he claims to have been unfairly dismissed from his job. In fact this system provides full legal service up to, but not including, representation in court or before a tribunal or arbitrator. Most problems can be solved without the need for representation: consumer grievances, landlord and tenant problems, divorce, maintenance and so on. Under this scheme a client can obtain the services of a solicitor for nothing or for a contribution (explained below), if he satisfies the means test (below) until the solicitor has performed work for which he would otherwise have charged for 2 hours. In the case of an undefended divorce or judicial separation the limit is 3 hours. Note, however, that the figures are revised from time to time. Under the Legal Aid Act 1988 the scope of the 'Green Form' scheme has been reduced. It no longer covers the making of wills or conveyancing, although there are some exceptions.

In order for a potential client to avail himself of the benefit of this scheme he should patrol the high street until a solicitor's office is found that displays the legal aid sign.

Having made an appointment with the client the solicitor will conduct the means test and give an instant reply about whether the applicant qualifies under the scheme. From 7 April 1997 the Green Form scheme has been available only to those in receipt of income support, family credit, or disability working allowance, or with a weekly disposable income not exceeding £77. There used to be a contribution system for those slightly above these levels, but reform has overtaken provision, for better or worse.

The calculation of disposable income relies upon deductions from gross figures reflecting obligations towards dependants: £28 is deducted for a partner, £16.90 for dependants under 11, £24.75 for those between 11 and 15, £29.60 for those aged 16 or 17, and for those aged 18 and over—£38.90. There is also a capital limit, so that even if the income hurdle is cleared the applicant can fall at the next test for having too many savings. Again, deductions are made, so that with no dependants the capital limit is £1000, it is £1335 with one, £1535 with two, and £100 more for each additional dependant.

The solicitor requires permission from the Legal Aid Board before he can exceed the 2 hours (or 3 hours) limit of work, or where the applicant has already been given assistance under this scheme, on the same matter, by another solicitor.

Assistance by way of representation

This is an extension of the Green Form scheme. With the Green Form another is completed by the solicitor, and if the Legal Aid Board feels that it would be reasonable for the client to obtain assistance by way of representation then the solicitor is able to prepare the case and represent his client.

To qualify for what is known as ABWOR the same income levels apply, except that the calculated disposable income can be up to £166. With an income of between £69 and £166 a contribution system survives the reforms. Broadly, those within these limits pay a contribution of one third of the excess over £69.

There is a capital hurdle for ABWOR too. The limits are: £3000 with no dependants, £3335 with one, £3535 with two and £100 more with each additional dependant.

LEGAL AID FOR CIVIL COURT PROCEEDINGS

Legal aid, if you qualify, covers work leading up to and including civil court proceedings and representation by a solicitor and/or a barrister, as necessary.

Legal aid covers the House of Lords, Court of Appeal, High Court, county courts, the Employment Appeal Tribunal, the Lands Tribunal, and others, but it does not cover coroners' courts, defamation actions or any other tribunal work (although legal advice and assistance, above, covers virtually everything, so some help may still be available). In the magistrates' courts legal aid certificates are rare nowadays. The 'assistance by way of representation' scheme (noted above) is replacing them in practice.

It can take weeks to obtain a legal aid certificate. The solicitor cannot act until it is granted; neither can it be backdated. There is provision for emergency legal aid if the case is very urgent which can be granted at once, but it lasts only until the full application for legal aid has been dealt with. The applicant must agree to co-operate fully with the DSS assessment officer. Furthermore, the full cost of the case must be paid if it is found that the applicant does not qualify for free legal aid, or if an offer of legal aid with a contribution payable is turned down by the applicant.

The solicitor, in normal cases, fills in and sends off the application form. An assessment officer from the local DSS usually interviews the applicant to assess financial resources—a means test.

The local Legal Aid Office assesses the chances of the case succeeding. Legal aid will only be granted if it would be reasonable to do so, i.e. the case has a reasonable chance of success. The financial and quality tests have both to be passed. The financial test involves the calculation of savings and income. Savings (disposable capital) are all added together. The lower capital limit is £3000. The upper limit is £6750 (£8560 for personal injury). Gross income is scaled down to reflect dependants as follows: £1460 for the partner, £881 for dependants under 11, £1291 for those between 11 and 15, £1543 for those aged 16 or 17, and £2028 for those aged 18 and over. The lower income limit is £2563 and the upper limit is £7595 (£8370 for personal injury). Contributions are required if the capital exceeds £3000. A monthly contribution from income is required of 1/36th of income over £2563 for the lifetime of the certificate. Those on income support qualify free of contribution.

Once the applicant has satisfied the DSS of his (lack of) means, and the Legal Aid Office about the quality of his case, then if he is to be awarded free legal aid he is issued with a certificate to that effect. If he is to be expected to contribute towards the costs of his actions, he is offered a certificate.

If the action proceeds and is successful then the property or money recovered can be affected by the controversial statutory charge under which the Legal Aid Office can deduct the costs of having aided the applicant. This would not happen if the losing party were ordered to pay both parties' costs.

LEGAL AID FOR CRIMINAL COURT PROCEEDINGS

The defendant in a criminal case may obtain legal guidance from a legal advice centre of some kind (e.g. a Citizens' Advice Bureau) or under the Green Form scheme. Many magistrates' courts also have a system of duty solicitors who are able to take instructions from defendants who realise they need legal advice only after they arrive at court.

In any event, there is a special scheme of legal aid in criminal cases.

A standard form for applications has been laid down: the details required include the defendant's financial circumstances (including full details of his own income and that of any members of his household), his dependants, and any outstanding payments such as hire-purchases and bank loans. The form is normally considered first by the Clerk to the Justices or one of his professionally qualified assistant clerks; if the application comes within the statutory financial limits (*see* below) and is one where the now reformed 'Widgery criteria' would justify the grant of legal aid, the certificate will be granted by the Clerk.

The 'Widgery criteria' were so named because Lord Chief Justice Widgery was a member of the committee which said in its report in 1966 that it was in the interests of justice that (subject to any requirements based on financial circumstances) legal aid should be granted in certain cases. These 'criteria' have been put into statutory form (and slightly amended) by the Legal Aid Act 1988, s.22. In general terms these are the cases:

1 where the charge is a grave one (e.g. involves serious damage to the defendant's reputation or might lead to him losing his liberty); or
2 where the charge involves substantial questions of law; or
3 where the defendant may not be able to follow the proceedings properly (e.g. where the defendant cannot speak English or he is disabled in some way); or
4 where witnesses need to be traced or expert witnesses need to be cross-examined; or
5 where legal representation is required for some other reason (e.g. it is most undesirable for the defendant to cross-examine a child witness in a case about sexual offences against the child).

The financial limits are now set out in the appropriate legal aid regulations. Once the amount of an applicant's income and capital have been assessed (using the details on the form) he will be required to pay a contribution towards the costs of the legal advice he gets. The money will be ordered to be paid into the court office in twenty-six weekly instalments. The amount to be paid is worked out on the basis of the income in the three months before the date when the form is completed. If the case ends before the twenty-six-week period expires the justices have the power to remit any future payments (which means that there will be nothing more to pay) but they cannot waive any 'arrears' of payments which should have been made. Payments made by defendants who are later acquitted may be ordered to be refunded (and this will normally be done).

Failure to pay the necessary contributions may lead to the Clerk revoking the legal aid certificate after he has given the defendant the opportunity to explain why the payments have not been made.

Examples may help to show the way the system works:

1 The defendant is charged with a number of road traffic matters and intends to plead not guilty, but no questions of law appear to be involved and the facts seem to be straightforward: on the basis of the criteria the application may be expected to be unsuccessful. (This would be so regardless of the financial questions since they would need to be considered only if there was any need to decide how much ought to be paid by the defendant.)

2 The defendant is charged with theft of goods from a shop and has no previous convictions; he intends to plead not guilty. The criteria apply (*see* type **1** above) and the financial assessment will need to be done. His 'disposable income' is between £52 and £58 per week but he has no 'disposable capital'. The regulations require a contribution of £1 per week to be paid by him for twenty-six weeks.

3 The defendant is charged with selling an unroadworthy vehicle (a summary offence) and intends to plead not guilty; significant arguments about the law are expected. The criteria (item **2** above) apply and the financial assessment will need to be done. His 'disposable income' need not even be considered because he is drawing income support.

If a certificate is not granted by the Clerk there is power for the matter to be referred to other authorities to consider. If the case is about a summary offence the application is referred to the magistrates by the Clerk but the applicant and his solicitor are not (normally) invited to attend to make the application. If the refusal is made solely on the grounds of the applicant's means there is no appeal available. There is a right of appeal to a Criminal Legal Aid Committee of the Legal Aid Board.

One of the constant problems about legal aid for a long time has been the different rates of grant/refusal which appear in the national statistics. The most serious difficulty about these figures, however, is that they do not contain an adequate assessment of the nature of the cases in which applications have been made, so it is impossible to decide how serious the situation really is. The 1981 refusal rate in Warrington was seven times as high as it was for the same period in Macclesfield. In 1982 the figures were even more emphatic: the refusal rate in Warrington was then 41 per cent but in Macclesfield it was only 3 per cent. But who can tell whether this was simply because the solicitors in the one area (and their clients) asked for legal aid in many cases where the criteria clearly excluded their cases? Furthermore, updating such figures as these is something between difficult and impossible because the data published by the Lord Chancellor's Department show little evidence of detailed monitoring.

Applications for legal aid to cover cases going on to the Crown Court may be heard and decided by magistrates' courts; the most common order, indeed, covers the proceedings at the magistrates' own court as well as at the Crown Court and financial contributions are collected in a similar way for these. It will be remembered that cases may go through to the Crown Court because (among other things) the defendant relies on his right to jury trial (if available) or because the magistrates consider that the defendant's record and general background make it necessary to impose a greater punishment than they have the power to order: legal aid for the further hearing may be (and usually is) ordered by the magistrates.

The system of criminal legal aid is under review. The Lord Chancellor's Department issued a circular (MCD [921] 1) to justices' clerks setting out guidelines 'to ensure the efficient, effective and economic administration of legal aid in the magistrates' court', suggesting, amongst other things, that 13 weekly payslips be required before legal aid is granted. This document projected the cat into the pigeonloft. The Law Society challenged it as unlawful. From the chaos emerged a consultation document suggesting changes. It was issued on the 17 December 1992. Replies had to be in by the 29 January 1993. There seems little doubt that changes are on the way.

Those who are not quite in poverty find themselves outside the system.

On the 22 July 1928 Judge Sturgess said 'Justice is open to everybody, in the same way as the Ritz Hotel'. Perhaps he was right.

An alternative to legal aid – the contingent fee system

In July 1995 a 'contingent fee' system was introduced in England and Wales. It is unlike the 'contingent' or 'no win, no fee' system in the United States in that, there, a lawyer is entitled to a percentage of any damages gained by his client, whereas, here, the Courts and Legal Services Act 1990 provides for conditional fee agreements in all types of case except family and criminal proceedings where the lawyer stands to get a maximum 'uplift' (additional fee for taking the risk) of 100 per cent—thus double his usual fee, if the case succeeds. Conditional fees were initially available in three types of proceedings: personal injury cases, insolvency actions and cases before the European Court of Human Rights.

In late September 1997 it was announced by the Parliamentary Secretary at the Lord Chancellor's Department, Geoff Hoon MP (after the publication of a survey carried out by the Policy Studies Institute) that the Government is considering how the use of conditional fees might be extended to cover more areas of litigation. Mr Hoon said:

. . . the aim of the conditional fee legislation was to widen access to justice, in particular for those without vast resources who fall outside the legal aid eligibility limits . . . We can take a great deal of encouragement from the results of this survey. Conditional fees would seem to be thriving as a means of gaining access to the courts and, whilst there are areas into which we will wish to carry out further research, there would not appear at present to be any major problems with the scheme. The question now must be: "Where to from here?" . . . When conditional fees were introduced, Lord Mackay of Clashfern [the then Lord Chancellor] wished to proceed cautiously in an area which was so new and controversial. He therefore introduced a fairly limited scheme which would allow observation of how conditional fees were working in practice before extension to other types of proceedings was considered . . . My initial reaction to those findings is very positive . . . I would find it hard to justify maintaining the exemptions on conditional fees and effectively limiting access to justice for a large number of people . . . The question, therefore, is rapidly becoming not whether they should be extended but how far? . . . But I do not think that our thoughts should rest with looking at whether the present arrangements should simply be extended. The debates about conditional fees largely took place some eight years ago. The market for legal services has changed and is changing . . . Options which may not have suited at the time the Courts and Legal Service Act was being debated may now be worth a second look . . . A system based on payment by proportion of damages does have the benefit of ensuring that all of the client's damages are not swallowed up in payment of the uplift. However, concern has been expressed in the past that relating a lawyer's fee too closely to an amount of damages would effectively remove his objectivity in providing advice to his client. I wonder if the time has come to re-examine these arguments and to consider whether contingency fees may in fact have a place in our legal sysyem?

One might be drawn to the conclusion that the future of the Legal Aid system is not rosy, however, in November 1997 Mr Hoon (speaking at a Legal Action Group Conference) denied that the demise, if it is to come, will come quickly:

We have no intention of reducing the money already committed to legal aid covering the next three years. Poorer people will be able to benefit from conditional fees in money recovery, while at the same time benefiting from the existing legal aid budget. The final picture is one of more access to justice, not less. Everyone criticises the civil justice system: 'It costs too much.' 'Expenditure on it is out of control.' 'It costs more but is delivering less.'—those are just headlines. The real story is the suffering of people who need legal help but cannot afford it. We must make justice affordable to the great majority of people who are not so poor that they do not qualify for legal aid. Secondly, we must transform legal aid to make the very best use we can of the available resources in meeting the needs of the less well-off and the wider community. I have heard it said that what we are proposing is too radical—too dramatic a change. To bring about real change people have to be aware of the consequences of continuing with the status quo. Unless they are, they will hang on, hoping the world will remain unchanged and doing what they can to hinder progress. But the change in business terms will be steady. Lawyers with cases in the pipeline under legal aid will continue to be paid on the current basis. Over two or three years their income from legal aid at income will steadily decline as they switch to conditional fee agreements, and income from that source will begin to climb. It will need to be carefully managed, but I see no reason at present to think it will be impossible to sustain.

The legal aid scheme must be transformed. Instead of being a bill-paying machine for the work that lawyers choose to do, it needs to become a positive system for buying the services that people need.

Reform of the legal aid system

In July 1996 the then Lord Chancellor introduced a Government White Paper entitled *Striking the Balance: The Future of Legal Aid in England and Wales*. He wrote the foreword, giving a clue to the nature and content of the proposals:

> the legal aid scheme was a vital contribution to the provision of justice . . . but concerns that it is not working as well as it might to target resources on those in most genuine need and on the most cost-effective services cannot be ignored.

He asserted that:

> the public see legal aid as wasteful in supporting too many weak and undeserving cases; as over-priced, with taxpayers on moderate incomes, who would not qualify for legal aid if they sought it, paying what appear to them to be huge lawyers' fees; and as unfair to the opponents of legally aided people who too often feel that they have to give in on cases that they would have a good chance of winning.

The proposals for change included:

- replacing the present open-ended approach to resources with pre-determined budgets that can be allocated to meet local demand within national priorities;
- extending the scheme to new types of providers and services;
- introducing contracts between providers of services and the Legal Aid Board for specified services of defined quality at an agreed price;
- introducing a new test for deciding whether civil cases should be given legal aid in order to target available resources on the most deserving cases;
- changing the rules governing financial conditions to increase the potential liability of assisted persons to contribute to their own and, in civil cases, their opponents' costs.

Some figure are undeniable. In 1995–96, legal aid cost the taxpayer £1.4 billion, twice as much as five years earlier. Further, the average cost of legal aid bills continues to rise faster than inflation. Some changes were made immediately: the funding of advice agencies was made a permanent part of the legal aid scheme and negotiations with agencies and lawyers were opened to bring advice services under contracts as soon as possible. Consultations began with the profession about setting standard fees for civil cases as a prelude to moving to bulk contracts with fixed prices in due course. A Special Investigations Unit was set up to look into the finances of apparently wealthy applicants.

However, with a change of government there came a change of Lord Chancellor, and, as we saw above in the proposed reforms of the civil justice system, a new review of these proposed changes in the legal aid system has been instituted. Sir Peter Middleton is steering the review. His terms of reference include:

- to consider whether existing proposals for reform are the right way to gain better control of cost of legal aid, better value for money for the resources available, and the ability to target those resources on the areas of greatest need.
- to make recommendations on whether the current proposals are workable, whether they are likely to be cost-effective, what the priorities should be for their implementation (where appropriate), and whether there are alternative approaches that ought to be examined further.
- and in particular to consider the means by which the cost of legal aid can be kept within limits which society can afford and is willing to pay in the context of the overall public expenditure ceilings to which the Government is committed, while giving the fullest possible weight to the important values of legal aid as a rights-based entitlement equally available throughout the country and to see how far relevant aspects of the reforms (for example, involving the not-for-profit sector, information services, use of ADR) might be developed to lay the foundations for a Community Legal Service.

So it seems that while the system may be tinkered with, there is to be no revolution—yet.

Indicative question

1 (a) What is the main difference between 'legal advice' and 'legal aid'? (*2 marks*)

(b) Apart from a solicitor's office, name two other places a person can go for advice about a legal problem and say where these places are generally located. (*4 marks*)

(c) (i) Where are applications for legal aid made to, in civil cases **and** in criminal cases? (*2 marks*)

(ii) How is it decided whether or not these applications are successful? (*4 marks*)

(d) State the purposes of having a system of legal aid and advice. (*2 marks*)

(e) Discuss whether the present system of legal aid and advice is adequate. (*6 marks*)

SEG

2 **A1** In which court or tribunal would the following cases first be heard?

(a) Maintenance for a spouse

(b) A breach of the provisions of the Health and Safety at Work Act

(c) A defended divorce application

(d) An application for Bail which had been refused by the Magistrates' Court

A2 What considerations are taken into account when deciding whether **criminal** legal aid will be granted?

A3 What are **three** of the traditional differences between a barrister and a solicitor?

A4 How would a person demonstrate in law that their marriage had irretrievably broken down?

A5 What are the **differences** between judicial separation and divorce?

NEAB Summer 1997 (Foundation)

CHAPTER 9

Legal Personality

NATURAL AND LEGAL PERSONS

The word person derives from Latin: *per* (through) and *sonare* (to sound). It seems that the idea of a *persona* comes from the mask worn by an actor through which he spoke to the audience. A person in law does not need arms and legs. Obviously we are all persons in law, but so are entities like registered companies. Any entity which is capable of separate legal identity—as the possessor of legal rights, responsible for the performance of legal duties—is a person as far as the law is concerned. However, it is usual to speak of natural persons when dealing with humans and to speak of legal or juristic persons when dealing with separate entities like companies. Partnerships, clubs and trade unions are not legal persons. They have no legal existence apart from the people of whom they are composed. The identity of such legal persons as companies will be probed more deeply in the next chapter.

NATURAL PERSONS

Status and capacity

Status is like a badge. It denotes membership of a particular class or grouping of people. There is no problem about wearing several badges at once: Jenny is twenty years old and married, with two daughters. She was born in Plymouth. She has at least four statuses (badges): adult, married, British, parent. Each status carries with it certain rights and duties under the law. Each brings a capacity to do certain things—to make a will, vote and so on.

Status and capacity are closely interwoven—if Jenny were a barrister by profession then she would be unable to sit as a juror—despite being qualified to do so through her adult status.

This chapter briefly inspects a few tapestries of status and capacity.

Nationality

Nationality is the link between an individual and a state. A person may have dual or even triple nationality, derived from parents and place of birth, or none at all—stateless. Nationality is most important where the rules of public law (*see* Chapter 1) are concerned. For example, only a British citizen (or a citizen of the Republic of Ireland) can vote in British elections. Aliens need work permits if they are employed in Britain, and they can be deported. Lack of status means lack of capacity.

British citizenship is controlled by the highly complicated British Nationality Act 1981.

Under this Act a child born in the UK is British if either parent is British or settled in Britain. A new born baby found abandoned in the UK is deemed to be British unless the contrary is shown. If neither parent is British at the child's birth in the UK, but later becomes a British citizen, or settles in Britain, then the child can be registered as British. Even if this does not happen registration is an entitlement if the child lives in Britain until he is ten years old.

A child adopted by a British citizen becomes British too, from the date of the United Kingdom court order.

A child born abroad is British at birth if either parent is British (otherwise than by descent) or if either parent is abroad on Crown (or other designated) service. This means that a child born of British parents abroad is British but his own children will not automatically be British. This is said to maintain connections with the UK. Naturally, Crown servants working abroad are not affected by the limit on citizenship by descent to those born abroad. Similarly, a child born abroad can be registered as British within twelve months if he has a British parent (British by descent) where that parent had a parent who was British otherwise than by descent. This is allowed only if the child's British parent had spent at least three years in the UK at any time before the birth. If the registration is not made within the year, then it is possible later in the child's life if the child and both his parents subsequently live in the UK for three years. Again these regulations are designed to reflect a connection with Britain.

British Dependent Territory citizens (e.g. those from the Cayman Islands), and British Overseas citizens can register as British citizens after five years' residence in the UK.

British citizenship can also be acquired by naturalisation. This means that the applicant must satisfy the Home Secretary that he has resided in the UK or colonies or been abroad on Crown service for a sufficient length of time—usually four of the last seven years, including the one before the application. Further, he must show that he is of good character, and is competent in the English language (or Welsh) and he intends (if allowed) to remain in the UK (or colony or on Crown service abroad). The naturalisation can be revoked (as can registration, if it has been obtained by fraud).

Domicile and residence

Most people live in the country of which they are citizens. Some do not. They decide, or their employers decide, that overseas there are better places to live. If a permanent home is set up there then while nationality may be British, domicile is not. A person's domicile is a matter of fact, although legal consequences follow. He is in a particular country, he intends to stay there (called *animus manendi*). It is his domicile. Everybody has a domicile. Nobody has more than one. It might be:

1 a domicile of origin—a legitimate child has the father's domicile, and an illegitimate one has the mother's, a foundling has the domicile of the place where he was found; or

2 a domicile of choice. The domicile of origin is changed as the person chooses to be domiciled elsewhere. Anyone over 16 can make such a choice. A married woman at one time took her husband's domicile, but the Domicile and Matrimonial Proceedings Act 1973 provides the choice for her too, although on marriage her domicile will generally be that of her husband, at least to start with. If a married couple split up and a child goes or stays with the mother, then her domicile becomes the child's too. Sometimes this is called the domicile of dependent persons.

This idea of domicile is important. For example, if a person is domiciled abroad then the laws of that country apply to him. If legal formalities are undertaken there, in accordance with that law, for example, marriage or divorce or making a will, then despite the fact that the English law has not been followed (e.g. only one witness to a will required there, but two in England), the result of the operation of that law (divorce, marriage, distribution of property after death) will be recognised by the English courts as valid.

So a change of domicile means a change of rights, duties, obligations etc. in accordance with the legal system in the new homeland.

Residence is another matter of fact. A person's residence is a narrower concept than that of his domicile. It has nothing to do with his nationality. For example a man domiciled in England has his residence in Plymouth. He is subject to the general law of England, and in so far as that law has a more localised nature, his residence will be important; for example he will probably be on the electoral roll for the constituency in Plymouth in which he resides (perhaps Devonport), he will be subject to the localised jurisdiction of the Plymouth County Court, and Plymouth Magistrates' Court. His taxes will be inspected and collected by those responsible for Plymouth, and so on. A lady living in Stoke-on-Trent would be subject to the same general law, but to different localised details.

Obviously, a person's residence is a very important factor in determining his domicile. Residence will not change where only temporary changes are made, e.g. for holidays.

Minors

The Family Law Reform Act 1969 set the age of majority at eighteen. The law protects young people, restricting their capacity in various ways:

1 a minor cannot own land, but he can own personal property;
2 before the age of eighteen a minor cannot vote, make a will (with one exception, see Chapter 17), make a contract which binds him (with two exceptions, see Chapter 13), get married without someone else's consent (see Chapter 16), see an '18' rated film at a cinema (see Chapter 11), order alcoholic drinks on licensed premises, enter a betting shop, or a sex shop, be tattooed (except by a qualified medical practitioner) or (generally) work night shifts.

The legal capacity of children is measured by age. Under ten a child is incapable of crime (*doli incapax*) and will not be charged, although care proceedings could be brought if his parents cannot or will not control him. Under twelve he cannot be sold an animal as a pet. Under thirteen he cannot generally be employed. Under fourteen (but over ten) he is criminally responsible if he can be shown to have understood the wrongful nature of the action in question (*see*, e.g. *A* v. *DPP* (1992)). Under fifteen a child cannot enter a knackers yard. Under sixteen a child cannot buy liqueur chocolates or cigarettes, education is compulsory (from five) and restricted part-time employment is allowed. Under seventeen a child cannot hold a pedlar's licence and, since October 1997, fireworks cannot be sold to those under eighteen.

There are progressive minimum ages for driving motor vehicles; sixteen (moped, mowing machine, invalid carriage, small agricultural tractor), seventeen (motor-cycle, small passenger and goods vehicles, some road rollers), eighteen (medium sized goods vehicles) and twenty-one (other road vehicles, e.g. most heavy goods vehicles).

There are no age requirements for liability in tort, except when some intent is required and the child is too young to have formed such an intent.

Persons suffering from mental disorder

In the law of tort mentally disordered persons occupy much the same position as minors. There is generally no motive element in tortious activity and so the lack of mental capacity is not directly relevant. Obviously, in the exceptional cases where motive is necessary, and the incapacity precludes formation of intent, then no tortious liability arises.

There is protection in the law of contract. A contract is an exercise of free will, so if the person understood nothing of what was going on, and if the other party to the alleged contract was aware of his infirmity, then the contract can be made void (avoided or cancelled) at his option. This means that he can, if he wishes, choose to carry on with it. The contract is valid, but voidable. If he ratifies the contract when he knows what he is doing (during a lucid interval) then the contract is no longer voidable.

If the person in question is so ill as to be within the scope of the Mental Health Act 1983, and his property has been put under the control of the court (called the Court of Protection) under a s.93(2) of the Act, then he cannot make contracts involving that property.

Where contracts for necessaries (e.g. food, clothing, shelter) are made then a reasonable price is payable for them. This is much the same as with minors (*see* Chapter 13).

These basic, common law rules of contract law apply in a similar manner to those who are only temporarily lacking in capacity like drunkards and (presumably) those under the influence of drugs etc.

Marriage (which is discussed in more detail in Chapter 16) must also be an act of free will, so if a person is unaware of the circumstances then consent cannot be said to be genuine and the marriage is voidable (it can be undone). The Matrimonial Causes Act 1973 provides:

12 A marriage celebrated after 31 July 1971 shall be voidable on the following grounds only, that is to say . . .

(*c*) that either party to the marriage did not validly consent to it, whether in consequence of duress, mistake, unsoundness of mind or otherwise;

(*d*) that at the time of marriage, either party, though capable of giving a valid consent was suffering (whether continuously or intermittently) from mental disorder within the meaning of the Mental Health Act 1983 of such a kind or to such an extent as to be unfitted for marriage.

Furthermore, to make a will a person needs to understand the nature of what he is doing, as Cockburn C J said in *Banks* v. *Goodfellow* (1870):

As to the testator's capacity, he must, in the language of the law, have a sound and disposing mind and memory. In other words, he ought to be capable of making his will with an understanding of the nature of the business in which he is engaged, a recollection of the property he means to dispose of, of the persons who are the objects of his bounty, and the manner in which it is to be distributed between them. It is not necessary that he should view his will with the eye of a lawyer, and comprehend its provisions in their legal form. It is sufficient if he has such a mind and memory as will enable him to understand the elements of which it is composed, and the disposition of his property in its simple forms.

It seems, then, that a will can only be made during a lucid interval. The person need not be cured. He could revert to illness the following day, but his will must be made when he had capacity to do it. (There is more about wills in Chapter 17.)

As for the criminal law, the mentally disordered person's position must be regarded in line with the statutory provisions, particularly the Mental Health Act 1983. If a minor offence has been committed the police might well choose not to charge the mentally disordered person at all, but allow him to return to his relatives or enter an appropriate hospital informally (voluntarily). Alternatively he might be committed compulsorily to hospital on a medical certificate without going through the criminal courts. If the alleged crime is more serious, and the person has been charged, and remanded in custody, then, again under the 1983 Act, he can be transferred to hospital. If he is taken to court for trial, he may be declared unfit to plead or unfit to stand trial if he does not understand what is happening. He can then be sent to hospital (under the Criminal Procedure (Insanity) Act 1964). If he can plead, but his defence at the trial is insanity, and if it succeeds, he can be sent to hospital. Even if he does not raise the defence, or if it is raised and not accepted by the jury he can still be sent to hospital by the judge. If he is sentenced to imprisonment he can be later transferred to hospital.

The defence of insanity is governed by rules called the M'Naghten Rules, after a case in 1843 where Daniel M'Naghten shot Sir Robert Peel's secretary. He was acquitted because of his insanity and committed to hospital. The Rules emerged from a House of Lords debate on the case. The leniency of the result had caused a public outcry. The House requested that the judges clarify the requirements of the insanity defence. These are, briefly, the Rules they laid down:

1 everyone is presumed sane until proved otherwise;

2 it is a defence to prove that when committing the alleged offence the accused was labouring under such a defect of reason, from disease of the mind, as not to know the nature and quality of his act, or (if he did know it) that what he was doing was wrong;

3 where an act is committed by someone under an insane delusion about what is going on around him, and this prevents him from understanding what he is doing, then his responsibility is measured in accordance with his appreciation of the circumstances, i.e. that which he imagined as true, was accurate.

Where the defence is raised, because of the general presumption of sanity, the defence counsel must establish (on a balance of probabilities) that the accused was insane. If this works, the accused is not guilty by reason of insanity, and hospitalised, unless he appeals, for an unlimited time. The defence is not often raised, perhaps three or four times each year.

Against a charge of murder there is a statutory defence called diminished responsibility contained in the Homicide Act 1957. If successful it has the effect of reducing a conviction for murder to a conviction for manslaughter (and the result is not automatically life imprisonment nor indefinite detention in a mental hospital). In order to establish the defence it must be shown (on a balance of probabilities) that at the time of the crime the accused (1957 Act, s.2.):

> was suffering from such abnormality of mind (whether arising from a condition of arrested or retarded development of mind or any inherent causes of induced by disease or injury) as substantially impaired his mental responsibility for his acts and omissions in doing or being a party to the killing.

So, for example in *R.* v. *Byrne* (1960) the defence was successfully raised on behalf of a man who had strangled a young woman in a YWCA hostel and then horribly mutilated her body. It was established that from an early age he had been subject to perverted violent desires and that these had become an 'irresistible impulse' to commit the offence. Incidentally, despite successfully having his conviction altered from murder to manslaughter, his sentence to life imprisonment was confirmed. Barbara Wootton commented: 'Logic, experience and the Lord Chief Justice thus all appear to lead to the same conclusion—that is to say, to the impossibility of establishing any reliable measure of responsibility in the sense of a man's ability to have acted otherwise than as he did. After all, every one of us can say with St Paul (who, as far as I am aware, is not generally suspected of diminished responsibility) 'the good that I would, I do not: but the evil which I would not, that I do.'

In *R.* v. *Egan* (1992) it was held that a man who was bordering on mental subnormality and also drunk when he attacked and killed an old lady was guilty of murder. His defence of diminished responsibility would only have succeeded if the jury had been satisfied that even had he been sober his mental condition would have been substantially impaired.

Further, in *R*. v. *Ahluwalia* (1992) an Asian wife in an unhappy and very violent arranged marriage poured petrol on her husband and burnt him to death. Her defence of provocation was unsuccessful. Her appeal concerning that defence failed—but the court ordered a retrial so that diminished responsibility could be pleaded on her behalf. This was successful.

CHAPTER 10

Corporations and Unincorporated Associations

LEGAL PERSONALITY

In the last chapter we considered the differences between natural and legal (or juristic) persons. Each has its own identity and capacity. In this chapter we look more closely at precisely what legal persons are, how they are created, and how they differ from other groups and associations, like partnerships and social clubs.

A legal person is created by the process of incorporation. It is a corporation—from the Latin *corpus*, a body. It has a separate legal identity apart from the human beings who work for it. As Lord Halsbury LC said (in *Salomon* v. *Salomon and Co. Ltd.* (1897)):

> It seems to me impossible to dispute that once the company is legally incorporated it must be treated like any other independent person with its rights and liabilities appropriate to itself and that the motives of those who took part in the promotion of the company are absolutely irrelevant in discussing what those rights and liabilities are.

The people come and go, but the corporation lives on, unless it is brought to an end by the proper legal processes. Sometimes this survival capability is called perpetual succession.

Corporations come in two types: corporations sole and aggregate. A corporation sole is an official position which has a separate legal identity from the man or woman who occupies it from time to time, like the monarch or the Archbishop of Canterbury. There is a great deal of property vested in such positions. It may be used by the incumbents, but it is not their personal property. When the job changes hands there is no need to revest the property in the new occupant because the corporation lives on continuously through the change (perpetual succession). New corporations sole are not easily created; it can only be done by statute; they are not common.

On the other hand, corporations aggregate are everywhere. For example, there are almost a million companies registered in England and Wales. Such corporations are usually classified according to method of creation.

CREATING CORPORATIONS

By royal charter

This is issued by the monarch after a request (called a petition) to the Privy Council. Trading corporations are not formed by charter today although the East India Co. and the Hudson Bay Co. were set up in this way (in 1600 and 1670). Examples of modern-day chartered corporations are the BBC, the Institute of Chartered Accountants and the Chartered Institute of Secretaries and Administrators. Liability of members is not usually limited, but since trading is not usual either this is not important.

By Act of Parliament

Statutory corporations are generally large bodies of a public nature. The nineteenth-century railway and canal companies were created in this way. They were created by an Act of Parliament which set out their powers (e.g. borrowing) and duties. Such incorporation is now rare. Economic activity is too swift to create each company by means of a separate Act. However, the remaining nationalised operations, such as British Coal, are statutory corporations.

By registration

This is done under the Companies Acts and is the way most trading corporations are established.

INCORPORATION BY REGISTRATION

This method of creating a corporation, a registered company in this case, involves the deposit of certain documents with the Registrar of Companies at 55 City Road, London EC1, or Crown Way, Maindy, Cardiff. It is usual to take them along by hand, but it can be done by post. These documents are as follows.

1 The Memorandum of Association. This document will regulate the external affairs of the company. It is a sort of charter. Those who are considering dealing with the company can refer to it. It includes the name of the company, the address of the registered office, the objects of the company (the purpose for which it is created), a statement of how liability is limited, the amount of share capital and its division into shares (a public company must have at least £50 000 with 25 per cent of the nominal value and the whole of any premium paid up), and the association clause. This is the declaration of the members that they wish to be associated as a company. Each subscriber takes at least one share, the rest are distributed later, according to the contract between the members. Each must sign and the signature must be dated and witnessed by at least one person, who must also sign.

2 The Articles of Association. This document must also be formally executed by the members. It is the internal document, containing the regulations for internal management. It can be written especially, or the model set out in Table A of the Companies

(Tables A to F) Regulations 1985 could be adopted. The document will contain rules about the issue and transfer of shares and dividends, general meetings, voting rights, accounts, audits, the appointment and powers of directors, the managing director and the secretary.

3 A statement of names. These are those of the proposed first directors and secretary, signed by or on behalf of the subscribers and containing the director's consent to act.

4 A statement of the share capital.

5 The statutory declaration. This is usually made by the solicitor who is acting for those setting up the company. The declaration is that the registration requirements have been satisfied. The Registrar may be satisfied with this as sufficient evidence of compliance. When he is satisfied he issues a certificate of incorporation, and publishes the fact in the *London Gazette*.

There are significant advantages to incorporating a business, particularly in the area of limited liability. In exchange, the company must regard itself as being open to public scrutiny. The documents deposited with the Registrar are public. They can be inspected by anyone who has paid the appropriate fee. Furthermore, each year after incorporation a company issuing share capital must make an annual return to the Registrar. This must include such matters as the address of the registered office, a summary of the position regarding the issue, holding and transfer of shares, the extent of the company's indebtedness; details of the directors and secretary, and the accounts and reports as presented to the annual general meeting.

CAPACITY OF CORPORATIONS

It is important to keep in mind the artificial nature of the personality of corporations when considering matters of legal capacity.

In the criminal law, for example, it is difficult to imagine a company being held criminally liable for activities that require the accoutrements of the human body, for example, perjury, bigamy, rape. However, there is a principle within the criminal law called identification. It has been developed along the fictional lines that the minds of certain superior officers within a corporation compose its personality and their acts are its acts.

Lord Denning said (in *Bolton* v. *Graham* (1957)):

A company may in many ways be likened to a human body. It has a brain and nerve centre which controls what it does. It also has hands which hold the tools and act in accordance with directions from the centre. Some of the people in the company are mere servants and agents who are nothing more than hands to do the work and cannot be said to represent the mind or will. Others are directors and managers who represent the directing mind and will of the company, and control what it does. The state of mind of these managers is the state of mind of the company and is treated by the law as such.

While it may be mildly diverting to imagine a company being jailed for incest, it is important to note that there have been heavy fines levied on corporations for criminal offences which involve commercial fraud. Indeed the Law Commission has issued a Working Paper, No. 44, on the Criminal Liability of Corporations, and at the Labour Party Conference in October 1997 the Home Secretary announced plans to change and clarify the law in order to create liability for company directors. Furthermore, a corporation can be vicariously liable for the crimes of its servants which do not require a mental element (called *mens rea*; *see* Chapter 15). The doctrine of identification is not the same as holding an employer liable for his/its employees' activities. It actually equates the acts of the superior officers of the company with the company itself. Their crimes are the company's own acts for which it can be punished, not those of someone else for which it must answer. The case *R. v. P & O European Ferries (Dover) Ltd* (1991) arose out of the deaths of four of the 193 people who died on March 6th 1987 when the *Herald of Free Enterprise* capsized outside Zeebrugge. The case collapsed because the assistant bosun and chief officer were not regarded as senior enough to be identifiable as the company itself. However, in 1994 OLL Ltd was convicted of manslaughter after the deaths of four teenagers who were killed while canoeing off Lyme Bay.

In the law of tort the position is quite similar. Of course, corporations can be held vicariously liable for torts committed by their employees while they are acting within the course of their employment (*see* Chapter 12 and, as illustration, consider the offences of strict liability which are contained in s.1 of the Trade Descriptions Act 1968, below, Chapter 14), but corporations have been held personally liable too. In *Lennards Carrying Co. v. Asiatic Petroleum* (1915) the managing director was found to have been the 'directing mind and will of the corporation'. In general, corporations can own and dispose of land and all other property just as natural persons can, provided that the source of its status (charter, statute or memorandum of association) permits it.

For capacity in the law of contract, again reference must be made to the status source. A chartered corporation will have powers from its charter, but in theory it has the full contractual capacity of a natural, sane, adult, despite any limits within the charter. However, and naturally, if it persists in acting beyond its power (*ultra vires*), then it risks having its charter revoked. Short of that, any member can seek an injunction to stop the activity. This was seen in *Jenkin v. Pharmaceutical Society* (1921) where the Society was prevented by such an injunction from setting up an industrial committee, a trade union activity which was outside its charter of 1843. It was similarly prevented from organising an insurance scheme.

A statutory corporation's activities outside its statutory powers are *ultra vires* and void.

On the face of it, that would appear to be the position with a registered company's activities outside the objects clause within its memorandum of association. After all, the registered documents are public, and so those who contract with companies are presumed to be aware of the contents of their objects clauses, that is, of what the company was set up to do.

However, these objects clauses are often very widely drawn. For example, in *Bell Houses Ltd* v. *City Wall Properties Ltd* (1966) a company in housing development had drafted part of its objects to read:

> To carry on any other trade or business whatsoever which can in the opinion of the board of directors be advantageously carried on by the company in connection with, or as ancillary to, any of the above business or the general business of the company.

This was held to cover the mortgage broking in which the company had dabbled. Further to wide objects clauses, the European Communities Act 1972 (and now the Companies Act 1985, s.35) implementing a directive designed to harmonise company law amongst the European Community, provides:

> 9(1) In favour of a person dealing with a company in good faith, any transaction decided on by the directors shall be deemed to be one which it is within the capacity of the company to enter into, and the power of the directors to bind the company to enter into, and the power of the directors to bind the company shall be deemed to be free of any limitation under the memorandum or articles of association; and a party to a transaction so decided on shall not be bound to enquire as to the capacity of the company to enter into it or as to any such limitation on the powers of the directors, and shall be presumed to have acted in good faith unless the contrary is proved.

It follows from this that, if someone makes an *ultra vires* contract with a company, not aware that it is *ultra vires*, then provided that it has been decided upon by the board of directors or (presumably) someone delegated by them specifically for the purposes of that contract, it is deemed to be within the powers of the company, but only from his point of view. He can enforce it. The company cannot. He must, of course, have acted in good faith; that is, without actual notice of the limitations of the objects clause. His good faith is presumed, unless the company can show otherwise.

This lack of good faith was established as one of several grounds for the benefit of s.9(1) not being available in *International Sales and Agencies Ltd* v. *Marcus* (1982).

The Companies Act 1989 is designed to simplify the *ultra vires* rules. There is a new s.3(a) for the Companies Act 1985. It provides that where The Memorandum of Association of a registered corporation shows the company's object as a 'general commercial company' then it can carry on any trade or business and indeed it can do other things which are 'incidental' or 'conducive' to that activity as well. S.4 of the 1985 Act is also amended to remove restrictions on altering the objects of a company.

Although the company directors are still bound to observe restrictions on their powers which appear in the Memorandum, the *ultra vires* rule with regard to third parties was abolished by the 1989 Act. If such a third party contracts in good faith, the company is bound.

COMPARISON BETWEEN CORPORATIONS AND UNINCORPORATED ASSOCIATIONS

Formation

A registered company, as we have seen in this chapter, is formed by the deposit of certain documents with the Registrar of Companies, whereas a partnership is formed by agreement. It can be express or implied. It can be written, oral, put into a deed or inferred from the conduct of the parties. However, joint ownership of property is not enough, nor is just sharing the income (particularly if it is simply the recovery of an existing debt or taken as a salary or an annuity).

The Partnership Act 1890 is very important here. Unless the agreement provides to the contrary, its contents will form the legal framework of the partnership firm. The definition within the 1890 Act, s.1(1), is:

> Partnership is the relation which subsists between persons carrying on a business in common with a view of profit.

Number of members

A public company must have at least two members; there is no upper limit. A private company, by virtue of the implementation of an EC Directive in July 1992, can be formed by one person and be limited by shares or guarantee. A partnership firm will generally be limited to a maximum of 20 members (under the Companies Act 1985), however solicitors, accountants and those making a market on the stock exchange can exceed 20 members. Furthermore, regulations can enable other professionals to exceed the limit such as patent agents, actuaries, surveyors, auctioneers, estate agents, consulting engineers and (under 1992 Regulations) member firms of the International Stock Exchange of the United Kingdom and the Republic of Ireland Limited.

Separate personality

A company has, as has been noted, a legal identity quite separate and apart from those who set it up. As Lord Mcnaghten said (in *Salomon* v. *Salomon and Co. Ltd* (1897)):

> The company is at law a different person altogether from the subscribers to the memorandum, and though it may be that after the incorporation the business is precisely the same as it was before, the same persons are managers and the same hands receive the profits the company is not in law the agent of the subscribers or trustee for them.

This famous case was about a boot business. Mr Salomon set up a limited company, with himself and his wife and children as shareholders. The company bought the business from him for about £40 000. £10 000 of this was paid with debentures. These are loan shares which are repaid before unsecured creditors if a company fails. This company did fail owing about £7800 to unsecured trade creditors. The assets were only about £6000. The unsecured creditors were left unpaid because the debenture holders had to be paid first. Mr Salomon was one. The company was a different legal person.

This veil of incorporation, as it is known, is lifted sometimes, when the court suspects particularly scurrilous activity. For example, in *Daimler* v. *Continental Tyre and Rubber Co.* (1916) the principle of separate identity was disregarded in order to expose a trading organisation controlled by the enemy in wartime.

The tendency to 'lift the veil' has increased in recent years. In *Goodwin* v. *Birmingham City Football Club* (1980), for example, a club manager and the company he formed and to which he supplied his services (so that employing football clubs contracted with the company) were regarded as one and the same 'person'.

By contrast a partnership firm has no separate identity apart from the members who comprise it. It may, however, sue and be sued in the firm's name. The partners own the firm's property and they are liable on the firm's contracts.

Spheres of activity

A company may only trade in accordance with the objects clause within its memorandum of association. Although this might in fact be very widely drawn, as we have seen, it can, also, be altered if the appropriate procedures are followed. Furthermore, the impact of the European Communities Act 1972 and the promised impact of the Prentice Report, also seen earlier in this chapter, must be taken into consideration.

With a partnership the objects will have been agreed between the members of the firm. If there is a formal document they will most probably be included in it. By a (unanimous) resolution they can be changed. They cannot be discovered from public registered documents by outsiders and potential traders with the firm. Privacy is an advantage of partnerships.

Agency

A member of a company is not thereby qualified as its agent. Agents must be specially appointed before they can bind the company by their acts.

However, each general partner is an agent of the firm—as the 1890 Act, s.5, says:

> Every partner is an agent of the firm and his other partners for the purpose of the business of the partnership; and the acts of every partner who does any act for carrying on in the usual way of business of the kind carried on by the firm of which he is a member bind the firm and his partners, unless the partner so acting has in fact no authority to act for the firm in the particular matter, and the person with whom he is dealing either knows that he has no authority, or does not know or believe him to be a partner.

The transfer of shares

A public company is one (*a*) which is limited by shares (or by guarantee) and has a share capital (whichever is the case, the share capital must meet a minimum requirement, currently £50 000); and (*b*) whose memorandum states that the company is public, and which has been properly registered as a public company (Companies Act 1985, s.1). The name of a public limited company must always end with 'Public Limited Company' (plc will do). Shares are usually freely transferable, subject only to restrictions in the articles of association.

Any company not meeting the definition of 'public' will be a private company. Again, shares are transferable, but much less freely. There are likely to be far greater restrictions in the articles.

A partner cannot transfer his share in the firm without the consent of all the other partners. The firm is the product of an agreement between the specific individuals initially and each is individually involved. A share, however, can be 'assigned'. This might be, for example, as security for a loan. The 1890 Act, s.31(1), provides that the assignee does not take the full place of the partner:

> An assignment by any partner of his share in the partnership, either absolute, or by way of mortgage or redeemable charge, does not, as against the other partners, entitle the assignee, during the continuance of the partnership, to interfere in the management or administration of the partnership business or affairs, or to require any accounts of the partnership transactions, or to inspect the partnership books, but entitles the assignee only to receive the share of profits to which the assigning partner would otherwise be entitled, and the assignee must accept the account of profits agreed to by the partners.

Management

The members of a company are not entitled to participate in management unless they are appointed onto the board of directors from whom this work is expected. Partners are entitled to share in management, unless their agreement stipulates otherwise.

Liability

A company can be expected to pay its debts, until its assets are exhausted. Limitation of liability applies to members, not the company itself. The extent to which this protection is effective depends upon the way the company was created. It could be a company limited by shares.

This is the usual kind of limited liability company. Each shareholder is liable only to the extent of his shareholding. If he has paid for the shares he holds no further call can be made upon him; if he has not, then he is responsible only for the amount that he still owes. Alternatively, the company might be limited by guarantee, where the members guarantee to pay a particular amount in the event of the company going into liquidation. The size of the guarantee will be stated in the memorandum of association. This is the extent of the members' liability provided that no shares are issued by the company. If shares are issued, then their liability extends to them. This is very rare. Limited liability is the most obvious advantage of incorporation (there are very few companies with unlimited liability). A member of such a company is liable for its debts without limit.

General partners are liable to the extent of their personal wealth for the debts of the firm.

It is possible to set up a limited partnership under the Limited Partnerships Act 1907. They are rare. They must be registered. A statement signed by all the members must be sent to the Registrar. It must contain the firm's name, the nature and general place of business, the full name of each partner, when the firm was created and (if it is set) its duration, the particulars of contribution whether in cash or otherwise of each limited partner and a statement that the firm is a limited partnership. The limited partner is liable only to the extent of his contribution. He cannot participate in management, only advise. He cannot bind the firm. Any limited partnership must contain at least one

Partnership Agreement

THIS AGREEMENT is made the .... day of ......

BETWEEN

(1) (name) of (address)
and
(2) (name) of (address)

(together called 'the partners')

IT IS AGREED as follows:

The Firm

1. The Partners shall carry on business in partnership as (business) under the firm name of (name) at (address) or at whatever other place as shall be agreed by the Partners

2. The partnership shall commence on the date of this agreement and shall continue until ended as provided within this agreement

Relationship of the Partners

1. Each Partner will be just and faithful to the other and his/her best efforts and whole time shall be devoted to the firm's business.

2. Each Partner shall be entitled to take (number) weeks holiday each year at a time or times agreed with the other Partner.

3. Neither Partner shall, without the consent of the other:
a) engage in any business other than that of the firm, or
b) engage of dismiss any of the firm's employees, or
c) lend any partnership money or property, or
d) release any debt due to the firm, or
e) except in the ordinary course of business, draw, accept or endorse any cheque or other bill of exchange or give any security or promise for the payment of money.

The opening clause of a typical Partnership Agreement

The Companies Act 1985

COMPANY LIMITED BY SHARES

Memorandum of Association

OF

LIMITED

1. The Company's name is "

                                          LIMITED."

2. The Company's registered office is to be situated in England and Wales.

3. The Company's objects are:—

(A)

(B) To carry on any other trade or business which can, in the opinion of the Board of Directors, be advantageously carried on by the Company in connection with or as ancillary to any of the above businesses or the general business of the Company.

(C) To purchase, take on lease or in exchange, hire or otherwise acquire and hold for any estate or interest any lands, buildings, easements, rights, privileges, concessions, patents, patent rights, licences, secret processes, machinery, plant, stock-in-trade, and any real or personal property of any kind necessary or convenient for the purpose of or in connection with the Company's business or any branch or department thereof.

Memorandum of Association; reproduced by kind permission of the Solicitors' Law Stationery Society Ltd

general partner, whose liability, of course, is unlimited. Limited partnerships never really caught on. In the same year, 1907, a Companies Act was passed which reduced the minimum number of members required to form a private company to two. So it followed that in the first five years to 1912 only 492 limited partnerships were formed.

Taxation

The dividends paid to the members of a company are always taxed as investment income—although directors' salaries will be earned income, whereas partners' income from the firm is taxed (usually) as earned income.

Accounts and auditors

Companies, as we saw earlier in this chapter, must make an annual return. Their accounts must be audited by professionally qualified auditors, whereas partnership accounts are private, and need not be audited professionally, although they usually are.

Termination

A company, having been created by process of law, must be legally 'killed' (wound up). It possesses perpetual succession, that is, it survives all involved natural persons, until it is wound up. This could be a voluntary winding-up by the members (if the company can meet its debts) or by creditors (if it seems unable to meet them). Alternatively, the winding-up could be compulsory—ordered by the court. This will be on the petition of the company, a creditor or a contributory (someone who is liable to pay in on winding-up). Petitions by contributories are very rare. There are seven grounds upon which a company might be compulsorily wound up (Insolvency Act 1986, s.122):

1 it is unable to pay its debts;
2 the number of members has fallen below the minimum;
3 the company was registered as a public company, but it failed to satisfy the minimum capital requirement;
4 the company does not commence business within a year of being incorporated;
5 the company suspends business for a whole year;
6 the members have passed a special resolution to have the company wound up (this is unusual because it would be cheaper and easier to wind up voluntarily); and
7 the court is satisfied that it would be just and equitable to wind the company up.

By contrast a partnership firm is dissolved. This might be achieved with or without the aid of a court, and subject to the partnership agreement. The 1890 Act, s.32, provides for dissolution, without the aid of the court:

Subject to any agreement between the partners a partnership is dissolved—
(a) if entered into for a fixed term, by the expiration of that term;
(b) if entered into for a single adventure or undertaking, by the termination of that adventure or undertaking;
(c) if entered for an undefined time, by any partner giving notice to the other or others of his intention to dissolve the partnership.

Note also that by virtue of s.33(1):

> Subject to any agreement between the parties, every partnership is dissolved as regards all the partners by the death or bankruptcy of any partner.

Further, by virtue of s.34 of the Act, a partnership is in every case dissolved by the happening of any event which makes it unlawful for the business of the firm to be carried on or for the members of the firm to carry it on in partnership.

On the other hand, s.35 provides that on application by a partner the court may decree a dissolution of the partnership in any of the following cases:

(*a*) (This paragraph concerned the insanity of a partner and has been replaced by the Mental Health Act 1983, s.96(1)(*g*), under which a judge can dissolve a firm if one member is a patient within the Act, i.e. broadly speaking, mentally too disordered to manage his affairs);

(*b*) when a partner, other than the partner suing becomes in any other way permanently incapable of performing his part of the partnership contract;

(*c*) when a partner, other than the partner suing, has been guilty of such conduct as, in the opinion of the court, regard being had to the nature of the business, is calculated to prejudicially affect the carrying on of the business;

(*d*) when a partner, other than the partner suing, wilfully or persistently commits a breach of the partnership agreement, or otherwise so conducts himself in matters relating to the partnership business that it is not reasonably practicable for the other partner or partners to carry on the business in partnership with him;

(*e*) when the business of the partnership can only be carried on at a loss;

(*f*) whenever in any case circumstances have arisen which in the opinion of the court render it just and equitable that the partnership be dissolved.

TRADE UNIONS

Union membership reached a peak in 1979, at 13.29 million. By the end of 1986 it had fallen by 2.5 million, nearly 20 per cent. In 1979 55 per cent of the workforce was unionised. In 1989 only 40 per cent were union members. In late 1997 union membership was 6.7 million. There were 519 unions in 1973. There were 335 in 1986. Amalgamations are inevitable in days of falling membership. There are now 75 unions enrolled into the Trades Union Congress.

Trade unions were originally seen as unlawful conspiracies. Now they enjoy a special status in the law. They are not corporations, they have no separate legal personality, but they can make contracts and their property is held by trustees for them. They are capable of suing and being sued in their own names. Their liability in tort is covered by the Trade Union and Labour Relations (Consolidation) Act 1992. It is constantly under review. Presently where an action is not taken in contemplation or furtherance of a trade dispute, tortious liability can exist for negligence, nuisance, breach of statutory duty, etc. which has resulted in personal injury, or which arises from a breach of duty involving the occupation, ownership, possession, control or use of property. Under this legislation, individuals are enabled to bring actions in tort against trade unions for damages and/or injunctions. The 1992 Act exposes unions to liability for the actions of officials or committees whether or not they are authorised to act. The policy seems to be to ensure that unions take quick and effective steps to discuss them!

Under the Employment Act 1980 immunity was removed in respect of secondary action, unless the action was aimed at supplies to or from the employer involved in the dispute. Lawful picketing was restricted to the employees' own place of work. Immunity has been removed from virtually all secondary action.

The 1992 Consolidating Act also concentrates on the way in which a call to strike (or to other industrial action) is made. It makes a postal strike ballot compulsory in the case of official action. The Act requires the balloting of self-employed trade union members. Without a ballot, anyone adversely affected by the action can sue the union. For example, in *Falconer* v. *ASLEF* (1986), Angus Falconer sued the union in the Sheffield County Court before Judge Henham. The plaintiff had been left stranded in London by a strike called without a ballot by ASLEF. He was awarded £53 special damages, the cost of his hotel in London, and also £100 general damages for the breach of his contract with British Rail. The judge said 'the defendants were reckless in that they knew and appreciated the result of their actions on the plaintiff and others, but nevertheless they pursued it.' This simple step of a procedural requirement before the tortious immunity will apply has had a considerable effect. Union members can obtain orders from the High Court to restrain action if the balloting requirements are not met. There is now a Commissioner for the Rights of Trade Union Members to assist in the enforcement of individual members' rights.

Under the Trade Union and Labour Relations (Consolidation) Act 1992, collective agreements between a trade union and an employer about wages, hours, conditions of work etc. are presumed not to be legally enforceable, unless they are written and they state that they are to be legally binding.

Trade unions are required to keep properly audited accounts, and to make an annual return to the Registrar of Friendly Societies.

CHAPTER 11

Freedom under the Law

RIGHTS OR LIBERTIES?

In English law there is no written constitution nor any Bill of Rights to enshrine individual freedoms. Indeed, the idea of rights may not be entirely appropriate here. It is a matter of liberties rather than rights. Professor Williams wrote:

> A liberty . . . means any occasion on which an act or omission is not a breach of a duty . . . A right exists where there is a positive law on the subject; a liberty where there is no law against it.

Furthermore it is tempting to examine the topic of civil liberties from a comfortable point of view. Professor O'Higgins wrote:

> A basic question is whether the effectiveness with which civil liberties are protected should be assessed from the point of view of a conventional middle-class citizen comfortably employed with conventional politics or whether it should be assessed from the point of view of the black; the poor; the subversive; the atheist; the 'lunatic fringe' etc.

So while it is true to say that all societies require limitations upon total individual freedom to do, say, write, meet, etc., and it is also true that any civilised society will attempt to maximise the liberty and minimise the restriction upon an individual's freedom, it must be borne in mind that such pure theory may not be reflected every day, on the streets. Nevertheless, over time, a pattern may develop in the law which reflects the development of a view within a society. One example here is the changing status of women within the English law: the Equal Pay Act 1970, the Sex Discrimination Act 1975, the Abortion Act 1967, the Prohibition of Female Circumcision Act 1985 and other provisions surely must reflect more than the 'one-off' legislative provisions seen elsewhere. Moreover, whereas our discussion centres upon civil liberties in the United Kingdom there is an international context into which our liberties must be placed. Since the Second World War a number of international agreements, treaties, conventions and so on have been drawn up to protect, stabilise and increase civil liberties.

As examples, consider the following:

1 the Universal Declaration of Human Rights—United Nations Organisation. This was adopted by the General Assembly on 10 December 1948;

2 the European Convention on Human Rights and Fundamental Freedoms 1950—Council of Europe. This is not an institution of the European Community, but an international organisation of twenty-one west European states which was formed in 1949; it was the first post-war attempt at unifying Europe. Twenty of the twenty-one are parties to the convention—Liechtenstein being the exception. The convention came into force on 3 September 1953. In May 1997, the newly elected Government promised formally to incorporate the Convention into English law.

This promise was repeated by the Lord Chancellor in his first interview after taking office (*The Observer* 27 July 97). He added that a model closer to that in New Zealand (where the courts cannot strike down Acts of Parliament) would be adopted rather than that in Canada (where they can). In the late autumn of 1997 the Bill was duly introduced into the House of Lords. On 28 November, in a speech about the Human Rights Bill, at a conference organised by a huge firm of London solicitors, the Lord Chancellor focused on three main issues:

- the way in which the Bill provides for incorporating the thinking behind the European Convention on Human Rights into English law;
- the constitutional balance between Parliament and the Courts;
- the way in which the Bill is designed to protect the citizen from the power of the State in a time of change.

He said:

> The challenge in incorporating the Convention was to find a way to do so which respected Parliamentary sovereignty and gave further effect to Convention rights directly in our domestic courts—without interfering with the balance of powers between the legislative, executive and judicial arms of the State. We have achieved this through a unique scheme which has met with almost embarrassing approval in debate so far in the House of Lords. The aim of the Bill is to 'bring rights home'. We wanted to allow the Convention rights to be relied upon, and adjudicated on, in the United Kingdom courts.

He noted that the Bill proposes a judicial remedy which is wholly original—the 'declaration of incompatibility'. "That will be a statement," he said, "that, even after the process of interpretation has been carried as far as it can, there remains a stumbling block which cannot be got over without repealing or amending the legislation. And at that point, under our scheme, the question is handed back to Parliament, where in our view it properly belongs." The Lord Chancellor explained that because of its importance, the power to make a declaration would be limited to the higher courts:

> The power goes with the level of the court, not with the level of the individual judge. Confining the power to the High Court and above also makes it easier to

allow the Crown to intervene, so that the courts may have before them any argument which the Crown feels should be drawn to their attention. The declaration of incompatibility triggers a fast-track procedure for making a remedial order. The appropriate Government Minister will be able to amend the legislation by Order so as to make it compatible with the Convention. In cases where there is a particularly urgent need to amend the legislation, the Order will take effect immediately, but will expire if it is not approved by Parliament within 40 sitting days. The Minister is not obliged to make an Order, and Parliament is not obliged to approve it. Just as the courts are left free to decide whether to make a declaration of incompatibility, so Parliament is left free to decide whether to amend the legislation. In this way, the Bill respects the central sovereignty of Parliament.

Lord Irvine then addressed the way in which the Bill protects the citizen from the power of the State. He said:

Clause 6, one of the main building blocks of the Bill, provides that it is unlawful for a public authority to act in a way which is incompatible with one or more of the Convention rights. We have opted for a wide ranging definition of public authority, because we want to provide as much protection as possible for the rights of individuals against the misuse of power by the State. The provisions in the Bill tie in with the existing provisions for judicial review but enable them to be expanded in a way which is consistent with the aims of the Bill. Clause 6 makes it clear that 'public authority' includes a court and a tribunal which exercises functions in relation to legal proceedings. It imposes on them a duty to act compatibly with the Convention. We believe that it is right as a matter of principle for the courts to have the duty of acting compatibly with the Convention. They will be under this duty not only in cases involving other public authorities but also in developing the common law in deciding cases between individuals.

The Lord Chancellor also addressed the issue of privacy:

I would not agree with any proposition that the court, as public authorities, will be obliged to fashion a law on privacy because of the terms of the Bill. The courts may not act as legislators and grant new remedies for infringement of Convention rights unless the common law itself enables them to develop new rights or remedies. I believe that the courts will be able to adapt and develop the common law by relying on existing domestic principles in the laws of trespass, nuisance, copyright, confidence and the like, to fashion a common law right to privacy. I say this because members of the higher judiciary have already themselves said so. My view is that any privacy law developed by the judges will be a better law after incorporation of the convention because the judges will have to balance and have regard to Articles 10 and 8—giving Article 10 its due high value.

Lord Irvine summed up by saying that Strasbourg's position as the custodian of the Convention will not be affected by the passing of the Human Rights Bill:

It is right that our courts and tribunals should apply the Convention rights in a way which reflects Strasbourg case law. Taking account of Strasbourg decisions will mean that, as happens with our common law, interpretations of the Convention articles will develop over time. It is a living set of values to be developed for changing times. It also means that our courts, will have to balance the various rights in the Convention when arriving at their decisions. Our judiciary is adept at balancing competing interests and values when deciding particular cases. Its impact on English law will be considerable and positive. It will enable individuals to have access to rights here that at present they have to seek in Strasbourg. It does bring human rights home.

If and when incorporation takes place the problems that surfaced in *R.* v. *Khan* (Sultan) (1996) should be avoided. Here, the police obtained incriminating evidence that Khan was involved in the importation of illegal drugs by 'bugging' private premises while he was there. Khan claimed that this 'bugging' constituted a breach of his right to privacy under Art. 8 of the Convention When the case reached the House of Lords, Lord Nolan said, "we are not concerned with the view which the European Court of Human Rights might have taken of the facts of the present case. Its decision is no more part of our law than the convention itself". However, he also said "that is not to say that the principles reflected in the Convention are irrelevant . . . they could hardly be irrelevant, because they embody so many of the familiar principles of our own law and of our concept of justice". So, in *Murray* v. *UK* (1996), the European Court of Human Rights held that the unjustified delay in allowing access to a solicitor during questioning was a breach of Art.6(3) of the European Convention on Human Rights, which guarantees the 'minimum right' of 'legal assistance . . . when the interests of justice so require'.

PERSONAL LIBERTY

An individual is allowed to move freely. His personal liberty can only be curtailed on specific and narrowly defined grounds:

1 he is unfit to plead to a criminal charge in court, or is detained otherwise through mental illness;
2 he has been sentenced to imprisonment;
3 he has been committed to jail for contempt of court;
4 he is detained in pursuance of another court order;
5 he is detained in order to bring him before a court (i.e. arrested and not granted bail, *see* Chapter 15);
6 he has been granted bail but neglected to present himself at the appointed hour (*see* warrant above);
7 he is a minor under a care order;
8 he is detained to prevent the spread of serious illness;
9 he is an illegal immigrant or awaiting deportation or extradition.

A person wrongfully detained can sue for false imprisonment and/or malicious prosecution as appropriate. These are essentially actions which follow the event. During wrongful imprisonment the prerogative writ called *habeas corpus* may be applied for. This was considered in Chapter 4 when we were dealing with the supervisory jurisdiction of the Divisional Court of the Queen's Bench Division. It is to this court that applications for *habeas corpus* are made.

FREEDOM OF ASSOCIATION

People join together in association for various reasons, of which the following are examples:

1 to facilitate the expression of a collective viewpoint (get their points across more powerfully); and/or
2 to increase job security or the quality and conditions of work; and/or
3 for social reasons.

There are few restrictions on the freedom of individuals to associate, provided that neither the purpose of their association nor the means it employs are against the general law (e.g. to overthrow the government by force). The European Convention on Human Rights provides, in Article 11:

> Everyone has the right to freedom of peaceful assembly and to freedom of association with others.

However, it goes on to say:

> No restrictions shall be placed on the exercise of these rights other than such as are prescribed by law and are necessary in a democratic society in the interests of national security or public safety, for the prevention of disorder or crime . . . or the protection of the rights and freedoms of others.

Such rights are the result of compromise and balance.

Some professions restrict the activities of individuals; for example, in the Police Act 1964, s.47(1), it is provided as follows:

> Subject to the provision of this section, a member of a police force shall not be a member of any trade union, or of any association having for its objects, or one of its objects, to control or influence the pay, pensions or conditions of service of any police force.

Otherwise, the general law has basic controls within it. The crime of conspiracy (under the Criminal Law Act 1977, as amended by the Criminal Justice Act 1987) applies to those who agree together to commit a crime, to defraud or to act so as to outrage public decency or corrupt public morals. There is also a tort of conspiracy. This is committed where a group of people decide to do something unlawful, or to do something lawful using unlawful means with the object of injuring someone else. If he is injured he can sue them. In *Huntley* v. *Thornton* (1957) the plaintiff obtained £500 compensation. He had refused to go out on a strike called by his union. The district committee (whom he had described as 'a shower') expelled him. The national executive did not ratify this decision, but the district committee made it impossible for the plaintiff to carry on his trade in the area. This amounted to tortious conspiracy. They had set out to injure him, not to protect their own interests.

There are also restrictions on association which are placed in the interests of preserving public order. Under the Public Order Act 1936 for example:

> any person who in any public place or at any public meeting wears uniform signifying his association with any political organisation with the promotion of any political object shall be guilty of an offence.

The police can allow the wearing of uniforms, but only where the peace is not likely to be disturbed. This section was designed to combat the rise of the fascists. In R. v. *Charnley* (1937) successful prosecutions were brought against 'blackshirts'. These actions show that full regalia is not required for a uniform here. Armbands, emblems, etc., are enough. Members of the Ku Klux Klan were prosecuted in 1965, IRA supporters in 1975.

The Prevention of Terrorism (Temporary Provisions) Act 1989 (as elaborated by the Prevention of Terrorism (Additional Powers) Act 1996) continues the legality of special powers of interrogation, detention and exclusion from mainland Britain along with offences connected with membership and support of proscribed organisations. The 1989 Act even extends to banks. It is now a crime to lend or arrange a loan to any person for the purposes of terrorism. The original Act was passed in forty-eight hours in November 1974, within a week of the dreadful Birmingham pub bombings, when 21 people died and over 180 were injured. Orders are made each year to keep the 1989 Act in force, and to provide an opportunity for debate.

This was last seen on 10 March 1997 when the House of Lords approved the Prevention of Terrorism (Temporary Provisions) Act (Continuance) Order without a vote. In the Commons, a week earlier, most of the Labour Party's MPs abstained and a handful of backbenchers opposed renewal. Having once been the Home Secretary, Lord Merlyn-Rees questioned the need for two pieces of anti-terrorism legislation covering the province. He said the Northern Ireland (Emergency Provisions) Act was already 'tailored to the needs of Northern Ireland' and questioned the need to use the UK-wide Prevention of Terrorism Act 'to such a degree' in Ulster, 'given the fact that there is separate legislation which is the lineal descendant of legislation that was put through Parliament by Mr Gladstone in the last century'. Lord Merlyn-Rees warned that people would have to wait 'a jolly long time' for peace in Northern Ireland. Lord McIntosh of Haringey, for Labour, repeated party pledges to scrap exclusion order powers to stop individuals travelling between Ulster and the mainland. He said exclusion orders had 'revived a power which has not existed in this country since the time of Henry VIII – the power of internal exile'. He called for judges to be involved in the extension beyond 48 hours. 'We will see to it that judicial intervention is introduced as soon as possible.' Then a Home Office Minister of State, Baroness Blatch, said the Prevention of Terrorism Act contained 'different powers' from the Emergency Provisions Act. She added:

> Sometimes the circumstances are such that we have to accept measures that in normal circumstances we would not contemplate. Exclusion order powers are an important part of our defences against this threat. The Government believes it would be irresponsible to abandon them whilst the need for them so clearly remains.

Now that there has been a change of government it will be interesting to watch for a change of policy.

FREEDOM OF ASSEMBLY

There are many restrictions on the freedom to hold public assemblies—meetings and processions. They fall into two categories: control of the place of assembly and control over the conduct there once the assembly has gathered.

Location

The highway

The use of the highway is controlled by the criminal law and the law of tort.

The key criminal provision is the Highways Act 1980, s.137, which states:

1 If a person, without lawful authority or excuse, in any way wilfully obstructs the free passage along a highway he shall be guilty of an offence.
2 A constable may arrest without warrant any person whom he sees committing an offence against this section.

The power of arrest is important. It is in daily use at demonstrations. The local authority cannot give permission for an obstruction of the highway. The fact that only part of the highway is blocked, and not for long, is not a defence. The use being made of the highway is relevant. In *Nagy* v. *Weston* (1965) a lay-by was used for five minutes by a hot-dog salesman. This was not a reasonable use. Lord Parker CJ said:

> It depends upon all the circumstances, including the length of time the obstruction continues, the place where it occurs, the purpose for which it is done, and of course whether it does in fact cause an actual obstruction as opposed to a potential obstruction.

It was a busy road. The lay-by also contained a bus stop. Lajors Nagy was convicted. Similarly convicted was a club tout who repeatedly stopped groups of pedestrians, trying to entice them into his employer's establishment: *Cooper* v. *Metropolitan Police Commissioner* (1985). The Criminal Justice and Public Order Act 1994, s.70, controls 'trespassory assemblies', especially on land of 'historical, archaeological or scientific importance', or on the highway. In *DPP* v. *Jones* (1997) a demonstration on a roadside verge near Stonehenge, even though peaceable and non-obstructive, was 'nothing whatever to do with the right of passage' and therefore an offence.

The controls contained in the civil law of tort, on the other hand, are less commonly seen. They include the torts of trespass, public nuisance and private nuisance. The landowners of the highways are (usually) the highway authorities. An assembly on a highway would not be the purpose for which access to the land is permitted, thus (technically) a trespass. A public nuisance is caused by unreasonable use of the land affecting the public at large. What is unreasonable will depend on local circumstances: in *Gillingham Borough Council* v. *Medway (Chatham) Dock Ltd* (1991) the local residents could not assert as a public nuisance the disturbance caused by a commercial port where planning permission had been granted for that use. The disturbance was then a fact of local life. Unless an individual has been especially injured (beyond the general effect on others) an action in public nuisance can be brought only by the Attorney-General. In private nuisance, the individual whose reasonable use of his property is adversely affected can sue; this may occur as a result, for example, of blocking an access. In *Hubbard* v. *Pitt* (1976) a firm of estate agents obtained an injunction against a group of pickets (from the Islington Tenants Campaign) who were standing around outside their offices. This case was applied in a picketing context in *Mersey Dock & Harbour Co.* v. *Verrinder* (1982).

Open spaces

These usually belong to the Crown or to a local authority. Under the Local Government Act 1972, s.235, district and London Borough Councils are enabled to make byelaws for the good rule and government of their areas. (We saw this in Chapter 3, when considering delegated legislation.) There are likely to be regulations about assemblies in open spaces. It is likely that the written permission of the local authority will be necessary.

A popular open space in this context is Hyde Park in London. The Department of the Environment, Royal Parks Division, published in 1969 a document of 'Policy and Procedure for the Use of Hyde Park for Special Events':

> Applications may be considered from any organisation (religious, political or otherwise) for permission to hold assemblies and events in Hyde Park. Normally, the Speaker's Corner/Reformer's Tree areas will be used for assemblies/rallies, but for special events other areas are permissible (e.g. Cockpit, Serpentine Road).

The formal regulations are to be found in the Royal and Other Parks and Gardens Regulations 1977.

The fact that there was no right to assemble in Hyde Park, at Speaker's Corner or anywhere else, was pointed out by Cockburn CJ (in *Bailey* v. *Williamson* (1873)):

> Whatever enjoyment the public have been allowed to have of these parks and royal possessions for any purpose has been an enjoyment which the public have had by the gracious concession of the Crown.

Trafalgar Square, similarly, may be used only in accordance with regulations, the Trafalgar Square Regulations 1952. They contain a list of prohibited acts (which include bathing and paddling) and acts for which written permission is required (which include 'organising, conducting or taking part in any assembly, parade or procession').

Near Parliament

Under the Seditious Meetings Act 1817, s.23, no meeting of fifty people or more could take place within a mile of Westminster Hall 'for the purpose or on the pretext of considering or preparing any petition, complaint, remonstrance, declaration or other address to the king . . .' or to the Houses of Parliament for 'alteration of matters in Church or State' when either or both Houses is sitting. Any such gathering was an unlawful assembly. There was an even older provision, the Tumultuous Petitioning Act 1661, under which it was an offence for more than ten persons at any one time to repair to the Queen or to Parliament to present any address. On April Fool's Day 1987, both of these provisions were repealed by Schedule 3 of the Public Order Act 1986.

Apart from these statutes, every session Parliament directs the Metropolitan Police Commissioner to see to it that free access to the Houses is maintained. Under the Metropolitan Police Act 1839, s.52, sessional orders are made under which police constables 'take care that the passages leading to this House be kept free' and they 'disperse all assemblies or processions of persons causing or likely to cause obstruction or disorder'.

Meetings in public buildings

At election time the Representation of the People Act 1983, s.95(1), provides:

> A candidate at a parliamentary election shall be entitled for the purpose of holding public meetings in furtherance of his candidature to the use at reasonable times between the receipt of the writ and the date of the poll of—
> (*a*) a suitable room in the premises of any school to which this section applies;
> (*b*) any meeting room to which this section applies.

The section applies to local authority, publicly funded properties. Notice must be given and a fee can be charged. A deposit against damage can be required. In 1934 a meeting of the British Union of Fascists was cancelled because of the size of the deposit required for using the White City Stadium in London. At other times a reasonable policy must be followed. A set of rules against particular groups or parties might be challenged in the courts as an improper use of public property, or an arbitrary use of discretion. See, for example, *Webster* v. *Southwark LBC* (1983), where a ban on a National Front meeting was declared unlawful.

Processions

Processions are popular but it is often said that we need to maintain the delicate balance between peace on the streets and the freedom to associate and express opinions.

Part II of the Public Order Act 1986 creates a new framework of law for the holding of processions, demonstrations and assemblies. There is a requirement for the organisers of most marches to give seven days' notice to the police. Broadly, this is directed at marches of a political nature. The idea is that the organisers and the police will be able to discuss the nature and route of the demonstration. Existing powers to impose conditions were widened to include measures to avoid serious disruption or coercion. Similar police powers exist to control the numbers, the location and the duration of other demonstrations and assemblies in the open air. The powers cover everything from mass political gatherings in Trafalgar Square to a modest protest by parents to call for a pedestrian crossing outside a school. The debate on this part of the Act was fierce. Incidentally, the organisers of demonstrations which are called at short notice are only required to give such notice 'as is practicable'.

The conduct of those who attend the assembly or procession

Those who take part in public meetings or processions, and those who seek to disrupt them, could commit any from a range of criminal offences:

1 assaulting a constable in the execution of his duty, or anyone assisting the constable (Police Act 1964, s.52(1));
2 resisting or wilfully obstructing such an officer or assistant (1964 Act, s.51(3));
3 obstruction of the free passage along a highway (Highways Act 1980, s.137(1));
4 destruction of or damage to another's property, without lawful excuse (Criminal Damage Act 1971, s.1). While it remains impressive, the consent of God is no defence here. This was established in *Blake* v. *DPP* (1993) where, as a protest against the Gulf war, a biblical quotation was written on a pillar near Parliament;
5 possession of offensive weapons in public places (Prevention of Crime Act 1953, s.1);
6 trespass upon consular or diplomatic premises (Criminal Law Act 1977, s.9);
7 threatening behaviour—as revised and extended by Part I of the Public Order Act 1986, i.e. using threatening, abusive or insulting words or behaviour which is intended or likely: (*a*) to cause another person to fear violence or (*b*) to provoke the use of violence by another. This was well illustrated in *Winn* v. *DPP* (1992) where a man who was attempting to serve a county court summons was punched and also threatened with a child's pot!
8 affray (again, under the 1986 Act), which is committed when one, two or more persons use or threaten violence against another in such a way as could cause a person of reasonable firmness to fear for their personal safety—such as fights outside pubs and clubs;
9 disorderly conduct (1986 Act), which is committed by anyone who uses threatening, abusive, insulting or disorderly behaviour within the hearing or sight of another person likely to be caused alarm, harassment or distress. This is a new offence which has been designed to give the police powers to control, and if necessary arrest, hooligans;
10 violent disorder (1986 Act), where three or more people are behaving violently in such a way as would cause a person of reasonable firmness if present to fear for his personal safety, each person using or threatening unlawful violence will be guilty of this offence;
11 riot (1986 Act) where twelve or more people are using or threatening violence to persons or property for a common purpose in such a way as would cause a person of reasonable firmness if present to fear for his personal safety, each person using unlawful violence will be guilty of riot. (It seems likely that violent disorder will be used for coping with group violence, whereas riot will be kept aside for the really serious cases.) Under the Riot (Damages) Act 1886, where the assembly has been tumultuously as well as

riotously gathered together, there can be paid compensation for property damage out of the police rate (i.e. from public funds);

12 acting in a disorderly manner so as to break up a public meeting is an offence (Public Meetings Act 1908, s.1), as is inciting others to do so. This Act does not apply to election meetings, but a similar offence is to be found within the Representation of the People Act 1983, s.97.

FREEDOM OF SPEECH AND EXPRESSION

Professor Dicey, one of our greatest constitutional lawyers, wrote in 1885:

> Freedom of discussion is . . . in England little else than the right to write or say anything which a jury, consisting of twelve shopkeepers, think it expedient should be said or written. Such 'liberty' may vary at different times and seasons from unrestricted license to very severe restraint, and the experience of English history during the last two centuries shows that under the law of libel the amount of latitude conceded to its expression of opinion has, in fact, differed greatly according to the conditions of popular sentiment.

So it is today. The extent of the freedom of the individual to say what he likes or write what he feels is far from an absolute right. There are both civil and criminal law restrictions on these freedoms. The restraint upon the spoken word depends not just on what is said, but on where it is said and the job the person voicing his opinion has. In Parliament, for example, there is a great deal of freedom from actions in the tort of defamation. On the other hand, people like to discuss their work, but if the work is covered by the Official Secrets Acts 1911–1939 and 1989, then his freedom of discussion is very restricted.

Even if a person is free to express his opinions he may not be able to find anyone to listen to them; reasons for this include:

1 no-one will hire him a hall; or
2 public open spaces are not available; or
3 the police threaten to prosecute for obstruction of the highway; or
4 the police disperse the assembly to avoid a breach of the peace; or
5 newspaper editors burn his letters; or
6 publishers return his manuscript for books; or
7 private printers refuse to take on his work; or
8 printers have had his work printed but he cannot post it to his audience because it is offensive, obscene or prejudicial to public safety or to security; or
9 booksellers and libraries refuse to stock the work; or
10 the advertising media refuse his copy; or
11 a licence to broadcast is refused.

Perhaps the media do wish to publish a person's views. There are many restrictions (short of outright censorship) which might prevent it—the law on obscenity, contempt of court, official secrets, 'D' notices, treason, sedition, incitement to disaffection, racial and sexual discrimination, privacy, criminal and blasphemous libel and the tort of defamation. Even if put into dramatic form, there are limits on freedom of expression in theatres and cinemas.

1 **Obscenity** There are criminal offences contained in the Obscene Publications Acts 1959 and 1964, including the offence of publication of obscene material. The Acts were designed to protect works of art and outlaw pornography. The tastes of juries and magistrates and the massive profits to be had from publishing pornography despite criminal sanctions have reduced their effectiveness.

A related statute is the Children and Young Persons (Harmful Publications) Act 1955, which is designed to outlaw horror comics—illustrating crimes, violence, cruelty, 'incidents of a repulsive or horrible nature'—which would tend to corrupt the young.

2 **Contemptof court** There are, of course, various restrictions upon the reporting of trials (e.g. the general ban on publishing the name of the accused in a youth court), but this topic of contempt is wider and more vague. It seems to be an offence to publish material which may be prejudicial to a fair criminal trial, or civil proceedings, scandalising the court (like abusing the judge), contempt in the face of the court, and material which interferes with the course of justice. The most recent changes in the law on this matter were made by the Contempt of Court Act 1981 and the County Court (Penalties for Contempt) Act 1983.

3 **Official secrets** The Official Secrets Acts 1911–1939 and 1989, cover offences involving the disclosure of matters undermining national security at one extreme and the unauthorised release of even the broadest detail of official information at the other. They cover everybody who holds a public office: ministers, civil servants, the armed forces, even the royal gardeners.

4 **'D' notices** These are confidential letters, sent at the request of government departments to newspapers, periodicals, and radio and television news editors requesting that certain material not be published in the interests of national defence or security. To ignore a 'D' notice is not an offence, but it might be evidence of a breach of the Official Secrets Acts. Anyway, they are rare and virtually always obeyed.

5 **Treason** This ancient common law crime (in theory still carrying the death penalty) is committed by a person who conspires or incites the murder or overthrow of the monarch, levies war against her or adheres to her enemies (e.g. by broadcasting enemy propaganda). There is a marginally less serious offence called treason felony which involves inviting foreigners to invade British territory or inciting rebellions against the monarch.

6 **Sedition** This is a very broad common law crime, committed by expressing opinions with the intent as Sir James Stephen wrote:

to bring into hatred and contempt, or excite disaffection against . . . the government and constitution . . . either House of Parliament, or the administration of justice . . . or to raise discontent or disaffection among Her Majesty's subjects, or to promote feelings of ill-will and hostility between different classes of such subjects.

So it seems to cover any criticism of the existing structure of authority within the state, provided that it is expressed with sufficient force. Examples of this offence are very rare nowadays.

7 **Incitement to disaffection** There exist a number of statutory offences generally related towards those who attempt to persuade members of the armed forces or the police away from their duties: the Incitement to Mutiny Act 1797, the Army Act 1955, the Air Force Act 1955, the Naval Discipline Act 1957, the Aliens Restriction (Amendment) Act 1919, the Incitement to Disaffection Act 1934 and the Police Act 1964. Recent instances include the cases in the mid 1970s involving Pat Arrowsmith and her friends who distributed leaflets to soldiers suggesting leaving the army or deserting rather than serving in Northern Ireland.

8 **Racial and sexual discrimination** The Race Relations Act 1976 and the Sex Discrimination Act 1975 seek to outlaw unjustifiable discrimination on the grounds of sex or race. They each provide a mechanism of complaint for the victim of such action. Furthermore, Part III of the Public Order Act 1986 creates a variety of offences which are concerned with stirring up racial hatred. These include activities such as using threatening, abusive or insulting words or behaviour, the display, publication or distribution of written material, plays or broadcasts where stirring up racial hatred is intended.

9 **Privacy** As long ago as 1880 Dr Cooley described privacy as 'the right to be let alone'. There is no general right to privacy in English law. Protection against interference is piecemeal and includes the torts of defamation, trespass to land, and nuisance, breach of copyright and breach of confidence. There have been many suggestions for a more general law, for example the famous Younger Report in 1972, but little has been achieved. In the 1988–89 Parliamentary session two private members' bills were debated: one on privacy and the other on the 'right to reply'. Neither became law.

10 **Criminal and blasphemous libel** The tort of defamation will be dealt with in Chapter 12. Libel is generally a tort, but if it is likely to lead to a breach of the peace, then it can be the subject of a criminal prosecution. Blasphemous libel, on the other hand, is committed where a person publishes in a permanent form any matter attacking the Christian doctrine or the Bible, or the doctrine of the Church of England, or God, Christ or other sacred persons. *Gay News* and its editor, Mr Lemon, were convicted of this offence (*R.* v. *Lemon* (1979)). However, in *R.* v. *Chief Metropolitan Stipendiary Magistrate ex parte Chaudhury* (1991) the court refused to find the book *The Satanic Verses*, by Salman Rushdie criminally blasphemous, as had been claimed by Muslims. It was held that to try to protect all religious beliefs:

would encourage intolerance, divisiveness and unreasonable interferences with freedom of expression. Fundamentalist Christians, Jews or Muslims could then seek to invoke the offence of blasphemy against each other's religion.

11 **The censorship of plays** Theatre censorship was abolished by the Theatres Act 1968, but the presentation of obscenity is still criminal.

12 **An example in more detail – film censorship: The British Board of Film Classification** The British Board of Film Classification is an independent, non-governmental body which, for over 80 years has participated in the execution of responsibilities concerning the cinema, which the law attaches to local authorities.

The licensing of cinemas was introduced by the Cinematograph Act 1909 in order to ensure the physical safety of cinemagoers. Pubs and music halls were already licensed by the local councils, and the law now extended those powers to public cinemas as well, provided only that the conditions laid down by the licence were reasonable ones. In 1911, the courts ruled that the prior censorship of films was a reasonable condition and in 1952, this power became a duty as far as the protection of children was concerned when for the first time the Cinematograph Act 1952 required local authorities to prohibit the admission of children to films classified as unsuitable for them. At this time the law laid down that such classification might be either by the local authority itself or by 'such other body as may be specified in the licence', an oblique reference by Parliament to the fact that film classification was by then carried on almost exclusively by the British Board of Film Censors, as the BBFC was then called.

The Board had been set up by the film industry in 1912 in order to bring a degree of uniformity to the standards of film censorship imposed by the many very disparate local authorities. The object was to create a body which, with no greater power than that of persuasion, would seek to make judgements which were acceptable nationally. To this end, the Board has needed ever since to earn the trust of the local authorities and also of Parliament, the press and the public. It must not only be independent, but be seen to be so, taking care, for example, that the film industry does not seek to influence Board decisions and that, similarly, pressure groups and the media are permitted to comment but not to determine the standards set by the Board for the public at large.

Statutory powers remain with the local councils who may overrule any of the Board's decisions on appeal, passing films that have been rejected, banning films that have been passed, and even waiving cuts, instituting new ones, or altering categories for films exhibited under their own licensing jurisdiction.

In 1982, Parliament decided to follow the recommendation of the Williams Committee and close the loophole which had permitted bogus cinema clubs to evade both censorship and fire and safety regulations by offering 'instant membership' at the door. The Cinematograph Act required the licensing of all cinema exhibitions which operated for private gain, which meant that all films shown in commercial clubs were now subject to scrutiny. For these premises, a new film category, the 'R18', was introduced, to be used for films containing more explicit sexual depictions than would be acceptable in the public adult category. Non-profit organisations, such as film societies, are still permitted to hold exhibitions without prior certification. All three Cinematograph Acts have now been consolidated in the Cinemas Act 1985.

In 1984, the Video Recordings Act 1984 introduced the statutory requirement that, subject to certain exemptions, video recordings offered for sale or hire commercially in the UK must be classified by an authority designated by the Home Secretary. In July 1985, the President and Vice Presidents of the BBFC were so designated and charged with applying the new and additional test of 'suitability for viewing in the home'. For the first time the BBFC found itself exercising a statutory function on behalf of central Government, and one on which it is expected to make an Annual Report to Parliament. In 1994, the Criminal Justice Act extended this responsibility further (from 1 April 1996) to include laserdiscs, CD-i, CD video MPEG and other formats. All formats of recordings have to be classified for them to be available for sale or hire in the UK.

In order to preserve its independence of judgement, the BBFC does not receive any subsidy from the film industry or from Government. Its income is derived solely from fees it charges for its services, calculated by measuring the running time of films or video works submitted for certification. The average film costs around £600. The Board is not organised for profit and its fees are adjusted only as required to cover its costs. Examiners are chosen from a wide range of ages and backgrounds, including some from the ethnic communities, for whom many foreign-language videos are now classified.

If a film or video is obscene within the meaning of the Obscene Publications Act or offends against other provisions of the criminal law in such a manner that in the view of the BBFC no amount of cutting can make it acceptable for national distribution, then the work will be refused a certificate. In the 1960s and early 1970s, it was usual for 20 or 30 films to be rejected each year. By contrast, only sixteen films were rejected throughout the 1980s.

BBFC certificates – and the relative content!

'E' (Exempt) – exempt from classification

Some types of video are exempt from classification. These include some sport and music videos. They are given an E certificate which has no restrictions.

'U' (Universal) – suitable for all

Contains no theme, scene, action or dialogue that could be construed as disturbing, harmful or offensive. Although not equally suitable for all ages, it could not be described as unsuitable for persons of any age.

'Uc'	A video-only category denoting particular suitability for very young or pre-school children.
'PG' (Parental Guidance) – General viewing, but some scenes may be unsuitable for young children	Mild violence; occasional non-sexual nudity; bed scenes, but no serious suggestion of sexual activity; limited scatological language, but no sexual expletives; no drug use or condoning of immoral behaviour unless clearly mitigated by context (for example, comedy); no undue emphasis on weapons (for example, flick-knives).
'12' – Passed only for persons of twelve years and over	Implications of sex (within a relationship); stronger language, but only a rare sexual expletive; more realistic violence but limited in length and intensity; no drug use. (Introduced for the cinema in 1989 for *Batman*. Introduced for video on 1 July 1994.)
'15' – Passed only for persons of fifteen years and over	Themes requiring a more mature understanding. Full-frontal nudity in a non-sexual context; brief or impressionistic sex; more extensive use of expletives; mildly graphic violence and/or horror, but limited gore. Soft drugs may be seen in use, but not so as to condone or normalise. As with categories above, no details of harmful or criminal techniques.
'18' – Passed only for persons of eighteen years and over	Themes requiring an adult understanding (e.g. complex sexual relationships, controversial religious subjects); simulated sex (or in some educational contexts real sex); full nudity in a sexual context; unglamourised use of hard drugs; no censorship of sexual expletives, although pornographic descriptions may be cut; graphic violence provided it does not encourage sadistic pleasure nor glamorise dangerous weapons.
'R18' (Restricted 18)	Consenting, non-violent sex depicted with a degree of explicitness limited only by the law. No censorship of pornographic language, provided it does not encourage or incite to sexual crime.

(These paragraphs were drawn from materials issued by the BBFC and found on the internet).
Source: BBFC

Indicative questions

1 The United Kingdom is said to be a free country and it is widely recognised that its citizens have various rights and freedoms. However, these rights and freedoms are not absolute: they may be restricted where the needs of society generally are seen to be more important than the rights of the individual.

Examine *each* of the following situations. State which right or freedom is involved and explain whether it would be restricted in that situation.

(a) Jill, who works for the Ministry of Defence, tells the newspaper the date of the arrival of a nuclear submarine from the USA. The information is secret.

(2 marks)

(b) Bill organises a march through the streets to protest about the laws on abortion. Many people in the procession take the opportunity to cause damage and to steal from local shops. (*2 marks*)

(c) Michael, a private citizen, sees Alan throwing a brick through the jeweller's shop window. Michael arrests Alan and takes him to the local police station. (*2 marks*)

SEG

2 (a) What are the main 'freedoms' generally recognised as part of English Law? (*10 marks*)

(b) Why is it necessary for these freedoms to be restricted in various ways? Give examples of such restrictions in your answer. (*15 marks*)

SEG

3 We live in a free society and individuals in the United Kingdom have certain freedoms. Most freedoms of the individual, however, are subject to some restriction. The freedom of speech and the freedom to hold meetings may be affected by the torts of trespass, nuisance or defamation.

Now consider the following situation which involves the freedom of speech and the freedom to hold meetings.

Jean held a meeting on a field without the permission of the owner, Mrs Windermere. The purpose of the meeting was to form a society for the protection of wild flowers.

In *each* of the following instances, explain whether or not Jean is protected by the above-named freedoms, and if Mrs Windermere has any legal claim against her.

(a) Jean, in her own opening address, falsely accused Mrs Windermere of deliberately planning to build on the field in order to damage the wild flowers that grew there. (*4 marks*)

(b) The crowd attending the meeting was small and caused no damage to the field. (*4 marks*)

SEG

4 All societies exist within a legal framework. That framework creates rules which individuals in society must live by. Those rules restrict individual freedom for the good of society as a whole. Such restrictions are laid down either by the criminal law or civil law.

In **each** of the following situations:

identify the particular freedom concerned and comment on how it might be restricted.

Your answer should make clear whether any restriction you identify is **civil** or **criminal**, or both civil and criminal, in nature.

(a) Ahmed appears before his local Magristrates' Court charged with a serious assault on his wife. The case has to be adjourned and the magistrates have to make a decision as to whether Ahmed can be released or not before his next hearing. *(5 marks)*

(b) During the course of a debate in the House of Commons, Bertram, a Member of Parliament, accuses another MP of taking bribes. He then repeats the accusation to a group of press reporters outside the House of Commons. His comments are widely reported in the press the following day. *(5 marks)*

(c) Carolyn is a member of an organisation which campaigns against the use of animals in scientific experiments. One night she breaks into a research establishment and removes some papers which, she claims, show evidence of cruelty. As an afterthought, she also releases some animals from their cages. The animals escape and are not recovered. *(5 marks)*

SEG Summer 1996 (Higher)

CHAPTER 12

The Law of Tort

TORT: GENERAL ISSUES

A tort is a civil wrong. We met the law of tort first in Chapter 1 while classifying the law as between civil and criminal law. Sometimes students new to legal study have difficulty with the word tort. Professor Williams wrote:

> This word conveys little meaning to the average layman, and its exact definition is a matter of great difficulty even for the lawyer; but the general idea of it will become clear enough if one says that torts include such wrongs as assault, battery, false imprisonment, trespass, conversion, defamation of character, negligence and nuisance. It is a civil wrong independent of contract: that is to say, it gives rise to an action for damages irrespective of any agreement not to do the act complained of.

The point of taking action in tort is to obtain compensation. There are other ways: private insurance, social insurance, compensation for criminal injuries, welfare benefits, etc., but if your legal rights have been infringed, then you can sue for compensation in a tort action. Your rights are the key—not your injury.

There is no automatic right to compensation in tort law simply because the plaintiff has suffered injury. A corner shop going out of business because of the pressure of a supermarket brings about financial injury and loss, but no legal right has (usually) been infringed, so no action lies. On the other hand, there are certain rights which the law takes so seriously that if they are infringed an action can be brought. There is no need to establish injury. *Damnum* means physical or financial damage or loss, *injuria* means the infringement of a legal right. It follows from the above that *damnum sine injuria* (physical etc. loss without the infringement of a legal right) is not actionable, whereas *injuria sine damno*, the opposite, is.

For example, in the famous case of *Bradford Corporation* v. *Pickles* (1895) Mr Pickles had excavated a hole on his land so as to reduce the water supply to the corporation waterworks down the hill from the spring up the hill. (He claimed to be working minerals.) The gesture was made, it was alleged, so as to induce the corporation to buy his land. He had, obviously, caused injury, but no legal right had been infringed.

This case also highlights another general principle of the law of tort: that (with only a few exceptions, which we will consider later) it is not much concerned with motive. Broadly, tort law is about what the defendant did, not why he did it, and what the plaintiff suffered as a reasonably foreseeable consequence. Lord Halsbury said, in this case:

> This is not a case in which the state of mind of the person doing the act can affect the right to do it. If it was a lawful act, however ill the motive might be, he had a right to do it. If it was an unlawful act, however good his motive might be, he would have no right to do it.

On the other hand, there are a number of cases in libel (a form of defamation) where the plaintiff has not really suffered much at all. Similarly in trespass to land. The law regards these wrongs as especially bad and tends to compensate beyond loss. Indeed actual loss need not be proved. Such torts are said to be actionable *per se*.

There are also instances where the courts have awarded exemplary damages, where the activity of the defendant has been regarded as especially outrageous, but such events are very rare. In *Sutcliffe* v. *Pressdram* (1989) the court removed an award which they regarded as exemplary, and decided to replace it with an amount which represented only compensation. The broad line of policy in tortious liability is founded on fault—that the defendant should answer for loss which is his fault. This fault must be proved. It is argued that much of the money available to compensate for, say, road accident injuries, is soaked up in proving that the plaintiff's injuries are attributable to the defendant's fault.

There are instances where the defendant is liable even where the injury was clearly not his fault. These include the liability of an employer for the torts of his employees (called vicarious liability), and those instances where liability is said to be strict. These include actions under the tort named after the case *Rylands* v. *Fletcher* (1866) which concerned the flooding of mine shafts by a reservoir of water built on the instructions of the defendants. Blackburn J said:

> The person who for his own purposes brings on his land and collects and keeps there anything likely to do mischief if it escapes, must keep it in at his peril, and, if he does not do so, is prima facie answerable for all the damage which is the natural consequence of its escape.

VICARIOUS LIABILITY

This is the liability of one person for acts committed by someone else. In tort law the usual instance is the liability of an employer for the torts of his employee. It is important to note that the employer is not liable instead of the employee, but liable as well. In practice the point may not matter to a plaintiff faced with an employer carrying an insurance policy and an impecunious employee. The justifications for this liability have been various:

1 the plaintiff has a financially sound defendant (usually with insurers who will pay, raise the premiums generally, so everybody who insures pays; at least it spreads the load);
2 the potential of vicarious liability will increase standards of training, supervision and safety within the enterprise;
3 the employee is merely an extension of the employer, taken on as the business grew and diversified, so the torts are really those of the employer, committed indirectly.

The employer will not be answerable for all the torts of everyone he employs. In strange terminology, a distinction is drawn between servants and independent contractors, so that the employer is not usually liable for the torts of his independent contractor.

Servants and independent contractors

We know that the distinction is important, but how is it made? There is no single test. There are various guidelines which emerge from the cases. (Each case is decided on its own facts.) These guidelines include the so-called control test; that is, the servant can be told what to do and how to do it, but the independent contractor only what to do. This test is not much use in an age of accelerating technology. The employee may have been chosen for his special expertise, he probably was. The employer does not really control his methods of work. Any control in an overall sense would not separate out the independent contractor. There are other tests:

1 the method of payment (servants by wage or salary, independent contractors by lump sum);
2 the supply of tools, premises, etc.;
3 taxation (servants on PAYE, independent contractors taking care of their own tax);
4 pension schemes;
5 the power of appointment and dismissal (called the right to hire and fire; an employer would have individual powers of this kind over servants); and
6 the integration test, suggested by Denning LJ (in *Stevenson, Jordan and Harrison Ltd* v. *MacDonald and Evans* (1952)):

It is often easy to recognise a contract of service when you see it, but difficult to say wherein the difference lies. A ship's master, a chauffeur, and a reporter on the staff of a newspaper are all employed under a contract of service; but a ship's pilot, a taxi-man, and a newspaper contributor are employed under a contract for services. One feature which seems to run through the instances is that, under a contract of service, a man is employed as part of the business, and his work is done as an integral part of the business; whereas, under a contract for services, his work, although done for the business, is not integrated into it but is only accessory to it.

The lack of any single test leads to apparent inconsistencies. For example, in *Morren* v. *Swinton and Pendlebury UDC* (1965) an engineer was held to be the servant of a local authority despite the lack of control over his work, because his contract of employment made him part of the organisation. Whereas, in *Market Investigations* v. *Minister of Social Security* (1969) a lady interviewer was held to be a servant because the manner of her interviewing was controlled, yet she was hardly integrated: she could work when she wanted, and for other similar organisations as well if she chose to.

This distinction is always made when required, but not always in a predictable way. Its importance, as we noted, lies in the fact that only very rarely does an employer find himself answering vicariously for the torts of his independent contractor. However, it is not the case either that he will always have to answer for the torts of his servant.

Servants

An employer is vicariously liable for the torts of his servants committed during the course of their employment. This is another problem: was the act which injured the plaintiff done while the employee was within his course of employment or not? Where an employee was outside the course of his employment he is often said to have been 'off on a frolic of his own'. The answer to this course of employment question, from the cases, seems to be based more on degree than logic. This may reflect the policy (quite widely advocated) that wherever an injury can be compensated by insurance it ought to be—and if this means stretching the course of employment, well . . . One judge actually said 'this court looks around to see who is best able to pay.'

The measure of the course of employment is readily visible in *Hilton* v. *Thomas Burton* (1961) where some demolition contractors decided to take the employer's van (they had permission) to a cafe eight miles away, for tea. They left the site at about 3.30 p.m. When they reached the cafe it was time to finish work. They drove back again. The driver's negligence resulted in one of his colleagues being killed. His widow sued. The employer's insurers claimed that the men were outside the course of their employment. Diplock J said:

> I think that the true test can best be expressed in these words: was the second defendant doing something that he was employed to do? If so, however improper the manner in which he was doing it, whether negligent or fraudulently, or contrary to express orders, I have got to look at the realities of the situation. What were the circumstances, and what was the purpose for which this journey to the cafe and back was taken. Looking at the realities of the situation, it seems to me to be clear beyond a peradventure that what happened was this: the four men having taken the view that they had done enough work to pass muster, were filling in the rest of their time until their hours of work had come to an end. They decided to go to the cafe after sitting and chatting on the job for some time, to fill in the time until they could go home and draw their pay. This seems to me to be a plain case of what, in the old cases, was sometimes called going out on a frolic of their own. It had most tragic consequences; but it does not seem to me that it is possible to hold (though I would like to do so if I could), looking at the realities of the situation, that on the course of that journey the second defendant was doing anything that he was employed to do.

It is interesting to compare this case with the decision in *Rose* v. *Plenty* (1976) where a Co-op milkman in Bristol, in the face of an express prohibition from his employers, used a boy, Leslie Rose, thirteen years of age, to help him on his round. The boy's leg was broken when the float was driven negligently. Despite the prohibition, the employers were held vicariously liable. Lord Denning said:

> In considering whether a prohibited act was within the course of the employment, it depends very much on the purpose for which it is done. If it is done for his employers' business, it is usually done in the course of his employment, even though it is a prohibited act.

This would seem to echo the true test mentioned at the beginning of what we noted from the judgment of Diplock J in *Hilton* v. *Thomas Burton* (1961).

Independent contractors

As we have noted, vicarious liability here is rare and limited. It could arise where the tortious activity was authorised or done under the employers' instructions; or where the instructions were carelessly given, or where the tort was one of strict liability (like *Rylands* v. *Fletcher*, noted earlier in this chapter), or where the work ordered is of exceptional danger to the public (like work on the highway) or where the duty the work has been commissioned to fulfil is not delegable to anyone else (like the employer's duty to provide proper equipment, premises and staff—it is a personal duty).

GENERAL DEFENCES

There are special defences available to the defendant when faced with allegations of particular torts. We will note some of them later, but there are also a number of general defences which are available to combat allegations of many torts. It is important to realise that when dealing with particular torts the tendency is to look from the plaintiff's point of view (i.e. what must the plaintiff prove in order to succeed, etc.), whereas here we are looking from the reverse angle. We are about to consider the defences that might be raised in reply.

Volenti

This is one of the most important of the general defences. It is properly called *volenti non fit injuria*. Recalling that *injuria* means the infringement of a legal right and not injury in the usual sense, this phrase means 'to one who consents, no harm is done'.

Sometimes the defence is considered as falling into two parts: certain harm and accidental harm. If you climb into the boxing ring to fight a boxer you are likely to be punched. If this took place elsewhere it would be actionable as a tort, but if you were to sue the boxer you would lose because you would be taken to have consented to the normal consequences of boxing. This was so in the case of *Simms* v. *Leigh Rugby Football Club* (1969), where a player whose leg was broken in a tackle lost his action. The accident was within the rules of the game. On the other hand, of course, if the tackle had been outside those rules then he might not have been taken to have consented. In *Gilbert* v. *Grundy* (1978), for example, almost £4000 in damages and costs were awarded to the owner of a broken leg following 'deliberate and/or reckless foul play outside the laws of the game'. Similarly, in

Condon v. *Basi* (1985), where, during a football match between Whittle Wanderers and Khalsa Football Club in the Leamington local league the plaintiff's leg was broken by a tackle executed 'in a manner which constituted serious foul play, and for which he was sent off by the referee'. £4900 was awarded in the county court, and the decision was upheld by the Court of Appeal. Interestingly, the Master of the Rolls, Sir John Donaldson, noted that a higher degree of care will be required of a first division player than one in the fourth division. (Can that be right?) This issue was not crucial to the case in hand since the tackle here fell below the standard of care reasonably expected in any match.

The question of accidental harm is more subtle. Where the plaintiff places himself in a position where, if an accident were to happen he might well be injured, then in general he will be taken to have consented to run the risk of it happening. In *Hall* v. *Brooklands Auto Racing Club* (1933) a spectator was badly injured when a car crashed off the track. The court was satisfied that reasonable precautions had been taken by the organisers. They took the plaintiff to have consented to run the risk of accidental harm in attending a race-track and standing near the railings. (No car had left the track before in the twenty-three year history of the club.) More recently, in *Morris* v. *Murray* (1990) the plaintiff was flown in a light aircraft by a pilot with whom he had been drinking—hard and long. He was well aware of the state of the pilot. The plane crashed. The pilot was killed and the plaintiff was seriously injured, but the court held that he had consented to run the risk. The action failed.

There are two groups of people who are not generally taken to consent to run the risk of accidental harm in what they do: employees and rescuers.

In *Smith* v. *Baker* (1891) we can see the employee, a man drilling holes in rock for railway contractors, carrying on working despite the fact that he knew that a nearby crane was carrying rocks over his head. Almost inevitably he was struck by a falling rock. His action was defended with *volenti*. Lord Halsbury said:

> I think that a person who relies on the maxim must show a consent to the particular thing done. Of course, I do not mean to deny that a consent to the particular thing may be inferred from the course of conduct, as well as proved by express consent; but if I were to apply my proposition to the particular facts of this case, I do not believe that the plaintiff ever did or would have consented to the particular act done under the particular circumstances.

Thus it is said that knowledge of the risk is not enough, the plaintiff must have actually consented to run it. It seems that the only employees who do that will be those who are handsomely paid to take risks, like test pilots, racing drivers, and so on. It is plain that an employer owes his employees a duty of care in the workplace. However, recently the cases have moved to a consideration of whether this duty extends beyond the worker and to his wife. In *Gunn* v. *Wallsend Slipway and Engineering Co. Ltd* (1989) and *Hewett* v. *Alf Brown's Transport Ltd* (1992) where the employees' wives were injured by hazardous substances carried into the home on their husbands' working clothes, the courts held that no duty was owed to them by the employers.

The rescuer can be seen in *Haynes* v. *Harwood* (1935) where horses and a van had been left unattended by the defendants. The horses bolted when a boy threw stones at them, and a policeman was badly injured when he caught one of them to save bystanders, including many children, from injury. One of the defences raised was *volenti*. It was held that where a situation of danger is brought about by negligence and someone is put at risk and a rescue is made or attempted, then the rescuer acts out of a spirit of moral duty rather than of consent to run the risk, and *volenti* cannot be used against him. It would be unacceptable to (in effect) punish a rescuer for helping his fellow human being.

Statutory authority

It may be that the defendant admits that he did the act complained of as causing the plaintiff's injury, but that he has authority within a statute to carry on with that activity. The extent of the defence depends entirely upon the interpretation put upon the statute in question by the court. They might see the authority as absolute—something in the nature of a duty. This happened in *Vaughan* v. *Taff Vale Railway* (1860) where sparks escaped from a steam engine causing extensive damage. The statute under which the railway was operated afforded a defence. Had the company not taken all reasonable precautions, been negligent, it might have been otherwise. Alternatively, the statute might be seen as just permissive, so that an activity can be carried on provided the rights of others are observed. This happened in *Metropolitan Asylum District* v. *Hill* (1881) where the construction and operation of a hospital in Hampstead as a reception centre for smallpox and other infectious and contagious diseases was held to constitute a nuisance to those nearby, and an injunction was awarded.

Act of God

In *Tennent* v. *Earl of Glasgow* (1864) Lord Westbury defined this defence as involving 'circumstances which no human foresight can provide against and of which human prudence is not bound to recognise the possibility'. The defence is almost unknown today, Professor Rogers wrote:

> not because strict liability is thought to be desirable but because increased knowledge limits the unpredictable.

The case of *Nichols* v. *Marsland* (1876) is an illustration. A rainstorm 'greater and more violent than any within the memory of witnesses' caused damage when some ornamental lakes overflowed. The defence of act of God was successfully pleaded.

Necessity

This is another rare defence. The defendant admits the activity, but claims that it was done in order to prevent greater harm. In *Cope* v. *Sharpe* (1912), for example, a gamekeeper deliberately destroyed some of the plaintiff's heather in order to create a fire-break and stop a fire spreading to the land where his pheasants were kept. The fire was extinguished before it reached the fire-break, but the defence of necessity was accepted by the court. His fear had been reasonable; so had his action. Much more recently, in *Rigby* v. *Chief Constable of Northamptonshire* (1985), the plaintiff owned a gun shop. A dangerous psychopath had broken in, and in order to encourage him to leave, the police fired in a canister of CS gas. A fierce fire followed and the shop was considerably damaged. The action against the police for trespass, nuisance, *Rylands* v. *Fletcher* and negligence failed for various reasons including the successful plea in defence of necessity. However, the claim based in negligence did succeed, because at the time the gas was fired the fire brigade had been called away and had left via a police road block.

Inevitable accident

This is virtually unknown, of dubious value, but is quoted in some books as a general defence. It depends upon an injury having been sustained as a result of an accident which no reasonable man could have been expected to provide against. The difference between this and the act of God defence is that here the elements are not the exclusive players. There are people around. *Stanley* v. *Powell* (1891) is cited. It concerned a hunting accident where a shot fired at a pheasant ricocheted off an oak tree and injured one of the party. The court held that in the absence of negligence the defendant, who fired the gun, was not liable.

Contributory negligence

This is not strictly a general defence since it only serves to reduce liability, it does not enable the defendant to escape it. We will include it in our examination of the tort of negligence.

REMOTENESS OF DAMAGE

The court must be able to see a clear link between what the defendant did and what the plaintiff suffered. Without it the damage is said to be too remote a consequence, and the action fails. It is not quite the same thing as pleading a defence.

If several things happen between the activity of the defendant and the injury complained of the chain of events is called a chain of causation. Provided it remains unbroken the necessary connection between the action and injury exists. Anything which breaks the chain of causation is called a *novus actus interveniens*.

These principles can be applied to a very old case, *Scott* v. *Shepherd* (1773). It was the fair day at Milborne Port, 28 October 1770, in the evening. The defendant threw a lighted gunpowder firework into a crowded covered market. It fell onto Yate's gingerbread stall. A bystander called Willis, in order to protect himself and Yate's goods, picked it up and threw it across the market. It landed on Ryal's stall. He picked it up and threw it to another part of the market, where it exploded in the plaintiff's face, and he lost an eye. There was a lengthy chain of causation, but no break, no *novus actus interveniens*. Nothing had happened which was not a natural consequence of the defendant's act.

However, in *McKew* v. *Holland & Hannen & Cubitts (Scotland) Ltd* (1969) the chain was broken. The plaintiff was injured at work. The defendants were responsible. As a result, sometimes, and without much warning, he temporarily lost the use of his left leg. He had been out to look over a flat with his wife, child and brother-in-law. The access to it was a steep flight of stairs, without a handrail. On the way down he felt his leg give way, he pushed his child out of the way, and in order not to fall head first he jumped, and broke his right ankle. He claimed for this injury too. Lord Reid said:

> If a man is injured in such a way that his leg may give way at any moment he must act reasonably and carefully. It is quite possible that in spite of all reasonable care his leg may give way in circumstances such that as a result he sustains further injury. Then that second injury was caused by his disability which in turn was caused by the defender's fault. But if the injured man acts unreasonably he cannot hold the defender liable for injury caused by his own unreasonable conduct. His unreasonable conduct is *novus actus interveniens*. The chain of causation has been broken and what follows must be regarded as caused by his own conduct and not by the defender's fault or the disability caused by it.

The test of remoteness

Apart from a strictly factual approach to causation (it either followed or it did not), the courts also set a limit to the defendant's liability for what he has actually caused. He will be called to account only for the damage which is of a kind that the reasonable man should have foreseen—not the precise nature, nor the precise manner in which it was inflicted—but the kind of damage which should reasonably have been foreseen. So his liability is not limited by the extent of the loss, provided the kind of loss was foreseeable.

The rule comes from an Australian case called *The Wagon Mound* (1961) in which the defendants spilt oil on to seawater. Sparks from welding nearby set the oil alight and the plaintiff's wharf was destroyed. The damage was a direct result of the spillage, but the kind of damage, fire damage, was not reasonably foreseeable. It seems that to ignite this oil on that water is not easy. Obviously, clogging up the wharf with oil would have been foreseeable.

The case of *Hughes* v. *Lord Advocate* (1963) is also instructive. Some Post Office workmen were away at tea. They were working on cables reached by a ladder, down through a manhole. They had a tent over the manhole. They put a tarpaulin over the entrance to the tent, having lifted out the ladder and left it nearby. Two boys (eight and ten) went exploring. They went down the manhole, using the ladder and one of the paraffin lamps the men had set to mark the site. On the way out of the tent one of the lads knocked the paraffin lamp into the manhole. There was a violent explosion. Flames reached thirty feet. The boy fell into the hole and was badly burnt. He was able to recover damages because it was foreseeable that a child might get onto the site, break a lamp, and be burnt. The lamp exploding was not foreseeable, but the type of injury was.

The importance of the foreseeability was recently re-emphasised in *Cambridge Water Co* v. *Eastern Counties Leather PLC* (*The Times*, 9.12.93) in the House of Lords where Lord Goff said that reasonable foreseeability of harm of the type complained of (here contamination of water by chemicals stored on nearby land) was an essential element of the rule in *Rylands* v. *Fletcher*.

The point about the extent of injury enabling the defendant to escape liability, provided the type of injury is foreseeable, is nowhere clearer seen than in the so called thin-skull cases. In *Smith* v. *Leech Brain & Co.* (1962), for example, the plaintiff's husband was burnt on the lip by molten metal. It was the defendant's fault. The burn set off a latent cancer in him, and he died. The kind of injury, the burn, was foreseeable, the extent was not, but the defendants were liable for all his injury.

NEGLIGENCE

Negligence is the most important of the torts. It is committed when a person fails to live up to a standard of care expected of him, as a matter of law, and someone else is injured as a result. It is often claimed that in order to succeed in an action for negligence the plaintiff must prove:

1 that the defendant owed him a duty of care; and
2 that he acted in breach of that duty; and
3 that as a result the plaintiff suffered. (This resultant damage, of course, is subject to the issues about remoteness which we considered earlier in this chapter.)

So the action could be regarded as something of a hurdle race: duty, breach, resulting damage. It is a neat and convenient way to examine the tort, but, as Lord Pearson said (in *Home Office* v. *Dorset Yacht Co.* (1970)):

> The analysis is logically correct and often convenient for purposes of exposition, but it is only an analysis and should not eliminate consideration of the tort of negligence as a whole.

We will return often to the idea of negligence (for example in Chapter 15 it will be seen as an element in some crimes), but here we consider it as a matter which is actionable in itself, as a tort.

The duty of care   The foundation stone of much of the modern development of the tort is a case called *Donoghue* v. *Stevenson* (1932) which arose from the events of 28 August 1928, in Vincenti Minchella's ice cream parlour in Paisley, near Glasgow. Mrs May Donoghue drank some ginger beer, bought for her by her friend, only to discover, in the opaque bottle, the remnants of a decomposing snail. She had not bought the product, so a breach of contract action was not possible for her, so she sued the manufacturer for negligence. The case that finally wound its way into the House of Lords, and thereafter into English law (remember that the law in Scotland is different), was based upon the question whether the manufacturer owed her, a consumer not a buyer, a duty of care.

The judgement of Lord Atkin is very important. It goes wider than the set point, it explores generally when a duty of care is owed, by whom, and to whom. Unless the plaintiff can show himself to have been owed such a duty of care by the defendant, his action in negligence will fail (fall at the first hurdle, as it were). Lord Atkin explained the law in terms of neighbours—not necessarily the person next door, but the person whose welfare in the circumstances in question ought to have been of concern to the defendant. It is, of course, an application of the Biblical entreaty, 'love thy neighbour'. Lord Atkin said:

> The rule that you are to love your neighbour becomes in law, you must not injure your neighbour; and the lawyer's question, 'Who is my neighbour?' receives a restricted reply. You must take reasonable care to avoid acts or omissions which you can reasonably foresee would be likely to injure your neighbour. Who, then, in law, is my neighbour? The answer seems to be—persons who are so closely and directly affected by my act that I ought reasonably to have them in contemplation as being so affected when I am directing my mind to the acts or omissions which are called in question.

Clearly, then, the manufacturer, David Stevenson, owed the consumer a duty of care. This principle seems fairly predictable in the 1990s, but it was established by the narrowest of majorities: 3:2 in the House of Lords in 1932. The category of persons to whom a duty of care can be owed has been extended to children who were unborn when the incident took place but towards whom the duty 'crystallised' upon birth: *Burton* v. *Islington Health Authority; de Martell* v. *Merton and Sutton Health Authority* (1992). This is not to say that there are no limits to set to the size of neighbourhood. There is a case popularly called the pregnant fishwife case, *Bourhill* v. *Young* (1943) which shows a plaintiff who was not owed a duty of care. Euphemia Bourhill was a pregnant (eight months) fishwife getting off a tram in Edinburgh. Her basket of fish was being lifted onto her back by the driver of the tram. She was standing at the rear offside of the tram. John Young was a motor cyclist. He overtook the tram on the inside and crashed into a car which was turning right, in front of the tram. He was killed. Mrs Bourhill heard the crash. She did not see it. She saw the blood on the road. Her child was still-born. She blamed the motor cyclist, and sued his estate. To win, she would first need to establish that John Young had owed her a duty of care at the time of the crash. Lord Russell said:

> In considering whether a person owes to another a duty a breach of which will render him liable to that other in damages for negligence, it is material to consider what the defendant ought to have contemplated as a reasonable man.
>
> Can it be said that [the motor cyclist] could reasonably have anticipated that a person, situated as was the [plaintiff], would be affected by his proceeding towards Colinton at the speed at which he was travelling? I think not. His road was clear of pedestrians. The [plaintiff] was not within his vision, but was standing behind the solid barrier of the tramcar. His speed in no way endangered her. In these circumstances I am unable to see how he could reasonably anticipate that,

if he came into collision with a vehicle coming across the tramcar into Glenlockhart Road, the resultant noise would cause physical injury by shock to a person standing behind the tramcar. In my opinion, he owed no duty to the [plaintiff] and was, therefore, not guilty of any negligence in relation to her.

She was beyond the area of foreseeable danger; as was the plaintiff mother in *King* v. *Phillips* (1953). She was 70–80 yards away, upstairs in her house, from the taxi which was reversing over her son's tricycle. Naturally the boy screamed in protest, but he was hardly hurt at all. The boy was owed a duty of care, but not the mother. These cases have to be read now in the light of the House of Lords decision in *McLoughlin* v. *O'Brien* (1982) where a mother was held to have been owed a duty of care even though she was not at the scene of the road accident which injured her husband and two of her children, and killed the third child. Lord Wilberforce placed a new line of limitation on claims. He said that it is necessary to take into account:

1 the class of persons claiming (relative, friend, bystander);
2 their proximity to the accident (in time and space); and
3 the means by which the nervous shock, which forms the basis of cases like these, was caused.

The mother here satisfied these three considerations.

An important elaboration of these principles flowed from the tragedy at the FA Cup semi-final between Liverpool and Nottingham Forest at Hillsborough on the 15 April 1989. At the ground the Lepping Lanes pens had become very overcrowded. People were crushed against the fence around the pitch. 95 people died, more than 400 needed hospital treatment. Thousands saw the events at the ground. Millions were watching on television. Inevitably, many people suffered from what they had witnessed.

16 cases were brought to test the liability of the Chief Constable, whose responsibility it had been to police the ground. These were representative of 150 similar claims.

The matters reached the House of Lords as *Alcock* v. *Chief Constable of the South Yorkshire Police* (1991). From the case the following requirements must be met before a duty of care can arise in nervous shock cases:

1 there must be a sufficiently close relationship of love and affection with the victim, so that it would be reasonably foreseeable that the plaintiff might suffer nervous shock at the injury;
2 there must be a sufficient proximity to the accident, or its immediate aftermath, in terms of time and space;
3 the nervous shock must have resulted from seeing or hearing the accident, or its immediate aftermath. It is doubted that watching television would normally be enough.

Having considered some of the limits which have been placed upon the expansion of the neighbour principle, we must note the remarkable manner in which it has been instrumental in the spread of negligence liability. At the (considerable) risk of over-simplification, we could examine several different threads of development.

Acts causing physical damage

In *Dutton* v. *Bognor Regis UDC* (1972) (and similarly in *Anns* v. *London Borough of Merton* (1977)) the plaintiff recovered for damage to her house due to inadequate foundations which ought to have been spotted by the local council building inspector. However, Anns was expressly and completely over-ruled by the House of Lords in *Murphy* v. *Brentwood District Council* (1990). The facts are very similar. The court over-ruled not to free local authorities from liability, but more to cut down the broad statements about duty of care that had been made by Lord Wilberforce in Anns. It is clear from Murphy that the test for a duty of care is much closer to the proximity principles set out so long ago in *Donoghue* v. *Stevenson*.

In *Smith* v. *Bush; Harris* v. *Wyre Forest DC* (1989) a surveyor who was carrying out a survey for a building society, knowing that a copy would be given to the prospective mortgagor, was held to owe a duty to that mortgagor.

Acts causing financial loss

In *Ross* v. *Caunters* (1979) a solicitor drew up a will, but used the husband of a beneficiary as a witness. Under the Wills Act 1837, s.15, the gift in the will could not go to the beneficiary, so she sued the solicitor in negligence, and won.

In *Junior Books* v. *Veitchi* (1982) specialists laid a floor in a factory inadequately. It was not dangerous but it needed replacing. It had cracked badly. The plaintiffs wanted the cost of replacing it, and compensation for the cost of shifting the machinery to do it, and loss of profit while the machinery was out of use. The House of Lords allowed all this, because, as specialists, they ought to have known what was required and the consequences of not supplying it.

This *Junior Books* case seemed at the time to have been a remarkable step in the law—liability of a third party for shoddy goods. The courts have since appeared to be retreating from it. In *Muirhead* v. *Industrial Tank Specialities Ltd* (1985), for example, a manufacturer was held liable for the loss of a stock of lobsters which had died as a result of the pumps they supplied having failed to do the job of circulating oxygenated sea water, and for the consequent loss of profit. However they were not answerable for 'pure economic loss' (i.e. profits lost while replacing the equipment) because they were not proximate enough to have been relied upon to a sufficient degree. This is contrary to the *Junior Books* decision, which was distinguished in this case as having been decided 'strictly on its own facts'—a very restrictive comment to make about such a potentially important precedent. A further opportunity to expand the law in line with *Junior Books* was rejected in *Leigh & Sullivan* v. *Aliakmon Shipping* (1986) where compensation was denied to a party who was the 'risk carrier' because he was not the owner of the damaged goods. From these cases, and others, it seems clear that the tort of negligence is going through a period of consolidation rather than development, a point which has been further confirmed in *D and F Estates* v. *The Church Commissioners* (1989) where the cost of repairing a defectively plastered ceiling was not recoverable in that it was 'pure' economic loss. In *Murphy*, while the House of Lords expressly over-ruled *Anns*, they did not over-rule *Junior Books*.

Nevertheless, *Murphy* is a very significant contraction in the scope of the duty of care in economic loss cases.

Statements causing physical damage

In *Clay* v. *Crump* (1964) land was being redeveloped. An architect said a particular wall could be left standing but did not examine it. It fell on the plaintiff, who was an employee of the building contractors on the site. Lord Justice Ormerod applied the words of Lord Atkin (which we noted earlier in this chapter); he said:

> The question is . . . whether, according to established principles of law, the architect owed a duty to the plaintiff. Is this a case in which it can be said that the plaintiff was so closely and directly affected by the acts of the architect as to have been reasonably in his contemplation when he was directing his mind to the acts or omissions which are called in question? In my judgment, there must be an affirmative answer to that question.

Statements causing financial loss

In the very important case of *Hedley Byrne* v. *Heller and Partners* (1964) a new stream of authority arose, but it was based on Lord Atkin's neighbour principle. The plaintiffs were advertising agents. They needed to enquire into the financial stability of a company called Easipower Ltd to whom they were advancing credit. The plaintiffs asked their bankers to enquire. They asked Easipower's bankers, who provided a favourable reference, but carrying an exclusion clause: 'for your private use and without responsibility on the part of this bank or its officials.' The plaintiffs relied on the references. Easipower went into liquidation and the plaintiffs lost £17 661.92 ¹/₂. They sued Easipower's bankers but lost because of the effectiveness of the exclusion clause. The central importance of the case lies in the discussion in the judgments of the House of Lords about what the position would have been without the exclusion clause.

Lord Reid commented upon the impact of Lord Atkin's neighbour principle in *Donoghue* v. *Stevenson* (1932); he said:

> I would think that the law must treat negligent words differently from negligent acts. The law ought so far as possible to reflect the standards of the reasonable man, and that is what *Donoghue* v. *Stevenson* sets out to do. The most obvious difference between negligent words and negligent acts is this. Quite careful people often express definite opinions on social or informal occasions even when they see that others are likely to be influenced by them; and they often do that without taking that care which they would take if asked for their opinion professionally or in a business connection. The appellant agrees that there can be no duty of care on such occasions . . . A reasonable man, knowing that he was being trusted or that his skill and judgment were being relied on, would, I think, have three courses open to him. He could keep silent or decline to give the information or advice sought: or he could give an answer with a clear qualification that he accepted no responsibility for it or that it was given without that reflection or inquiry which a careful answer would require: or he could simply answer without any such qualification. If he chooses to adopt the last course he must, I think, be held to have accepted some responsibility for his answer being given carefully, or to have accepted a relationship with the inquirer which requires him to exercise such care as the circumstances require.

In recent cases there has been an attempt to introduce a form of *caveat emptor* into reliance on information supplied. In *Caparo*

Industries v. *Dickman* (1990) the audited accounts of a company were relied upon, shares were bought and the company was taken over. The accounts showed a pre-tax profit of £1.3 million whereas they ought to have revealed a £4 000 000 loss. It was held by the House of Lords that the extent of the duty of care owed by those preparing the accounts was limited to the company members (shareholders), to enable them to exercise proper control over the company. Those engaged in take-overs should either take independent advice or make their own enquiries. A similar result was seen in *James McNaughten Paper Group Ltd* v. *Hicks Anderson & Co.* (1991). Here draft accounts prepared for a company chairman were relied upon by a bidder. No duty of care was owed to the bidder.

On the other hand, and perhaps leaving the installation of *caveat emptor* incomplete, we have *Morgan Crucible Co.* v. *Hill Samuel Bank Ltd* (1991) where it was held that *Caparo* could be distinguished in that the statements relied upon were made after the plaintiffs had emerged as bidders.

Breach of duty

While the existence of a duty of care owed by defendants to plaintiffs is a complex and developing matter of law, if such a duty was owed, then the issue of its breach (the second hurdle) is a matter of fact in each case. Broadly, the court will look at what the defendant did and what the plaintiff suffered and judge the risk that the defendant was running of causing the plaintiff's injury, and the measures which would have been necessary to prevent that risk being run. In short, the court will ask itself whether the defendant acted reasonably in the circumstances. One definition of negligence describes it as 'doing what a reasonable man would not do, or failing to do what a reasonable man would do'. You do not have to be perfect, just reasonably careful.

In *Bolton* v. *Stone* (1951) the plaintiff was injured by a cricket ball which had travelled so far and so high that it sailed over the defendant cricket club's perimeter fence (seventeen foot high, and seventy-eight yards from the wicket). It was a straight drive. A ball had left the cricket ground only five or six times before, and never hit anyone outside. There was a risk. There were measures which could obviate it—close the ground perhaps. Lord Oaksey said:

> The standard of care in the law of negligence is the standard of an ordinarily careful man, but in my opinion an ordinarily careful man does not take precautions against every foreseeable risk. He can, of course, foresee the possibility of many risks, but life would be almost impossible if he were to attempt to take precautions against every risk which he can foresee. He takes precautions against risks which are reasonably likely to happen.

So the duty of care which the club owed to those in the neighbourhood of their activities had not been breached. They had acted reasonably.

In *Paris* v. *Stepney Borough Council* (1951) a council fitter had sight in only one eye. He was using a hammer to move a bolt on a vehicle when a chip of metal flew into his good eye, and he was blinded. The defendants had not provided goggles. It seems that it was not usual for that kind of job. On the facts (and only by a majority) the House of

Lords held that the duty of care had been breached. The seriousness of the risk (total loss of sight) and the foreseeable chance of it happening on the one hand, and the simple precaution (goggles being provided) necessary to obviate it on the other, were regarded, on balance, as sufficient evidence to show lack of reasonable care in this case.

Resulting damage

The third element or hurdle is that the damage the plaintiff complains of must have resulted from the breach of the duty that was owed him by the defendant. Again, it is a matter of fact, the damage resulted or it did not. In Barnett v. *Chelsea and Kensington Hospital Management Committee* (1968) a nightwatchman came to the casualty department of the hospital, complaining of vomiting after having drunk tea. The nurse contacted the doctor, a Dr Banerjee, by telephone, who recommended that he go home to bed and call his own doctor. A few hours later he died of arsenical poisoning. His widow sued. Clearly a duty of care was owed. Plainly, in not even examining the man, the duty had been breached, but, on the evidence it seems that when he called at casualty he was already bound to die. There was nothing which could have been done for him which would have saved his life. This sad case shows that if the damage does not, in fact, result from the breach of the duty owed, then the plaintiff's case in negligence must fail.

Contributory negligence

Where a plaintiff is in part the cause of his own injury then the blame is shared, on a percentage basis, and he receives less from the defendant than he would have had he not been contributorily negligent. This is the position today, under the Law Reform (Contributory Negligence) Act 1945. Before the 1945 Act contributory negligence was a complete defence.

The matter is topical with the discussion of the compulsory wearing of seat belts both in the front and back of cars. Even before the criminal law was changed in January 1983, an action for injury sustained in a road accident could result in reduced damages if the plaintiff had failed to wear a seat belt where, had it been worn, his injuries would have been less serious. These were the circumstances in *Froom* v. *Butcher* (1975). The plaintiff here had his damages reduced by 20 per cent. Lord Denning explained:

> Negligence depends on a breach of duty, whereas contributory negligence does not. Negligence is a man's carelessness in breach of duty to others. Contributory negligence is a man's carelessness in looking after his own safety.

When the discussion turned towards the plaintiff and his claim that he was free not to wear his seat belt (free from criminal prosecution—at the time) Lord Denning added that he was indeed:

> free in the sense that everyone is free to run his head against a brick wall . . . But it is not a sensible thing to do.

A popular case in this area is *Sayers* v. *Harlow UDC* (1958). Eileen Sayers had popped into a public convenience before catching the bus to London. On discovering that she could not get out, she shouted and waved for fifteen minutes and then tried to climb out. She put her left foot on the seat, her right on the toilet-roll holder, grasped the cistern pipe with her left hand and the top of the door with her right. She gave up. As she was returning to ground level the toilet roll rotated and she fell, and was injured. Her climbing attempt was unsuccessfully argued as a *novus actus interveniens*, breaking the chain of causation (we considered such things earlier in this chapter). The defendants were held liable in negligence, but Eileen Sayers was found 25 per cent to blame, and her damages were reduced accordingly.

Res ipsa loquitur

Sometimes the plaintiff suffers in such a way that it appears fairly obvious that the defendant must have been negligent—*res ipsa loquitur* (the thing speaks for itself). This is a rule of evidence law. Where the plaintiff can show:

1 that the defendant was in control of the activity which caused his injury; and
2 that the injury was of such a kind as would not have occurred unless someone had been negligent;

then the burden shifts, very unusually in English law, to the defendant to show that he had not been negligent. If he can give another reasonable explanation for the plaintiff's injuries then the burden shifts back to the plaintiff to establish negligence in the normal way. An early example is *Scott* v. *London and St Katherine Docks* (1865) where a customs officer going about his business was hit on the head by six bags of sugar as he passed by the defendant's warehouse. They had no explanation to offer. Erle CJ said:

> There must be reasonable evidence of negligence. But where the thing is shewn to be under the management of the defendant or his servants, and the accident is such as in the ordinary course of things does not happen if those who have the management use proper care, it affords reasonable evidence, in the absence of explanation by the defendants, that the accident arose from want of care.

Similarly, and more recently, in *Ward* v. *Tesco Stores* (1976) the company was held responsible for the injury sustained by a customer who fell over in a puddle of yoghurt on the floor of their branch in Smithdown Road, Liverpool. They said that the floor was cleaned regularly. But they were unable to establish when it had last been cleaned before Mrs Ward fell over.

OCCUPIERS' LIABILITY

The liability of an occupier for injuries sustained by someone on his premises depends upon whether that person was a lawful visitor or a trespasser.

All lawful visitors are protected by the Occupiers' Liability Act 1957, but the protection does not extend to trespassers. There are three categories of lawful visitor:

1 persons with an express permission to visit the occupier's premises (e.g. friends invited for a party);
2 persons with an implied permission to visit the occupier's premises (i.e. persons not specifically excluded such as customers in a shop, door-to-door salesmen);
3 persons who enter by operation of law (e.g. police in execution of a search warrant, gas and electricity meter reading).

Under the Occupiers' Liability Act 1957, s.2(2), the occupier owes a common duty of care to all his visitors. It is defined as:

> a duty to take such care as in all the circumstances of the case is reasonable to see that the visitor will be reasonably safe in using the premises for the purposes for which he is invited or permitted to be there.

This is not an absolute duty and can therefore be discharged by the occupier taking reasonable care; what this means will depend on all the circumstances of the case. For example, it was held in *Cunningham* v. *Reading Football Club* (1991) that a football club could face liability under the Act to injured visitors if it knew that football 'fans' would break off bits of concrete from the structure of the ground to use as missiles if they could, and the club did nothing to remove or minimise the risk.

The occupier is the person who has sufficient degree of control over the premises to be expected to take responsibility for them. For example, in a block of rented flats the tenants are occupiers of their living accommodation but the landlord is occupier of the hall/landings, stairway and lifts. However, where the injury is attributable to danger arising from the defendant's activities (rather than from the state and condition of the land) the defendant will owe a common law duty rather than that within the Act. In *Revill* v. *Newbery* (1996) an 82-year-old man shot a burglar who returned to break into his shed. The old man was sleeping there to protect a television and washing machine, and was frightened, especially when (as his counsel put it) the burglar banged on the shed shouting, 'If the old bastard's in there, we will do him.' The old man was liable in damages, however, to the burglar, but the burglar was held to have been two-thirds contributorily negligent. Interestingly, it seems that burglary is not so illegal as to raise the defence of *ex turpi causa* (nobody should benefit from his own wrongdoing)!

An occupier may attempt to exclude or limit his liability by putting up a notice. The notice may state 'Trespassers will be prosecuted' and is an attempt to keep people off the premises. What is the effect of such a notice? As far as it concerns children who go on such premises and are injured it would probably have little or no effect. As far as adults are concerned the Occupiers' Liability Act, s.2(4), states that if damage is caused to a visitor by a danger of which he has been warned, the fact of a warning notice is not enough. The warning notice must be brought to the visitor's attention and the contents of the notice must be so clear as 'to enable the visitor to be reasonably safe'. In law, in fact, it will only very rarely be possible for the occupier to prosecute trespassers; the normal remedy is to sue for damages for the tort of trespass to land.

If the visitor enters as a result of a contract, e.g. to watch motor racing or to watch a film, then a further restriction on notices is imposed by the Unfair Contract Terms Act 1977, s.2. This prevents an occupier from excluding or restricting his liability for death or personal injury resulting from his being in breach of the common duty of care under the Occupiers' Liability Act 1957, e.g. at a motor race in failing to erect an adequate safety barrier. This position has been modified somewhat by the Occupiers' Liability Act 1984. Where the occupier has permitted the use of his land by visitors, and this use is nothing much to do with his business activity on that land, then he is able to exclude liability. An example would be a farmer allowing a party of student geologists or rockclimbers onto his land.

Towards the trespasser no statutory duty is owed under the 1957 Act. Particularly, towards the trespassing adult. It has been said that there is no duty owed towards trespassing adults at all—but this goes too far. There is a duty. It is referred to as a duty of common humanity. It is, of course, far less onerous than that imposed by the Occupiers' Liability Act 1957, but it nevertheless exists. In the famous old case of *Bird* v. *Holbrook* (1828), for example, the defendant set a spring gun in his garden to protect his tulips. The plaintiff entered to retrieve a pea-hen, and was severely injured when the gun went off. The plaintiff received damages. He was a trespasser, but was owed the duty of common humanity, which, in this instance might have been satisfied by warning signs. The 1984 Act seems to have added little to this approach.

Liability towards children

The Occupiers' Liability Act 1957 states that the occupier must be prepared for children to be less careful than adults. Therefore, if the occupier expects children to enter his premises as visitors, e.g. a public park or a children's playground, then those premises must be safe for their use since he owes them the common duty of care. This requires that the characteristics of children be taken into account so that if there is an allurement on the land that can injure children the occupier will be liable. An allurement is something which is 'fatal and fascinating'.

In *Glasgow Corporation* v. *Taylor* (1922) a child of seven died after eating poisonous berries in a public park. The berries looked like cherries and were very tempting to children. Because the shrub had no warning notice or anything which prevented the children reaching the berries the occupiers were held liable.

If, however, the child is not a lawful visitor, but a trespasser, then the 1957 Act does not apply, and the plaintiff is left to establish that the basic duty of common humanity has been breached. There was a milestone of a case decided on this point: *British Railways Board* v. *Herrington* (1972). Here a six-year-old boy called Peter Herrington ran from land belonging to the National Trust onto the property of British Railways through a hole in the fence. He was severely injured on the electric line. The employees of the defendants had been aware of the hole in the fence for weeks, perhaps months, and yet had done nothing effective to mend it. Lord Reid said:

> An occupier does not voluntarily assume a relationship with trespassers. By trespassing they force a 'neighbour' relationship on him. When they do so he must act in a humane manner—that is not asking too much of him—but I do not see why he should be required to do more. So it appears to me that an occupier's duty to trespassers must vary according to his knowledge, ability and resources.

So, to satisfy the duty of common humanity the fence ought to have been repaired—especially in the light of the occupier's knowledge that children played nearby. The defendants were liable to Peter Herrington.

Generally, whether this duty has been discharged will depend on the particular facts. In *Pannet* v. *McGuiness and Co Ltd* (1972) the defendants were demolishing a warehouse. This involved lighting large bonfires which employees of the defendants were supposed to supervise but failed to do. A child of five, trespassing on the property, fell into one of the fires and was badly burned. The Court of Appeal held the defendants liable. This was because the fires were attractive to children, and the defendants knew that children trespassed on the site. To discharge their duty of common humanity the defendants should have ensured that the fires were properly supervised at all times.

This developing rule in the *Herrington* case has now been put into a statutory form by the Occupiers' Liability Act 1984. An occupier of premises owes a duty to trespassers under this Act if he is aware (or ought to be) of danger, or if he knows (or has grounds to believe) that the trespasser is or may be in the vicinity of that danger, and may reasonably be expected to offer some protection to the trespasser against the danger. The duty imposed by this Act is said to be to take such care as in all the circumstances is reasonable to see that the trespasser does not get injured. A warning sign might be enough, and, incidentally this injury does not include injury to property, only to the person. This vague expression of duty will leave the courts to go through the decided cases before the Act.

The cases decided immediately before the 1984 Act show the courts taking a rather less protective stance towards children and one more inclining towards a recognition of parental responsibility for their welfare. In *Ryan* v. *London Borough of Camden* (1982), where a child was hurt by hot pipes in a council dwelling, and *Simkiss* v. *Rhondda Borough Council* (1983), where the injury was sustained while sliding down a steep slope on a blanket, the occupiers were not held liable.

NUISANCE

The tort of nuisance concerns the unjustifiable interference with your right to enjoy your land (i.e. to live there reasonably comfortably). The tort has a public and private category.

Public nuisance

Public nuisance, logically since its effect is so broad, is usually a crime, but it is actionable in tort by an individual too where he has suffered more than the public have generally. As to the general aspect of public nuisance, Denning LJ (as he then was) sat in a case called *Attorney-General* v. *PYA Quarries* (1957), which concerned the public nuisance of blasting, flying stones, dust and vibrations from a quarry. He said:

> A public nuisance is a nuisance which is so widespread in its range or so indiscriminate in its effect that it would not be reasonable to expect one person to take proceedings on his own responsibility to put a stop to it, but that it should be taken on the responsibility of the community at large.

If no single person can show particular injury there can still be a prosecution. This was seen in *R.* v. *Johnson* (1996) where the accused was convicted of making hundreds of obscene phone calls to different women in a particular area. Concerning the individual bringing an action, note that in *Castle* v. *St Augustine's Links Ltd* (1922) a taxi driver on the way from Deal to Ramsgate was severely injured when a golf ball, driven from the 13th tee of a golf course smashed his windscreen. The evidence showed that balls often went into the road. 'The 13th' was declared a public nuisance, and the taxi driver, because he had especially suffered, was able to obtain individual compensation.

Private nuisance

There are a number of characteristics which make up an actionable private nuisance, but it has none of the general character of public nuisance. It concerns the complaint of one person about another person or persons' activity.

The activity complained of must interfere with the plaintiff's enjoyment of his land. It is usually a general state of affairs rather than one isolated act (a large bonfire, an all night party, an explosion). The interference must be unreasonable; we live in towns, on estates, and there are certain activities we have to put up with. The alleged nuisance must have either been created by the defendant or be the result of his neglect of some specific duty imposed by the law, or it must be carried on (continued) by him, having been created by someone else. Usually actual damage must be proved. The plaintiff must be someone with an interest in the land over which the alleged nuisance is having an effect.

So that in *Malone* v. *Laskey* (1907) the injured woman was the wife of the manager of the company who was the subtenant of the house. It was unfortunate that the cistern in the lavatory had fallen on her head, but this was not actionable in nuisance. She had no interest in the land. Similarly, in *Hunter* v. *London Docklands Development Corp.* (1997) no action could be brought for dust damage caused by roadworks where the plaintiff had no proprietary interest. This event illustrates another aspect of the tort. Although the injury followed a single event, the reason for it lay in the continuing state of the property caused by vibrations from the defendants' machinery in the adjoining premises.

S.C.M. v. *Whittall* (1971) concerned a power cut and consequent loss of production when a cable was cut by a workman. Referring to the need for a continuing characteristic in nuisance, Thesiger J said:

> While there is no doubt that a single isolated escape may cause the damage that entitles the plaintiff to sue for nuisance, yet it must be proved that the nuisance arose from the condition of the defendants' land or premises or property or activities thereon that constituted a nuisance. I am satisfied that one negligent act that causes physical damage to an electric cable does not thereby constitute a nuisance.

The defendant must have been acting in an unreasonable manner. This is not easy to assess, but it concerns the measure of what one must put up with in a social environment, and what exceeds that. Furthermore, there are standards of comfort and convenience which are more than one can expect.

In *Andreae* v. *Selfridge* (1938), for example, the plaintiffs ran an hotel. Nearby, the defendants, who were demolition contractors, were busily at work. This was an actionable nuisance not in itself but to the extent that it developed an excessive amount of dust and noise, over and above what is normally to be expected in such circumstances. However, in *Bridlington Relay* v. *Yorkshire Electricity Board* (1965) the plaintiffs demanded a high standard of interference-free television reception. They traded in relaying the signal to the public. The defendants' power lines nearby disturbed reception. Buckley J said:

> In my judgment, the plaintiff could not succeed in a claim for damages for nuisance if what I may call an ordinary receiver of television by means of an aerial mounted on his own house could not do so. It is, I think, established by authority that an act which does not, or would not, interfere with the ordinary enjoyment of their property by neighbours in the ordinary modes of using such property cannot constitute a legal nuisance.

So the plaintiffs were expecting too much.

Another factor taken into account is the character of the neighbourhood. One arrogant judge once said '. . . what would be a nuisance in Belgrave Square would not necessarily be so in Bermondsey'. Furthermore the motive for the activity complained of is relevant. In *Christie* v. *Davey* (1893) a woodcarver, who did not much enjoy music, retaliated when piano and singing lessons were given next door. He blew whistles, knocked on trays and boards, hammered, shrieked and shouted. His neighbours' use of their property was held to be reasonable, his was not. (This is a rare example of the motive for action being counted as relevant in tort.)

There are various defences that can be raised by the defendant in the face of a private nuisance action. We considered most of them earlier in this chapter: *volenti*, statutory authority and act of God. In addition he might claim that the nuisance was created by a third party (someone else), or he might allege the right to be a nuisance by 'twenty years' user'. This interesting defence arises where an activity has been carried on for so long (twenty years at least) that it has hardened into a right—despite the fact that it might have been actionable as a nuisance over the years. It is now too late.

The point was raised in *Sturges* v. *Bridgman* (1879), where the plaintiff, a doctor in Wimpole Street, London, had built a consulting room in his back garden which was close to the workshop of the defendant's confectionery business. The plaintiff complained of the interference. The defendant raised 'twenty years' user' because the machinery had been in use for many years. The defence failed. The extra room had only just been built. The interference there was in question. The time had only just begun to run.

The obvious remedies for nuisance are damages and/or an injunction. It may well be that damages are not enough in this tort. An injunction will be wanted to stop the activity. (We considered the common law nature of damages and the equitable remedy of injunction in Chapter 2.) Further to these, the plaintiff could abate (put an end to) the nuisance himself. No unnecessary damage can be done. If it involves going onto the defendant's property then notice of the intention must be given, unless, of course, it is an emergency.

TRESPASS

Trespass is one of the oldest actions in English law. It is concerned with the direct infringement of the plaintiff's rights. (An indirect infringement might be actionable in nuisance.) It is likely that the infringement will have been made intentionally. Careless infringement is probably now part of the empire of negligence, but since there is no need for the plaintiff to specify the tort in his action this does not matter much. Actual damage must be proved if the infringement was careless. (It must usually be proved if the infringment was indirect.) Intentional, direct infringement of the plaintiff's rights is actionable *per se*, i.e. without proof of damage. These are some of the rights taken very seriously by the law. We considered such matters earlier in this chapter. Broadly, trespass falls into three categories which will be examined in turn.

To land

This has been defined as the unjustifiable, direct, intentional interference with the plaintiff's possession of land. So the plaintiff must be in possession of the land affected. He need not be the owner. The one in control, who intends to exclude others is in possession (a tenant perhaps, but probably not a bed and breakfast customer).

The interference must be direct. It could be entry, or refusal to leave having been invited in (say to a party) and asked to go. It could be placing things on the land (perhaps tossing garden pests like slugs into next-door's vegetable patch). It could be tunnelling under the ground, or flying above it. Here, however, the Civil Aviation Act 1982, s.76(1), gives immunity to aircraft flying at a reasonable height, although it also makes them strictly liable for any damage they cause. It was suggested in *Bernstein* v. *Skyviews* (1977) that constant surveillance from the air may be outside this statutory protection and actionable as a nuisance.

The main defences are that the defendant entered because there is a public or private right of way across the land, or because the person in possession gave permission, or under the Civil Aviation Act 1982, or because (as may be pleaded by an official such as a policeman or electricity board meter reader) another statute gives him the right to enter (this is the defence of statutory authority again). Further defences are necessity, or entering to put a stop to (abate) a nuisance, or that the defendant entered to recover his own goods of which he had been deprived by the plaintiff.

Of the remedies available to the plaintiff, damages are the most obvious. An injunction might be appropriate. There are various self-help remedies, like ejectment (using only reasonable force) of the trespasser. This was used in *Hemmings* v. *Stoke Poges Golf Club* (1920), where the plaintiff and his wife were ejected from a cottage which had been let to them in connection with their employment. Proper notice to quit had been given but the plaintiffs refused to leave. They were removed, as was their furniture, but no unreasonable force was held to have been used. There used to be problems with 'squatters' in that trespass actions had to be mounted to remove them. The matter has now been absorbed into the criminal law. The Criminal Law Act 1977 created a variety of crimes connected with opening and remaining in property to which someone else was entitled as possessor.

In the summer of 1986 (and, it seems, every year since) there was a great deal of fuss about a so-called 'peace convoy' of 'travellers'' vehicles which crossed the south west and from time to time stopped on farmland and had to be removed using the civil courts and the tort of trespass. As a reaction to this the government made a last minute addition to the Public Order Act 1986, under Part V of which is created a new police power. Where two or more persons are present on land, and a senior police officer reasonably believes that they have entered as trespassers, that the occupier of the land has asked them to leave, and that they have a common purpose of residing, he will be able to direct them to leave the land when any one of three tests is breached: where any of the trespassers has caused damage to property, used threatening, abusive or insulting behaviour to the occupier, his agent or family, or where the trespassers have brought between them twelve or more vehicles onto the land. Anyone who fails to comply with such a direction to leave will be committing a criminal offence, for which the maximum penalty is three months' jail and/or a £1000 fine. During the debate on this matter in Parliament the government ministers stressed that they had no intention of criminalising the tort of trespass. In subsequent summers the fuss has been less, although the problem of people choosing to pitch camp on private land has not been solved.

To the person

This category of trespass can be considered in three parts: assault, battery and false imprisonment. Assault and battery will be considered in Chapter 15 because they overlap to an extent with the criminal law.

Briefly, an assault is committed where the defendant puts the plaintiff in fear of an imminent battery, and a battery is the intentional, direct application of force to the plaintiff's body. So, in *Tuberville* v. *Savage* (1669), when the defendant said 'If it were not assize-time, I would not take such language from you', with his hand placed upon his sword, this did not amount to an assault. This was because it was assize-time and the judges were in town and so the plaintiff knew he was not about to be filleted. The opposite was held to be the case in *R.* v. *Cotesworth* (1704) when someone who spat in a doctor's face was found to have committed a battery (which involves some physical contact).

False imprisonment consists of an unlawful restraint directly and intentionally being placed upon the plaintiff's liberty. It is not clear whether an intention to do an act that results in imprisonment or an intent to imprison is required for false imprisonment. It seems the former (of wider scope) should suffice as the liberty of the person is constitutionally important. If so, the bus driver who drives past a compulsory bus stop falsely imprisons passengers who wished to alight there and could, in principle, be arrested for the offence as it is now an arrestable offence. In general, though, suing would not be worthwhile. The restraint need not be by lock and key, but it must be such that liberty is confined. As Patterson J explained in *Bird* v. *Jones* (1845):

> Now the facts of this case appear to be as follows. A part of Hammersmith Bridge which is ordinarily used as a public footway was appropriated for seats to view a regatta on the river, and separated for that purpose from the carriage way by a temporary fence. The plaintiff insisted on passing along the part so appropriated, and attempted to climb over the fence. The defendant, being a clerk of the Bridge Company, seized his coat, and tried to pull him back: the plaintiff, however, succeeded in climbing over the fence. The defendant then stationed two policemen to prevent and, they did prevent, the plaintiff from proceeding forwards along the footway; but he was told that he might go back into the carriage way, and proceed to the other side of the bridge, if he pleased. The plaintiff would not do so, but remained where he was above half an hour; and then, on the defendant still refusing to suffer him to go fowards along the footway, he endeavoured to force his way, and, in so doing, assaulted the defendant: whereupon he was taken into custody . . . I have no doubt that, in general, if one compels another to stay in any given place against his will, he imprisons that other just as much as if he locked him up in the room: and I agree that it is not necessary, in order to constitute an imprisonment, that a man's person should be touched. I agree, also, that compelling a man to go in a given direction against his will may amount to imprisonment. But I cannot bring my mind to the conclusion that, if one man merely obstructs the passage of another in a particular direction, whether by threat of personal violence or otherwise, leaving him at liberty to stay where he is or to go in any other direction if he pleases, he can be said thereby to imprison him.

The person imprisoned, it seems, need not know about it at the time. In *Meering* v. *Graham-White Aviation* (1919) the plaintiff was unaware of the two men outside the room in which he was being quizzed about thefts from the factory. They would have hindered his departure. This amounted to false imprisonment.

Obviously, if there is a justification for the restraint, then it is not false; for example, lawful arrest, sentence to imprisonment by a court, confinement under the mental health legislation, reasonable chastisement by parents, are all lawful restraints.

The remedy would be damages, perhaps an injunction. *Habeas corpus* might be available (*see* Chapters 4 and 11). Self-help could be appropriate (breaking out, using only reasonable force).

Trespass and other interference with goods

Under the Torts (Interference with Goods) Act 1977, interference includes trespass to goods, conversion of goods, negligence or any other tort so far as it results in damage to goods or to an interest in goods.

Trespass to goods is an intentional, unjustifiable, direct interference with the plaintiff's possession of goods. It could be damage to goods, moving them somewhere else, or just messing around with them. The defendant can sometimes plead that a third party has a better right than the plaintiff to the goods. An interesting case on trespass to goods is *Kirk* v. *Gregory* (1876) where the 'master of the house' died in a state of delirium tremens. There was a party going on, and the deceased's sister-in-law decided to move some of his valuables (jewellery, etc.) from where he was lying to a place of safety, from where some of it was stolen. She was held to have trespassed with regard to those goods, despite her good faith.

Conversion consists in the defendant acting in such a way in connection with goods that it amounts to a complete denial of, or is totally inconsistent with, the plaintiff's ownership of them. (Interference with possession will not do.) This might be taking, destroying, or selling the goods.

As a remedy the plaintiff might claim damages, perhaps an injunction; the court can order the return of the goods, indeed the plaintiff could take them back himself (a course called recaption) provided that only reasonable force is used.

DEFAMATION

This is not an easy tort to define. Professor Winfield offered:

> It is the publication of a statement which tends to lower a person in the estimation of right-thinking members of society generally; or which tends to make them shun or avoid that person.

The tort falls into two categories: libel and slander. Libel is defamatory material published in a permanent form—like writing, photographs, films, waxworks, statues, records etc. and broadcasting for general reception (because the Defamation Act 1952 says so). Libel is actionable *per se* (without proof of damage). If it tends towards a breach of the peace it could also be a crime (slander cannot be). Slander is defamatory material published in a temporary (or transient) form like speech, gestures etc. It is regarded rather less seriously. Damage must be proved, except in the following four instances where slander is also actionable *per se*:

1 where there is an imputation of (imprisonable) crime;
2 where there is an imputation of contagious or infectious disease;

3 where there is an imputation of unchastity or adultery in a woman (under the Slander of Women Act 1891, s.1);

4 where there is an imputation designed to disparage the plaintiff in any office, profession, trade or business held or carried on by him when the material was published (under the Defamation Act 1952, s.2).

So with these exceptions, the plaintiff in a slander action needs to show loss. It must be monetary or calculated in money terms—like loss of a job. Otherwise, defamation is actionable without proof of damage.

The plaintiff has to prove three other things to establish the action, and we shall examine each in turn.

Defamatory nature of the publication

The plaintiff must show the statement was defamatory. Insults and jokes can be defamatory. All the circumstances must be taken into consideration. For example, in *Berkoff* v. *Burchill* (1996) an article described an actor as 'hideous-looking'. The Court of Appeal rejected the defendant's claim that this could only amount to injury to feelings and not to reputation. In *Charleston* v. *News Group Newspapers* (1995) the *News of the World* showed headlines: 'Strewth! What's Harold up to with our Madge?' and 'Porn Shocker for Neighbours Stars' above a photograph of a man and woman nearly naked and seemingly engaged in sexual activity. Superimposed over the heads of the apparently coupling people were pictures of the plaintiffs, an actress and actor in an Australian television 'soap' series. Having commented about the photographs, the newspaper then sided with the actors by complaining about a 'sordid computer game' made without the actors' consent and showing similar photographs to those which the newspaper had shown. The issue was whether the headlines and photographs alone were libellous, given that, as Lord Bridge put it: 'a significant number of readers will not trouble to read any further', or would 'right-thinking members of society' not form a judgement before reading the article? The House of Lords agreed with the latter argument, quoting from an 1835 case that 'the bane and antidote must be taken together'. The statement might be overtly defamatory, a bald statement which fulfils the requirements of Winfield's definition above. Or it might be an apparently innocent statement which carries a defamatory meaning called an innuendo. Lord Reid explained (in *Lewis* v. *Daily Telegraph* (1964)):

> Sometimes it is not necessary to go beyond the words themselves, as where the plaintiff has been called a thief or a murderer. But more often the sting is not so much in the words themselves as in what the ordinary man will infer from them, and that is also regarded as part of their natural and ordinary meaning . . .

A famous case on innuendo is *Tolley* v. *Fry* (1931). The plaintiff was a famous amateur golfer. The defendants made chocolate. They published advertisements in the *Daily Sketch* and *Daily Mail* which included a caricature drawing of the plaintiff with a bar of chocolate sticking out of his pocket. There was also a limerick:

> The caddy to Tolley said, 'Oh Sir,
> Good Shot, Sir! That ball, see it go, Sir.
> My Word, how it flies,
> Like a cartet of Fry's,
> They're handy, they're good, and priced low, Sir.'

The golfer sued for libel. He said that people would think that he has taken money, and lost his amateur status. The action succeeded.

Reference to the plaintiff

The statement must be understood to refer to the plaintiff. People must be able to spot who is being referred to. In *Hulton* v. *Jones* (1910) a newspaper published a story about Artemus Jones who was having a pretty good time in Dieppe with a French lady, despite being a churchwarden from Peckham. The publishers thought the name fictitious. They were mistaken. A barrister of the same name sued successfully. He showed that people had taken the tale to refer to him.

Under the Defamation Act 1952, s.4, it is possible to make an offer of amends in cases like this, if the publication was done innocently and without carelessness and a suitable apology is published. It is not uncommon to see disclaimers in books and at the cinema—'all characters fictitious' and so on. Of course, they do not protect a careless publisher.

It is not every 'entity' that can sue in defamation. It was held in *Derbyshire County Council* v. *Times Newspaper Ltd* (1992) that while in general a corporation can sue in defamation to protect its reputation, a corporation that takes the form of a non-trading public authority cannot do so in the face of criticism of the standard of its governmental or administrative activities. This would be contrary to the right of free speech enshrined in the European Convention on Human Rights. It does, however, have the right to bring an action for malicious falsehood.

Publication

The statement must have been published. This means that someone other than the plaintiff must be made aware of the statement. Otherwise the effect in Winfield's definition (above) could not be achieved.

Publication to the plaintiff's spouse is publication. Everyone who repeats the publication is a potential defendant, from the newspaper proprietor to the paper boy. Every new publication constitutes a fresh cause of action. (However an agent such as a newspaper seller can claim to have been an innocent disseminator, and thus avoid liability for having published the statement if he can establish that he did not know about the libel, and would not have known if he had been carrying on his business properly.)

In *Huth* v. *Huth* (1915), however, an improper opening of a letter by a butler was held not to constitute publication. 'Publishing ill of the dead' is not defamation; nor is it possible to defame a 'class' of people (e.g. by saying that all lawyers are crooks) unless the class is so small that each member can claim to be identifiable, when each can sue. However, legal aid is not available for defamation (*see* Chapter 8), so if you must defame people, be sure they are poor! Elton John (£1m out of court settlement with *The Sun*) and Jeffrey Archer (£500 000 from another newspaper) arguably do not need the money, but could afford to sue. In March 1990, Viscount Linley, the Queen's nephew and the first member of the Royal Family to sue for defamation for 60 years, was awarded £35 000 against the *Today* newspaper. The judge had given the jury some guidance. He suggested that they choose one of five figures: the equivalent of the cost of a house, a Porsche, a clapped-out Volvo, a good holiday, or something 'quite small'. Later the viscount waived the award.

Defences

Apart from the defendant simply denying that the statement was defamatory, or that it referred to the plaintiff, or that it had been published, there are certain special defences available in this tort.

Justification

The defendant produces evidence that the statements are true both in substance and in fact. Slight inaccuracies, especially where lists of allegations are published, will not render the defence useless, provided that the bulk of the statement was true. This is provided for in the Defamation Act 1952, s.5, and in cases like *Alexander* v. *North-Eastern Railway Co.* (1895), where a sign was exhibited which read:

> North-Eastern Railway. Caution. J. Alexander . . . was charged before the magistrates of Darlington, on 28 September for riding in a train from Leeds for which his ticket was not available and refusing to pay the proper fare. He was convicted in the penalty of £9 1s 10d, including costs, or three weeks' imprisonment.

The said Mr Alexander had actually only been ordered to spend two weeks in jail. He sued for libel, and lost.

This can be a risky defence to raise, because in effect it is an emphatic repetition of the allegedly defamatory statement. If the defence fails, damages escalate.

Fair comment on a matter of public interest

Opinion is free, and its expression (on matters of public interest) is not actionable—unless it is activated by malice. Lord Denning explained the need for and the nature of the defence in *Slim* v. *Daily Telegraph* (1968):

> The right of fair comment is one of the essential elements which go to make up our freedom of speech. We must ever maintain this right intact. It must not be whittled down by legal refinements. When a citizen is troubled by things going wrong, he should be free to 'write to the newspaper': and the newspaper should be free to publish his letter. It is often the only way to get things put right. The matter must, of course, be one of public interest. The writer must get his facts right: and he must honestly state his real opinion. But that being done, both he and the newspaper should be clear of any liability. They should not be deterred by fear of libel actions.

The requirement of honesty here involves an absence of malice (spite, ill-will) In *Thomas* v. *Bradbury* (1906) the plaintiff published a book called *Fifty Years of Fleet Street*. There appeared an extremely critical review in the magazine *Punch*, which was owned by the defendants.

The plaintiff successfully sued. The defence of fair comment failed because, on the evidence, the reviewer was seen to have been motivated by malice. This can be compared to *Telnikoff* v. *Matusevitch* (1991), an argument between two Russian emigrés conducted in the columns of the *Daily Telegraph* and concerning the BBC Russian service. Here it was held that, in the absence of evidence of express malice, a jury would be bound to accept a plea of fair comment.

An important distinction between justification and fair comment as defences here is that when raising justification the truth or accuracy of the statement must be established, whereas when raising fair comment the essential feature is that the opinion was honestly held. It need not be true.

Privilege

This is a defence in that certain statements made at certain times cannot amount to actionable defamation. It is not that the individual involved does not suffer; it is simply that the public interest in the statement being made is seen to outweigh the injury to the individual. Privilege might be absolute or qualified.

Absolute privilege is as wide as it sounds. Anything can be said or written. Nothing can be done about it. This complete freedom of speech is closely confined to several occasions:

1 statements made by members of either House within Parliament (under the Bill of Rights 1688), reports, papers, votes and proceedings ordered to be published by either House (under the Parliamentary Papers Act 1840). It is an interesting discussion point to consider the origin of this freedom of speech and whether it does, or indeed whether it should, extend to broadcasting what is said in the exercise of this freedom on radio and television. If broadcasting is not to be a protected medium, then what is the point of permitting freedom of expression in Parliament?

2 all statements made in the course of judicial proceedings, whether by the judge, barrister or solicitor, jury member, witness or a party to the case, provided that the statement relates to the proceedings;

3 communications between senior 'officers of state' (probably not below the rank of minister);

4 fair, accurate and contemporaneous reporting in newspapers and on radio and television of judicial proceedings in the United Kingdom, (under the Law of Libel Amendment Act 1888).

It was interesting to see that in *Church of Scientology* v. *Johnson-Smith* (1972), Hansard, the verbatim report of proceedings in Parliament, could not even be referred to as providing evidence of ill-will sufficient to defeat the defences of fair comment and qualified privilege. The case arose from statements made outside Parliament, in a television interview.

The other aspect of the defence is qualified privilege. It affords less protection than absolute privilege, but it is better than nothing. There are a number of occasions when it can be relied upon. They have in common a quality of reciprocity, as Lord Atkinson explained (in *Adam* v. *Ward* (1917)):

Where the person who makes a communication has an interest or a duty, legal, social or moral, to make it to the person to whom it is made, and the person to whom it is made has a corresponding interest or duty to receive it. This reciprocity is essential.

So there must be a relationship of this kind between the maker of the statement (a duty to make it) and the person to whom it is made (an interest in receiving it). where a statement is made in circumstances such as these, then it is protected. It is not actionable as defamation. An example of such a relationship would be that between your present or previous employer or school master or course tutor and a prospective employer, when writing a reference about you.

Fair and accurate reports of parliamentary proceedings, judicial proceedings and the meetings of other public bodies (like local authorities and the United Nations) are also protected by qualified privilege.

A crucially important point about this kind of qualified privilege is that it can be defeated with evidence of malice in the maker of the statement. In *Egger* v. *Viscount Chelmsford* (1964) the plaintiff was a judge of Alsatian dogs whom, in a letter to a dog club in Northern Ireland, the committee of the Kennel Club refused to approve, despite the fact that she was on their list of judges. The action for libel succeeded against the five members of the committee whose protection in qualified privilege had been destroyed by evidence of their malice. It failed against the three who were not shown to have been motivated in that way (their defence was successful). The other two members of the committee died before the verdict. In *Horrocks* v. *Lowe* (1974), a Labour councillor in Bolton, Lancashire said that a Conservative councillor had 'misled the town' and should be removed from a committee. The Conservative sued and lost. Lord Diplock said that councillors:

may be swayed by strong political prejudice, they may be obstinate and pig-headed, stupid and obtuse; but they were chosen by the electors to speak their minds on matters of local concern.

Offer to make amends

Within the Defamation Act 1996, s.2, the defendant can make the plaintiff an 'offer to make amends', i.e. to correct the statement, apologise and pay agreed or determined damages. The plaintiff can accept or reject the offer, but the offer is a complete defence under s.4 if made by a defendant who has innocently defamed, or innocently but without negligence referred to, the plaintiff.

No responsibility for publication

Within the Defamation Act 1996, s.1, a printer or distributor (i.e. not an 'author, editor or publisher') who took reasonable care in relation to the content of the publication has a defence if he neither knew nor ought to have known of its defamatory content.

Damages

Damages are awarded by juries and have amounted to very large sums in the past, e.g. £1 500 000 for libel (later reduced by consent) in *Lord Aldington* v. *Tolstoy and Watts* (1989), £150 000 for slander in *Smith*

v. *Houston* (1991), and £350 000 in *John* v. *Mirror Group* (1996). The reason is clear. The jury not only wishes to compensate the plaintiff but also to punish the defendant. The Courts and Legal Services Act 1990 now gives the Court of Appeal power to decrease an extravagant jury award. In this last case they did so—to £75 000. They went on to call upon the judges at first instance to indicate to juries that damages should be equated to those for personal injuries. There, for example, the most serious of quadroplegic (non pecuniary) injury is awarded around £125 000. On the other hand, juries have awarded 'contemptuous' damages. In *Newstead* v. *London Express* (1939), for example, the award was one farthing. They agreed that the law was on the plaintiff's side but, nevertheless, thought that the plaintiff was more interested in the money than to clear his name.

The Defamation Act 1996 now provides for a summary procedure where a judge sitting alone can dispose of a defamation matter, declare the statement in question to be false and defamatory and make an order for correction, apology, damages of up to £10 000 and an injunction, or any of these or, indeed, dismiss the application.

Indicative questions

1 Private nuisance is the direct interference with someone's enjoyment or use of their land.

Trespass to land is the direct, intentional entering onto someone's land without lawful permission.

The problem
Charles and Kate are neighbours. Kate, to annoy Charles, always has a bonfire on a Monday, which is Charles's washday. One Monday, Charles's washing is badly marked by smoke from Kate's bonfire since the wind was blowing in the direction of his washing line. In order to prevent further damage he went round to Kate's garden and stamped out the fire.

(a) Explain whether Charles may sue Kate for the tort of nuisance. (*8 marks*)

(b) Explain whether Kate may sue Charles for trespass. (*6 marks*)

(c) If Charles consults a solicitor about suing Kate for the tort of nuisance, he will probably be advised not to take the case to court even though he appears to be in the right.

Why do you think the solicitor would give this advice? (*8 marks*)

(d) Is it possible to make changes in the law of trespass and nuisance in order to prevent Kate from spoiling Charles's washday while, at the same time, maintaining her rights to use her own property? Explain your answer.
(*8 marks*)

SEG

2 The tort of trespass to the person can take three different forms: assault, battery and false imprisonment.

Explain what form or forms of trespass may have occurred in the following situations, giving your reasons.

(a) Jean creeps up behind Gary and hits him on the head with a tree branch.
(*2 marks*)

(b) Jo, a heavyweight wrestler, backs Jeremy, a small frightened man, into a corner and proceeds to slap him on the face. (*2 marks*)

(c) Julie, aged 13 years, is told to go to her room and to close the door behind her. Her parents refuse to let her come out for an hour. (*2 marks*)

SEG

3 In an action for negligence, the principles of vicarious liability and contributory negligence may affect who is made liable and how much compensation is paid.

In the following situations explain how these principles may apply.

(a) Charles is employed by a transport firm as a lorry driver. While delivering goods for them, he carelessly mounts the pavement and knocks down and injures Fiona. (*2 marks*)

(b) Jane, a private motorist, negligently knocks down and injures Bill, a pedestrian. However, it is shown that Bill was not paying attention when he walked into the road. (*2 marks*)

SEG

4 Study this extract and then answer questions (a) to (e) which follow.

Threats by hippy leaders to hold an illegal midsummer festival near Stonehenge could provide the first test of a new law to protect land-owners. If there is a mass trespass by hippies who refuse to move when directed to do so by the police they face prosecution for a new offence under the 1986 Public Order Act. Landowners seeking to evict hippies from their land may also benefit from changes in the civil law which will speed up the legal procedures for recovering possession. The new Act, though a useful piece of law reform, has not changed the law as regards public or private nuisance.

(Adapted from *The Daily Telegraph*, 2 June 1987)

(a) What is the definition of the tort of trespass to land? (*2 marks*)

(b) Give *two* examples of the kind of conduct which could constitute this tort.
(*4 marks*)

(c) In what circumstances is it permissible to enter the land of another?
(*4 marks*)

(d) Explain the civil remedies available for trespass to land. (*5 marks*)

(e) Set out the legal differences between public and private nuisance. How useful is an action in Public Nuisance? (*10 marks*)

LEAG

5 The *Daily Examiner* newspaper published a report of the trial and conviction for theft of John Dawson, who was caught stripping lead from the local church roof. Dawson was described in the report as 'a local man with church connections'. In fact, his father is a vicar.

Unfortunately, the local churchwarden is also called John Dawson and he has sued the *Daily Examiner* for defamation.

During the trial, the judge mentioned three elements that have to be proved in defamation:

(a) the statement must be defamatory;

(b) it should refer to the plaintiff;

(c) it must have been published.

Choose *one* of these elements and show how it was significant in this case.

(*4 marks*)

SEG

6 Six months ago Susan had an appendix operation. For a few weeks afterwards she felt fine, but then gradually she started to have pains in her stomach and began to feel dizzy and sick.

On visiting her family doctor, she was referred back to hospital, where she was immediately operated upon. The surgeon discovered that a small needle, of the type used to put stitches into patients, had been left inside her stomach during her appendix operation.

She is now quite well again and wants some legal advice.

(a) What type of legal action could Susan bring? (*2 marks*)

(b) What main elements would need to be proved for this action to succeed?

(*3 marks*)

(c) Explain to her the principles of *res ipsa loquitur* ('the thing speaks for itself'). Would this principle help her in her action? (*8 marks*)

(d) Explain to her the principle of vicarious liability. How is it relevant in this case? Give reasons for your answer. (*7 marks*)

7 A tort is a civil wrong committed by one individual against another. Under English Law, there are a number of well-established torts. These include:

> negligence, involving a breach of duty of care;
> occupiers' liability, an extension to the law of negligence;
> trespass, in a variety of forms;
> nuisance, both public and private.

The Problem
Cheryl, aged 17, lives with her parents in a large house on the edge of town. Cheryl's birthday was to be in two weeks' time and she had planned a big party at her home, including a disco and fireworks. Cheryl decided to invite about 200 people.

On the night of the party, a number of incidents occurred.

1. Guests' cars were parked on the road outside the house, completely blocking the road all evening.

2. Noise from the party upset Dagmar who lives next door. Dagmar claims that she could not sleep at all that night.

3. Errol, one of Cheryl's guests, was injured by a firework after Cheryl's father, Fergus, ignored the safety instructions.

4. Gordon, a small boy, sneaked into Fergus' garden to watch the fireworks. He then fell down a large hole in the garden which had been dug for a swimming pool. The hole was not fenced or covered, though there was a warning notice by the hole. Gordon suffered a broken arm.

(a) Explain which tort may have been committed as a result of the blocked road. (*4 marks*)

(b) Dagmar has since gone to see her solicitor who discussed with her a potential action for private nuisance.
  (i) Explain and illustrate what is meant by private nuisance. (*4 marks*)
  (ii) Briefly explain one reason why Dagmar's solicitor may have advised her not to sue. (*2 marks*)

(c) Discuss Fergus' potential liability if he were to be sued by Errol:
  (i) in the tort of negligence; (*6 marks*)
  (ii) in the tort of occupiers' liability. (*4 marks*)

(d) (i) State which tort Gordon would have been committing when he sneaked into Fergus' garden. (*2 marks*)
  (ii) Discuss whether or not Fergus could be held liable for Gordon's injury. (*4 marks*)
  (iii) Comment on whether or not an occupier should ever be held liable for injuries caused to a person who is unlawfully on the occupier's land. (*4 marks*)

SEG Summer 1997 (Foundation)

8 Negligence is a tort based on a breach of a duty of care, as a result of which the plaintiff suffers loss. The plaintiff will then be awarded damages based on the extent of that loss unless he has in some way contributed to that loss, in which case the damages may be reduced.

In some cases, negligence is so obvious that the defendant then has to prove that he was not negligent.

The Problem
Donald has been given a ticket to see his favourite rock group, Exodus, at Kings Court in London. The concert is being broadcast live both on TV and national radio.

Donald goes to the concert and takes his seat in a temporary stand which has been erected by the group's road crew. Just as the group is coming on stage, the audience leaps to its feet and the people in the stand, Donald included, start jumping up and down and stamping their feet.

The stand, which has been badly erected, collapses and Donald is thrown to the floor and badly injured.

(a) Donald is considering suing for negligence. Discuss what he would need to prove and the likely outcome if he were to sue the following:
  (i) Exodus;
  (ii) Kings Court Ltd, which owns the concert hall. (*10 marks*)

(b) Explain why Donald may be in a better position to sue if the court were to see this as an obvious case of negligence. (*4 marks*)

(c) Discuss whether or not Donald is likely to be awarded the full amount of damages based on the injuries he has suffered. (*4 marks*)

(d) Donald's wife, Emily, is watching the concert on TV at home and sees the stand collapse. She rushes to the local hospital and sees Donald in intensive care. She suffers nervous shock. Discuss whether or not she has a claim in negligence. (*4 marks*)

(e) Donald's uncle, Fergal, is listening to the concert on the radio and hears the stand collapse and the announcer describing what has happened. He also hears the screams of the injured people. He fears for his nephew's safety and also suffers nervous shock. Discuss whether or not he has a claim in negligence. (*4 marks*)

(f) Comment on whether or not a defendant should be responsible in negligence for people who are not physically present and who are in no physical danger. (*4 marks*)

SEG Summer 1996 (Higher)

CHAPTER 13

The Law of Contract

THE FORMATION OF CONTRACTS

A contract is an agreement which the law will enforce. It is at least an agreement. There are other requirements too. It is sometimes said 'all contracts are agreements but not all agreements are contracts'. A contract consists of five basic elements. The two most basic ones, offer and acceptance, form the agreement. In addition, both parties must contribute something to the bargain. This contribution (e.g. money, work, goods) has the special name of consideration. Unless a promise is put into a deed it will not be binding upon the person who has made it (called the promisor) unless the other party (the promisee) has also contributed to the bargain (provided consideration). Thus 'I promise to deliver' is not binding on me, but 'I promise to deliver in return for your promise to pay' probably would be.

So offer, acceptance, and consideration are three of the essential ingredients. Further to these the parties must intend to make the sort of bargain which has legal overtones; they must intend to be legally bound. If a young man asks a girl out for the evening and she agrees but neglects to attend at the appointed place and time, then he would be disappointed certainly, but hardly in the position to sue for breach of contract. It was a social agreement. Such agreements are presumed not to carry the intention to be legally binding which is another essential ingredient for a contract.

The fifth requirement is that both parties must be able to make contracts. The law protects the weak and the infirm, those of less than full contractual capacity—the mentally disordered (permanently or not), the drunk, those under the influence of drugs, and the young.

So the five elements in any 'simple' contract are offer, acceptance, consideration, the intention to be legally bound and capacity.

It is important to note that the common law of contract is developed through the cases, through the activities of real people. If a dispute has reached the courts there must be something worth arguing about, and it may not fit easily into the 'simple' categories so often set out in text books! Take the matter of agreement as an example. Over the years judges have indicated a willingness to depart from the 'traditional' approach, usually in an effort to recognise commercial realities. In

Gibson v. *Manchester City Council* (1978), Lord Diplock observed: "there may be certain types of contract, though I think they are exceptional, which do not fit easily into the normal analysis of a contract as being constituted by offer and acceptance." In the same case, Lord Denning, then the Master of the Rolls, stressed that the circumstances as a whole should be investigated when attempting to discover whether or not an agreement had come into being. More recently, Lord Steyn in *Trentham Ltd* v. *Archital Luxfer* (1993) placed emphasis on giving effect to the "reasonable expectations of sensible businessmen". In this case both parties to a contract had performed their obligations—the defendants had supplied and installed aluminium windows and doors and the plaintiffs had paid for them. When sued for defective performance the defendants claimed that no binding contract had ever come into being. It was nevertheless held that an executed contract came into existence during performance, even if it could not be analysed precisely in terms of offer and acceptance.

OFFERS

The party making the offer is called the offeror; the party to whom it is made is called the offeree. An offer is a statement of the terms by which the offeror is prepared to be bound. If an offer is accepted then the agreement exists. If the other three elements are present, a contract exists. The person who has offered to buy and the person who has agreed to sell are bound. If either fails to do as he has promised it might amount to a breach of contract.

Some statements, however, are not offers, though they may look like them. They cannot be accepted so as to form contracts.

Most of the law of contract is common law. That is, it has been developed over the years by the judges, case by case, by analogy with earlier cases. (We examined this in Chapter 3.) It follows, then, that whenever a statement of a point of contract law is made it is usually based upon the decision of a judge in a case brought before him. Therefore, when examining contract law it is very important to examine (and remember) cases. They are the basis of the contract law.

For example, on this point of statements which are not offers, but look like them, clearly, there must be at least one case in which one party was alleging the existence of a contract and the other denying it on the basis that there was no offer made, thus no acceptance and thus no contract. Such a case is *Pharmaceutical Society* v. *Boots* (1953). Here it was alleged that in a supermarket shop layout the sales were made at the shelves. It was defended on the basis that a contract is made at the cashdesk. It was important because the sale of certain medicines must be made under the supervision of a pharmacist. The Pharmacy and Poisons Act 1933 said so. The pharmacist was near the cashdesk not the shelves. This is what the judge, Somervell LJ said:

> Is a contract to be regarded as being completed when the article is put into the receptable, or is this to be regarded as a more organised way of doing what is

done already in many types of shops—and a bookseller is perhaps the best example—namely, enabling customers to have free access to what is in the shop, to look at the different articles, and then ultimately, having got the ones which they wish to buy, to come up to the assistant saying: 'I want this'? The assistant in 999 times out of 1000 says: 'That is all right,' and the money passes and the transaction is completed. I agree with what the Lord Chief Justice has said, and with the reasons which he has given for his conclusion, that in the case of an ordinary shop, although goods are displayed and it is intended that customers should go and choose what they want, the contract is not completed until, the customer having indicated the articles which he needs, the shopkeeper, or someone on his behalf, accepts that offer. Then the contract is completed. . . . On that conclusion the case fails, because it is admitted that there was supervision in the sense required by the Act and at the appropriate moment of time.

Judgements are not often as lucid as this. Wherever possible the cases should be read in law reports or casebooks. They are the raw material of the law.

It follows from this case that price tags in shops are not offers. They are called invitations to treat. It is the same if the goods are not on the shelves inside but in the window on display. This was established in *Fisher* v. *Bell* (1960). Here the outcome of the case depended upon whether goods (flick-knives) on display in a shop window were being offered for sale. If it had been so then the shopkeeper would have been guilty of an offence under the Restriction of Offensive Weapons Act 1959; but it was not so. Lord Parker said:

It is clear that, according to the ordinary law of contract the display of an article with a price on it in a shop window is merely an invitation to treat. It is in no sense an offer for sale, the acceptance of which constitutes a contract.

Similarly, a classified advertisement is an invitation to the readers to make offers. So that if a car is advertised in the classified advertisements columns of the local evening paper at, say, £500 and if there are fifty replies from people who are willing to buy the car, then is there to be one sale followed by forty-nine breach of contract actions? No, the advertisement is an invitation to treat, so the replies must be offers. Now the advertiser can choose between the offers as to which he will accept. Of course, he is still free not to sell at all, should he so choose. An interesting case on the point is *Partridge* v. *Crittenden* (1968) where a man was acquitted of offering for sale a bramblefinch, contrary to the Protection of Birds Act 1954, on the basis that the display of an advertisement in *Cage and Aviary Birds* constituted an invitation to treat and not an offer.

This advertisement in the paper must be distinguished from a reward poster on a wall. In the paper the reader makes an offer, if he is interested. With a reward case the reader is asked to do something—give information leading to a murderer, find a lost cat—and if he does then the advertiser is bound to pay the reward. Problems with rewards are rare, but it is important to understand that the nature of the transaction is very different. An advertisement is an invitation to treat. A reward poster is an offer—'if you do this, I will pay'.

The position was dramatically illustrated by the famous case of *Carlill* v. *Carbolic Smoke Ball Co.* (1893). Medicine was advertised—

the carbolic smoke ball. Full page advertisements were placed in such papers as the *Illustrated London News*:

> Coughs cured in 1 week
> Snoring cured in 1 week
> Whooping cough relieved the first application
> Hay fever cured in every case

There were eighteen such claims. The advertisers went further, they said: '£100 reward', and they named their deposit account. It was a very substantial sum in 1892. The reward was to be paid to anyone who bought and used the smoke ball, and caught influenza. There was an epidemic. Mrs Carlill bought and used a smoke ball and caught 'flu, claimed the £100, and was refused. She sued. Bowen LJ said:

> We were asked to say that this document was a contract too vague to be enforced. The first observation which arises is that the document itself is not a contract at all, it is only an offer made to the public. The defendants contend next, that it is an offer, the terms of which are too vague to be treated as a definite offer, inasmuch as there is no limit of time fixed for the catching of the influenza, and it cannot be supposed that the advertisers seriously meant to promise to pay money to every person who catches the influenza at any time after the inhaling of the smoke ball. It was urged also, that if you look at this document you will find much vagueness as to the persons with whom the contract was intended to be made—that, in the first place, its terms are wide enough to include persons who may have used the smoke ball before the advertisement was issued; at all events, that it is an offer to the world in general, and, also, that it is unreasonable to suppose it to be a definite offer, because nobody in their senses would contract themselves out of the opportunity of checking the experiment which was going to be made at their own expense. It is also contended that the advertisement is rather in the nature of a puff or a proclamation than a promise or offer intended to mature into a contract when accepted.
>
> But the main point seems to be that the vagueness of the document shows that no contract whatever was intended. It seems to me that in order to arrive at a right conclusion we must read this advertisement in its plain meaning, as the public would understand it. It was intended to be issued to the public and to be read by the public. How would an ordinary person reading this document construe it? It was intended unquestionably to have some effect, and I think the effect which it was intended to have, was to make people use the smoke ball, because the suggestions and allegations which it contains are directed immediately to the use of the smoke ball as distinct from the purchase of it. It did not follow that the smoke ball was to be purchased from the defendants directly, or even from agents of theirs directly. The intention was that the circulation of the smoke ball should be promoted, and that the use of it should be increased . . .
>
> Was it intended that the £100 should, if the conditions were fulfilled, be paid? The advertisement says that £1000 is lodged at the bank for the purpose . . . it was intended to be understood by the public as an offer which was to be acted upon. But it was said there was no check on the part of the persons who issued the advertisement. The answer to that argument seems to me to be that if a person chooses to make extravagant promises of this kind he probably does so because it pays him to make them, and, if he has made them, the extravagance of the promises is no reason in law why he should not be bound by them.
>
> It was also said that the contract is made with all the world—that is, with everybody; and that you cannot contract with everybody. It is not a contract made with all the world. There is the fallacy of the argument. It is an offer made to all

CARBOLIC SMOKE BALL

WILL POSITIVELY CURE

COUGHS Cured in 1 week	**CATARRH** Cured in 1 to 3 months.	**HOARSENESS** Cured in 12 hrs.	**THROAT DEAFNESS** Cured in 1 to 3 months.	**INFLUENZA** Cured in 24 hrs.	**CROUP** Relieved in 5 minutes.
COLD IN THE HEAD Cured in 12 hours.	**ASTHMA** Relieved in 10 minutes.	**LOSS OF VOICE** Fully restored.	**SNORING** Cured in 1 week.	**HAY FEVER** Cured in every case.	**WHOOPING COUGH** Relieved the first application.
COLD ON THE CHEST Cured in 12 hours.	**BRONCHITIS** Cured in every case.	**SORE THROAT** Cured in 12 hours.	**SORE EYES** Cured in 2 weeks.	**HEADACHE** Cured in 10 minutes.	**NEURALGIA** Cured in 10 minutes.

As all the Diseases mentioned above proceed from one cause, they can be Cured by this Remedy.

£100 REWARD

WILL BE PAID BY THE

CARBOLIC SMOKE BALL CO.

to any Person who contracts the Increasing Epidemic.

INFLUENZA,

Colds, or any Diseases caused by taking Cold, after having used the **CARBOLIC SMOKE BALL** according to the printed directions supplied with each Ball.

£1000 IS DEPOSITED

with the ALLIANCE BANK, Regent Street, showing our sincerity in the matter.

During the last epidemic of **INFLUENZA** many thousand **CARBOLIC SMOKE BALLS** were sold as preventives against this disease, and in no ascertained case was the disease contracted by those using the **CARBOLIC SMOKE BALL**.

THE CARBOLIC SMOKE BALL,

TESTIMONIALS.

The DUKE OF PORTLAND writes: "I am much obliged for the Carbolic Smoke Ball which you have sent me, and which I find most efficacious."

SIR FREDERICK MILNER, Bart., M.P., writes from Nice, March 7, 1890: "Lady Milner and my children have derived much benefit from the Carbolic Smoke Ball."

Lady MOSTYN writes from Curshalton, Cave Crescent, Torquay, Jan. 16, 1890: "Lady Mostyn believes the Carbolic Smoke Ball to be a certain check and a cure for a cold, and will have great pleasure in recommending it to her friends. Lady Mostyn hopes the Carbolic Smoke Ball will have all the success its merits deserve."

Lady ERSKINE writes from Sunton Hall, Northampton, Jan. 1, 1890: "Lady Erskine is pleased to say that the Carbolic Smoke Ball has given every satisfaction; she considers it a very good invention."

Mrs. GLADSTONE writes: "She finds the Carbolic Smoke Ball has done her a great deal of good."

Madame ADELINA PATTI writes: "Madame Patti has found the Carbolic Smoke Ball very beneficial, and the only thing to prevent her cough at rest well at night when having a severe cold."

AS PRESCRIBED BY

SIR MORELL MACKENZIE, M.D.,

HAS BEEN SUPPLIED TO

H.I.M. THE GERMAN EMPRESS.

H.R.H. The Duke of Edinburgh, K.G.
H.R.H. The Duke of Connaught, K.G.
The Duke of Fife, K.T.
The Marquis of Salisbury, K.G.
The Duke of Argyll, K.T.
The Duke of Westminster, K.G.
The Duke of Richmond and Gordon, K.G.
The Duke of Manchester.
The Duke of Newcastle.
The Duke of Norfolk.
The Duke of Rutland, K.G.
The Duke of Wellington.
The Marquis of Ripon, K.G.
The Earl of Derby, K.G.
Earl Spencer, K.G.
The Lord Chancellor.
The Lord Chief Justice.
Lord Tennyson.

TESTIMONIALS.

The BISHOP OF LONDON writes: "The Carbolic Smoke Ball has benefited me greatly."

The MARCHIONESS DE SAIN writes from Pidworth House, Reading, Jan. 14, 1890: "The Marchioness de Sain has daily used the Smoke Ball since the commencement of the epidemic of Influenza and has not taken the Influenza, although surrounded by those suffering from it."

Dr. J. RUSSELL HARRIS, M.D., writes from 6, Adam Street, Adelphi, Sept. 24, 1891: "Many obstinate cases of post-nasal catarrh, which have resisted other treatment, have yielded to your Carbolic Smoke Ball."

A. GIBBONS, Esq., Editor of the Lady's Pictorial, writes from 172, Strand, W.C., Feb. 14, 1890: "During a recent sharp attack of the prevailing epidemic I had some of the unpleasant and dangerous catarrh and bronchial symptoms. I attribute this entirely to the use of the Carbolic Smoke Ball."

The Rev. Dr. CHICHESTER A. W. READE, LL.D., D.C.L., writes from Banstead Downs, Surrey, May 1890: "My duties in a large public institution have brought me daily, during the recent epidemic of influenza, in close contact with the disease. I have been perfectly free from any symptom by having the Smoke Ball always handy. It has also wonderfully improved my voice for speaking and singing."

The Originals of these Testimonials may be seen at our Consulting Rooms, with hundreds of others.

One **CARBOLIC SMOKE BALL** will last a family several months, making it the cheapest remedy in the world at the price—10s., post free.

The **CARBOLIC SMOKE BALL** can be refilled, when empty, at a cost of 5s., post free. Address:

CARBOLIC SMOKE BALL CO., 27, PRINCES ST., HANOVER SQ., LONDON, W.

Reproduced by kind permission of *The Illustrated London News*

the world; and why should not an offer be made to all the world which is to ripen into a contract with anybody who comes forward and performs the condition?

When an offer is accepted an agreement (and perhaps a contract) is made. If it remains unaccepted it will not last for ever. There are various ways in which an offer might be brought to an end.

Rejection

This is self-explanatory.

Revocation

This is the withdrawal of the offer by the offeror. Provided that revocation is effectively communicated to the offeree—by the offeror or a reliable third party—and provided this is done before acceptance—then the offer is revoked. It no longer exists to be accepted.

Counter-offers

If an offer is answered with another offer then the first offer is destroyed. In *Hyde* v. *Wrench* (1840) a farm was offered at £1000; the offeree suggested £950 (a counter-offer); the offeror refused (whereupon the counter-offer died); the offeree then suggested £1000—as an acceptance of the first offer. The court held that this had been destroyed by the counter-offer. Careful businessmen always check that both sides are agreed at the end of negotiations.

Lapse of time

Obviously, if an offer is open for a fixed time it lapses afterwards. If it is not, then it lapses after a reasonable time, and this depends on the circumstances. In *Ramsgate Victoria Hotel Co* v. *Montefiore* (1866) an offer to buy shares on 8 June 1864 was held to have lapsed by 23 November when the offeree tried to accept.

Delays

There have been cases which involve delays between offer and acceptance during which the goods involved have been damaged. Such a case was *Financings* v. *Stimson* (1962) where, while the offeror was awaiting a finance company's response to his offer to buy a car on hire purchase terms, the vehicle was wrecked by thieves. The offer lapsed then. It was held that the offer was made to buy the car in its condition when inspected.

Death

The general rule is that the death of either offeror or offeree terminates negotiations. If the subject matter does not involve the dead party's personal activity—if his executors could carry out the deal—and if the offeree had not heard of the death when he accepted, then a contract might be made.

ACCEPTANCE

An acceptance is the unconditional assent of the offeree to all the terms of the offer. Obviously a conditional acceptance is not good enough. Counter-offers can be regarded as conditional acceptances, as in *Hyde* v. *Wrench* above.

Sometimes the phrase 'acceptance subject to contract' is used, typically when houses are being bought and sold. The parties agree 'subject to contract'. Both then go away and contact surveyors, building societies, etc. Meanwhile, the contract will be prepared, a process which will also require certain enquiries before contract to be made (*see* p. 203). The court will not hold the parties bound by such an agreement, as Jessel MR said (in *Winn* v. *Bull* (1877):

> It comes, therefore, to this, that where you have a proposal or agreement made in writing expressed to be subject to a formal contract being prepared, it means what it says; it is subject to and is dependent upon a formal contract being prepared.

Meanwhile the estate agent's board outside the house might say 'under offer' or 'sold—subject to contract'. A contract is envisaged, but not yet made. The buyer needs time to get a survey done, raise a mortgage, etc. The seller may get a better offer. If he accepts it he is not in breach of contract. There is no contract with the first 'buyer', only an agreement. 'All agreements are not contracts.' Making this second agreement is called gazumping. Anyway, the seller is likely to be the buyer in another deal somewhere else. House sales are usually done in 'chains'.

When an offeree decides to accept the offer he must communicate his decision. The offeror must know he is now a party to an agreement. This can be seen in the case of *Felthouse* v. *Bindley* (1862) where a horse was to be sold by auction. The seller's uncle had offered to buy it. He said, 'if I hear no more about him, I consider the horse mine at £30 15s.' As Willes J explained:

> The nephew might, no doubt, have bound his uncle to the bargain by writing to him: the uncle might also have retracted his offer at any time before acceptance. It stood an open offer; and so things remained until 25 February, when the nephew was about to sell his farming stock by auction. The horse in question being catalogued with the rest of the stock, the auctioneer (the defendant) was told that it was already sold. It is clear, therefore, that the nephew in his own mind intended his uncle to have the horse at the price which he (the uncle) had named, £30,15s.: but he had not communicated such his intention to his uncle, or done anything to bind himself. Nothing, therefore, had been done to vest the property in the horse in the plaintiff down to 25 February, when the horse was sold by the defendant. It appears to me that, independently of the subsequent letters, there had been no bargain to pass the property in the horse to the plaintiff, and therefore that he had no right to complain of the sale.

The action was brought by the disappointed uncle against the auctioneer—alleging that he had bought the horse from his nephew and so the auctioneer had no right to sell it. He lost. There had been no contract formed between uncle and nephew. No acceptance had been communicated. The rule is sometimes phrased: 'silence does not constitute acceptance'. A similar argument applies to situations where books, records, etc., are sent unrequested to householders with notes saying 'if you do not tell us you do not want this we will send you the bill'. Now we have the Unsolicited Goods and Services Act 1971 which provides that where goods do arrive unsolicited they become the

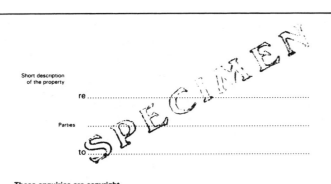

— *OYEZ* —
ENQUIRIES
BEFORE CONTRACT

In cases of property subject to a tenancy, forms **Con 291** (general business and residential tenancies) *or* **Con 292** (agricultural tenancies) should also be used.

Short description of the property

re ....

Parties ....

to ....

These enquiries are copyright and may not be reproduced

Please strike out enquiries which are not applicable

Replies are requested to the following enquiries.

Proposed buyer's solicitors.

Date .... 19.......

GENERAL ENQUIRIES

The replies are as follows.

Proposed seller's solicitors.

Date .... 19.......

REPLIES

These replies, except in the case of any enquiry expressly requiring a reply from the Seller's solicitors, are given on behalf of the proposed Seller and without responsibility on the part of his solicitors their partners or employees. They are believed to be correct but the accuracy is not guaranteed and they do not obviate the need to make appropriate searches, enquiries and inspections.

1. Boundaries
(A) To whom do all the boundary walls, fences, hedges and ditches belong?

(B) If no definite indications exist, which has the Seller maintained or regarded as his responsibility?

2. Disputes
(A) Is the Seller aware of any past or current disputes regarding boundaries, easements, covenants or other matters relating to the property or its use?

(B) During the last three years, has the Seller complained or had cause to complain about the state and condition, or the manner of use, of any adjoining or neighbouring property? If so, please give particulars.

3. Notices
Please give particulars of all notices relating to the property, or to matters likely to affect its use or enjoyment, that the Seller (or to his knowledge, any predecessor in title) has given or received.

4. Guarantees etc.
(A) Please supply a copy of any of the following of which the Buyer is to have the benefit:

agreement, covenant, guarantee, warranty, bond, certificate, indemnity and insurance policy,
relating to any of the following matters:
the construction of the property, or any part of it, or of any building of which it forms part;
any repair or replacement of, or treatment or improvement to the fabric of the property;
the maintenance of any accessway;
the construction costs of any road (including lighting, drainage and crossovers) to which the property fronts, and the charges for adopting any such road as maintainable at the public expense;
a defective title;
breach of any restrictive covenant.

(B) (i) What defects or other matters have become apparent, or adverse claims have been made by third parties, which might give rise to a claim under any document mentioned in (A)?

(ii) Has notice of such defect, matter or adverse claim been given? If so, please give particulars.

(iii) Please give particulars of all such claims already made, whether or not already settled.

Enquiries before contract; reproduced by kind permission of the Solicitors' Law Stationery Society Ltd
Note: Many solicitors now use the Law Society's 'conveyancing transaction protocol' which involves a number of new forms.

property of the recipient after six months. He need not pay anything. If he takes the step of informing the sender, then unless they are collected within thirty days, the goods become his. Meanwhile they should be kept reasonably safe (i.e. not left out in the rain). Incidentally, book and record clubs often use an 'opt out' approach, where they send their 'selection of the month' or other item, unless you say you do not want it. Such goods are not unsolicited. This is the performance of the existing contract, not the formation of a new one.

There are two exceptions to the rule that acceptance must be communicated. The first one we have already met. It concerns rewards. The offeror of a reward does not expect to be told—indeed he does not need to be in order to be bound to pay up. In *Carlill* v. *Carbolic Smoke Ball Co*, which we considered earlier in this chapter, another unsuccessful excuse put forward was that the company had not been told that the plaintiff had bought and was using the smokeball. That is, that acceptance had not been communicated. But this was a reward case, and, as Bowen LJ said:

> If I advertise to the world that my dog is lost, and that anybody who brings the dog to a particular place will be paid some money, are all the police or other persons whose business it is to find lost dogs to be expected to sit down and write me a note saying that they have accepted my proposal? Why, of course, they at once look for the dog, and as soon as they find the dog they have performed the condition. The essence of the transaction is that the dog should be found, and it is not necessary under such circumstances, as it seems to me, that in order to make the contract binding there should be any notification of acceptance.

The other exception is about the post. Where the post is the appropriate means of communication between the parties then, unless the parties have agreed otherwise, the following rules apply.

1 The letter containing the offer is effective when the offeree receives it. Obviously, you cannot accept an offer you have not heard about. (Consider returning a lost cat out of the goodness of your heart and then finding a postcard on a tree offering a reward for its recovery. Can you claim it?)
2 A letter of revocation is effective when it is received—because the revocation (withdrawal) of an offer must be communicated to the offeror before acceptance.
3 A letter of acceptance is valid as soon as it is posted, or put into the hands of a post office employee who can take letters for posting.

This third rule might seem a bit strange. It applies even if the letter of acceptance goes astray in the post, so the offeror is not told he is bound in a contract. However, the rule comes from the judgments in difficult cases like *Byrne* v. *Tienhoven* (1880). Here the defendants, in Cardiff, posted an offer to the plaintiffs in New York on 1 October. On 8 October, however, they had changed their minds, and they posted a letter of revocation. Meanwhile, the plaintiffs had received the offer and had accepted by telegram on 11 October, and sent a letter confirming acceptance on 20 October. The letter of revocation did not arrive until 25 October. The court was faced with two innocent parties. One regarded the offer as revoked, the other was convinced that he had accepted it. The court held that the letter of acceptance was valid when posted, and so the revocation arrived too late. The contract had been formed, probably on 11 October, but if not by the telegram certainly by the letter of 20 October. Both were sent before the revocation arrived. As has been noted, the parties can avoid this rule if they wish. In *Holwell Securities* v. *Hughes* (1974) the offeror said that he required 'notice in writing' of the acceptance. Thus the letter of acceptance had to reach him before the contract could be formed.

CONSIDERATION

As was explained earlier in this chapter, consideration is the technical name given to the contribution each party makes to the bargain—'I promise to pay if you promise to deliver'—'You can be the proud owner of this car for £1500', and so on. Lord Dunedin defined consideration (in *Dunlop Pneumatic Tyre Co* v. *Selfridge* (1915)) like this:

> An act or forbearance of one party or the promise thereof is the price for which the promise of the other is brought and the promise thus given for value is enforceable.

In practical terms, consideration is the point of making the bargain. It is what you wanted to get out of it. If you do not receive it (if the consideration fails) then it usually amounts to a breach of contract. Professor Atiyah wrote:

> Consideration means a reason for the enforcement of a promise. Nobody can seriously propose that all promises should become enforceable; to abolish the doctrine of consideration, therefore, is simply to require the courts to begin all over again the task of deciding what promises are to be enforceable.

There have been many cases over the years which have developed the idea of consideration to such an extent that there seem to be several rules which must be obeyed before consideration can properly be said to exist. This is crucial, of course, because it is one of the five essentials of a contract. Without any one of them no contract exists. Again, in practical terms, this means that while I may promise to do something for you unless that promise is part of a contract, unless I receive something in return, then I can break my promise. There is nothing you can do. With very few exceptions (e.g. promises in deeds), a promise for nothing (a gratuitous promise) is not binding. Let us return to these developed rules.

The first is that 'consideration must be valuable but it need not be adequate'. This means that provided something of value is given, in the absence of fraud or improper pressure, then it will be enough. In *Thomas* v. *Thomas* (1842) £1 each year towards the ground rent of a house was held to be enough to bind a promise to allow a woman to live in her late husband's house. It was not a market price, but it had value. His natural love and affection for her was not enough. It has no commercial value. But £1 would do.

Similarly, in *Chappel & Co.* v. *Nestlé's* (1960), the issue arose whether three chocolate bar wrappers, which were later thrown away by a record company, could be of value as consideration, and thus part of a deal where the wrappers and 1s. 6d. formed the price paid for a copy of a record called 'Rockin' Shoes'. Lord Somervell said:

> The question, then, is whether these wrappers were part of the consideration . . . I think they are part of the consideration. They are so described in the offer. 'They', the wrappers, 'will help you to get smash hit recordings'. They are so described on the record itself—'all you have to do to get this new record is to send three wrappers from Nestlé's 6d. milk chocolate bars, together with a postal order for 1s.,6d.'. This is not conclusive but, however described, they are, in my view, in law part of the consideration. It is said that when received the wrappers are of no value to Nestlé's. This I would have thought irrelevant. A contracting party can stipulate for what consideration he chooses. A peppercorn does not cease to be good consideration if it is established that the promisee does not like pepper and will throw away the corn. As the whole object of selling the record, if it was a sale, was to increase the sales of chocolate, it seems to me wrong not to treat the stipulated evidence of such sales as part of the consideration.

Consideration, however, cannot exist in doing what you are already bound to do in a contract with the same other party (called existing contractual duty) although if you do more you could expect extra payment. In *Stilk* v. *Myrick* (1809) a sailor could not recover extra pay he was promised (the promise was not binding) for working on a voyage to cover for two deserters out of a crew of eleven. On the other hand, in *Hartley* v. *Ponsonby* (1857), on similar facts, the sailor did get his extra pay because the desertion was nineteen of thirty-six, leaving only four or five able seamen. He had done more than his existing contractual duty. He had 'bought' the promise of extra pay. This point has been further considered in *Williams* v. *Roffey Bros.* (1990) where a firm of subcontractors was paid extra money to finish a job on time (their existing duty) thus freeing the main contractors from the liability they would otherwise have incurred under a penalty clause. This was held to amount to valuable consideration. This decision would appear to undercut *Stilk* v. *Myrick*, but the court said that the rule was refined not revoked The law now seems to be that the performance of an existing contractual duty can be consideration enough to bind a promise of extra payment in the absence of duress and fraud and provided that the other party obtains some extra benefit from the performance.

Since *Williams* v. *Roffey* the courts seem to have limited its application. In *Re Selectmove* (1994) it was held that a promise to accept part payment of a debt to the Inland Revenue in settlement of it all was not binding on them despite the fact that they may have gained an advantage from the arrangement.

Concerning the part payment of debts, it is of no extra value to be paid less than you are owed. So it was that in *D & C Builders* v. *Rees* (1965) the builders' promise to accept £300 in full settlement of a debt of £482 was not binding on them, and they could successfully sue for the balance. It would not be the same, of course, if part payment were to be made early or in a different form (e.g. £300's worth of bricks) or with a chattel (£300 and a bucket) or by a third party (A owes B but B accepts less from C)—all with the agreement of the creditor—because none of these is 'straight' part payment. They all contain a little extra and, as we know, three second-hand chocolate bar wrappers will do. If a little extra is paid the promise is binding but straight part payment will not discharge a debt. It has no value. Consideration must be valuable.

The second of these so-called rules is that 'consideration must not be past'. The rule sounds strange, but it is not difficult. Suppose I sell you a horse. After we have agreed the price and I have the cash and you have the horse you ask me about its temperament. I say that the horse is 'sound and free from vice'. This turns out to be less than accurate. The horse bites you and you want to enforce my promise against me. You cannot. At the time I made my promise about the horse the deal was over. You can only sue me for a broken binding promise (part of a contract). This promise was not binding. At the time I made it the only possible consideration from you (the money for the horse) was already in the past—used up. The rule is sometimes stated as 'past consideration is no consideration', and the facts of this story happened in *Roscorla* v. *Thomas* (1842).

Similary, in *Re McArdle* (1951) a man left his house to his widow in his will, for her life, and then to his children. There were improvements made to the house, for which the children subsequently promised to pay a contribution. This they neglected to do. Nothing could be done. When the promise was made the improvements had already been done. It was a gratuitous promise.

On the other hand, suppose I ask you to work for my company. You do so for a while. Later I promise to pay you. Since (*a*) I asked you to do it, and (*b*) it is the kind of thing that would normally be paid for, then despite the fact that I promised after you worked I have to pay. In a sense my request carried an implied promise of payment. These were the circumstances of *Stewart* v. *Casey* (1892) (which is sometimes called *Re Casey's Patents* (1892)). It followed a very old case called *Lampleigh* v. *Braithwait* (1615) in which a man asked another to travel to the king and beg a reprieve from hanging for him. It was successful. The man promised to pay £100. He failed to do so, but he was held bound by his promise to pay for the act since it had been performed at his request.

The final rule has an even stranger name: 'consideration must move from the promisee'. It is part of a doctrine of contract law called privity. Only the parties to a contract have rights under it, and only they have obligations. There are very few exceptions to this. In *Tweddle* v. *Atkinson* (1861), for example, a couple were engaged. Their parents promised each other that they would each pay some money to the couple when they married. One set of parents paid, the other did not; the father died before he had had a chance to. The couple sued his estate. The action failed, because the only appropriate plaintiffs were the other set of parents. The couple had provided no consideration.

They were not parties to the contract. They could not, therefore, sue on it.

In Chapter 2 we discussed the nature of equity. We observed that it is composed of a number of principles developed over the years in the interests of justice and fairness between the parties when a strict observance of the common law rules would lead to unfairness and injustice. In *Central London Property Trust Ltd* v. *High Trees House Ltd* (1947), commonly called *High Trees*, such a principle emerged when the argument concerned consideration. A landlord had gratuitously promised to halve the rent he could legally have demanded from a company renting the whole of a block of flats from him. It was wartime and it was proving difficult for the company to let the flats and pay the full rent. After the emergency the landlord wanted to restore the position and claim the full rent. He also questioned his ability to claim the back rent. Strictly, he had a right to the money, but the court said that they would not have allowed it if formally asked. This was on the basis of the unfairness to the company who had relied on the promise, which had been made knowing it would be relied upon (they cut the rents to fill the block). This rare and very limited principle of equity is called estoppel. Where it is recognised, it can make a gratuitous promise binding provided, generally, that it was relied on and acted upon by the promisee.

THE INTENTION TO BE LEGALLY BOUND

This is the fourth essential ingredient in any simple contract. For example, a 'letter of comfort' was held not to carry an intention to be legally bound (*see Kleinwort Benson* v. *Malaysian Mining Corp.* (1989)). In order to assist the courts to decide whether or not an intention to be legally bound exists two presumptions are made.

1 That in social and domestic agreements there is no intention to be legally bound. This was seen in *Balfour* v. *Balfour* (1919). The defendant was a civil servant stationed in Sri Lanka. He and his wife came to England on leave. When it was time to return, he left his wife in England for the good of her health. They agreed that he would pay her £30 per month while they were apart. Later the wife divorced him and he stopped paying. She sued him, unsuccessfully. As Atkin LJ said:

> It is necessary to remember that there are agreements which do not amount to contracts . . . it is quite common and it is the natural and inevitable result of the relationship of husband and wife that the two spouses should make arrangements between themselves . . . They are not contracts because the parties did not intend that they should be attended by legal consequences.

However, it is only a presumption and not a rule. When the court sees fit it will hold social agreements to have been contracts. For example, in *Simpkins* v. *Pays* (1955), an old lady, her grand-daughter and the lodger jointly entered a competition. The entry was made in the old lady's name. The grand-daughter won £750 but the lodger had to sue

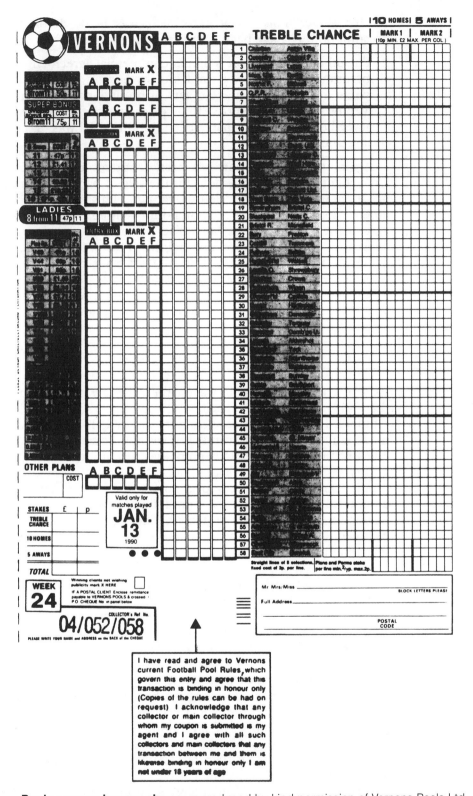

Pools coupon honour clause; reproduced by kind permission of Vernons Pools Ltd

for his share. This social agreement was held, despite the usual presumption, to have been a contract. He was paid.

2 The other presumption is that in commercial agreements there is an intention to be legally bound. So, in *Edwards* v. *Skyways* (1964), where a promise to make a sort of redundancy payment to some surplus pilots was referred to as ex gratia (out of goodwill), it was nevertheless held to have been binding. It was a commercial agreement.

Again, the presumption has been rebutted. In *Rose & Frank* v. *Crompton* (1923) an agreement for the sale of paper tissues contained an 'honourable pledge' clause stating: 'This arrangement is not entered into, nor is this memorandum written, as a formal or legal agreement, and shall not be subject to legal jurisdiction in the law courts.' The parties were not bound. This was because they had expressly agreed not to be. This kind of clause is found in football pools agreements. In *Jones* v. *Vernons Pools Ltd* (1938), the action for an unpaid win was lost, because the agreement was not a contract. If you 'do the pools' check the rules for such an honour clause as this.

CAPACITY

As was discussed earlier in the chapter, the law protects those of less than full contractual capacity. The mentally disordered (whether temporarily through drink or drugs or mentally ill) can avoid contracts made while unaware of events, if it can be shown that the other party knew of the incapacity. This point was recently confirmed in *Hart* v. *O'Connor* (1985) where a contract was made by someone who was insane, but who did not appear to be so to the other party to the contract. It was held that the contract was not voidable.

Minors are also closely protected. They are people under the age of eighteen. Contracts involving minors are usually considered under the following three headings.

Valid, binding contracts

These are made either for necessaries (like food, clothing, shelter and education) or they are beneficial contracts of service. If it is alleged that a minor is bound in a contract for necessaries, two things must be proved. First that the goods or services could (as a matter of law) have been necessaries; secondly, that they were (as a matter of fact) actually necessary. So in the famous case of *Nash* v. *Inman* (1908) a minor was not bound in a contract for clothing, not because the goods could not have been necessaries (clothing) nor because they were unsuitable for him (he was an undergraduate at Cambridge), but because he already possessed a large number of such clothes. The lesson to the tailor was not to sell children goods they do not need. Even if they had been necessaries the price payable would have been a reasonable price only, whatever the agreed price might have been.

The other type of (potentially) binding contract is a 'beneficial contract of service'. That is, a good apprenticeship or something similar, as in *Doyle* v. *White City Stadium* (1935) where a licence to box was held to be binding according to the rules of the British Boxing Board of Control. This was so even though it meant the minor (a boxer) would lose his fight fee. He had been disqualified in the second round. The apprenticeship agreement, or whatever other arrangement is in question is scrutinised by the court; if, taken as a whole, it is regarded as being reasonable, and for the minor's benefit, then it is binding. Otherwise, it is not. Here, the boy wanted to fight for a living. This fight was for the Heavyweight Championship of Great Britain. Taken as a whole the contract was for his benefit. He had to learn to fight fairly.

Valid but voidable contracts

Where the contract is of one of four kinds, the minor can avoid it. Up until the time it is avoided the contract is valid, so that any liability under it arising before then must be met. The four types are said to concern property of a permanent kind which involves continuing obligations, they include contracts concerning land (particularly buying or renting it, e.g. renting a flat), contracts subscribing for or buying company shares, partnership contracts and marriage settlements.

There is a further class of voidable contracts, including contracts entered into by an infant during the course of his trade or profession. These are now rare since the age of majority was reduced to 18. The Minors' Contracts Act 1987 (repealing the Infants' Relief Act 1874) re-established the old common law rules. A minor, on attaining majority, can ratify contracts that are unenforceable against him or voidable at his option. The Act enables a minor, on reaching the age of eighteen, to ratify a contract for a loan made during infancy; guarantees made by adults to secure the debts of minors are now binding on the adults and goods other than necessaries can now, on a court order, be recovered in all cases (not just where the minor had retained them by fraudulent activity, as was previously the case).

THE CONTENTS OF CONTRACTS

While negotiating the contract the parties will make many statements. Not all of them will be part of the contract. Those which induce the deal but do not form part of it are called representations. If they prove to have been lies (or just inaccurate) then the innocent party might consider action for misrepresentation. This will be considered later in this chapter. It is easy to tell which statements have become terms of the contract when it takes a written form; but there are millions of oral contracts made every day. It is more difficult to establish whether or not a particular statement formed part of an oral contract. Every statement which did form part of the contract, written or oral, is a contractual term.

These terms are not all of equal importance. The major ones are called conditions, the minor ones warranties. The innocent party to a breach is entitled to damages for a breach of either sort of them. For a breach of condition he is also entitled to cancel the contract and regard himself as free of it.

Express and implied terms

The terms within a contract will comprise many, but not necessarily all, of the statements made by the parties during negotiations: 'I want some boots fit for fell walking', 'this car has done 50 000 miles' and so on. Collectively all these terms can be referred to as express terms. In *Baldry* v. *Marshall* [1925], for example, a buyer ordered a car 'suitable for touring purposes'. The dealers supplied a racing car

There may well be more in the contract than the express terms. Terms are implied into contracts by statutes, and also by the courts. A common example of a statute which does this is the Sale of Goods Act 1979. Sections 12–15 of that Act imply terms about the title of the seller of goods, the quality of those goods, correspondence with description and so on. These will be examined more closely later. There are other statutes which imply terms into contracts. They include the Trading Stamps Act 1964, the Defective Premises Act 1972, the Carriage of Goods by Sea Act 1971 and the Marine Insurance Act 1906.

The courts are not keen to imply terms into contracts. They will only do so where:

1 the parties are in the same trade and the term required is commonly accepted in the trade as usual, or
2 the contract would not make business sense without it.

In these cases their policy is based on the idea that the term is already part of the deal, although it has not been included expressly. This is how three judges have explained it.

In *Reigate* v. *Union Manufacturing Co* (1918), Scrutton LJ said:

A term can only be implied if it is necessary in the business sense to give efficacy to the contract, i.e. if it is such a term that it can confidently be said that if at the time the contract was being negotiated someone had said to the parties 'What will happen in such a case?' they would both have replied: 'Oh, of course, so and so will happen; we did not trouble to say that; it is too clear.'

In *Shirlaw* v. *Southern Foundries (1926) Ltd* (1939), MacKinnon LJ said:

Prima facie that which in any contract is left to be implied and need not be expressed is something so obvious that it goes without saying; so that, if while the parties were making their bargain an officious bystander were to suggest some express provision for it in their agreement, they would testily suppress him with a common, 'Oh, of course'.

In *Trollope & Colls Ltd* v. *North West Metropolitan Regional Hospital Board* (1973), Lord Pearson said:

An unexpressed term can be implied if and only if the court finds that the parties must have intended that term to form part of their contract. It is not enough for the court to find that such a term would have been adopted by the parties as reasonable men if it had been suggested to them: it must have been a term that went without saying, a term which although tacit, formed part of the contract which the parties made for themselves.

The case called *The Moorcock* (1889) is a good illustration. In this case the problem concerned a river bed. A mooring had been hired for a steamship called *The Moorcock* in the tidal part of the Thames. When the tide ebbed she grounded and was damaged. The owners of the jetty claimed no responsibility for the river bed or its condition. It was under the control of the Thames Conservators. The contract had made no mention of the river bed, but both parties realised that the tide would go out. So the question which arose was whether the court ought to imply a term into the contract about the condition of the river bed. Bowen LJ said:

> I think if they let out their jetty for use they imply that they have taken reasonable care to see whether the berth, which is the essential part of the use of the jetty, is safe, and if it is not safe, and if they have not taken such reasonable care, it is their duty to warn persons with whom they have dealings that they have not done so.

The court implied the term. The owners could then be liable for breach of it.

Exclusion clauses

An exclusion (or exemption) clause is a term which, if found to be part of a contract and effectual, will enable one party to avoid liability he would otherwise carry. A limitation clause is similar, but, obviously, seeks to limit rather than exclude responsibility—'the company is responsible for the first £100 only of any loss' and 'all cars parked at owners' risk' are commonly found examples.

The courts frown on such clauses. They militate against the very nature of contracts—the assumption of rights and obligations. However, where the parties agree to their inclusion, the court must recognise their freedom of contract. Recent statutes have undermined this freedom to some extent. Some exclusion clauses, while they may be part of a contract, have been deprived of their effectiveness.

In order for an exclusion clause to be relied upon three points must be established:

1 that the clause was incorporated into the contract, and
2 that it covered the damage complained of, and
3 that it is not affected by statutory interventions or by common law rules of invalidity.

Incorporation can be achieved by signature or notice. Scrutton LJ said (in *L'Estrange* v. *Graucob* (1934)):

> When a document containing contractual terms is signed, then, in the absence of fraud or, I will add, misrepresentation, the party signing it is bound, and it is wholly immaterial whether he has read the document or not.

The courts are very strict about signatures. You are bound by what you sign, whether or not you have read the document, and if you have read it, whether or not you understand it. So an exclusion clause can enter a contract by means of a signature on a contractual document.

Otherwise, a notice must be used—a sign or a poster. This notice must be effectively brought to the attention of the other party to the contract, and this must be done before the contract is made, while the other party can still refuse to make a deal on the basis that the other party restricts his obligations under it.

As to effectiveness of communication, Lord Denning said (in *Thornton* v. *Shoe Lane Parking* (1971)):

> I do not pause to inquire whether the exempting condition is void for unreasonableness. All I say is that it is so wide and so destructive of rights that the court should not hold any man bound by it unless it is drawn to his attention in the most explicit way. In order to give sufficient notice, it would need to be printed in red ink with a red hand pointing to it—or something equally startling.

Even the most startling communication is useless if it comes too late. It must be before the contract is formed (pre-contractual, not post-contractual). In *Olley* v. *Marlborough Court Hotel* (1949), for example, a couple booked into an hotel for a week. They paid in advance, at the desk. When they went to their room they saw a sign which said 'the proprietors will not hold themselves responsible for articles lost or stolen unless handed to the manageress for safe custody'. The lady's furs were stolen. This clause was not part of the contract. The hotel could not rely on it. It had been communicated effectively enough, but post-contractually. The contract had been made at the desk.

Once the clause has been established as a term of the contract it must be shown to cover the damage complained of. In *Andrews* v. *Singer* (1934) a clause which read 'all conditions, warranties and liabilities, implied by statute, common law or otherwise' was useless to protect a breach of an express term. The contract was for 'new Singer cars'. One of the cars supplied was not new.

Finally, the clause must not be invalidated by statute or the various common law rules of invalidity. There are several statutes which disallow exclusion of liability. As examples: under the Road Traffic Act 1988, a driver cannot exclude his liability towards his passengers and this consolidating Act also makes passenger insurance compulsory. The Carriage of Passengers by Road Act 1974, the Transport Act 1962, the Carriage by Railway Act 1972 and the Public Passenger Vehicles Act 1981 all taken together provide that neither the buses nor the railway can exclude or limit liability for the death or personal injury of their passengers. They can limit liability for luggage, but only so far as would be held reasonable under the most recent and important statute of this kind: the Unfair Contract Terms Act 1977. This statute includes the following provisions:

> 2(1) A person cannot by reference to any contract term or to a notice given to persons generally or to particular persons exclude or restrict his liability for death or personal injury resulting from negligence.
>
> (2) In the case of other loss or damage, a person cannot so exclude or restrict his liability for negligence except in so far as the term or notice satisfies the requirement of reasonableness.
>
> 3(1) This section applies as between contracting parties where one of them deals as consumer or on the other's written standard terms of business.
>
> (2) As against that party, the other cannot by reference to any contract term—
>
> (a) when himself in breach of contract, exclude or restrict any liability of his in respect of the breach; or

(*b*) claim to be entitled—
    (*i*) to render a contractual performance substantially different from that which was reasonably expected of him or
    (*ii*) in respect of the whole or any part of his contractual obligation, to render no performance at all, except in so far as (in any of the cases mentioned above in this subsection) the contract term satisfies the requirement of reasonableness.

Furthermore, the 1977 Act provides, in s.6, that the terms implied into contracts for the sale of goods by the Sale of Goods Act 1979 cannot be excluded at all in a consumer sale, and only so far as would be reasonable in any other sale, for example, between a wholesaler and retailer. This reflects the protective attitude often taken towards the weaker party in situations of inequality of bargaining power. The Act says:

6(1) Liability for breach of the obligations arising from—
    (*a*) section 12 of the Sale of Goods Act 1979 (seller's implied undertakings as to title, etc.);
    (*b*) section 8 of the Supply of Goods (Implied Terms) Act 1973 (the corresponding thing in relation to hire-purchase), cannot be excluded or restricted by reference to any contract term.
    (2) Against a person dealing as consumer liability for breach of the obligations arising from—
    (*a*) section 13, 14 or 15 of the 1979 Act (seller's implied undertakings as to conformity of goods with description or sample or as to their quality or fitness for a particular purpose);
    (*b*) section 9, 10 or 11 of the 1973 Act (the corresponding things in relation to hire-purchase), cannot be excluded or restricted by reference to any contract term.
    (3) As against a person dealing otherwise than as consumer, the liability specified in subsection (2) above can be excluded or restricted by reference to a contract term, but only in so far as the term satisfies the requirement of reasonableness.

The attitudes of the courts towards this very important statute are beginning to emerge in the cases—at all levels. In the county courts we have *Waldron-Kelly* v. *British Railways Board* (1981), where a suitcase was lost. The Board relied on their limitation of liability (£27), whereas the value of the lost case was £320. The court held the limitation unreasonable. A similar result can be seen in *Woodman* v. *Photo Trade Processing* (1981), where wedding photographs were ruined and a limitation clause (just to replace the film) was held unreasonable. Incidentally, this case is an example of the Consumer Association's activity on behalf of its members. Their legal officer, David Tench (who had had a hand in the drafting and enactment of the 1977 Act) appeared in person at the Exeter County Court. (*See Warren* v. *Truprint Ltd* (1986), where very similar facts yielded a result in another county court which, if anything, seems stronger for the consumer. Whereas the processors appealed against an award of £50 compensation the judge said that he would, had it been his decision have awarded £150.)

At the other end of the scale we have *George Mitchell* v. *Finney Lock Seeds* (1983), where the House of Lords held a limitation clause unreasonable. It purported to limit to a replacement of seeds liability for having negligently supplied the wrong seeds to a grower, who, in consequence, lost a crop worth well over £60 000. The Unfair Terms in Consumer Contracts Regulations 1994 have been in force since the 1 July 1995. They implement Council Directive 93/13/EEC on unfair terms in consumer contracts. Where they apply to a particular contractual term the effect is simply that it is not binding on the consumer. This completely undermines the concept of freedom of contract! The Regulations are aimed at contractual terms which have not been 'individually negotiated', so the main target is the 'unfair' term in the 'standard form' contract so often presented to a consumer by a large business enterprise of one kind or another. To be regarded as 'unfair' the term must be contrary to the principle of 'good faith' in that it causes a significant imbalance in the rights and obligations of the parties to the contract, to the 'detriment' of the 'consumer'. Now a 'consumer' here is any 'natural' person (so not a company) who is not acting for the purposes of a trade, business or profession. Schedule 3 to the Regulations illustrates terms which may be unfair, but the list there is not exhaustive.

Article 7 of the Directive requires Member States to provide for enforcement by enabling organisations with a legitimate interest under national law in protecting consumers to take action before the courts or competent administrative bodies for a decision as to whether contractual terms are unfair so as to prevent their continued use. In 1995 the Government implemented Article 7 by placing a duty on the Director General of Fair Trading to consider complaints about unfair terms. He is able to accept undertakings from traders and, if necessary, to seek injunctions against the continued use of unfair terms.

The Consumers' Association had sought judicial review on the basis that it had a 'legitimate interest' too, and in June 1997 the new Government announced a change of policy, allowing bodies which represent consumers, like the Consumers' Association, to mount a legal challenge to contracts whose terms are unfair, such as terms which are baffling or illegible, or which allow the trader to change the contract or increase the price after the consumer has signed. The Director General of Fair Trading, John Bridgeman, commented:

> the decision to empower a wider range of bodies to tackle the serious and widespread problem of unfair terms is to be welcomed and was, in my view, inevitable. There was an argument for giving the Office of Fair Trading sole responsibility for implementing the Regulations in 1995. It enabled us to produce valuable guidance to ensure that the law is interpreted in a consistent way. Now we look forward to working with other bodies to deal with this priority area of consumer detriment.

It is important to note that these Regulations, and the exciting prospect of a variety of consumer organisations scanning standard form contracts for unfairness does not replace the Unfair Contract Terms Act. This is an addition to our law, perhaps partly overlapping, and certainly not an instalment in the implementation of a structured plan for law making. Perhaps it is a beneficial bolt-on!

As to limitations on effectiveness aside from statutes, exclusion clauses are not generally allowed to protect third parties. That is, if the contract is made between A and B, and it contains a clause purporting to protect C then that protection is (usually) ineffectual. Furthermore if the nature or extent of the clause is misrepresented by the party who later seeks to rely on it then its effect will be limited to his statement, despite the actual wording. So if he says it excludes X but in fact it seeks to exclude liability for X, Y and Z, the clause is likely to be held to protect only against X. This is not to say that there is an absolute policy against exclusion clauses—particularly where the parties are seen to be roughly equal in bargaining power. In *Photo Production* v. *Securicor* (1980), for example, a security company was able to rely upon an exclusion clause which protected them from liability when their employee burnt down the premises the company was hired to protect!

There was more damage by fire in *Norwich City Council* v. *Harvey* (1989) where an employee of sub-contractors negligently set fire with his blow torch to both a new extension and the existing buildings. Here the contract contained a term whereby the main building contractor had placed the risk of loss or damage by fire on the owner of the buildings, thus protecting the main contractor and his sub-contractor.

VITIATING ELEMENTS: THINGS THAT CAN GO WRONG AND SPOIL CONTRACTS

Having considered the formation of contracts, and their contents once formed, we now need to look at a collection of ways in which the contract could be spoilt (vitiated). These will include the lack of formality, where a contract needs to be made in a particular form, mistakes of various kinds, misrepresentation, duress, undue influence, illegality and vagueness.

Lack of formality Most contracts are just as valid and enforceable (given the evidence) whether they are made orally or in writing. However, formality is sometimes required:

1 conveyances of land, leases for longer than three years, the transfer of British ships, or shares in them all need deeds. The Law of Property (Miscellaneous Provisions) Act 1989 removed the need for a seal on the deed;
2 bills of exchange, promissory notes, marine insurance contracts, bills of sale and most consumer credit agreements are examples of transactions which need to be made in writing;
3 guarantees (where someone says he will answer for another's liability if he fails to do so) need written evidence of their existence before they can be enforced by court proceedings.

Since the Law of Property (Miscellaneous Provisions) Act 1989 guarantees are the only important contracts that need to be evidenced in writing.

Section 40 of the Law of Property Act 1925 required that contracts for the sale or other disposition of land needed to be evidenced rather than made in writing. The 1989 Act repealed this provision. Now such contracts must be made in writing, and the writing must contain all that has been agreed between the parties and both their signatures. Without the writing the contract is void. There are two exceptions to this: where the sale takes place at a public auction so that the contract is made when the hammer falls, and where the disposition is for a lease of less than three years and the tenant takes possession. Such leases can be granted orally.

Of course, many contracts that do not specifically require formality are made in a formal way. The importance of written evidence when starting an action for breach of contract, for example, cannot be overemphasised; but some contracts have special requirements without which they are not valid at all or (in the case of those needing written evidence) are unenforceable.

Mistake

Signed documents

We have already noted in this chapter the seriousness of the courts' attitude towards signatures on documents. It is settled that a mistake about the contents of a signed document will be no excuse. The signer is bound. In *Saunders* v. *Anglia Building Society* (1970), for example, a 78-year-old lady who had lost her reading glasses was held bound by her signature on a document which had been prepared by a crook and had the effect of transferring her house to him. Since this case, to escape the binding nature of your signature you would need to prove that the document signed was radically different from the one thought to have been signed; secondly, that the signing had not been done negligently (carelessly); thirdly, that had the true contents of the document been known, it would not have been signed. The old lady in the case could have established this last one, but not the others. The document was not radically different and she had been careless in that she had signed without asking independent advice about the contents which she could not read.

It seems that to escape liability you have to be blind, illiterate and without a friend—as Byles J explained (in *Foster* v. *MacKinnon* (1869)):

> It seems plain on principle and on authority that if a blind man, or a man who cannot read or who for some reason (not implying negligence) forbears to read, has a written contract falsely read over to him, the reader misreading to such a degree that the written contract is of a nature altogether different from the contract pretended to be read from the paper which the blind or illiterate man afterwards signs; then, at least if there be no negligence, the signature so obtained is of no force. And it is invalid not merely on the grounds of fraud, where fraud exists, but on the ground that the mind of the signer did not accompany the signature; in other words, that he never intended to sign, and therefore in contemplation of law never did sign, the contract to which his name is appended.

In *Lloyds Bank* v. *Waterhouse* (1991) an illiterate father signed a guarantee for his son's debts to his bank, believing that it covered the purchase price of a farm. Actually it covered all his son's liabilities to the bank. This mistake was held to render the document sufficiently different from that which he thought he was signing and there was no evidence of negligence on the part of the father.

Mistakes about the identity of the other party

If someone makes a contract with you and he is lying about who he is, should it matter? Moreover, if he sells the goods he has obtained from you to an innocent third party, should you be able to recover the goods from that third party who bought them in good faith? The answer seems to be no. Unless you can prove that the identity of the other party to the contract was so important to you that you would not have sold to anyone else, then your mistake does not matter, even though it might have been induced by fraud. Naturally, if you can trace the other person before he has time to sell the goods on, then you can recover them because of the fraud (misrepresentation which we will examine soon), but not because of the mistake alone. You would probably have sold to anyone who appeared to be able to pay you. It was really a mistake about creditworthiness not identity that has left you with a useless cheque, no goods and little hope of catching the crook.

The courts have had to deal with such cases. An example is *Lewis* v. *Averay* (1972) where the crook pretended to be Richard Greene, the actor (who used to play Robin Hood on television). A car was sold for a cheque with a film studio pass as evidence of identity. It was sold on to a student before the cheque bounced. The original owner sued the student to get the car back. He lost. He had to establish that the contract between himself and the crook was spoilt (made void) by his mistake, thereby preventing the ownership passing to the student on the second sale; that he had not parted with ownership, and so the crook could not sell it to the student. He failed. Lord Denning said:

> When a dealing is had between a seller like Mr Lewis and a person who is actually there present before him, then the presumption in law is that there is a contract, even though there is a fraudulent impersonation by the buyer representing himself as a different man than he is. There is a contract made with the very person there, who is present in person. It is liable no doubt to be avoided for fraud, but it is still a good contract under which title will pass unless and until it is avoided.

There have been cases where the identity of the other party to the contract has been recognised as having been essential to the contract. They are rare, and often criticised, because innocent third parties lose out. Such a case was *Cundy* v. *Lindsay* (1878) where linen was sold to a rogue, through the post. He called himself 'Blenkiron & Co.' The sellers were able to satisfy the court that they would only have dealt with that company, and not with the rogue, whose name was Alfred Blenkarn. Lord Cairns said:

> How is it possible to imagine that in that state of things any contract could have arisen between the respondents and Blenkarn, the dishonest man? Of him they knew nothing, and of him they never thought. With him they never intended to deal. Their minds never, even for an instant of time rested upon him, and as between him and them there was no consensus of mind which could lead to any agreement or any contract whatever.

It is worth observing that this was not a contract made after 'face to face' negotiations, as was the case in *Lewis* v. *Averay* (1972).

Mistakes about the subject matter

If you are misled you may be able to complain, but if you are just mistaken about the quality of what you buy, then the basic rule is *caveat emptor* (let the buyer beware). However, mistakes about the identity of the subject matter are sometimes recognised. In *Raffles* v. *Wichelhaus* (1864), for example, there was an agreement made concerning a cargo aboard a ship called the *Peerless*. The fact that there were two ships of that name in the harbour at the time, and the parties were at cross purposes about which ship was meant, led the court to the conclusion that no contract had actually been made at all. The parties were never truly agreed.

If the parties were mistaken about the existence of the subject matter, then this would be an operative mistake, enabling the court to conclude that no contract had been made. So in *Strickland* v. *Turner* (1852), where an annuity was taken out upon the life of a man who was already dead at the time, the court held that no contract had been made at all.

Misrepresentation

We noted earlier in this chapter that it is not every statement made during pre-contractual negotiations that becomes a term of the contract. Those that do not are called representations. If a representation proves false, it might be actionable as a misrepresentation. It must, however, have been a statement of fact, not opinion or future intentions, etc. and it must have been relied upon to the extent that it induced the contract. It must have been taken seriously.

In *Bisset* v. *Wilkinson* (1972) the statement in question was held just to have been an opinion. The seller of land had stated that it would support 2000 sheep, but he had never used it for that purpose; so, as Sim J said:

> In ordinary circumstances, any statement made by an owner who has been occupying his own farm as to its carrying capacity would be regarded as a statement of fact . . . This, however, is not such a case . . . In these circumstances . . . the defendants were not justified in regarding anything said by the plaintiff as to the carrying capacity as being anything more than an expression of his opinion on the subject.

In *Redgrave* v. *Hurd* (1881) statements made about income misled a solicitor into believing that a place in a partnership was worth more than documents produced to him showed. They were statements of fact. They had induced the contract. On the other hand, in *Attwood* v. *Small* (1838) the prospective purchaser sent surveyors in to check the accuracy of statements the seller had made about a mine. They were statements of fact too, but, obviously, they had not been relied upon.

Sometimes you can be liable for misrepresentation if you say nothing. Silence can amount to statements of fact. When completing a proposal for life assurance, for example, if you are silent about your fits and three dozen heart attacks, it amounts to misrepresentation.

Such contracts are called *uberrimae fidei* (of the utmost good faith). There is a duty to disclose all relevant facts in such contracts.

When a court allows you to plead your mistake the contract is void—it was not made—you were not truly agreed. When misrepresentation is the issue, the contract is valid but voidable at the option of the party misled. It is called a right to rescind the contract. It is a choice; if he wished he could continue with the deal. If the statement was made innocently, without fraud, and without negligence, then the court could grant the innocent party damages (money compensation), but this would be instead of rescission. If it had been an innocent but negligently made statement, damages are available as well as rescission. If it was fraudulent misrepresentation then the innocent party sues for deceit, which is a tort.

In *Royscot Trust Ltd* v. *Rogerson* (1991) it was settled that where the misrepresentation is negligent (i.e. under s.2(1) of the Misrepresentation Act 1967) or fraudulent, the measure of damages is based upon the principles of the tort of deceit rather than negligence. This means that all losses are recoverable, not just those which were reasonably foreseeable, as in negligence.

Rescission is a remedy from the area of law called Equity which we have noticed on several occasions already—particularly in Chapter 2. As an equitable remedy it is discretionary. It cannot be demanded. It will generally not be allowed after a long delay in applying for it (it looks as if the claimant has decided to carry on despite having been misled), nor if it would be unfair to an innocent third party (so in *Lewis* v. *Averay* (1972), above, the mistake was not allowed and nor was rescission because the car was in the hands of an innocent third party).

Some contracts contain exclusion clauses purporting to cover misrepresentation. The Misrepresentation Act 1967 (now amended by the Unfair Contract Terms Act 1977, which we met earlier in this chapter) says:

3 If a contract contains a term which would exclude or restrict—
   (*a*) any liability to which a party to a contract may be subject by reason of any misrepresentation made by him before the contract was made; or
   (*b*) any remedy available to another party to the contract by reason of such a misrepresentation,
   that term shall be of no effect except in so far as it satisfies the requirement of reasonableness as stated in section 11(1) of the Unfair Contract Terms Act 1977; and it is for those claiming that the term satisfies the requirement to show that it does.

So exclusion must be reasonable, and if the parties are not of equal bargaining power it is unlikely to be so.

Duress and undue influence

When negotiating a contract the parties must have been acting free of the threat of force (e.g. with a gun in one ear) and free of the unjustifiable influence of those who have power or authority over them. The use of threat of force is called duress and it prevents the formation of a contract, although some people argue that a contract is made but it is voidable. Undue influence does make contracts voidable. If the parties have a 'special relationship' (e.g. doctor and patient, solicitor and client, but not husband and wife—*Midland Bank* v. *Shepherd* (1988)) then any contract between them will be assumed to have been the result of undue influence, and therefore voidable—unless the stronger party can rebut the presumption. He might show, for example, that independent advice was taken by the weaker party. Where no such relationship exists undue influence must be proved. It will not be presumed.

This was discussed in the case of *Lloyds Bank* v. *Bundy* (1975) where an old man was freed of mortgages held by his bank on his house, his only asset. He had executed them in reliance on advice from his bank manager. Eventually the mortgages outweighed the value of the house. Lord Denning took the opportunity to review many of the earlier decisions in this area:

> Gathering all together, I would suggest that through all these instances there runs a single thread. They rest on 'inequality of bargaining power'. By virtue of it, the English law gives relief to one who, without independent advice, enters into a contract on terms which are very unfair or transfers property for a consideration which is grossly inadequate, when his bargaining power is grievously impaired by reason of his own needs or desires, or by his own ignorance or infirmity, coupled with undue influences or pressures brought to bear on him by or for the benefit of the other.

This fine general principle has been reconsidered and disapproved in the case of *National Westminster Bank* v. *Morgan* (1985) which concerned a mess of bank loans and mortgages. Mr Morgan's widow had executed a form of mortgage with her bank under what she claimed to be undue influence. The House of Lords disagreed, holding that before a transaction can be set aside by reason of undue influence, it has to be shown to be disadvantageous to the person influenced. Here it was not.

Tattered as the general principle of inequality of bargaining power may be in this context, it does still underpin much of the attitude of the law—especially the consumer law.

The impact of the *Morgan* decision seems likely to be widespread. There have been other cases which would repay study, both of which concern the alleged undue influence of a son over his parents. *Avon Finance* v. *Bridger* (1985) was heard before the *Morgan* case, but reported afterwards, whereas *Culdenell* v. *Gallon* (1986) comes after this important House of Lords ruling.

More recently still, *Barclays Bank plc* v. *O'Brien* (1993) shows a legal charge on a matrimonial home being set aside by the House of Lords in circumstances where the extent of the charge had been misrepresented by the husband to the wife, and the employee of the bank, contrary to his superior's instructions, failed to explain the transaction or to suggest that she take independent legal advice. The House of Lords in the later case of *CIBC Mortgages plc* v. *Pitt* (1993) took the same approach, that of considering the effect of the behaviour of the husband upon the contractual relationship between the wife and the creditor. In future, it seems that the treatment of cases such as these will depend upon considerations of notice, actual or constructive, of third party activity, although it appears from cases such as *Massey* v. *Midland Bank plc* (1995) and *Banco Exterior Internacional SA* v. *Thomas* (1997) that, providing the bank has good reason to believe that the wife has been properly advised by a solicitor, it need not enquire into the quality of the advice given.

Illegality

Some contracts are declared illegal by statute; some at common law have been declared illegal on the grounds of public policy by the judges over the years. As examples, agreements for the collective enforcement of conditions regulating the price at which goods may be sold (e.g. black lists) are illegal under the Resale Prices Act 1976, whereas agreements to commit a crime or a tort or fraud, to trade with the enemy in wartime, to prejudice international diplomacy, the administration of justice, or honesty in public life, to defraud the Inland Revenue or to promote immorality have all been declared illegal by judges.

When an illegal contract is made the general effects (with rare exceptions) are that neither party can take action upon it to force performance by the other and property transferred under such a contract cannot be recovered.

In *Parkinson* v. *College of Ambulance Ltd* (1925) one Colonel Parkinson placed £3000 into the coffers of a charity in return for the promise of a knighthood in the Honours List. No knighthood appeared. No money was refunded. The contract was 'prejudicial to honesty in public life' and illegal at common law. This case led to the passing of the Honours (Prevention of Abuses) Act 1925, which now governs the position.

Other contracts are not illegal but void of legal effect. The courts do not enforce rights and obligations in such deals. Again, they are identified by statutes and at common law. The Gaming Act 1845, s.18, says:

> All contracts or agreements, whether by parole or in writing, by way of gaming or wagering, shall be null and void; and no suit shall be brought or maintained in any court of law and equity for recovering any sum of money or valuable thing alleged to be won upon any wager or which shall have been deposited in the hands of any person to abide the event on which any wager shall have been made.

So losers cannot be made to pay, nor can stakeholders.

Void contracts at common law (declared so by the judges on grounds of public policy) include:

1 **Agreements to oust the jurisdiction of the courts** These are deals where the parties agree not to take disputes to court. The judges do not mind agreements to go to some form of arbitration before going to court—but agreements which seek to oust them altogether are simply ignored, and the complaining party is welcomed into court.
2 **Agreements prejudicial to the sanctity of marriage** These would include a promise to procure a marriage for a fee and other such deals. Incidentally the agreement to marry is no longer a contract (Law Reform (Miscellaneous Provisions) Act 1970, s.1(1)).

3 Contracts in restraint of trade These contracts are found in business where there seem to be good reasons for restricting an individual to trade freely. Where the restraint is regarded as reasonable by the courts (as between the parties and in the public interest) then they are allowed; but where they are held unreasonable (because they are too wide or last too long) then they are not allowed. They are void to start with; they remain so unless declared reasonable. Sometimes only part of a restraining clause will be declared reasonable and allowed. The other part is said to be severed from the contract. It has no effect. In *Goldsall* v. *Goldman* (1915), for example, the buyer of a business which made imitation jewellery sought to restrain the seller from selling such goods or real jewellery for two years within the United Kingdom and various other areas of the world. The restraint on imitation jewellery in the United Kingdom was held to be reasonable in the circumstances, but the restraint on other goods and overseas was not. It was therefore void.

These contracts in restraint of trade tend to fall into three categories:

1 between the buyer of a business and the seller;
2 between an employer and an employee, to stop him working for the competition; and
3 agreements (called solus ties) under which a garage or a public house might agree to take supplies from one petrol company or brewer in return for various financial advantages.

As examples of the employer-employee restraint consider the cases of *Fitch* v. *Dewes* (1921) where a solicitor was successfully restrained from working for another firm of solicitors within a seven mile radius of the town hall of Tamworth, and *Pearks* v. *Cullen* (1912) where a counterhand in a grocers in Southend was not restrained by the clause seeking to forbid employment for two years in any similar business within two miles of any of the chain of stores the company owned in which he had worked in the past twelve months. It was too much restraint. Validity seems to depend upon the importance of the employee and the trade the employer is trying to protect. From time to time we see entertainers and sportsmen bringing their contracts with their managers and promoters into court to have them tested for reasonableness of restraint. In *Watson* v. *Prager* (1991) for example, a three year tie to a man who was both the manager and promoter of a boxer might have been reasonable, but the option to renew it for a further three years made it unreasonable.

An interesting case on solus ties is *Esso* v. *Harper's Garage* (1968). Here there were two garages tied, one for four years and five months, the other for twenty-one years. The first was upheld as reasonable; the second was not reasonable; it was void.

Vagueness

The terms of a contract must be clear. The courts cannot enforce vague or ambiguous promises. Thus, in *Scammel* v. *Ouston* (1941), a statement that 'the balance of the purchase price can be had on hire purchase terms' was too vague to be enforceable. Similarly, it was held in *Walford* v. *Miles* (1992) that an agreement to negotiate only with one party (a 'lock out' agreement) without a time limit on those negotiations, is too vague to be enforced.

However, the courts are anxious to uphold a bargain whenever possible. So, if there is a way of clarifying uncertainty they will use it. In *Hillas* v. *Arcos* (1932) a vague term about an option to buy timber, which lacked such details as type and price, was clarified by reference to the previous course of dealings between the parties.

THE DISCHARGE OF CONTRACTS

Contractual liability does not go on forever. Contracts are brought to an end (discharged) in one of four main ways.

Performance

The contract ends when both parties have done as they agreed. I have paid, you have delivered. Our contract has been discharged by performance.

Obviously, the trouble starts where one party has not performed or he has tendered performance late when time was of the essence (i.e. an essential part of the agreement) of the deal, or has only partially performed. The general rule is that 'part performance is no performance'. That is, that in order to discharge the contract both sides must completely perform their side of the deal. It can be a harsh rule—as in *Cutter* v. *Powell* (1795) where a dead sailor's wife recovered nothing of her late husband's wages because he had died just before completing his voyage.

This rule has been mollified from time to time by the courts, in the interests of fairness, and several so-called exceptions now exist.

1 **Substantial performance** Where performance is nearly complete some payment is made to match the extent of the performance (on a basis called *quantum meruit* ('as much as he has earned'). One famous example is *Hoenig* v. *Isaacs* (1952) where a carpenter and decorator nearly completed a job, and did part of it badly. He was to be paid £750. He was awarded £750 less the cost of having the job put right—£56.

2 **Severable contracts** If a large contract can be seen as a series of smaller ones, for example instalment deliveries, then payment could be claimed (*quantum meruit* again) for the instalments actually delivered. Such a contract is sometimes called severable.

3 **Prevention** Obviously if the other party prevents full performance, then payment must be made for the performance achieved up to that time. The case of *Planche* v. *Colburn* (1831) involved an author commissioned to write a book about costume and ancient armour for a series called *The Juvenile Library*. He was to be paid £100. When the work was half-done the series was cancelled by the publishers. He recovered £50.

4 Part performance accepted If the other party accepts part performance (e.g. short delivery), then he must pay for what he has received.

Agreement

A contract is a creature of agreement. It can be discharged by agreement. The parties can just agree to end it. Technically this is binding because each side promises not to sue the other for breach. This compromises the necessary consideration.

There might be a slight problem, when one party has partly performed his side of the bargain. Here, the other party must compensate him in some way for what he has done before the contract can be discharged. This is called accord and satisfaction (i.e. agreement and compensation).

Breach

Any breach of contract qualifies the innocent party to recover damages. A serious breach will enable him to regard the contract as discharged and to regard himself as free of further obligations under it as well as claiming damages. Such a breach is a breach of condition. A condition, as has already been observed, is a major term in a contract. A warranty is not and its breach gives rise only to a claim for damages as compensation. A breach of warranty does not discharge the contract.

Frustration

If there is a period of time between formation and the date for performance then the contract could be discharged by frustration. It means supervening impossibility. For example:

1 The whole foundation of the deal may be destroyed: in *Taylor* v. *Caldwell* (1863) the music hall hired under the contract burnt down before the concert date. The contract was discharged.
2 The law might change: in *Re Shipton, Anderson and Co* (1915) the Army, Supply of Food, Forage and Stores Act 1914 had rendered the performance of the contract illegal. The contract was for wheat which had now been requisitioned because of the war.
3 Personal services may not be available: in *Condor* v. *Barron Knights* (1966) a drummer signed to play every night, but he fell ill. He could only play four nights each week. The contract was discharged.

However, increased difficulty or the prospect of loss on the deal cannot be enough. Performance must be made impossible by the unforeseen event. In *Davis Contractors* v. *Fareham UDC* (1956) the fact that shortage of materials and labour meant that the estate would cost the builders far more to build was not enough. In *Amalgamated Investment* v. *John Walker* (1976) a preservation order placed on a warehouse rendering a £1 750 000 development site worth only £200 000 did not discharge the liability to pay the contract price. (The order was issued the day after formation of the contract.)

REMEDIES FOR BREACH OF CONTRACT

Damages

The object of an award of damages is to put the parties where they could have been had the contract not been breached. In *Victoria*

Laundry v. *Newman* (1949) the breach was the late delivery of an extra boiler for the laundry. The loss claimed was two-fold. First the loss of extra business profit. Second the special loss of certain Ministry of Supply contracts. However, they had not told the boiler-makers about these special contracts. They would have been expected to foresee the loss of extra profits, but without information, they could not have been expected to foresee the further loss. Asquith LJ explained:

> It is well settled that the governing purpose of damages is to put the party whose rights have been violated in the same position, so far as money can do so, as if his rights had been observed . . . This purpose, if relentlessly pursued would provide him with a complete indemnity for all loss *de facto* resulting from a particular breach, however improbable, however unpredictable. This, in contract at least, is recognised as too harsh a rule. Hence, in cases of breach of contract the aggrieved party is only entitled to recover such part of the loss actually resulting as was at the time of the contract reasonably foreseeable as liable to result from the breach. What was at the time reasonably so foreseeable depends on the knowledge then possessed by the parties or, at all events, by the party who later commits the breach.

The rules about remoteness of damage emerged from a case called *Hadley* v. *Baxendale* (1854), where a replacement crankshaft for a mill was very late in being delivered. No damages were recovered because the carriers were unaware that no spare shaft was kept, and that the mill was at a standstill.

The plaintiff is always expected to keep his loss to a minimum (mitigate his loss). If I cancel my booking at your hotel you should at least try to relet, even at a lower rate. You can recover the difference from me later. It would amount to ordinary loss and have been reasonably foreseeable. Any extra loss could only be claimed if I had been made aware of the extra risk when we formed the deal.

In *The Heron II* (1967) a ship was chartered by the respondents to carry sugar. The ship arrived late and when the sugar was sold, because of a change in the market price, a poorer price was obtained. The House of Lords held that the fall in the market price was not too remote a consequence of the breach of contract in arriving late. Their Lordships suggested that the test for remoteness of damage should be 'real danger' or 'serious possibility' of the events occurring. Or the fact the respondents should have recognised a 'real danger' or 'serious possibility' of the price of sugar falling and so were liable for it.

Given that the object of awarding damages is to compensate the plaintiff not to punish the defendant, the measure of the money could be argued as reflecting: expectation loss (to put the plaintiff financially where he would have been if the defendant had performed the contract properly), reliance loss (to restore the plaintiff financially to the position he was in before he entered into the contract), and/or, and it has to be admitted, exceptionally, compensation for distress and disappointment, where the plaintiff is awarded damages to 'help him get over' what he has had to put up with as a consequence of the breach, such as a dreadful holiday (*Jarvis* v. *Swan Tours* (1973), *Jackson* v. *Horizon Holidays* (1975)).

An interesting combination of one principle—that the plaintiff should 'mitigate his loss' and thus not recover more than is reasonable, and another—that parties to a contract should perform what they bargained to do—is to be seen in *Ruxley Electronics & Construction Ltd* v. *Forsyth* (1995) where contractors had built a swimming pool to a maximum depth which was 9 inches shallower than that bargained for. The House of Lords, reversing the decision of the Court of Appeal, held that this defect did not affect the value of the pool. Furthermore, as the pool was still fit for its intended purpose, which included diving into the pool from the side, it was unnecessary to award the £21 560 claimed for reconstruction, so the only damages payable were £2500 for 'loss of amenity'. It was argued that here the higher figure (a 'cost of cure') would involve a 'consumer surplus' the rebuilding was not really necessary, and to permit such damages would be contrary to the principle that a plaintiff must mitigate his losses. But does this now mean that builders can cut costs and corners by missing the specifications in the knowledge that their liability will be minimal?

Other remedies

We have already met other remedies than just money compensation in Chapter 2. None can be demanded. Damages are available as a right. Only the amount (*quantum*) is open for discussion. Other remedies are from equity and therefore at the discretion of the court. They include:

1 **Specific performance**—to make me do what I promised (although it cannot be used to enforce personal services).
2 **Injunctions**—to stop me acting in breach of contract, like playing for another club when I have signed for you or, as in *Warner Bros.* v. *Nelson* (1937) where the actress Bette Davies was ordered not to breach her exclusive contract with the plaintiffs. Note here that specific performance would not have been available to make her act for the plaintiffs, but an injunction was granted to stop her acting for anyone else.
3 **Rescission**—which we considered with misrepresentation. It means undoing the contract and putting the parties (as far as possible) back in their precontractual position. Note the difference from the purpose of an award of damages.
4 *Quantum meruit*—where performance is rewarded according to worth—'as much as he has earned'.

With damages there are statutory time limits within which claims must be brought. For a simple contract this is six years; on a deed it is twelve years. Time runs from the cause of action arising or when the plaintiff ought reasonably to have realised it had arisen (Limitation Act 1980).

With equitable remedies there is less time for, as we have noted, 'delay defeats equity' (if in doubt *see* Chapter 2).

1 On 1st June, Susan wrote to Sam and offered him a full-time job, giving him seven days to accept. Having received the letter on 2nd June, Sam went on holiday for a week. He wrote accepting the job, posting his letter on 4th June, so that it was received by Susan on 6th June.

However, on 4th June, Susan had written to Sam cancelling her offer of the job. This letter reached Sam's home address on 5th June but was not seen by Sam until he returned home from his holiday on 9th June.

(a) Explain to Susan the difference between the normal rule on acceptance of an offer and the postal rules on acceptance. (*3 marks*)

(b) Explain whether Susan was legally bound to give Sam seven days to accept her offer. (*3 marks*)

(c) Advise Susan whether or not she has a binding contract with Sam. (*8 marks*)

(d) If Susan does employ Sam, what formalities will she need to satisfy concerning Sam's contract of employment? (*6 marks*)

SEG

2 In English contract law, not only does there need to be a genuine agreement supported by consideration, but the court has to be satisfied that the parties intended to create legal relations: in other words, that they intended their agreement to be legally binding.

State whether the courts would find such legal intention in the following examples, explaining your reasons.

(a) Arthur promises to pay his son, Julian, who is unemployed, £30 per week if he will continue to live at home. Later they argue and Arthur stops the payments. (*2 marks*)

(b) Sandra, a self-employed dressmaker, signs an agreement with a material supplier for the supply of rolls of cotton. The agreement contains this clause:

'This agreement is not entered into as a legal agreement and shall not be subject to legal jurisdiction in the courts.' (*2 marks*)

SEG

3 Contract

There are established rules in contract. One rule states that, if a minor enters into a contract to buy goods, that contract will only be binding if those goods are necessaries. Another rule states that a contract will only be binding if the parties intended to create legal relations.

The problem
Bernard, aged 17, agrees to buy his father's motor bike for £200 and to pay him back at £50 per month, starting at the end of the month. Bernard intends using the bike to travel to work instead of catching the bus. Before the end of the month, Bernard decides that he cannot afford to buy the bike.

(a) What is the legal significance of Bernard's age in this problem? (*8 marks*)

(b) Would your answer to (a) differ if there were no local bus service? Explain why. (*4 marks*)

(c) Will the fact that this agreement was made between father and son have any effect on whether the contract is legally binding?
Give your reasons. (*6 marks*)

(d) *Explain* why the law is reluctant to enforce agreements between members of a family. (*4 marks*)

(e) The aim of the law relating to minors' contracts is to protect the minor. Explain why this is so and say how well you think the law achieves this aim.
(*8 marks*)

SEG

4 There are established rules in contract. One rule states that a contract requires an offer by one party and an acceptance of that offer by the other. The law also distinguishes between an offer, which can be accepted, and an invitation to treat, which cannot. In addition, once the contract is entered into, only the two parties can sue or be sued under the contract.

In a contract for the sale or supply of goods or services, Parliament has passed a number of Acts, in 1979, 1982 and 1994, designed principally to protect consumers through the use of certain implied terms.

Following a breach of contract, an injured party will usually be entitled to sue for some form of remedy.

The Problem
Alma has gone shopping, looking for a birthday present for her husband Boris. In the window of the local camera shop, she sees a high quality camera priced at £25. Alma knows that the camera was priced at £250 last week.

Alma goes into the shop and insists on buying the camera for £25. The shop is reluctant to sell, pointing out that the price ticket was a mistake, but eventually the manager agrees to sell the camera at the price in the window.

Boris is happy with his birthday present until he tries to use the zoom facility on his camera which, unknown to Boris, does not work. Boris finishes the roll of film and Alma takes it to the local camera shop for developing.

The shop takes six weeks to develop the film because of a problem with its developing machine. This problem also leads to Boris' film being over-exposed and the pictures ruined.

Boris has since discovered the problem with the camera and returns to the shop to complain. However, the manager refuses to refund the cost of the camera, saying that it is the "manufacturer's fault". The manager also refuses to compensate Boris for the ruined photographs.

(a) (i) Explain and illustrate the difference between an offer and an invitation to treat. (*4 marks*)
    (ii) Discuss whether or not the shop was legally obliged to sell the camera for £25. (*4 marks*)

(b) Name the Act of Parliament which applies to the sale of a camera that does not work properly. Discuss how the Act could help the purchaser. (*4 marks*)

(c) Name the Act of Parliament that would apply to the six week delay in developing the film. Discuss how this Act would help the customer.
(*3 marks*)

(d) Name the Act of Parliament that would apply to the ruined photographs. Discuss how this Act would help the customer. (*3 marks*)

(e) Taking into account your answers to (b), (c) and (d), discuss whether:
   (i) Alms would have a right of action against the shop; (*3 marks*)
   (ii) Boris would have a right of action against the shop. (*3 marks*)

(f) (i) State the most likely remedy available in a case such as this. (*1 mark*)
   (ii) Name the court where this case would almost certainly be heard.
(*1 mark*)
   (iii) Comment on the advantages of using this court. (*4 marks*)

SEG Summer 1997 (Foundation)

5 There are established rules in contract. The law requires that both offer and acceptance must be communicated. An acceptance must conform exactly with the terms of the offer, otherwise it may well become a counter-offer.

Actual communication of acceptance is not required where the postal rules apply.

Where the plaintiff proves that the defendant is in breach of contract, the court will award a remedy. Possible remedies include an award of compensation or an order which requires the parties to carry out the terms of their contract.

The Problem
Alpha Co. Ltd (Alpha), knowing that Beta Co. Ltd (Beta) has previously expressed an interest in buying some of Alpha's machinery, writes to Beta offering to sell that equipment for £50 000.

Beta receives the letter the following day and is interested. Beta writes back expressing willingness to buy the equipment for £45 000.

Alpha replies saying that it is not prepared to sell at that price. Beta then writes, accepting Alpha's original offer, asking Alpha to confirm both price and delivery date 'in writing'.

Alpha writes to confirm both details, but the letter goes astray in the post.

Beta, not having heard from Alpha, assumes Alpha no longer wishes to sell and buys similar equipment from Ceta Co. Ltd.

Alpha is now claiming that it has a contract with Beta and is threatening to sue for breach of contract.

(a) Explain the legal implications of Beta's first letter indicating a price of £45 000. (*4 marks*)

(b) Explain what is meant by the postal rule as it applies to:
   (i) offers; (*2 marks*)
   (ii) a revocation of the offer; (*2 marks*)
   (iii) letters of acceptance. (*4 marks*)

(c) Comment on the appropriateness of the postal rule in a modern society.
(*4 marks*)

(d) Discuss whether or not, in the light of the facts given above, Alpha and Beta have a legally binding contract. (*6 marks*)

(e) What difference, if any, would it have made if Alpha and Beta had been communicating by fax? (*4 marks*)

(f) Alpha is threatening to sue Beta for breach of contract.
Assuming Alpha could prove a breach,

    (i) name two remedies from the court for which Alpha could apply;

                                        (2 marks)

    (ii) briefly discuss which remedy, of the two you have chosen, a court would be more likely to grant. *(2 marks)*

SEG Summer 1996 (Higher)

CHAPTER 14

The Consumer and the Law

The law often reflects the balance between competing interests, whether they are public or private. In the area of consumer protection, on the one hand there is the sanctity of freedom of contract and the right of tradesmen and retailers to get the best deal they can with the consuming public. On the other hand there is the need to protect the public from, e.g. defective products, unfair advertising and agreements which are too heavily biased in favour of the retailer.

Certain types of transactions are entered into by consumers every day—for example, the shopper visiting the supermarket to buy groceries, the handyman/woman who visits the DIY shop or car accessory shop, or the schoolboy who visits the sweet shop for a bar of chocolate. They all enter into contracts for the sale and supply of goods and, from a practical point of view, this is probably the most important type of contract. The basis of the contract is that money changes hands in return for the goods.

However, consumers may wish to acquire goods but do not have the immediate finance to pay for them. In recent years hire-purchase and other forms of credit buying have been an important feature of many consumer transactions. This is particularly true of the purchase of more expensive and long-lasting products. It is not unusual for a married couple, setting up home for the first time, to buy a suite of furniture, carpets, washing machine and other things on some form of credit terms.

These and other contracts have been taken away to some extent from the area of pure freedom of contract and *caveat emptor* (let the buyer beware). There have been several statutes passed over the years to regulate them.

Furthermore, there is sometimes felt the need to protect the consumer in a more general way than just by implying terms into his contracts. This has been regarded as best provided by the criminal law—and to some extent by the administrative law too. In this chapter we will look briefly at this consumer law — civil, criminal and administrative.

CIVIL CONSUMER LAW

Contracts for the sale of goods

These contracts contain express and implied conditions and warranties which are referred to as the terms of the contract. They set out the rights and obligations of the parties under the contract. So, for example, express terms are usually included in the contract by the parties themselves, whereas implied terms are often implied into the contract by statute, e.g. the Sale of Goods Act 1979.

Conditions

These are important contractual terms and a breach of them may enable the injured party to treat the contract as at an end. Often this means that the goods are returned to the seller and the buyer gets his money back. For example, on the sale of a car S says to B that the car is 1196cc and was made in 1995; if either of these statements is untrue there is a breach of an express term and an implied term—that the car will match its description.

Warranties

These are less important contractual terms and, in the event of a breach the buyer may be able to claim damages, e.g. the difference in value between what the buyer contracted for and what he actually got. For example, on the sale of the same car S says to B that it has been serviced in the last three months. If this statement is untrue there is a breach of warranty.

The retailer may attempt, in the contract, to exclude liability for breach of conditions or warranties whether express or implied. Because this would cause hardship to the consumer who may have no choice but to accept such an exclusion if he wishes to purchase the goods, protection has been given by both the common law and statute. This prevents the seller from including in contracts clauses which are very unfair to the consumer.

In *Karsales (Harrow) Ltd* v. *Wallis* (1956) the buyer saw a Buick car in excellent condition and entered into a hire purchase agreement to buy it. A week later the 'car' was delivered to his house. It had, in fact, been towed there; the tyres had been changed, the cylinder head removed and all the valves were burnt out. The car would not go. The contract contained a comprehensive exclusion of liability clause in favour of the seller (to the effect that he would not be liable for any defects howsoever caused). It was held by the Court of Appeal that the seller could not rely on the exclusion clause in the contract. The fact was that the buyer had agreed to buy a car and the sellers had agreed to sell him one. What was eventually delivered was not a car at all and there was such a complete breach of the contract that no exclusion clause could cover it.

THE SALE OF GOODS ACT 1979

More straightforwardly, there are terms implied, as we shall shortly see, into contracts for the sale of goods by the 1979 Act. In the last chapter we met the Unfair Contract Terms Act 1977. There we saw that, under s.6 of the 1977 Act, it is not possible to exclude these implied terms in a consumer sale. So the overall effect of the legislation is that the 1979 Act (only a consolidation of earlier measures and itself now amended) implies terms into contracts for the sale of goods, and the 1977 Act says that they stay there in consumer sales.

The 1979 Act deals mainly with rules governing the parties' obligations to each other and the transfer of the ownership of the goods. Contracts of sale are usually made without the need for any formal requirements, e.g. cash sale of goods in shops or food and drink sold in a restaurant.

The contract of sale is defined as

> a contract whereby the seller transfers or agrees to transfer the property in the goods to the buyer for a money consideration called the price.

This covers:

1 a sale—where ownership of the goods passes immediately to the buyer when he tenders the price (e.g. most transactions in shops);
2 an agreement to sell—where the parties agree that ownership is to pass in the future.

With certain exceptions the parties are free to make whatever sort of contract they wish. The obligations under the contract are largely a matter for the parties themselves to decide. In the absence of such express agreement the Act implies certain obligations.

The right to sell the goods

The implied terms form the cornerstone of consumer protection in the civil law. They come from sections 12–15 of the Act. Section 12 is concerned with the right of the seller to sell the goods. This is an obviously central part of the contract. The parties have made a deal whereby the seller will get the buyer's money ('a money consideration called the price') and the buyer in return will receive the ownership of the goods. Plainly then, the seller must have the right to sell them.

Section 12(1) of the 1979 Act states there is:

> an implied condition on the part of the seller that in the case of a sale, he has a right to sell the goods, and in the case of an agreement to sell, he will have such a right at the time when the property is to pass.

Therefore, if the seller has no right to sell the goods because, for example, they are stolen, he is in breach of this condition under the Act. In *Rowland* v. *Divall* (1923) a buyer who was sold a stolen car was held entitled to recover the full price from the seller when it had to be returned to its rightful owner.

Description

Next, there is implied a requirement that the goods will correspond with any description applied to them.

Section 13(1) states that:

> where there is a contract for the sale of goods by description there is an implied condition that the goods shall correspond with that description.

This applies to goods that are ordered from catalogues and brochures and to descriptions on the packaging of articles. There is a breach, for example, if the box refers to a blue double-size electric blanket, but when it's opened it contains a pink single-size blanket. In *Beale* v. *Taylor* (1967) a car was advertised as a white Herald Convertible 1961. It was purchased but the buyer later discovered that while the description fitted the rear end of the car it did not apply to the front. The seller was held to be in breach of the term implied by s.13. There does, however, need to be a sale by description. In *Harlingdon and Leinster Enterprises Ltd* v. *Christopher Hull Fine Art Ltd* (1990), a sale between dealers of a wrongly-attributed painting was held not to have been a sale sufficiently influenced by the description.

Quality and fitness for purpose

The requirement that the goods supplied under a contract should be of adequate, or in the terms used by the 1979 Act, 'satisfactory quality' lies at the very heart of civil consumer law. However, the matter is rarely as simple as this requirement.

If the contract is a private sale and the individuals are not contracting in the course of business then the Act implies no conditions on quality or fitness. An example would be a washing machine advertised in a local newspaper by a private seller and bought by a private buyer. This means that the maxim *caveat emptor* (let the buyer beware) applies, and it is up to the buyer to ask all the relevant questions to ensure that the goods work and will do the job required.

If, however, it is a business sale (e.g. between a retailer and a private individual, or between two retailers) then there is an implied condition as to quality and fitness for purpose.

S.14 (2) implies a term that where goods are sold in the course of a business the goods will be of satisfactory quality. (The word 'satisfactory' was introduced by the Sale and Supply of Goods Act 1994, replacing the Victorian expression 'merchantable'.)

S.14 2(A) provides that goods are of a satisfactory quality if they meet the standard that a reasonable person would regard as satisfactory, taking account of any description of the goods, the price (if relevant) and all other relevant circumstances.

S.14 2(B) states that the following (among other things) are, in appropriate cases, aspects of the quality of the goods:

- fitness for all the purposes for which goods of the kind in question are commonly supplied;
- appearance and finish;
- freedom from minor defects;
- safety;
- durability.

However, s.14 2(C) provides that the above does not extend to any matter making the goods of unsatisfactory quality:

1 which is specifically drawn to the buyer's attention before the contract is made;
2 where the buyer examines the goods before the contract is made, which examination ought to reveal; or

3 in the case of a contract for the sale by sample, which would have been apparent on a reasonable examination of the sample.

The quality of goods which a buyer is entitled to expect varies with all the circumstances. However, second-hand goods or goods bought in a sale must still comply with this condition though obviously they may be of lower quality than new or full-price goods.

In addition s.14(3) provides that:

> where the seller sells in the course of a business and the buyer expressly or by implication makes it known to the seller any particular purpose for which the goods are being bought, there is an implied condition that the goods supplied are reasonably fit for that purpose . . . unless the circumstances show that the buyer does not rely, or that it is unreasonable for him to rely, on the skill or judgement of the seller . . . .

Therefore if the buyer expressly or impliedly makes known to the seller the purpose for which he requires the goods the seller will be in breach of the section if he fails to supply goods that will fulfil that purpose. The more the buyer relies on the seller's skill and expertise the greater is the seller's responsibility.

However, in *Griffiths* v. *Peter Conway Ltd* (1939) the plaintiff bought a new tweed coat from the defendant. After wearing it for a while she developed a skin irritation, so she sued the defendant for breach of s.14(3). It was held that the garment was fit for its purpose for normal wear and as she had not made known to the seller that she had a sensitive skin and asked him to recommend a suitable coat, she was not able to sue.

On the other hand, in *Grant* v. *Australian Knitting Mills* (1936), Dr Richard Thorold Grant contracted dermatitis from a pair of woollen underpants. He was in bed for seventeen weeks, and, after a relapse, back in bed for a further five months. As Lord Wright said: 'he scratched the places till he bled'. It was established that the reaction was caused by a sulphite chemical which had been left in the wool, and unlike the idiosyncratic reaction of Mrs Griffiths, this chemical would have made anyone suffer. The pants were, clearly, not of the required quality.

Sale by sample

S.15(1) provides that:

> where goods are sold by sample, the bulk shall correspond with the sample and the buyer shall have a reasonable opportunity of comparing the bulk with the sample. Further, that the goods will be free from any defect which would make their quality unsatisfactory and which would not be apparent upon a reasonable examination of the sample.

This section applies, for example, to wallpaper, curtain material or a suit which may be ordered after looking at a retailer's pattern books.

In *Godley* v. *Perry* (1960) a boy was injured by a defective catapult purchased in a retail shop. The catapults had been bought by the retailer after being shown samples. It was held that the boy had a claim for breach of s.14(2) and (3) and the retailer had a claim against the wholesaler and the wholesaler against the importer for breach of s.15(2)(c). The boy, Nigel Godley, argued lack of quality in the toy, and the retailer and wholesaler argued that upon a reasonable examination of the sample provided of the toys, the defect was not visible. Edmund Davies J said, referring to the sale of a box of catapults to the retailer:

> I hold that this was indeed a sale by sample, and that the implied condition accordingly existed . . . That in breach of such condition, what I might call the accident catapult was so defective as to be unmerchantable is clear. Nevertheless, learned counsel ... submitted that a reasonable examination of the sample would have revealed its defects, and that accordingly no such condition could be implied . . . counsel demonstrated that by squeezing together the two prongs of the catapult in the hand they could be fractured, and further suggested that by holding the toy down with one's foot and then pulling on the elastic, its safety could be tested and, as I understand it, its inherent frailty would thereby inevitably be discovered. True, the potential customer might have done any of these things. He might also, I suppose, have tried biting the catapult, or hitting it with a hammer, or applying a lighted match to ensure its non-inflammability.

It was held that pulling back the elastic was a reasonable examination, and because that had not revealed the defect in the 'accident' catapult there had been a breach of the term implied by s.15(2)(c).

Ownership and risk Apart from implying terms into contracts for the sale of goods, the 1979 Act also provides for other matters which may not have been addressed by the parties in their pre-contractual negotiations. (In reality, of course, with consumer sales, such talks are often brief, to say the least!) One of these other aspects of the working of the Act concerns the important matter of the passage of the ownership of and the risk attached to the goods.

In a contract for the sale of goods it is important to know when the property in the goods passes from the seller to the buyer. With the passing of property often goes the passing of the risk of, e.g. the goods being destroyed or damaged. This means that with expensive items, the buyer would be well advised to insure against such a loss occurring. Generally, if the contract refers to a specific item (e.g. a particular car in a retailer's showroom) the property passes as soon as the contract is made. If, however, modifications have to be made to the goods the property passes only when this has been done and the buyer has been notified to this effect.

If the buyer takes goods on approval the property only passes to the buyer when he signifies to the seller his intention to keep the goods. If goods have not been set aside or specifically assigned to the buyer then property only passes to the buyer when this process has been completed.

If goods are sold by a seller who has no right to sell them, then he cannot give the buyer a good title to these goods. This is because the law states that no one can give what he does not have (*nemo dat quod non habet*). The strict application of this rule can therefore cause hardship to innocent buyers who purchase goods in good faith from sellers who may have no right to sell them. It is for this reason that a number of exceptions to the rule have developed where the innocent buyer will obtain a good title as against the true owner.

1 Estoppel. If the owner knows his goods are being sold by a seller without good title he will be prevented (estopped) from later denying the seller's right to sell.
2 Mercantile agent. If an owner deposits goods with a mercantile agent, whose ordinary business is to buy and sell goods, and the agent sells to an innocent buyer, the buyer obtains a good title.
3 Seller or buyer in possession. If a seller is allowed to retain possession of goods after a sale, and if he sells to a third party the third party obtains a good title. Likewise, if a buyer obtains possession of goods before he has paid for them, and if he sells them, the third party obtains a good title.
4 Seller with a voidable title. A sale by a seller with a voidable title (i.e. one which is valid until avoided) will give the buyer a good title provided that the title had not been avoided at the time of sale, and the buyer did not know of the defect in the title.
5 Motor vehicles subject to a hire-purchase agreement. A private buyer (not a motor trader) buying a motor vehicle which is subject to a hire-purchase agreement will obtain a good title to the vehicle if he had no knowledge of the agreement.

The rights of the parties

Once a contract for the sale of goods has been made the seller is under an obligation to deliver the goods. This can mean actual delivery or the buyer can be handed the means of access to the goods, e.g. the keys to a warehouse where the goods are stored. If the seller refuses to deliver the goods the buyer can:

1 sue for damages for any loss incurred by him arising out of the refusal; or
2 obtain an order for specific performance.

If the seller delivers the wrong goods then the buyer can accept or reject them as he sees fit. This right to reject the goods is very important for the buyer. If the goods do not match their description, or are not of satisfactory quality, and so on (i.e. if the implied terms which we discussed earlier have not been met by the seller), then his delivery cannot be a delivery of the correct goods, and the buyer can reject them (and probably obtain damages too, or at least a refund of the purchase price). However, this right to reject can be lost. It is lost where the buyer has accepted the goods (s.11(2)). But acceptance (s.35) does not always mean saying that the goods are all right. It can mean saying nothing—failing to exercise the right to reject the goods, for beyond a 'reasonable time'. So the unhappy consumer must act quickly or he will lose the right to reject. How long is a reasonable time? The question was asked, in *Bernstein* v. *Pamsons Motors* (1986), where a new car was driven for 143 miles. The engine seized up because of a manufacturing defect. The engine was replaced, but the buyer wanted to reject the car. Mr Justice Rougier refused him that right. He held that using the car for three weeks, driving it for the sole purpose of testing it out, for 143 miles, amounted to acceptance. He was allowed the costs involved in getting around while the car was repaired, but not to reject it.

If the buyer refuses wrongfully to accept delivery of the correct goods then he can be sued for damages. If the ownership of the goods has passed to the buyer and he refuses to pay then he can be sued for the price of the goods.

An unpaid seller may not have parted with possession of the goods when he learns of the buyer's refusal to pay the contract price. In this situation the seller has:

1 **a lien for the price** This means the seller can retain possession of the goods until he is paid;
2 **a right of stoppage in transit** This means that if the goods are in the process of being delivered to the buyer, the seller can stop them and retain possession until paid.

The Sale of Goods Act 1979, s.19, allows a seller to 'reserve the right of disposal' of the goods. This could enable him to recover possession of goods even if they have been delivered to the buyer if he has not been paid. However, since the *Romalpa* case (1976) it has been possible by including an appropriately worded clause in the contract of sale, for the seller to recover any goods still in the buyer's possession and the proceeds of any sales of the goods that have taken place. It meant that the property in the goods was not to pass to the buyer until the seller had been paid. The goods could be sold on but the second buyer was to regard the proceeds of sale as belonging to the unpaid seller.

The Consumer Protection Act 1987, Part 1

Apart from arguing upon a breach of contract as under the Sale of Goods Act as in terms of negligence (*see* Chapter 12), a consumer who can establish that a defendant produced (or imported into the European Community or is an own brander or seller with inadequate records of his own supplies) the product which caused his injury because it was defective, then a claim can be made under the Consumer Protection Act 1987, Part I. This combines the best of contract law (strict liability, no need to prove fault, with the best of the tort of negligence, protection for third parties and bystanders). However, life is rarely as rosy as it seems. There are significant defences which may prove to dilute this new protection. A clear candidate is the 'state of the art' defence in CPA s4. (CPA Part I constitutes the UK's implementation of the European Community Directive on liability for defective products.)

BUYING GOODS ON CREDIT

There are many ways in which a consumer can obtain credit. He may seek a loan or overdraft facilities from his bank, large stores may have their own credit arrangements or he may use his credit card, e.g. Barclaycard and Access. Or he may enter into a credit arrangement that takes one of the three following forms.

Hire-Purchase Agreement

regulated by the Consumer Credit Act 1974

This agreement sets out the terms on which you (the customer) agree to buy on hire purchase from us (the suppliers) the goods which are listed below

The customer

Full name

Address

The suppliers

Name

Address

List of goods
including details of any defects   £ | p

Total cash price of goods
including VAT at _____ %

  Take away total of part exchange £

  and cash deposits £

    total £

Balance of cash price/Amount of credit

Add total charge for credit

Annual percentage rate _____ %

Balance of total amount payable

Total amount payable
(includes total of part exchange and cash deposits)

Terms of payment for the balance of the total amount payable

_____ payments of £ ____ per _____

payable on the _____ day of each

starting _____ 19 ____

(and one final payment of £ ____ one ____ after)
Cross out if unnecessary

1 Termination: your rights
You have a right to end this agreement If you wish to do so, you should write to the person authorised to receive your payments We will then be entitled to the return of the goods and to half the total amount payable under this agreement, that is £
If you have already paid at least this amount plus any overdue instalments, you will not have to pay any more, provided you have taken reasonable care of the goods

2 Repossession: your rights
If you fail to keep your side of this agreement but you have paid at least one third of the total amount payable under this agreement, that is £
we may not take back the goods against your wishes unless we get a court order (In Scotland we may need to get a court order at any time) If we do take them without your consent or a court order, you have the right to get back all the money you have paid under the agreement

3 Important — you should read this carefully
 Your rights
The Consumer Credit Act 1974 covers this agreement and lays down certain requirements for your protection which must be satisfied when the agreement is made If they are not, we cannot enforce the agreement against you without a court order

The Act also gives you a number of rights You have a right to settle this agreement at any time by giving notice in writing and paying off all amounts payable under the agreement which may be reduced by a rebate

If you would like to know more about the protection and remedies provided under the Act, you should contact either your local Trading Standards Department or your nearest Citizens' Advice Bureau

4 By signing this agreement you are declaring that
● Your name and address shown on the left are correct,
● You have read and understood the terms of the agreement on the back,
● Any information that you may have given us is correct,
● You realise that we may rely upon that information to decide whether we should make this agreement

> This is a Hire-Purchase Agreement regulated by the Consumer Credit Act 1974 Sign it only if you want to be legally bound by its terms
>
> Signature of Customer(s)
>
> The goods will not become your property until you have made all the payments You must not sell them before then

Signature of witness

Address of witness

Occupation of witness

Signature by or on behalf of the suppliers

Date which shall be treated as the date of this agreement

➤ please turn over for the terms of this agreement

Hire purchase agreement; written and designed by the Plain English Campaign (Tel. 01663 734541)

Hire-purchase

This is a contract of hire which gives the hirer an option to purchase the goods at the end of the period of hire. (It is a bailment of goods with an option to buy.) During the hiring the purchase price plus interest is paid by instalments. The hirer has no right to sell the goods to a third party before all instalments have been paid. Therefore, the third party obtains no title to the goods except under Part III of the

Terms of the agreement

1 Payment for the goods

You agree to make the payments as shown overleaf to us or to our representatives. If you fall behind with the payments we have the right to charge daily interest, equivalent to the annual percentage rate shown overleaf, on all payments in arrears. Interest can be charged before and after any court judgment.

If you pay by post you do so at your own risk.

The word 'goods' includes any replacements, renewals or additions which we may make.

2 Who owns the goods?

The goods will belong to you only when you have made all the payments.

3 Selling or disposing of the goods

You may not sell or dispose of the goods and you may only part with the goods to get them repaired. You may not sell or dispose of your rights under the agreement. You may not use the goods as security for a loan or for some other form of credit.

4 Repair of the goods, insurance and licensing

You must keep the goods in good condition and repair. You must not take them apart. You are responsible for all loss or damage to them except fair wear and tear. You must insure the goods against loss or damage. You must get any licence for the goods required by law.

5 Change of address

You must tell us within 14 days if you change your address.

6 Our right to inspect the goods

You must allow us or our representatives to inspect the goods at all reasonable times.

7 Your right to end the agreement

You can end the agreement by the method shown in paragraph 1 overleaf. You must then return the goods to us at your own expense.

8 Our rights to end the agreement

We may end the agreement, after giving any written notice required by law, if

- You fail to keep any part of the agreement,
- You commit an act of bankruptcy (such as failing to pay a debt as ordered by a court), or
- You have given false information in connection with this agreement.

If we end the agreement, you immediately lose your right to possess the goods.

Instead of ending the agreement, we may take back the goods, but we will need a court order once you have paid at least one third of the total amount payable under this agreement (see paragraph 2 overleaf).

If we end the agreement or take back the goods you will have to bring your payments to half the total amount payable under this agreement (see paragraph 1 overleaf).

9 Automatic end of the agreement

This agreement, and your right to possess the goods, will end automatically if a landlord of the premises where the goods are kept threatens, or takes any step, to take them to satisfy a debt.

10 Our expenses

You must repay our expenses and legal costs for the following

- Finding you if you have changed address without notice, or finding the goods,
- Taking steps, including court action, to recover the goods or to obtain payment for them.

11 Relaxing the terms of the agreement

If we temporarily relax the terms of the agreement, we may at any time decide to enforce the terms strictly again.

12 Our right to assign the agreement

We may allow another person to take over our part of the agreement. That person will then take over all our rights and responsibilities under this agreement.

13 More than one hirer

If two or more people are named as the customer, the liability of each shall be joint and several. This means that each person can be held fully responsible for all the responsibilities set out in this agreement.

Hire purchase agreement continued

Hire-Purchase Act 1964 where the hirer sells a motor car to an innocent private purchaser.

Suppose, for example, that A wishes to buy a car from a garage. He asks for credit and completes a proposal form supplied by a finance company. The garage offers to sell the car to the finance company. If the finance company accepts both transactions it will buy the car from the garage and also enter into a contract with A to supply the car on instalment credit terms.

Credit sale

This is a contract for the sale of goods which means that in return for the price the seller promises to transfer to the buyer the property (i.e. the ownership) in the goods. The buyer will be entitled to take possession (i.e. delivery of the goods) immediately. The ownership will usually transfer to the buyer at or before the time he takes delivery. Therefore, if the buyer sells the goods he will be selling his own goods and the person buying them will have a good title (i.e. ownership) to them. It is a sale of goods with time to pay.

Conditional sale

This is also a contract for the sale of goods where the buyer takes possession immediately. However, the property (i.e. the ownership) in the goods does not transfer to the buyer until a condition has been fulfilled. This condition is usually that the buyer must complete the payment of all instalments under the agreement. Therefore, although the buyer obtains possession of the goods, until he has paid all the instalments the property (i.e. the ownership) of the goods remains with the seller. This means, in most cases, that a good title cannot be obtained by a third party if the goods are sold by the buyer prior to this date, except under Part III of the Hire-Purchase Act 1964, which as we have seen, concerns motor vehicles sold to private individuals.

The Consumer Credit Act 1974

All consumer credit agreements have now been brought within one statute, the Consumer Credit Act 1974. The aim of the statute is to provide reasonable protection for consumers. This aim is achieved in several ways:

1 it regulates the formation, terms and enforcement of credit agreements;
2 anyone engaged in the consumer credit business must be licensed to carry on the business;
3 an advertisement for credit must show the true cost of the credit;
4 restrictions are placed on door-to-door selling on credit; e.g. salesmen selling double-glazing on credit need to be licensed;
5 it creates new criminal offences, e.g. trading without the necessary licence;
6 it makes it impossible to contract out of the provisions of the Act.

The Act applies to 'consumer credit agreements'. These are defined in s.8 as credit agreements made between an individual (the 'debtor') and any other person (the 'creditor') by which the creditor provides the debtor with credit not exceeding £15 000. The term 'individual' includes partnerships and unincorporated bodies but not companies.

Credit agreements include hire-purchase agreements, conditional sale agreements, credit sale agreements, credit card agreements, loan agreements and bank overdraft agreements. In the Act these are all trading check and trading voucher agreements. In the Act these are all referred to as 'regulated agreements' and they must comply with the provisions of the Act and the regulations made under it. Not included within the definition are ordinary hire agreements where the hirer never becomes the owner of the goods, e.g. television rentals. Hire agreements are, however, covered by certain provisions of the Act.

Making a regulated agreement

This is made like any other form of contract. It is usually in writing, often using a standard form provided by the creditor. Certain formal requirements must be complied with to ensure that the debtor (customer) is aware of the nature and full cost of the transaction and that he has a copy of the final written agreement. These formalities are:

1 information on:
   (a) the total charge for credit;
   (b) the true annual percentage rate of charge (the APR);
   (c) the price for which goods could be bought for cash;
2 provision of a full and detailed written agreement covering all the terms of the agreement;
3 signature of the agreement by the debtor and credit should only take place when the agreement has been completely filled in;
4 the debtor must receive a copy of the agreement.

In the event of failure to comply with these formalities the creditor will not be able to enforce the agreement without seeking an enforcement order from the court; the county court is the usual place for these cases.

Cancellation of a regulated agreement

This covers mainly agreements made as a result of door-to-door salesmanship or agreements signed away from the creditor's business premises after 'oral representations' (sales chat), e.g. in the debtor's own home. To exercise his right of cancellation the debtor must send a written notice to this effect to the creditor within five days of receiving either his copy of the agreement or a notice of his cancellation rights.

The effect of cancellation is that the transaction is without effect and the debtor is entitled to the return of any deposit or the return of any goods traded in part-exchange. In return the debtor must either return the goods or make them available for collection by the creditor. (Incidentally, this right to cancel was extended in 1988 to cover cash sales, over £35. The consumer protection is broadly the same. The cooling off period is seven days. The new law came with the implementation of a European Community Directive on doorstep selling.)

Liability of the creditor

In a hire purchase agreement it is the creditor (i.e. usually a finance house) and not the dealer (e.g. the garage who sold the car) who will be liable if there is a breach of any of the conditions and warranties implied by the Supply of Goods (Implied Terms) Act 1973. Any attempt to exclude liability for such breaches would be ineffective.

These terms closely resemble those implied into contracts for the sale of goods by the 1979 Act. With credit sales and conditional sales the liability for breach of contract and misrepresentation is shared between the finance house and the dealer, under the Consumer Credit

Act 1974, ss.56, 75—provided that the finance house and the dealer had a 'business link' (e.g. Access and a shop with an 'Access accepted here' sign in the window).

Termination of regulated agreements

If the debtor is in breach of the agreement, e.g. through failure to pay instalments, then the creditor may wish to terminate the agreement. To do this, under s.87 of the Act he must first serve a default notice setting out:

1 the amount required to bring payments up-to-date;
2 the time by which payments must be made (subject to a minimum of seven days);
3 the consequences of failure to comply with the notice;
4 the provision of the agreement under which the agreement can be terminated;
5 the fact that if the breach is remedied the agreement will not be terminated.

If the notice is not complied with the creditor can exercise his right to terminate the agreement. The consequences of termination are:

1 the creditor may be able to recover possession of the goods unless it is a hire-purchase agreement and the debtor has already paid a third of the total price of the goods. Here the goods should not be taken without an order from the county court. They are called 'protected goods';
2 the creditor may be able to claim further sums of money from the debtor. These may be either damages or an amount stipulated in the agreement which is payable on termination.

Recovery of goods by the creditor

If an agreement is terminated the creditor is entitled to recover possession of the goods. However:

1 the creditor cannot, without the debtor's permission, or an order from the county court, enter premises to repossess the property;
2 if the goods are 'protected goods' then, unless the debtor is prepared to hand them over a court order is again necessary to repossess them. Goods become 'protected' when one-third of the payments due under the agreement have been made.

It is always open to the court on the application for a possession order by the creditor to make a 'time order' giving the debtor more time to pay.

Money claim by the creditor

In addition to claiming recovery of the goods the creditor may also be entitled to:

1 damages for repudiation of the contract by the debtor which aim to put the creditor in the position he would have been in if the contract had been completed;
2 the arrears in instalments plus any damages for the debtor's failure to take reasonable care of the goods;

3 a minimum payment stipulated in the contract provided it is not excessive in the light of the circumstances of the case.

Powers of the court

The court may make the following orders:

1 a time order giving the debtor extra time to pay;
2 a return order ordering the debtor to return the goods to the creditor;
3 a transfer order allowing the debtor to return part of the goods and allowing him to keep the other part.

Debtor's right of termination

Section 99 gives a debtor under a regulated hire-purchase or conditional sale agreement a statutory right of termination. He should give notice, in writing, of his intention to terminate, usually to the creditor. When the debtor has exercised his right of termination he has to return goods which are not protected goods. He must also pay:

1 any loss caused by his failure to take reasonable care of the goods; plus
2 all arrears due; plus
3 a sum sufficient to bring his payments up to half of the total price.

These are serious consequences for the debtor. Usually he would be better off agreeing to re-schedule his payments to the creditor.

The 1974 Act in general

The Consumer Credit Act 1974 is a long and complicated statute, but its aim is simple: 'truth in lending'. It is based on the Report of the Crowther Committee in 1971 which pointed out that:

> The use of consumer credit . . . enables individuals to enjoy the services of consumer durable goods sooner than they otherwise would and in a period of inflation offers them a real prospect of acquiring them more cheaply . . . Furthermore, some individuals, who lack the self-discipline to save up for the purchase of a consumer durable good but are nevertheless unlikely to break their contract with a creditor, are able to buy a consumer durable good which might otherwise never be theirs.

On the other hand, these days inflation is not as rampant as it has been, and the prospect of redundancy haunts the workforce. Credit is easy to obtain. Every year the Citizens' Advice Bureaux around the country report that the number of people in serious financial difficulties has increased. The old ideas of saving up and not buying what you cannot afford have been replaced with slogans like 'take the waiting out of wanting'. Some argue that a central registry of indebtedness might make things easier—enabling prospective creditors to check on the existing commitments of their prospective debtors. Others, hardly surprisingly, counter that this smacks of 'Big Brother', that it is too patronising, and that people should be allowed to choose for themselves whether they take on a credit agreement.

CRIMINAL CONSUMER LAW

Since the nineteenth century the criminal law has attempted to protect consumers by imposing sanctions for the breach of statutory obligations placed upon manufacturers and retailers. These obligations cover a wide range of activities, from maintaining high standards of public safety and hygiene to ensuring that weighing and measuring equipment for the sale of goods (e.g. a petrol pump,) is accurate. Prosecutions are normally brought by public officials, e.g. environmental health officers or trading standards officers, employed by local authorities. These prosecutions often arise from routine checks carried out by the officers or from complaints from consumers. Although the outcome of a successful prosecution is usually a fine, the criminal court may award compensation to the consumer for any personal injury, loss or damage resulting from the offence (Powers of Criminal Courts Act 1973, s.35). It should also be borne in mind that consumer protection may be afforded by the criminal law in an indirect way, e.g. imposing sanctions under the Theft Act 1968 for deception practised on a consumer. The following four sections deal with statutes which are of particular importance in protecting the consumer.

The Trade Descriptions Act 1968

It is an offence under the 1968 Act for any person, in the course of trade or business:

1 to apply a false trade description to goods (s.1); or
2 to supply, or offer to supply, goods with such a description (s.1); or
3 knowingly or recklessly to make a false statement as to the provision of any services, accommodation or facilities (s.14). (This offence, unlike the others, is not an offence of strict liability.)

For the avoidance of doubt (as lawyers say!), we will look a little more closely at some of this terminology.

False trade description

A trade description is an indication of any of the following:

1 quantity, size or gauge;
2 method of manufacture, production, etc.;
3 composition;
4 fitness for purpose, strength, performance, behaviour or accuracy;
5 physical characteristics not included above;
6 testing and the results thereof;
7 approval by any person or conformity with an approved type;
8 place or date of manufacture, production, etc.;
9 person by whom manufactured, produced, etc.;
10 other history, including previous ownership or use.

The description must be 'false to a material degree'. This means that it must have been capable of inducing the sale or supply of the goods. The meaning to be attributed to the description is essentially decided by considering its likely effect on the ordinary man, e.g. a 'beautiful' car has been held to indicate both its appearance and its running order.

The indication of the above matters may be either direct or indirect, and by any means. Thus oral representations, advertisements, mileometer readings, etc. are all capable of being trade descriptions. Indeed consumers in Britain are conned out of £100 million each year by those who 'clock' cars!

Sale or supply

The offence under s.1 of the 1968 Act is committed either by applying the false trade description of goods, or supplying, or offering to supply, goods to which such a description has been applied. Thus, if a manufacturer applies a label describing his sweaters as 'all wool' and this is untrue, both he and the retailer who sells these sweaters still bearing this label commit an offence. Even if the sweaters were not sold but merely displayed in the retailer's shop there would be liability, as exposing goods for supply is deemed by the Act to be an 'offer' to supply (s.6); it is not an invitation to treat as in the law of contract (*see* Chapter 13).

False statements as to services

There can be no liability under the Act of 1968, s.14, unless, at the time the statement was made, it was false and the defendant knew it, or was reckless as to whether it was false. Therefore a holiday brochure published at a time when the services advertised do not exist is an offence (as in *Wings* v. *Ellis* (1984), as is confirmation of an airline reservation when no seat was available owing to the airline's overbooking policy as in *Taylor* v. *British Airways Board* (1976).

The section does not apply to promises about future services only.

Defences

A person will have a defence to a charge under s.1 if he indicates by a disclaimer that the consumer should place no reliance on the trade description, e.g. a notice stating that the reading on a car's mileometer should not be taken as indicating its true mileage (unless he 'clocked' the car himself). It is also a defence to a charge of supplying goods with a false trade description for the defendant to show that he did not know, and could not with reasonable diligence have ascertained, that the goods did not conform to the description or that the description had been applied to them. As regards s.14 a trader will have a defence if he neither possessed the required knowledge nor was reckless at the time of the alleged offence. In addition to these defences there is a defence of general application contained in s.24. Under this section the trader can defend himself if *he* can prove that the offence was caused by:

1 his mistake; or
2 reliance on information supplied to him; or
3 the act or default of another person; or
4 an accident; or
5 some other cause beyond his control, and in any event that he took all reasonable precautions and exercised all due diligence to avoid the commission of the offence by himself or any person under his control.

An early, but very important illustration of the effect of s.24 is *Tesco* v. *Natrass* (1972). Here a branch of the famous supermarket chain had advertised washing powder at a discounted price. However, all the cut price packs had been sold, and the shelves inside the shop were stocked with packs at the full price. The manager had signed the 'special offers' book as if nothing were amiss. The company was prosecuted for the now repealed and replaced (by CPA 1987 Part III) offence, within s.11, of advertising goods at a price at which they were not prepared to sell them. They raised the defence 'act or default of another' (i.e. of the manager) and gave the necessary seven days' notice to the prosecution. The defence was successful. The firm had organised a suitable chain of command, and a system of control. It had taken 'all reasonable precautions and exercised due diligence' to avoid committing an offence. In *Harley* v. *Martinez & Co.* (1990) it was accepted as reasonable for a small wine retailer to rely on the information supplied by German producers about the alcohol content of wine.

The Consumer Protection Act 1987

Part II of this Act empowers the Secretary of State to make regulations concerning the safe design, construction, manufacture, assembly and packaging of products. Its aim is to try to ensure that consumer products are designed and built to high safety standards, e.g. that electrical appliances do not electrocute consumers.

The marketing of unsafe products may be prevented by the Secretary of State issuing:

1 a prohibition notice, which is a particular ban relating only to the trader upon whom it is served;
2 a notice to warn, which applies to the particular trader served and, unlike the above, concerns goods which he has already supplied. The notice can require the trader to publish a warning about unsafe products, e.g. an advertisement warning purchasers of a particular make of car that it has defective brakes which should be checked by the dealer.

Contravention of safety regulations or a notice to warn is a crime.

This Act is unusual among the criminal statutes giving consumer protection, in that it confers a specific civil remedy on an injured party. Thus he may bring an action for damages against a trader who has infringed a safety regulation or a prohibition order. There is no need to prove negligence and the right of action cannot be excluded by any exemption clause.

So it was that the Secretary of State issued the Scented Erasers (Safety) Order 1984 as a result of considerable concern in the media about pencil erasers in the shape of sweets, coke bottles and the like (based, as it turned out, on little or no evidence of injury). Indeed, this order was made under emergency provisions in the now repealed and replaced 1978 Act which were designed to enable swift action in the face of imminent danger. This step was challenged by a wholesaler, Ian Kynaston Ford, who had only 3 million erasers in stock (having distributed 4 million of them in 1982). The challenge failed (*R.* v. *Secretary of State for Trade and Industry, ex parte Ford* (1984)). Such orders as this last for a year. Within this time it is thought either that the danger will go away, be negotiated away, or regulations can be drawn up to cater for it. This order was replaced with the Food Imitations (Safety) Regulations 1985, which have subsequently been amended so as to exclude those products which are actually made from food!

Interestingly, the regulations do not ban the sale of pencil erasers that look and/or smell like food (pineapple and strawberry are popular smells). They control the minimum size that these things must be (40 mm), obviously, to try to ensure that small children will not manage to swallow them; meanwhile larger children and adults with strange tastes are still able to buy them. Not to mention the interests of the manufacturers and sellers.

In 1986 a private member's Bill, introduced by Conal Gregory, became the Consumer Safety (Amendment) Act 1986. This Act was also consolidated by the Consumer Protection Act. It provided for closer liaison between the Customs and Excise and trading standards officers to help keep rubbish out of the country, and for 'suspension orders' to be served on traders to keep it away from consumers if it gets past the border. These orders last six months. If they are wrongly imposed compensation can be ordered. This 1986 Act implemented most of the proposals set out in a White Paper published in 1984. It did not, however, include a 'general duty' on traders to deal only in safe goods. Consumer safety regulation is piecemeal and reactive. Nevertheless, just such a general safety duty is included in the Consumer Protection Act. This provides a safety net for the consumer who is injured by products which are unsafe but which do not happen to be covered by specific safety regulations. Before the introduction of the general safety duty the manufacturer whose products were not specifically regulated was freed of criminal consumer law. Now this is no longer so. If a product is supplied which does not comply with generally accepted safety standards, then that amounts in itself to an offence. This idea has been further extended by the General Product Safety Regulations 1994 implementing a European Directive (92/59 1992) which seeks to harmonise a system of consumer product safety across the Member States, including channels of communication, to protect consumers across the European Union from the dangers of unsafe products. This generality in the definition of criminal consumer law offences is visible once more in Part III of CPA which makes it a crime to give a false or misleading price indication. The generality is partially clarified with a code of practice—a non-statutory guide to 'good pricing policy and practice'.

The Unsolicited Goods and Services Act 1971

We met this statute in Chapter 13, when considering the rules about communication of acceptance in the formation of contracts. This statute is designed to prevent inertia selling, i.e. unordered goods sent to the consumer with the implication that he is expected to pay for them. The Act provides that six months after such receipt the goods are deemed to belong unconditionally to the recipient. If the recipient does not want to wait six months, he may send a written notice to the sender asking him to remove the goods. If thirty days elapse and the goods are not removed, they belong to the recipient.

The Act also contains criminal sanctions which are confined to persons acting in the course of a trade or business. It is an offence for such persons to demand payment for unsolicited goods without reasonably believing in a right to payment. In such cases it is also an offence:

1 to assert a right to payment; or
2 to threaten legal proceedings; or
3 to place, or threaten to place, the consumer's name on a default list; or
4 to invoke, or threaten to invoke, any other collection procedure.

The Consumer Credit Act 1974

As was noted above, this Act established a licensing system for those involved in the 'consumer credit industry'. To trade without the licence you need is a criminal offence. There are six classes of licence which were designed to encompass the whole of the credit industry. It has been difficult to operate the system. Hundreds of thousands of licences have been issued, all requiring some sort of supervision. Instead of increasing resources to handle the increasing workload, it has been suggested that the classes of traders requiring licences (showing them to be fit and proper persons) be reduced. This would undo much of the framework of protection which has been built up over the years since the Crowther Report was published, floodlighting the consumer credit jungle.

ADMINISTRATIVE CONSUMER LAW

As we have seen, the civil and criminal law together provide a framework of protection for the consumer. However, there remain certain traders who regard civil court judgments as a minor inconvenience and fines from criminal courts as something like a business expense. There have been instances in the past where the Attorney-General has acted against such people, as in *Attorney-General* v. *Harris* (1961) where a husband and wife had 237 convictions between them under the Manchester Police Regulation Act 1844, in connection with their business of selling flowers in the streets. An injunction was granted to stop them.

In 1973 the Fair Trading Act was passed. Most of the legislation we have discussed in this chapter resulted from prolonged consideration and consultation. The 1973 Act arrived 'out of the blue'. There was no Green Paper, nor was there a White Paper setting out the proposals for reform.

Much of the Act consolidates earlier measures concerned with monopolies, mergers and so on. This Act forms the basis of the administrative consumer law.

The post of Director-General of Fair Trading was created. The Director General can initiate changes in the law to ban 'undesirable trade practices' as and when they are brought to his attention. Further, he can act against undesirable traders. Under Part III of the 1973 Act, he can seek an 'assurance' from a trader who persistently breaks either the civil or criminal law, or both, to the detriment of consumers, promising that he will mend his ways. Should he neglect to do so he can be called to a court to make a similar assurance, breach of which will be contempt of court, and this can attract a fine and/or a jail sentence. See the ingenious way in which a trader could be jailed for persistently breaking the civil law. Many assurances have been sought, but few people have been jailed for breaking them. As the Director General wrote:

> Because of the underlying sanctions, a written assurance itself normally achieves the desired results, by which I mean either trading standards are improved or the trader decides he had better leave the field for a less demanding vocation.

Under s.124(3) of the Act the Director General is under a duty to encourage trade associations to prepare and to disseminate codes of practice. These can be very important to consumers. They usually provide that members of trade associations will deal with consumers in a manner over and above the minimum standards required by the law. They usually contain a procedure for grievance redress (arbitration or conciliation) which is more specialised and much cheaper than using the court system. The drawback, of course, is that these rights and remedies concern only trade association members and those who deal with them. The real rogues have long ago been expelled. Nevertheless, there are quite a few of these codes in a wide variety of businesses—from shoes to funeral directors. Each is publicised by the Office of Fair Trading (the operating arm of the Director General), and leaflets about them are available at Citizens' Advice Bureaux, public libraries and other places.

Indicative questions

1 Freda, a housewife, purchases a new shirt from the menswear department of a large store for her husband, who is at present unemployed. It has printed on the label that it is a size 15 collar, her husband's size, but she has no way of checking this before she gets home, as the shirt is neatly packed in a box.

When she gets home, her husband tries on the shirt and discovers that the collar will not fasten because it is much too tight. When he takes off the shirt, he accidentally pulls off a sleeve which was only half-stitched on.

When Freda returns to the store, the manager refuses to refund the money or exchange the shirt, as he claims that her husband clearly caused the damage to the shirt.

(a) Freda and her husband are living on unemployment benefit and are worried about the costs of going to see a solicitor. Advise them. (*4 marks*)

(b) Advise Freda on her contractual rights with regard to:
   (i) the incorrect collar size on the shirt;
   (ii) the half-stitched sleeve. (*6 marks*)

(c) Could the manager insist:
   (i) that Freda takes up the matter with the shirt manufacturer? (*2 marks*)
   (ii) that Freda accepts another shirt in return? (*2 marks*)

(d) If Freda is forced to take further legal action:
  (i) to which court would the case go? *(2 marks)*
  (ii) will she need the solicitor to bring the action for her? Give reasons for your answer. *(4 marks)*

SEG

2 Read the following extracts on **LAW IN THE COMMUNITY** and answer the questions that follow using the information in the extracts and any other information you may have to help you.

Extract A

The Sale of Goods Act, 1979, section 2 defines a contract of sale of goods as:

"a **contract** by which the seller transfers or agrees to transfer the property in goods to the buyer for a money consideration called the price".

The provisions of this Act (as amended) cover:
~ the right to sell the goods
~ the goods must **match the description**
~ the goods must be of **satisfactory quality**.

Extract B

"The normal rules of contract apply and the law recognises that it is necessary to make sure that the consumer is not at a disadvantage when dealing with a business. There are a number of Acts of Parliament which imply terms into such contracts. There are Acts designed to protect the consumer and among these are the Sale of Goods Act, 1979, the Supply of Goods and Services Act, 1982, the Consumer Protection Act, 1987, and the Sale and Supply of Goods Act, 1994."

Extract C

Imran went to Spendalot Superstore and was persuaded to buy a new Hi Fi system for £400. The Hi Fi system was advertised in the store as being a "slight second" as it had been on display at the front of the store for several months.

Imran could not afford to pay **all** the £400 at once so he made a deposit of £100 from his holiday fund and agreed to pay three more amounts of £100 each month to Spendalot Finance Dealers, with a final payment of £25 for the credit deal.

When Imran took the system home he realised that the casing on one of the speakers was damaged, so he telephoned the Spendalot Superstore to ask them to give him his money back. Jake, the manager of Spendalot Superstore, told Imran that as the Hi Fi system was sold as a "slight second" he should expect to have something wrong with it.

Imran set up his Hi Fi in his bedroom and used it, despite the damage to one of the speakers. After playing the Hi Fi for about a month, the other speaker stopped giving out any noise at all and the compact disc player would not operate.

Imran is not very pleased about this situation, and Spendalot Finance Dealers are demanding the next payment of the credit deal he made.

Read extracts A and B.

(a) What do you understand by the following terms?
   Give one example from a consumer law situation that helps to explain the word or term used.
   (i) Contract
   (ii) Match the description
   (iii) Satisfactory quality

Look at all the extracts.

(b) What does the law say about Imran's situation and what legal action could he take?

(c) What sources of help and advice are available to consumers who have a complaint about an item or a service they have bought?

Why would you advise a person to use those specific sources?

(d) To what extent would you agree that the rights of buyers and sellers of goods and services are "balanced" and what evidence would you give to support your viewpoint?

NEAB Summer 1997 (Foundation)

CHAPTER 15

The Criminal Law

INTRODUCTION

In Chapter 1 we considered the nature of the criminal law, when comparing it with the civil law. In Chapter 4 we considered the classification and range of criminal offences, when dealing with the jurisdiction of the various criminal courts. In Chapter 7 we examined the way in which a criminal trial is dealt with in those courts and in Chapters 9 and 10 we considered the criminal capacity of such persons as children, the mentally disordered and corporations (legal persons). In this chapter we shall examine a little of the substance of the criminal law itself.

The criminal law is in a very interesting stage of development. In 1985 the Law Commission published a report containing a draft code for the criminal law as a whole. A sub-committee of the Commission had been asked to undertake this daunting task of redefinition and elucidation. The team consisted of three of the most eminent of academic lawyers: J C Smith, I H Dennis and E J Griew. Their draft code is appended to the Law Commission Report (No. 143 (1985)). A refined version was published in 1989 (Law Com. No. 177). While it is unlikely that the criminal law will be codified within the next few years, this is important work.

THE DEFINITION OF CRIME

There are many definitions to be found in the books and cases. All have their uses and drawbacks and the right answer rather depends upon the points the writer wishes to extract from the definition he is framing. As a general definition, Professor Card offers:

> A crime or offence is an illegal act, omission or event, whether or not it is also a tort, a breach of contract or a breach of trust, the principal consequence of which is that the offender, if he is detected and the police decide to prosecute, is prosecuted by or in the name of the state, and if he is found guilty is liable to be punished whether or not he is also ordered to compensate his victim.

This brings out the 'public' nature of crimes, the usual agency of enforcement and the main point of the proceedings, to punish offenders. There are other agencies of enforcement, such as trading standards and Environmental Health officers, and there are other purposes to criminal proceedings, like deterrence.

CLASSIFYING CRIMES

There are various ways in which crimes can be classified:

1 As between offences created by Acts of Parliament and those common law offences developed by the judges over the years. Most crimes are statutory. They might be relatively new crimes—like the failure to wear a seat belt when required. This was created by means of the Motor Vehicles (Wearing of Seat Belts) Regulations 1982, which were made under the Road Traffic Act 1972 (consolidated in 1988 and much amended in 1991). (We examined such lawmaking powers in Chapter 3, when considering delegated legislation.) If they are not new crimes, they might be the result of a reworking of the common law, or a consolidation of earlier statute law. Such crimes are to be found in the Theft Act 1968 (which will be discussed later in this chapter). The classification might be between statutory crimes like these and common law crimes, such as murder, the basic definition of which has not changed for centuries; Sir Edward Coke wrote, in 1644:

> Murder is when a man unlawfully killeth . . . any reasonable creature in *rerum natura* (in being) under the King's peace with malice aforethought (intent to kill or to cause grievous bodily harm), either expressed by the party, or implied by law, so as the party wounded, or hurt, etc. die of the wound, or hurt, etc. within a year and a day after the same.

Murder, too, will be seen in more detail later in this chapter.

2 It is possible to classify crimes into 'arrestable' and 'non-arrestable' offences. Before 1967 the split was between 'felonies', which, generally, were serious crimes, and 'misdemeanours', which were not. However, the distinctions became blurred and this new classification was made possible by the Criminal Law Act 1967. This has been replaced by Part III of the Police and Criminal Evidence Act 1984. An arrestable offence is one for which the sentence is fixed by law (like murder), or one for which a person of twenty-one years of age or over could be sentenced to five years' jail on a first conviction. This includes burglary, theft, criminal damage, rape and unlawful possession of drugs. The Act adds a further list to these for which the sentence could be less: this includes taking a motor vehicle, going equipped for theft, indecent assault on a female, corruption and smuggling. It also adds attempting conspiring, inciting, aiding, abetting, counselling or procuring any of these to the list of arrestable offences. Some of these are 'serious

arrestable offences' for which the police have extra powers. We will look at this later.

3 It is possible to classify by mode of trial. Indeed we did so when dealing with the jurisdiction of those courts which deal with criminal trials at first instance—the magistrates' courts and the Crown Court.

CRIMINAL LIABILITY: THE ELEMENTS OF A CRIME

The general rule is: *actus non facit reum nisi mens sit rea,* which means that an act is not wicked in itself, it is not wicked unless the mind too is wicked. That is, each crime requires a 'prohibited act', something not supposed to be acceptable, and generally 'not done' (e.g. appropriating property belonging to another), and the requisite intention (e.g. appropriating *dishonestly* and with the intention of permanently depriving the true owner of it). This means that both *actus reus* and *mens rea* must usually be present before a crime can be said to have been committed. For example, in the crime of theft, the Theft Act 1968 says:

> A person is guilty of theft if he dishonestly appropriates property belonging to another with the intention of permanently depriving the other of it; and 'thief' and 'steal' shall be construed accordingly.

Can you pick out the *actus reus* (what you are not supposed to do) and the two parts of the *mens rea* (wicked state of mind) within this offence?

An *actus reus* could, of course, consist of an omission to act when a duty to act existed, e.g. to stop at a red traffic light.

The *mens rea* requirement, particularly within a statutory offence, is often signalled by words such as 'maliciously, knowingly, wilfully, permitting, suffering, etc.' It could consist of a particular intention (e.g. the 'intention permanently to deprive') or it might be sufficient that the accused was 'reckless' (e.g. speeding along the high street, with no intention to knock over anyone in particular, but not caring either). If the accused intended to commit an offence, then the reason why (the motive) is not usually relevant. Many of the defences we are to consider later in this chapter for a variety of reasons amount to little more than a reasoned argument of lack of *mens rea*. Thus they amount, if they are successful, to a variety of ways to show that the prosecution has not established the basic requirements of the offence charged.

STRICT LIABILITY OFFENCES

While most crimes require both *actus reus* and *mens rea,* there are some offences which require no *mens rea* at all. That is, just doing the prohibited act is enough. This is called an offence of 'strict liability' or an 'absolute offence'.

The courts have a working rule, a presumption, that unless a statute expressly states that a strict liability offence has been created, then it has not. This was seen in *Sweet* v. *Parsley* (1970) where Miss Sweet's conviction for being concerned in the management of premises which were used for the purpose of smoking cannabis (contrary to the Dangerous Drugs Act 1965, s.5) was quashed on the basis that she had no knowledge of these circumstances. She only visited to collect the rent. Lord Reid said:

> Our first duty is to consider the words of the Act; if they show a clear intention to create an absolute offence, that is an end of the matter. But such cases are very rare. Sometimes the words of the section which creates a particular offence make it clear that *mens rea* is required in one form or another. Such cases are quite frequent. But in a very large number of cases there is no clear indication either way. In such cases there has for centuries been a presumption that Parliament did not intend to make criminals of persons who were in no way blameworthy in what they did. That means that, whenever a section is silent as to *mens rea*, there is a presumption that, in order to give effect to the will of Parliament, we must read in words appropriate to require *mens rea*.

Strict liability offences are created from time to time. The justifications seem to vary. Either, the offences are so petty that lengthy submissions about *mens rea* would waste the court's time (e.g. many motoring and parking offences), or, and much more importantly, the offence might be so socially dangerous or hazardous that the law should outlaw the activity alone. It should not be concerned with the accused's intention. For example, in *Pharmaceutical Society* v. *Storkwain Ltd* (1986). The Medicines Act 1968, s.58(2), provides that no person shall sell as a retailer any of a list of products unless they appear on a prescription from an appropriate medical practitioner. Drugs were supplied by the defendant, on the strength of a prescription carrying the forged signature of a Dr Irani. There was no suggestion or finding that the defendants had acted dishonestly, improperly or even negligently. Their activity revealed no shortcoming whatever, but they were convicted, and the decision was upheld by the House of Lords.

DEFENCES TO CRIME

An accused might seek to undermine the prosecution by disputing an element of the offence charged. For example, he might claim that his taking of the property he is accused of stealing was not dishonest—'He said I could borrow it any time'—thus defeating an accusation of theft, because dishonesty is an essential ingredient of the offence.

On the other hand, the accused might raise a defence of a more general nature; one which is available in answer to many different criminal charges.

Insanity

We examined this defence earlier (in Chapter 9) when dealing with the criminal responsibility of the mentally disordered. We noted then that the defence is based upon the famous 'M'Naghten Rules'.

In *R.* v. *Kemp* (1957) the accused hit his wife with a mallet. He was suffering from arteriosclerosis (hardening of the arteries) which restricted the flow of blood to his brain, so that he did not know what he was doing when he hit her. The 'Rules' mention 'a defect of reason from disease of the mind'. The accused's illness was held to fall within this category because it was capable of affecting the mind. Kemp was found 'guilty but insane'. These days (since the Criminal Procedure (Insanity) Act 1964) the verdict would be 'not guilty by reason of insanity', but the accused could be hospitalised just the same. It might seem a little strange to the man in the street to hear diseases and conditions like arteriosclerosis (in *Kemp*), psychomotor epilepsy (as in *R.* v. *Sullivan* (1983)) and sleepwalking (as in *R.* v. *Burgess* (1991) being described as instances of insanity, but, as Lord Diplock said (in *Sullivan*):

> 'mind' in the M'Naghten Rules is used in the ordinary sense of the mental faculties of reason, memory and understanding. If the effect of a disease is to impair these faculties so severely as to have either of the consequences referred to in the latter part of the rules, it matters not whether the atiology of the impairment is organic, as in epilepsy, or functional.

Pleading insanity has not been a popular option. Success would mean being confined in a psychiatric hospital—having not been convicted of a crime. On the 1 January 1992 the Criminal Procedure (Insanity and Unfitness to Plead) Act 1991 came into force. Now a jury decides whether the accused is fit to plead. If they find him unfit, a different jury decides whether he committed the *actus reus* of the offence. If he did then the judge has a range of options from committal to a psychiatric hospital (still the only choice for murder) to absolute discharge, and a new order under this Act of supervision and treatment.

We also noted the statutory defence of 'diminished responsibility' in Chapter 9. It is available only against a charge of murder, and if it is successfully raised it only reduces the conviction from murder to manslaughter.

Automatism

If the accused had no mental contact with the activities that his body has been up to then he might be classed as an 'automaton' for the purpose of criminal liability. If his plea of automatism involves a disease of the mind then the M'Naghten Rules apply—it is regarded as a plea of insanity. This was confirmed in *R.* v. *Sullivan* (1983), where the accused attacked his victim during an epileptic fit. However, if there is no disease of the mind, if the action resulted from, say, a blow on the head (concussion), then the defence can lead to an acquittal. It relies upon the act having been involuntary. Sir Matthew Hale, a great seventeenth-century lawyer, wrote:

> If there be an actual forcing of a man, as if A by force take the arm of B and the weapon in his hand, and therewith stabs C whereof he dies, this is murder in A, and B is not guilty.

Here, of course, B's act was involuntary. In a similar way, if while driving you are attacked by a swarm of bees, then your subsequent and doubtlessly frantic movements could not truly be said to be voluntary, and the consequent wreckage could be held not to have been your fault. On the other hand, if you cause damage with your car because you have fallen asleep at the wheel it might easily be regarded as having been your fault. You must have felt drowsy. You ought to have pulled over. The court held just this in *Kay* v. *Butterworth* (1945). An interesting area of development here is the interrelationship of diabetes and the defence of automatism. A line of cases such as *R.* v. *Quick* (1973), *R.* v. *Bailey* (1983), *R.* v. *Hennessy* (1989) and *R.* v. *Bingham* (1991) has revealed distinctions between hyperglycaemia (too much sugar in the blood) and hypoglycaemia (too little). The latter seems to be automatism, yet the former is insanity!

Intoxication

Intoxication is a state of mind which can be achieved by various means: drink, drugs etc. Voluntary or self-induced intoxication is no defence to a criminal charge in itself. However, if the intoxication gives rise to a 'disease of the mind', then the M'Naghten Rules might apply. Furthermore, if the offence requires a specific intent (e.g. murder, criminal damage, theft, robbery, burglary, handling stolen goods) and if the accused was intoxicated at the time, then that state of mind will be taken into account by the court when assessing whether the necessary intention existed in him.

In *DPP* v. *Majewski* (1976) the appellant was involved in a brawl outside a public house and also assaulted police officers. In his defence he claimed he had been taking drugs and these had mixed with alcohol and he had no recollection of what had happened. The House of Lords held that unless the offence was one that required proof of specific or ulterior intent it was no defence that, by reason of self-induced intoxication, the appellant did not intend to do the act which constituted the offence.

It is clear that drinking for 'dutch courage', the ability to steel yourself to do an act which you would otherwise not be able to do, cannot be a defence. In *Attorney-General for Northern Ireland* v. *Gallagher* (1961) the accused had decided to kill his wife. Lord Denning said:

> He bought a knife for the purpose and a bottle of whisky—either to give himself dutch courage to do the deed or to drown his conscience after it. He did in fact carry out his intention. He killed his wife with the knife and drank much of the whisky before or after he killed her . . . this case differs from all others in the books in that the respondent, whilst sane and sober, before he took to the drink, had already made up his mind to kill his wife. This seems to me to be far worse—and far more deserving of condemnation—than the case of a man who, before getting drunk, has no intention to kill, but afterwards in his cups, whilst drunk, kills another by an act which he would not dream of doing when sober. Yet, by the law of England, in this latter case his drunkenness is no defence even though it has distorted his reason and his will-power. So why should it be a defence even though it has distorted his reason and his will-power. So why should it be a defence in the present case?

Sir Matthew Hale also wrote about drunkenness:

> This vice both deprives men of the use of reason, and puts many men into a perfect, but temporary phrenzy . . . by the laws of England such a person shall have no privilege by this voluntary contracted madness, but shall have the same judgement as if he were in his right senses.

In *R.* v. *Kingston* (1994) a homosexual with paedophiliac tendencies had had his drinks 'laced', but ended up being tried for indecently assaulting a fifteen-year-old boy. He was held to have had the necessary intent. The fact that the alcohol might have removed his ability to stop himself was an insufficient defence.

On the other hand, the courts do sometimes show a little sympathy. In *R.* v. *Hardie* (1984), for example, where the defendant was charged under the Criminal Damage Act 1971, after having set fire to the flat where his estranged girlfriend and her daughter were sitting in the lounge, he pleaded 'no *mens rea*' on the basis of some outdated valium tablets he had taken to calm himself down. His friend had told him that they would do him no harm. Parker LJ said:

> There was no evidence that it was known to the appellant or even generally known that the taking of valium in the quantity taken would be liable to render a person aggressive or incapable of appreciating risks to others or have other side effects such that its self-administration would itself have an element of recklessness.

Hardie's appeal against conviction was allowed.

The law in this area is complex. In the spring of 1993 the Law Commission published a consultation paper (No 127) examining the relevant rules in depth and opening two main questions for debate. Is it necessary to have special rules to ensure that those who are drunk escape the consequences of their acts? It is suggested from experience in Australia and New Zealand that almost all such defendants are sufficiently aware of what they are doing to be dealt with using the ordinary rules of law. Second, if special rules are needed, would it be better to develop (as the Butler Committee recommended in 1975) a special offence aimed directly at those who offend while dangerously drunk?

Necessity

This defence might arise where the accused admits the allegedly criminal act, but claims that he did it when defending himself or his property, or in order to prevent the commission of a crime of violence against someone else.

There is very little case law on the point. The Criminal Law Act 1967 provides an excuse for the use of reasonable force in the prevention of crime or in making an arrest. Obviously the use of force on another would usually, without this 'lawful excuse', be a crime. The Act says:

> 3(1) A person may use such force as is reasonable in the circumstances in the prevention of crime, or in effecting or assisting in the lawful arrest of offenders or suspected offenders or of persons unlawfully at large.

Another occasion upon which the defence might arise is when the accused has committed an allegedly criminal act, but he has done so simply to prevent harm to himself or to another or to property—where the act prevented would not have been a crime had it happened. (Thus the reaction is not the 'prevention of crime' within the 1967 Act.) It is thought that a general defence of necessity does exist in circumstances like this, but there is little evidence upon which to base such thought. Indeed, the Law Commission Report in 1977 on Defences of General Application recommended that necessity should not be a defence. Nevertheless, from *R. v. Martin* (1989) it appears that there may well be a general defence of necessity. The defendant was charged with driving while disqualified. He was driving, but he did so because his wife threatened suicide if he did not! Further, in *R. v. Pommell* (1995) the defendant was found in bed with a loaded firearm. He claimed to have disarmed someone and to be minding the weapon until he could 'hand it in' next morning: 'I took it off a geezer who was going to do some people some damage with it'. His conviction was quashed on appeal.

There is one directly relevant English case in which the defence failed—*R. v. Dudley and Stephens* (1884). The two accused with a cabin boy had been shipwrecked from a yacht called *Mignonette*. They had been adrift in an open boat for twenty days and had not eaten for eight days. Therefore they ate the cabin boy. Four days later they were rescued. The jury at their trial for murder thought that they would not have survived to be rescued had they not killed the boy, but the two were convicted and sentenced to death. Later their sentences were commuted to six months' imprisonment. Professor Williams wrote:

> The decision cannot be considered as final authority for the proposition that in no circumstances, whatever is at stake, can life be deliberately taken.

Mistake

Where the prosecution have to prove intention, recklessness or guilty knowledge in the accused as part of the alleged offence, then a mistake could be pleaded as a defence by him where it resulted in him lacking that requirement. The mistake need not be reasonable. In *DPP v. Morgan* (1976), for example, it was held that an unreasonable but honestly held belief that a woman was consenting would be a defence to rape. Consent must be lacking; it was, but the accused was mistaken about it. The jury (or the magistrates) must be satisfied about the error. The 1976 decision was given statutory form in the Sexual Offences (Amendment) Act 1976. This question of consent to intercourse became a matter of great public interest during the proceedings of *R. v. R.* (1991). It is now clear that a wife does not give her permanent consent to sex just because she enters a marriage.

If the accused is mistaken about a more general state of affairs rather than the circumstances within a single event, then his mistake will need to be reasonable if it is to excuse criminal liability. For example, in *R. v. Tolson* (1889), Mrs Tolson was charged with bigamy. Her husband had deserted her in 1881. In 1887 she went through a ceremony of marriage with another man. She honestly, reasonably but mistakenly believed that her first husband had been drowned at sea. The ship he was supposed to have been aboard, bound for America, had gone down with all hands. Had she waited just under a year longer the presumption of death after seven years' inexplicable absence would have protected her. As it was, the court was convinced of her good faith, and the reasonable grounds of her mistake. Her conviction was quashed on appeal.

Duress

Where the accused is charged with having committed any crime except murder and (possibly) some kinds of treason, but the allegedly criminal act was committed while under duress, then the accused has a defence. The position regarding murder was settled in *R. v. Howe* (1987) and, for reasons of logic, attempted murder in *R. v. Gotts* (1992) where a sixteen-year-old had stabbed his mother, intending to kill her. His defence was that his father had told him to, threatening to kill him if he disobeyed. The boy was convicted and placed on probation. Law reform is needed here. Perhaps duress should be a matter of mitigation rather than defence.

The threat under which he felt forced to act must have been of death or serious bodily harm. The accused must have been left no third alternative. That is, he must have been faced with either committing the allegedly criminal act or not doing so and facing the horrible consequences. So in *R. v. Hudson and Taylor* (1971) two girls were charged with perjury. They had been the principal prosecution witnesses in a 'wounding' trial. The accused there was called Wright. The girls failed to identify him. He was acquitted. When tried for perjury they explained that several large men, including one called Farrell who had a reputation for violence, had approached them before the trial and promised to 'cut them up' if they testified against Wright. Anxious to avoid being filleted they acceded to the request. They were convicted of perjury, but the verdict was quashed on appeal. It was thought that the defence of duress ought to be available to those who had no real choice. There had been a choice of seeking police protection here, but its potential effectiveness in all the circumstances had to be taken into account. It was an issue which ought to have been left to the jury. It had not been. The appeal was allowed. Incidentally, the Law Commission here recommended that duress should not be available where the accused has had an opportunity to seek 'official protection'.

PARTICULAR CRIMES

Theft

Having considered the broader aspects of criminal liability, we must now focus a little closer on some particular offences. Theft is defined in the Theft Act 1968, s.1(1), as follows:

> A person is guilty of theft if he dishonestly appropriates property belonging to another with the intention of permanently depriving the other of it; and 'thief' and 'steal' shall be construed accordingly.

We met this definition earlier in this chapter. The section continues:

(2) It is immaterial whether the appropriation is made with a view to gain, or is made for the thief's own benefit.

(3) The five following sections of this Act shall have effect as regards the interpretation and operation of this section (and, except as otherwise provided by this Act, shall apply only for purposes of this section).

Sections 2–6 are designed as aids to the interpretation of s.1, which contains the basic offence of theft. Section 2 expands the notion of dishonesty. It provides three 'excuses' for the accused. That is, there are three possible reasons set out (the accused may think of more) in the Act which, if believed by the jury or the magistrates (for dishonesty is a matter of fact for them to decide) will mean that the appropriation was not dishonest and theft had, therefore, not been committed.

Section 2 says:

(1) A person's appropriation of property belonging to another is not to be regarded as dishonest—

(a) if he appropriates the property in the belief that he has in law the right to deprive the other of it, on behalf of himself or of a third person; or

(b) if he appropriates the property in the belief that he would have the other's consent if the other knew of the appropriation and the circumstances of it; or

(c) (except where the property came to him as trustee or personal representative) if he appropriates the property in the belief that the person to whom the property belongs cannot be discovered by taking reasonable steps.

So, if he believes he has (a) a legal right to it (he thinks it is his bike), or (b) that the owner would not mind or (c) he finds it and cannot trace the owner, he is not dishonest, and therefore not a thief (if the jury believe his story). In *R. v. Holden* (1991) it was held that the accused need only show that he honestly believed he could take scrap tyres from his employer's premises.

However, saying that you will pay when challenged is not good enough; s.2 continues:

(2) A person's appropriation of property belonging to another may be dishonest notwithstanding that he is willing to pay for the property.

The '*actus reus*' of theft consists of 'appropriation', which means assuming the rights of an owner (selling, destroying etc.). Section 3 of the Act says:

(1) Any assumptions by a person of the rights of an owner amounts to an appropriation, and this includes, where he has come by the property (innocently or not) without stealing it, any later assumption of a right to it by keeping or dealing with it as owner.

It makes no difference that the appropriation was done with the consent of the owner. This is clear from *R. v. Lawrence* (1972) (a foreign student opened his wallet to a taxi driver) and *R. v. Gomez* (1993) (electrical goods were supplied for cheques which were accepted by the manager of the shop but which were later found to be stolen).

The goods taken must be 'property', but this will not usually include land; 'property' does include money and 'things in action'.

There are proprietary interests which can only be protected by taking legal action. They cannot be seen, touched or carried away, but they do have value (e.g. copyright, patents, shares). The Act says:

4(1) 'Property' includes money and all other property, real or personal, including things in action and other intangible property.

(2) A person cannot steal land, or things forming part of land and severed from it by him or by his directions, except in the following cases, that is to say—

(a) when he is a trustee or personal representative, or is authorised by power of attorney, or as liquidator of a company, or otherwise, to sell or dispose of land belonging to another, and he appropriates the land or anything forming part of it by dealing with it in breach of the confidence reposed in him; or

(b) when he is not in possession of the land and appropriates anything forming part of the land by severing it or causing it to be severed, or after it has been severed; or

(c) when, being in possession of the land under a tenancy, he appropriates the whole or part of any fixture or structure let to be used with the land.

Wild flowers, fruit and animals are not 'property' for this purpose, although there may be other offences committed by picking certain wild flowers (e.g. under the Wildlife and Countryside Act 1981, s.13). It is not theft, however, unless the 'appropriation' is done for commercial purposes:

4(3) A person who picks mushrooms growing wild on any land, or who picks flowers, fruit or foliage from a plant growing wild on any land, does not (although not in possession of the land) steal what he picks, unless he does it for reward or for sale or other commercial purpose.

For purposes of this subsection 'mushrooms' includes any fungus, and 'plant' includes any shrub or tree.

(4) Wild creatures, tamed or untamed, shall be regarded as property; but a person cannot steal a wild creature not tamed nor ordinarily kept in captivity, or the carcass of any creature, unless either it has been reduced in possession by or on behalf of another person and possession of it has not been lost or abandoned, or another person is in course of reducing it into possession.

This 'property' must 'belong to another'. It is sufficient that the other person has possession, control or any proprietary right or interest. So property can be stolen from anyone in possession or control, not just the owner.

If you 'profit' by another's mistake (e.g. by being given too much change in the supermarket) you ought not to keep the cash; because the Act says, in s.5(4):

Where a person gets property by another's mistake, and is under an obligation to make restoration (in whole or in part) of the property or its proceeds or of the value thereof, then to the extent of that obligation the property or proceeds shall be regarded (as against him) as belonging to the person entitled to restoration, and intention not to make restoration shall be regarded accordingly as an intention to deprive that person of the property or proceeds.

Finally, the accused must 'intend permanently to deprive' another of the property. This means that he intends to treat the property as his own, to dispose of as he chooses (selling it on, lending, destroying); the Theft Act 1968, s.6(1) says this:

> A person appropriating property belonging to another without meaning the other permanently to lose the thing itself is nevertheless to be regarded as having the intention of permanently depriving the other of it if his intention is to treat the thing as his own to dispose of regardless of the other's rights; and a borrowing or lending of it may amount to so treating it if but only if, the borrowing or lending is for a period and in circumstances making it equivalent to an outright taking or disposal.

This is important in cases such as the extended 'borrowing' of property which 'uses it up'—like a 'multiple-journey' bus ticket or a football season ticket. I 'borrow' it from you and give it back after so long (or so many journeys or games) that it has lost its value and despite the fact that you have it back in your hand, my activities amount to theft.

Robbery

Robbery is defined within the Theft Act 1968. Ten years' imprisonment is the maximum for theft, but it can be life for robbery. Section 8(1) says:

> A person is guilty of robbery if he steals, and immediately before or at the time of doing so, and in order to do so, he uses force on any person or puts or seeks to put any person in fear of being then and there subjected to force.

All the elements of theft must be proved ('if he steals') and the force must be directed towards 'the person', rather than the property being stolen, and this must be directly connected with the theft such as pointing a gun at the shopkeeper. Pointing it at another customer so as to persuade the shopkeeper to open the till is robbery too. Robbery is really just an aggravated form of stealing.

Burglary

Burglary is committed by trespassers. It is not 'breaking and entering', neither is it confined to stealing.

The 1968 Act, s.9, says:

> (1) A person is guilty of burglary if—
>   (a) he enters any building or part of a building as a trespasser and with intent to commit any such offence as is mentioned in subsection (2) below; or
>   (b) having entered any building or part of a building as a trespasser he steals or attempts to steal anything in the building or that part of it or inflicts or attempts to inflict on any person therein any grievous bodily harm.
> (2) The offences referred to in subsection (1)(a) above are offences of stealing anything in the building or part of a building in question, of inflicting on any person therein any grievous bodily harm or raping any woman therein, and of doing unlawful damage to the building or anything therein.

There is an aggravataed form of burglary within the 1968 Act. While fourteen years' jail is the maximum for burglary, life can be given for the more serious offence; by s.10(1):

> A person is guilty of aggravated burglary if he commits any burglary and at the time has with him any firearm or imitation firearm, any weapon of offence, or any explosive.

Taking motor vehicles and pedal cycles without authority

The Theft Act 1968 also contains offences short of stealing. Sometimes they are called 'joy riding', although the essence of the offence is not riding but depriving the owner, albeit temporarily, of his conveyance:

> 12(1) Subject to subsections (5) and (6) below, a person shall be guilty of an offence if, without having the consent of the owner or other lawful authority, he takes any conveyance for his own or another's use or, knowing that any conveyance has been taken without such authority, drives it or allows himself to be carried in or on it.
>
> (2) A person guilty of an offence under subsection (1) above shall on conviction on indictment be liable to imprisonment for a term not exceeding three years.
>
> . . .
>
> (5) Subsection (1) above shall not apply in relation to pedal cycles; but, subject to subsection (6) below, a person who, without having the consent of the owner or other lawful authority, takes a pedal cycle for his own or another's use, or rides a pedal cycle knowing it to have been taken without such authority, shall on summary conviction be liable to a fine not exceeding level three on the standard scale.
>
> (6) A person does not commit an offence under this section by anything done in the belief that he has lawful authority to do it or that he would have the owner's consent if the owner knew of his doing it and the circumstances of it.

Offences involving deception in the Theft Acts

There are two sections in the 1968 Act which are directly concerned with gains by deception. Further Theft Acts were passed in 1978 and 1996. The Theft Act 1978 created three new offences out of one small part of one of the sections in the 1968 Act, s.16(a), which it repealed and replaced.

The first of these sections in the 1968 Act, s.15(1), is concerned with the offence of obtaining property by deception:

> A person who by any deception dishonestly obtains property belonging to another, with the intention of permanently depriving the other of it, shall on conviction on indictment be liable to imprisonment for a term not exceeding ten years.

The Act goes on to explain what it meant by 'deception', in s.15(4):

> For purposes of this section 'deception' means any deception (whether deliberate or reckless) by words or conduct as to fact or as to law, including a deception as to the present intentions of the person using the deception or any other person.

In *R.* v. *Preddy* (1996) the House of Lords held that a defendant who by deception obtained a bank transfer of money to his bank account did not obtain the 'property of another'; rather, the payer's legal interest (a chose in action) was extinguished, and the defendant's interest (a separate chose in action) was created in his own bank. This loophole in s.15 was quickly filled by the Theft (Amendment) Act 1996, which created two offences within the 1968 Act: dishonestly obtaining a money transfer by deception (s.15A) and dishonestly obtaining a wrongful credit (s.24A).

An old favourite of a case on deception by conduct is *R.* v. *Barnard* (1837). It is still authoritative. The accused went into a shop in Oxford wearing academic dress, a cap and gown. He was not a member of the university, but the shopkeeper was fooled. He sold the accused goods on credit. The accused was convicted of the offence which this section of the 1968 Act replaced. The words of a judge in the case, Bolland B, are often quoted:

> If nothing had passed in words, I should have laid down that the fact of the prisoner's appearing in the cap and gown would have been pregnant evidence from which a jury should infer that he pretended he was a member of the university.

The other section in the 1968 Act involves obtaining what is called a pecuniary advantage by deception. Fortunately, s.16 of the Act explains:

> (1) A person who by any deception dishonestly obtains for himself or another any pecuniary advantage shall on conviction on indictment be liable to imprisonment for a term not exceeding five years.
> (2) The cases in which a pecuniary advantage within the meaning of this section is to be regarded as obtained for a person are cases where—
> [(a) any debt or charge for which he makes himself liable or is or may become liable (including one not legally enforceable) is reduced or in whole or in part evaded or deferred; or]
> (b) he is allowed to borrow by way of overdraft, or to take out any policy of insurance or annuity contract, or obtains an improvement of the terms on which he is allowed to do so; or
> (c) he is given the opportunity to earn remuneration or greater remuneration in an office or employment, or to win money by betting.
> (3) For purposes of this section 'deception' has the same meaning as in section 15 of this Act.

Section 16(2)(a) is placed in brackets here because it was repealed and replaced by the three new offences in the Theft Act 1978. The wording as it stood had given rise to uncertainty. It was referred to as 'a judicial nightmare'.

The new offences are called obtaining services by deception, evasion of liability by deception and making off without payment. The 1978 Act says:

> (1) A person who by any deception dishonestly obtains services from another shall be guilty of an offence.
> 2(1) . . . where a person by any deception—
> (a) dishonestly secures the remission of the whole or part of any existing liability to make a payment, whether his own liability or another's; or
> (b) with intent to make permanent default in whole or in part on any existing liability to make a payment, or with intent to let another person do so, dishonestly induces the creditor or any person claiming payment on his behalf of the creditor to wait for payment (whether or not the due date for payment is deferred) or to forgo payment; or
> (c) dishonestly obtains any exemption from or statement of liability to make a payment;
>
> he shall be guilty of an offence.

Consider also s.3(1), which says:

> A person who, knowing that payment on the spot for any goods supplied or service done is required or expected from him, dishonestly makes off without having paid as required or expected and with intent to avoid payment of the amount due shall be guilty of an offence.

So if I trick you into thinking I will pay you for painting the outside of my house I have obtained services by deception (s.1); if I use your nontransferable membership card to get into the ground to watch a home fixture, I have dishonestly obtained exemption (s.2(1)(*c*)); if I run off with my 'three number 42s' from the local Chinese 'take-away', I have made off without payment (s.3). (*See* for example, *R.* v. *Allen* (1985) where a man stayed in an hotel for 10 nights and then ran away.)

Blackmail

Blackmail is the stuff the movies thrive on. It has a wonderful definition in the 1968 Act; it is 'an unwarranted demand with menaces', as can be seen from the statutory provisions:

21(1) A person is guilty of blackmail if, with a view to gain for himself or another or with intent to cause loss to another, he makes any unwarranted demand with menaces; and for this purpose a demand with menaces is unwarranted unless the person making it does so in belief—
(*a*) that he has reasonable grounds for making the demand; and
(*b*) that the use of menaces is a proper means of reinforcing the demand.
(2) The nature of the act or omission demanded is immaterial, and it is also immaterial whether the menaces relate to action to be taken by the person making the demand.
(3) A person guilty of blackmail shall on conviction on indictment be liable to imprisonment for a term not exceeding fourteen years.

Handling

If the accused receives stolen goods or assists in their retention, removal, disposal or realisation, he is accused of handling within the 1968 Act. Colloquially referred to as 'fencing' or 'receiving', it is interesting to note that it carries a heavier maximum sentence than theft itself, fourteen years. The Act defines the offence; in s.22(1):

A person handles stolen goods if (otherwise than in the course of stealing) knowing or believing them to be stolen goods he dishonestly receives the goods or dishonestly undertakes or assists in their retention, removal, disposal or realisation by or for the benefit of another person, or if he arranges to do so.

There are eighteen methods described in this quotation of committing this one offence; try to pick them out!

Murder

Murder is the most heinous form of killing. The term homicide includes manslaughter, infanticide and causing death by dangerous driving as well as murder, but it is this form of killing that hits the headlines. In fact there are usually less than 200 murder convictions each year, whereas there are about 350 000 convictions for theft and handling. Murder is an extremely serious crime, but not as common as its media impact might indicate.

We met Coke's classic definition of murder earlier in this chapter:

Murder is when a man unlawfully killeth . . . any reasonable creature *in rerum natura* (in being) under the King's peace with malice aforethought (intent to kill or to cause grievous bodily harm), either expressed by the party, or implied by law, so as the party wounded, or hurt, etc. die of the wound, or hurt, etc. within a year and a day after the same.

From this definition there are five points to note:

1 'a reasonable creature' is a human, rather than a dog or a dolphin;
2 In *rerum natura* or 'in being' means alive rather than, for example, unborn. There is a crime called child destruction (created by the Infant Life (Preservation) Act 1929) which is designed to protect the life of the unborn but, as they say, viable child. No conviction can be brought upon an accused who acted in good faith in order to preserve the life of the mother. This offence overlaps, of course, with abortion—the intentional procuring of a miscarriage. There are grounds upon which an abortion can be lawful, under the Abortion Act 1967;
3 'Under the King's peace'—not an enemy in wartime;
4 'malice aforethought'—as has been added in parentheses, this amounts to the *mens rea* for murder. The intent to kill is required, or at least the intent to cause really serious bodily harm (grievous bodily harm). In *R. v. Errington* (1838), for example, the accused covered a man in straw, threw hot cinders over it, and killed him. Despite the lack of evidence of intent to kill, the accused was charged with murder. There was evidence that the accused intended to cause serious bodily injury. This formulation of the *mens rea* for murder was reconsidered and confirmed by the House of Lords in *R. v. Moloney* (1985), where a shot was fired in the small hours after a ruby wedding party. It seems that the accused and his stepfather, who had both been drinking for hours, had been discussing, in rather heated tones, whether or not Moloney should stay in the army. The men then decided to race each other at loading and firing a shotgun. Moloney won the race. He was convicted of murder, but his conviction was reduced to manslaughter on appeal. The guidelines given in Moloney were criticised in *R. v. Hancock and Shankland* (1986), where the murder convictions of two miners (who threw a 46lb concrete block and a 65lb concrete post through the windscreen of a taxi, killing the driver) were also reduced to manslaughter;
5 'within a year and a day'—this is just a matter of causation, of establishing that it was the accused's activity which caused the death. Given the advances in both forensic science and the ability to establish a cause of death, the requirement that the death must occur 'within a year and a day' of the last act causing death was abolished by the Law Reform (Year and a Day Rule) Act 1996.

However, the consent of the Attorney-General is required before a prosecution can be brought three years or more after the last act allegedly causing the death or where the defendant was convicted and sentenced to at least two years' imprisonment for the act or omission now alleged to have caused the death.

Since the Murder (Abolition of Death Penalty) Act 1965, the fixed penalty for murder is life imprisonment. The judge will often add his recommendations about minimum periods of servitude. This seems illogical, but the prisoner is unlikely to be given any hope of release on any basis before the expiry of this period of time. It has often been argued that this fixed penalty be made discretionary.

Manslaughter

This is killing a human too, but this time without the malice aforethought required for murder. All unlawful homicides other than murder, causing death by dangerous driving and infanticide are classified as manslaughter. Furthermore, as we saw in Chapter 9, and earlier in this chapter, the success of a defence of diminished responsibility to a murder charge will result in a conviction for manslaughter.

Where a defence of provocation is accepted by a jury in a murder trial, their verdict will be manslaughter. The Homicide Act 1957, s.3, says:

> Where on a charge of murder there is evidence on which the jury can find that the person charged was provoked (whether by things done or by things said or by both together) to lose his self control, the question whether the provocation was enough to make a reasonable man do as he did shall be left to be determined by the jury; and in determining that question the jury shall take into account everything both done and said according to the effect which, in their opinion, it would have on a reasonable man.

Several recent cases concerned with the so-called 'battered wife syndrome' have illustrated this defence: *R.* v. *Thornton* (1996) is a good example. After a history of beatings the woman 'snapped' and stabbed her husband to death.

A conviction for manslaughter is also the appropriate result of a trial for murder where a suicide pact (an agreement where all agreed that they had the urge to die), leaves a survivor who was instrumental in the death of another party to the agreement, and himself had a 'settled intention of dying in persuance of the pact' (1957 Act, s.4). Since the Suicide Act 1961, suicide itself is no longer a crime, but it is an offence to aid, abet, counsel or procure the suicide of another.

Killing as the result of an unlawful and dangerous act is unlikely to amount to murder, but it is tried as manslaughter. The dangerousness of the act is measured by the standards of a reasonable man. Would he agree that pushing supermarket trolleys off multi-storey car parks at night in virtually deserted city centres amounts to an unlawful and dangerous act? Or, as in *R.* v. *Dawson* (1985), holding up a petrol station attendant to rob him (he died soon afterwards of a heart attack). Killing through gross negligence is manslaughter too, like the signalman who forgets to close the gates. This criminal negligence must amount to a wanton disregard for others. It is more than inadvertence.

If a woman kills her baby who is less than one year old because of post-natal depression or some related cause, then the charge will probably be infanticide (under the Infanticide Act 1938). If it is murder, the jury can return a verdict of infanticide—it is thus a kind of defence. Infanticide has the same extremely broad sentencing freedom as manslaughter. There are only about five convictions for infanticide each year. Probation is the usual sentence.

Assaults and woundings

An assault comprises any intentional or reckless activity which has the effect of inducing in another the fear of immediate and unlawful personal violence.

Assault and battery are often mentioned together. A battery is the actual application of force to another. Thus, you could assault without battery, if you miss with the punch; and you could batter without assault, if you attack from behind. They are different things. Nevertheless, in criminal law contexts, the word assault is often used to include a battery.

There are some assaults which are justifiable, although for this to be so only reasonable force (in all the circumstances of the case) must have been used. They include: assault in the furtherance of legal duties, like making lawful arrests (discussed later in this chapter), the use of lawful correction, like a father smacking his son, self-defence, the defence of your husband or wife, child or someone else who is dear to you, and the defence of property.

There are various kinds of assault. The basic offence is a common law crime but statutes have created variations on the theme:

1 **Common assault** Under the Offences against the Person Act 1861, s.42, the individuals involved in this type of offence sometimes initiate proceedings. The police will only intervene to prevent a breach of the peace. This is merely procedural (see *R. v. Harrow JJ* (1985)). *R. v. Ireland* (1997) was a case concerning the making of telephone calls during which the defendant said nothing. The Court of Appeal said that:

> with an assault 'the act' consists in the making of the telephone call, and it does not matter whether words or silence ensue.

The defendant had made a series of calls of this nature to three women, but the court made it clear that even a single call could amount to an assault, and that:

> repetitious telephone calls of this nature are likely to cause the victims to apprehend immediate and unlawful violence.

2 **Aggravated assault** Under s.43 of the 1861 Act a common assault becomes more serious if violence is used upon a boy under fourteen or any female.

3 **Actual bodily harm** Under s.47 of the 1861 Act, there is an offence where the assault interferes with the health and comfort of the victim, but falls short of grievous bodily harm. It was settled in *R. v. Brown* (1992) that consent is no defence here—even where the assault amounted to the satisfaction of a sado-masochistic libido. It was further settled in *R. v. Chan-Fook* (1993) that actual bodily harm includes psychiatric injury but it does not include emotional impact such as fear, distress or panic.

4 **Assault intending to resist arrest** is an offence under s.38 of the 1861 Act.

5 **Unlawful and malicious wounding or infliction of grievous bodily harm** under s.20 of the 1861 Act, whether or not an instrument is used.

6 **Grievous bodily harm** with intent under s.18 of the 1861 Act. It is an offence unlawfully and maliciously to wound, or cause grievous bodily harm to that person or to prevent or resist the lawful arrest or detention of any person.

7 **Assaults on the police.** Here the Police Act 1964, s.51, applies. It creates a variety of possibilities including assault, wilful resistance and obstruction of a constable in the execution of his duty. Of more serious consequence than the assault itself is wounding the victim.

Terminology

In order to avoid doubt and confusion, we ought to look at the terminology used in these offences:

1 for a 'wound' the skin needs to be broken. A bruise alone will not do;
2 'grievous bodily harm' means really serious bodily harm;
3 'maliciously' here means either an intention to do what was done, or recklessness about it, so that the accused must have foreseen that the harm might be done, but he went ahead anyway, not caring about it. Recklessness also includes deliberately refusing to consider a risk which might well exist ('shutting one's eyes to the risk' is a commonly used expression).

Criminal damage

This is a collection of crimes against property. The law is mainly found in the Criminal Damage Act 1971. 'Property' for this purpose is defined in s.10 of the 1971 Act. It includes all property of a tangible nature, whether real or personal, including money, tamed wild animals and (from *R. v. Whiteley* (1991)) computer files. (But see now Computer Misuse Act 1990.) Property does not include wild flowers, fruit and fungi.

There are three main offences: destroying or damaging property, threatening to destroy or damage it and possessing anything with the intention of destroying or damaging property. The Act says:

1 A person who without lawful excuse destroys or damages any property belonging to another intending to destroy or damage any such property or being reckless as to whether any such property would be destroyed or damaged shall be guilty of an offence.

2 A person who without lawful excuse destroys or damages any property, whether belonging to himself or another—

(*a*) intending to destroy or damage any property or being reckless as to whether any property would be destroyed or damaged, and

(*b*) intending by the destruction or damage to endanger the life of another or being reckless as to whether the life of another would be thereby endangered shall be guilty of an offence.

3 An offence committed under this section by destroying or damaging property by fire shall be charged as arson.

So, under s.1(1) there is no offence committed if the property destroyed belongs to the accused. This point was raised in *R. v. Appleyard* (1985), a case about a fire deliberately set to a storehouse. The accused was not able to avoid the conviction; he was the managing director of the company but not the owner of the property.

Note, however, that under s.1(2) any property will do. I am fed up with my moped. It will not start. So I decide to blow it up with a left over firework. You are pruning your roses next door, but I have no thought for your wellbeing in my anger. Both the moped and the roses are destroyed. Section 1(2) might apply, but, because I am using fire as my instrument of destruction, the likely charge appears in s.1(3). The Act continues:

2 A person who without lawful excuse makes to another a threat, intending that the other would fear it would be carried out:

(*a*) to destroy or damage any property belonging to that other or a third person, or

(*b*) to destroy or damage his own property in a way which he knows is likely to endanger the life of that other or a third person, shall be guilty of an offence.

3 A person who has anything in his custody or under his control intending without lawful excuse to use it or cause or permit another to use it:

(*a*) to destroy or damage any property belonging to some other person, or

(*b*) to destroy or damage his own or the user's property in a way he knows is likely to endanger the life of some other person, shall be guilty of an offence.

CRIMINAL LAW ARREST

An arrest is the taking or restraining of a person, depriving him of his liberty, so that he is available to answer an accusation of crime. We met the definition of arrestable offences earlier in this chapter, when classifying crimes as between them and non-arrestable offences, but the power of arrest is a far more complex matter than just a consideration of arrestable offences, and it has been made even more so by the Police and Criminal Evidence Act 1984, the Public Order Act 1986 and the Criminal Justice and Public Order Act 1994.

An arrest can be effected by anyone authorised by a warrant which has been lawfully issued and signed by a magistrate or other judicial authority. The complications arise when we turn towards the power to arrest without a warrant. The 1984 Act provides that anyone (a policeman or a private citizen) can arrest without warrant anyone who is in the act of committing an arrestable offence or anyone whom he has reasonable grounds for suspecting to be committing an arrestable offence. Where an arrestable offence has been committed any person may arrest without warrant anyone who is guilty of the offence or anyone whom he has reasonable grounds for suspecting to be guilty of it. It follows that if no arrestable offence (e.g. shoplifting (theft)) has been committed then a private citizen (e.g. a store detective) would not be making a lawful arrest, and could face a civil action for false imprisonment (*see* Chapter 12). No such problem arises for the police, however, because where a constable has reasonable grounds for suspecting that an arrestable offence has been committed he may arrest anyone whom he has reasonable grounds for suspecting to be guilty of the offence. Furthermore, a constable may arrest without warrant anyone who is about to commit an arrestable offence or anyone whom he has reasonable grounds for suspecting to be about to commit an arrestable offence.

The lawfulness of an arrest is obviously a centrally important issue for a policeman. Proceedings for unlawful arrest or false imprisonment could follow an improper exercise of his power to arrest. Plainly, the lawfulness of his action will depend to a large extent upon its reasonableness. In *Dumbell* v. *Roberts* (1947), for example, Scott LJ said that:

> the constable shall before arresting satisfy himself that there do in fact exist reasonable grounds for suspicion of guilt. That requirement is very limited. The police are not called upon before acting to have anything like a prima facie case for convicting.

Lord Devlin added (in *Hussein* v. *Chong Fook Kam* (1970)):

> to give power to arrest on reasonable suspicion does not mean that it is always or even ordinarily to be exercised. It means that there is an executive discretion. In the exercise of it many things have to be considered besides the strength of the case. The possibility of escape, the prevention of further crime and the obstruction of police enquiries are examples.

More recently, in *Ward* v. *Chief Constable of Avon & Somerset Constabulary* (1986), the Court of Appeal held that, where a constable's reasons for suspicion were sufficient, he was under no obligation to go looking for further evidence or to probe every explanation before exercising his power of arrest.

The reasonableness of police conduct in making arrests was tested in *G.* v. *Chief Superintendent of Police, Stroud* (1986), where it was held that allowance must be made for the fact that a 'spur of the moment' decision has often to be made, and again, in *Castorina* v. *Chief Constable of Surrey* (1988) where a company's premises had been burgled. The police thought it was an 'inside job'. The plaintiff had just been dismissed, and the papers taken were said to have been useful to someone with a grudge. She was arrested, sued and won damages at the trial. The judge said that the police should have made further enquiries. However, the Court of Appeal reversed the decision, saying that there was no need to 'probe every explanation' or 'make all presently practicable enquiries'. Most recently in *O'Hara* v. *Chief Constable of the RUC* (1997), an action in tort for a wrongful arrest, the House of Lords confirmed that the law requires the arresting officer to have in his own mind reasonable grounds for suspicion. Here the officer had attended a briefing by his superior officer about a murder. The information given at the briefing was held at the trial to have been sufficient to give the officer reason to suspect the plaintiff.

We noted earlier that an arrestable offence is one for which the sentence is fixed by law (like murder) or one for which the first conviction of someone of twenty-one years or more could be five years' jail or one which is declared to be arrestable; so, included here are most offences under the Theft Acts, the Criminal Damage Act, the Offences against the Person Act and the Protection from Harassment Act 1997 (but not the common law offences of common assault and battery).

Some arrestable offences are classified as serious arrestable offences. They include: treason, murder, manslaughter, rape, kidnapping, incest with a girl under thirteen, buggery with a boy under thirteen or with someone who has not consented, some offences of gross indecency, some firearms and explosives offences, various sexual offences, death by dangerous driving, hostage taking and highjacking. The point of this classification is that the police have extra powers in such cases. For instance, they can set up road blocks, search powers are increased, they can detain a suspect for up to ninety-six hours without charging him (or her) and they can deny access to a solicitor for up to thirty-six hours.

As if all this were not enough, there are certain so-called general arrest conditions under which a constable can arrest for any offence at all. If he has reasonable grounds for suspecting that anyone has committed or is about to commit any offence, then, if any one of the following conditions applies, he has the power to arrest that person without warrant. The conditions are: that the suspect's name is not known and cannot readily be found out; that the name given is believed to be false; that the suspect has failed to supply an address, or has not supplied an address which is satisfactory for serving a summons or which the police have reasonable ground for doubting is satisfactory; that the suspect will not stay at an address given for long enough for a summons to be served, and no-one else will be there who could receive the summons; that it is believed that arrest is necessary to prevent the person causing injury to himself or to others, suffering injury, causing loss or damage to property, committing an offence against public decency, unlawful obstruction of the highway; or to protect a child or other vulnerable person from the suspect. These 'general arrest conditions' were tested in *Nicholas* v. *Parsonage* (1987). Here a boy persisted in riding his bike with no hands after having been told by two policemen not to. He refused to give his name and address and was arrested. It was held that the arrest was correct. The policemen had informed him that he was committing a road traffic offence (for which he was subsequently convicted). It was not necessary to say why they wanted his name and address.

Under s. 117 of the 1984 Act a constable may use reasonable force in the exercise of these powers.

There are various other powers of arrest which exist at common law. For example, for breach of the peace.

The Police and Criminal Evidence Act 1984 (usually called PACE), together with Codes of Practices published under it, govern what happens after an arrest.

Bail

Once a person has been deprived of his liberty, the question arises (under PACE, s.47) whether he should be detained. He may be released on bail before trial (*see* Chapter 7) or before committal for trial (*see* Chapter 4), by the police or by the magistrates or by the Crown Court.

'Bail' used to mean the security put up by a third party (called a surety) to ensure that the accused turned up at the court. Now, however, the position is rather more complicated. The key piece of legislation is the Bail Act 1976, although it has been much amended—by the Criminal Justice Act 1988, the Criminal Justice Act 1991, the Bail (Amendment) Act 1993, the Magistrates' Court Act 1980 and, most recently, by the Criminal Justice and Public Order Act 1994. The general principle is that bail should be granted. If it is to be refused then this is exceptional and good reasons must be given. At the police station, following arrest but before charge, the custody officer may refuse bail in specified circumstances, grant unconditional bail, or impose conditions if they are felt to be necessary to secure that a suspect will return (surrender), that he does not commit an offence while on bail and that he does not interfere with witnesses or obstruct justice. Further conditions can be added, such as to require residence at a bail hostel or elsewhere for mental treatment.

After having been charged, an accused may be refused bail: where his name and address cannot be ascertained or reasonable grounds exist to believe those supplied are false; where the custody officer reasonably believes that he will fail to attend court; where (on arrest for an imprisonable offence) reasonable grounds exist for believing that detention is necessary to prevent the commission of other offences; to prevent the accused from causing injury to another or loss or damage to property; so as to prevent interference with the administration of justice or the investigation of offences; or where it is reasonable to detain him for his own protection. Conditions may be varied by another custody officer at the same police station, but either more or less favourable conditions may result. A further application for variation may then be made to the magistrates' court. Where someone fails to answer police bail, e.g. to attend the police station at an appointed time, he can be arrested without a warrant. At the magistrates' court the presumption is still in favour of bail. The magistrates' courts not only deal with bail from the time of first appearance but may confirm, vary or remove any conditions of police bail or remand a defendant in custody.

By s.25 of the 1994 Act bail will be refused where the defendant is charged with or convicted of murder, attempted murder, manslaughter, rape or attempted rape if previously convicted of such an offence or if the previous offence was manslaughter and a custodial sentence was imposed. Section 26 provides that a defendant need not be granted bail if the offence is indictable or triable either way and it appears to the court that he was on bail in criminal proceedings at the date of the offence.

If new information comes to light after the original police bail decision the prosecution may apply to the magistrates' court to have bail revoked or to have conditions imposed. The prosecution may appeal against bail decisions under the Bail (Amendment) Act 1993.

Indicative questions

1 **Theft is defined as the dishonest appropriation of property belonging to another person with the intention of permanently depriving the other of it.**

In each of the following examples, explain whether or not theft has occurred, **and** give reasons for your answer.

(a) Ann, because it is raining, takes Brian's umbrella and returns it a week later.
(*4 marks*)

(b) Clare finds a £5 note which she believes she can keep as she does not think she can discover the owner. (*4 marks*)

(c) Davis puts the price label from a cheap bottle of wine on to an expensive bottle, puts the more expensive bottle in his supermarket basket, and pays the lower price. (*4 marks*)

SEG

2 Read the following passage carefully, and then answer the questions which are based upon it.

James has a car which is twelve years old, and he has still to pass his driving test. He is nineteen years of age. One evening three friends suggest a trip to the beach for a late swim after work, and James offers to drive them all there in his car. Robin, who passed the driving test three weeks previously, is the only qualified driver among them. The car, which was due for an MOT test the previous week, has been giving trouble for some time, and James knows that the brakes do not work very well. The group of four friends sets off along the motorway, and after ten miles they realise that they have missed the exit for the beach. Finding a gap in the central reservation, James takes a chance and executes a quick U-turn to change direction. In so doing, he causes Mark, another driver, to swerve and crash, injuring a ten-year-old passenger who was sitting in a rear seat and was not wearing the seat-belt which was fitted there. James tries to brake, but the brakes fail and he collides with the central reservation, killing Robin and injuring himself. Robin's mother, who has a weak heart, collapses and dies of heart failure when she sees news of the crash for the first time, on the television.

(a) What criminal offences, if any, have been committed? (*6 marks*)

(b) In which court or courts might these offences be tried? (*3 marks*)

(c) Consider whether Robin's father will receive any compensation, and from whom. (*6 marks*)

(d) Explain what other actions may be brought to obtain compensation in this case. (*5 marks*)

SEG

3 People can break the law in a number of ways. A wrong committed against an individual is known as a tort and will be dealt with by civil action. A wrong committed against the State will be prosecuted as a crime.

A person charged with an offence or sued in tort may be able to plead a defence and thus escape liability.

In *each* of the following situations, explain whether the appropriate person(s) would be sued or prosecuted **or** both sued **and** prosecuted.

Your answer should also discuss whether or not that person would have a valid defence.

(a) Ann, a journalist, writes a newspaper report about the trial of Peter who was charged with rape. Peter is upset when, following his acquittal, Ann reports certain remarks made by the judge during his summing-up which could have suggested that Peter was guilty.

Peter is considering legal action against both the judge and Ann. (*5 marks*)

(b) Humphrey, a civil servant, reveals some classified information to Jim after Jim threatened Humphrey and claimed that he and his friends were holding Humphrey's family as hostages. (*5 marks*)

(c) Megan is a spectator at a football match and is furious when she sees her favourite player, Ryan, injured by a bad tackle from Derek, a member of the opposing team.

Megan rushes onto the pitch and throws a punch at Derek who retaliates by kicking Megan, causing severe bruising. (*5 marks*)

SEG Summer 1997 (Higher)

CHAPTER 16

Family Law

MARRIAGE

Getting engaged   'Will you marry me?' said the lovelorn lad; 'Yes,' she said. It is an agreement, but it is not a contract. Neither can sue the other for breach of promise of marriage—not since the Law Reform (Miscellaneous Provisions) Act 1970, s.1(1), which provides:

> an agreement between two persons to marry one another shall not under the law of England and Wales have effect as a contract giving rise to legal rights and no action shall lie in England and Wales for breach of such an agreement, whatever the law applicable to the agreement.

Of course, the problems may not end there. The couple might have started buying those absolute essentials for the home (e.g. sheets, microwave oven, compact disc player) and there remains the question of the ring. Property issues should be solved informally when the couple split up. If the engagement was formal, however, it might be that a certain formality is appropriate. In any event, provided there was an agreement to marry there is sufficient reason for a court to deal with property matters, despite the unenforceability of the agreement (*Shaw* v. *Fitzgerald* (1992)). The law provides the same mechanisms as are used between a husband and wife to ascertain the rights over individual items of property. The ring stays with the lady, unless it was given conditionally on the wedding (which is not likely and would be very difficult to prove). It is a rebuttable presumption that an engagement ring was an absolute gift. Furthermore it is unlikely that either party, or their parents, could recover the costs incurred in preparing for the 'big day': booked hotel room, honeymoon in the sunshine, wedding dress, cake, flowers, cars, confetti and the disco. All may have been paid for in advance, but unless some formal agreement was made such that the expense would be shared if the whole thing were to be called off, then the bills must be paid or negotiated away by those who incurred the expense. On the other hand, wedding presents will usually have to go back—because it is assumed that they were given conditionally on the wedding taking place. Should the donor not want the toaster back, however, it is generally assumed that the party whose 'side' gave the gift can keep it.

Just living together

Apart from whatever moral standpoint might seem appropriate to the couple and those close to them, the law distinguishes between married and unmarried couples living together. For example, the man is under no duty to support his girlfriend, only his wife—unless they have children, then he has to support them all. Children born to unmarried parents are, of course, illegitimate. This affects the issue of custody if the couple split up. If they were married the court will choose the more appropriate parent; usually the mother but neither has a better right to custody before the order is made. With illegitimate children the mother has the basic right to custody and the father would need to apply to a court for custody or access. The law does recognise that the co-habitee can be a 'parent' for the exercise of many of the responsibilities within the Children Act 1989. Illegitimate children could not inherit from relatives, other than their parents, within the intestacy rules. However, this, along with most of the other disadvantages attached to being illegitimate, has been removed by the Family Law Reform Act 1987. The unmarried woman cannot inherit from her man either under those rules, although she could claim from his estate as a dependant.

Unless the house is in joint names, or the unmarried woman has materially contributed towards it (or if it is protected under the Rent Acts), she has no right to remain in a house owned or rented by her man. The wife is far better protected. Finally, many social security benefits are not available to the unmarried (e.g. widows' benefits), but income support or family credit can be claimed (*see* Chapter 19). There are a number of other distinctions to be drawn between the legal positions of those who are married and those who are not. For example: concerning income tax—until 1990 married couples were usually taxed together, but an unmarried couple were always taxed separately. Yet capital transfers between an unmarried couple may attract inheritance tax. An unmarried woman cannot claim a state pension relying on her partner's paid contributions, as can a wife. Whereas married people can insure against each other's death, an unmarried couple can only insure against their own death and assign the benefit. On the other hand, should the unmarried couple get fed up with each other there is no need for the often prolonged and usually painful process of separation or divorce. A combination arrangement can be ended without notice—one partner can just walk out (although there may be difficulties over property distribution, much like those after a divorce).

Generally, though, the law is moving towards a recognition that people choose not to marry and yet achieve very stable relationships. The distinctions are fading, and in some countries legislation exists that specifically deals with cohabiting situations that have resemblance to marriage—that is, they seem to have the same 'commitment' or other characteristics that are traditionally attributed to marriages; in Australia, for example, where the De Facto Relationships Act 1984 was enacted in New South Wales.

The requirements

The classic definition of marriage is that of Lord Penzance (in *Hyde* v. *Hyde* (1866)):

I conceive that marriage as understood in Christendom, may . . . be defined as the voluntary union for life of one man and one woman to the exclusion of all others.

So marriage in England is monogamous (one spouse only), and it is intended by both parties, at the time it takes place, to last for life. Anything else is not recognised as a marriage, if it is made in England. We considered the concept of domicile in Chapter 9. Broadly, it involves the link of an individual with a particular legal system. Nobody domiciled in England can make a valid marriage anywhere, unless it meets Lord Penzance's definition.

Furthermore the parties to the marriage must have the necessary legal capacity. Age is crucial. Before 1929 a boy could marry at fourteen, a girl at twelve, but the Age of Marriage Act 1929 raised the age to sixteen for both. Between the ages of sixteen and eighteen everybody (except a widow or widower) requires consent to marry. Often it is stated that parental consent is needed, and if refused a court can give it. However, it may not be so simple (one may perhaps not have any parents). The person whose consent is required can be found by examining the Marriage Act 1949, Sched. 2. It is a detailed matter! Once the correct person has been identified and asked, then on refusal of consent the court can be approached. The usual court is the magistrates', although the High Court and county courts also have jurisdiction. The parties attend at the magistrates' domestic court. The public is excluded and the powers of the press restricted. There are three justices usually and there should be a man and a woman deciding the case. Everybody involved is given notice of the hearing. There is a case that says there is no appeal, but it is probably no longer a reliable authority.

It may be an exaggeration to describe parental consent as a requirement for marriage, because the absence of it does not invalidate the marriage. The parties are married—but there must have been fraud of some kind (forged documents etc.) so they can expect trouble. For those who revel in Royal trivia, the following may be of interest. Under the provisions of the Royal Marriages Act 1772, the consent of the Sovereign in Council is required before the marriage of descendants of George II will be valid. Since the children of princesses who have married into foreign families have been exempted from the 1772 Act, however, there are very few members of the Royal Family to whom this Act still applies.

Apart from considerations of age, there is a requirement for a valid marriage that the parties are not too closely related to each other already. This could be a relationship by blood or marriage. The restrictions are called the prohibited degrees of kindred and affinity. A marriage within the prohibited degrees is void. They are set out in the Marriage Act 1949, Sched. 1. (as amended by the Marriage (Prohibited Degrees of Relationship) Act 1986). It is a long and complicated list of two columns, to the effect that a man may not marry anyone listed in the left-hand column, and a woman may not marry anyone listed in the right-hand column. For example, a man may not marry his mother or daughter or sister or mother-in-law (unless his former wife and father-in-law are dead!), and a woman may not marry her father or son or brother or father-in-law (unless her former husband and mother-in-law are dead!). There are many other restrictions.

It is a fairly obvious requirement of the parties to a marriage that they are not already married to someone else. Any earlier marriage must have been terminated by death or by a decree of nullity or divorce. (After the implementation of the divorce provisions in the Family Law Act 1996 there will be a divorce order.) If either is already married then the second marriage is void and the crime of bigamy may have been committed (contrary to the Offences against the Person Act 1861, s.57). The maximum punishment is seven years' imprisonment. In fact, bigamy prosecutions are quite rare. The crime will probably not be prosecuted if the only purpose in the marriage was to let the couple live together 'respectably', as they say. Only about 20 per cent of cases of bigamy end up in the criminal courts. However, if the alleged bigamist believed in good faith, and on reasonable grounds, that his first marriage had been dissolved, or annulled, or that his first wife was dead, but he was wrong, this belief might constitute a good defence. In *R.* v. *Tolson* (1889) Mrs Tolson was deserted by her husband in 1881 and she believed he was drowned. She re-married in 1887. Even though her first husband reappeared it was held that she was not guilty of bigamy since she had reasonable grounds for believing he was dead.

If his wife had been continuously absent for seven years, and if he had no cause to believe that she was still alive, then an application could be made to the court for a decree called a presumption of death and dissolution of marriage (under the Matrimonial Causes Act 1973, s.19). With one of these the second marriage would be valid, even if the first wife did turn up, and bigamy would not have been committed.

The couple must not be of the same sex. It is not possible under English law to contract a homosexual or lesbian marriage and a person is regarded as the sex they were designated at birth for their sex at the time of their marriage. This has caused a little difficulty: *Corbett* v. *Corbett* (1970), *Rees* v. *UK* (1987) and *Cossey* v. *UK* (1991). In some countries, like Denmark, Norway and Sweden, same sex couples may register their partnerships and their relationship is given some limited legal protection.

The formalities
The precise arrangements will depend upon whether the couples are to be married in accordance with the rites of the Church of England, or on the authority of a superintendent registrar's certificate. English courts will also recognise the validity of marriages conducted abroad, provided local laws and/or customs were followed (a Ghanaian marriage in *McCabe* v. *McCabe* (1993)).

FORMALITIES

Church of England weddings
Before the ceremony of marriage one possible course is for banns to be read in the church which is the usual place of worship of the parties.

This is done three times, and consists of an announcement of the forthcoming wedding and an instruction to the congregation that if any of them knows of a cause or just impediment to the marriage 'ye are to declare it'. The names used by the clergyman when publishing the banns should be those by which the parties are generally known. In *Dancer* v. *Dancer* [1949], for example, the name used for the bride-to-be was 'Roberts'. The name of her parents when she was born was 'Knight'. Her mother had moved in with Mr Roberts, and taken his name. Despite the fact that the name used was inaccurate it was the one she was generally known by.

If banns are not read, a common licence could be issued by or on behalf of a bishop. The couple swear that no impediment exists. They can then marry in a church or chapel in the area either of them has lived in for the previous fifteen days.

A further option is for a superintendent registrar's certificate to be issued, allowing (subject to the agreement of the clergy) the marriage in either party's local church. The residence requirement is only seven days, but before the certificate is issued, there must be a notice of marriage written into a book which is open to public inspection, and left there for twenty-one days. Again, the parties make a solemn declaration about lack of impediment. The authority of a superintendent registrar's certificate can be used, under the Marriage Act 1983, to permit the marriage of those who are housebound, or in hospital, or in prison.

The final possibility is the special licence which is issued by or on behalf of the Archbishop of Canterbury. If granted (there are about 500 each year), a wedding can take place immediately and anywhere. This power comes from the Ecclesiastical Licences Act 1533.

The ceremony itself is laid down in the Book of Common Prayer or in the Alternative Services Book. Two witnesses must be present, apart from the clergyman.

Weddings with a superintendent registrar's certificate

If it is not to be a Church of England wedding, the parties need a certificate. Notice must be given to the local superintendent registrar, and the solemn declaration of no impediment is made. With a certificate the couple can be married in a registered building (i.e. registered as suitable by the Registrar General) by a registrar or another authorised person (usually the appropriate minister of the chosen religion). A solemn declaration of no impediment must be included in the ceremony somewhere.

Alternatively, with a certificate, the wedding could take place in a register office (office of the superintendent registrar). Weddings in registered buildings and register offices must have at least two witnesses and take place between 8 a.m. and 6 p.m. The doors must be left open while the ceremony is conducted.

A certificate will also permit a wedding in accordance with the customs of the Society of Friends (Quakers) or those of the Jewish faith. These can be behind closed doors, at any time and without witnesses.

Where the circumstances are extraordinary, (e.g. deathbed marriages), the Registrar General can issue a licence for a wedding

CERTIFICATE AND LICENCE FOR MARRIAGE
Marriage Act 1949, Section 32(2)
(Form prescribed by the Registration of Marriages Regulations 1986)

RD 235948

I,..Superintendent Registrar of the district of...in the
....hereby certify that on the‡...day of.......................................19......notice was
duly entered in the Marriage Notice Book of the said district of the marriage intended to be solemnized between the parties hereinafter named and described.

Name and Surname (1)	Age (2)	Marital status (3)	Occupation (4)	Place of residence (5)	Period of residence (6)	Church or other building in which the marriage is to be solemnized (7)	District and country of residence (8)
	years						
	years						

SPECIMEN

I further certify that the issue of this certificate has not been forbidden by any person authorised to forbid the issue thereof.
Now therefore I, the said Superintendent Registrar, grant to the above-named parties licence to contract and solemnize their intended marriage.

Date of issue.. Signature ....
Superintendent Registrar

NOTE: This certificate and licence will be void if the marriage is not solemnized within 12 months from the date of entry of notice give above (See ‡)
The marriage must be solemnized on or before..
*The Serial No. in the Marriage Notice Book must be entered in this space.
†When the marriage has been solemnized the No. of the Entry in the Marriage Register Book must be entered in this space.
Form 264 (Revised)

CERTIFICATE FOR MARRIAGE *WITHOUT* **LICENCE**
Marriage Act 1949, Section 31(2)
(Form prescribed by the Registration of Marriages Regulations 1986)

PH 517859

I,..Superintendent Registrar of the district of.., in the
....hereby certify that on the‡...day of.......................................19......notice was
duly entered in the Marriage Notice Book of the said district of the marriage intended to be solemnized between the parties hereinafter named and described.

Name and Surname (1)	Age (2)	Marital status (3)	Occupation (4)	Place of residence (5)	Period of residence (6)	Church or other building or residence in which the marriage is to be solemnized (7)	District and county of residence (8)
	years						
	years						

SPECIMEN

I further certify that the issue of this certificate has not been forbidden by any person authorised to forbid the issue thereof.

Date of issue.. Signature ....
Superintendent Registrar.

NOTE: This certificate will be void if the marriage is not solemnized within 12 months from the date of entry of notice give above (See ‡)
The marriage must be solemnized on or before..
*The Serial No. in the Marriage Notice Book must be entered in this space.
†When the marriage has been solemnized the No. of the Entry in the Marriage Register Book must be entered in this space.
Form 262 (Revised)

Superintendent registrar's certificates; Crown copyright reproduced by kind permission of the Controller of Her Majesty's Stationery Office

somewhere other than a registered building or a register office. Since April 1995 (under the Marriages Act 1994) couples choosing a civil wedding ceremony have been able to make their vows in a range of premises which have licenses for the solemnisation of marriage, not just register offices. These are called 'approved premises'. Many grand houses and homes have become 'approved'. Unsurprisingly, they tend to be the sort of places that host wedding receptions.

Proposals for reform

The Law Commission has recommended certain reforms in the formalities for marriage (Report No. 53 (1973)). These include: that civil preliminaries should be standardised; that banns should not be a legal requirement; that marriage by common licence be abolished; that the complications concerning premarital consent be revised; and that the various statutes in the field be consolidated into a new Marriage Act.

VOID AND VOIDABLE MARRIAGES

A void marriage is one which never happened. There was such a serious defect in the circumstances that the marriage never took effect. In a sense, therefore, it is not a variety of marriage at all. There is no need to ask a court for a decree of nullity, although if the circumstances are disputed, then the court will settle the matter.

The Matrimonial Causes Act 1973, s.11, sets out the defects which are regarded as sufficiently serious to render the marriage void—to prevent it happening at all.

A marriage celebrated after 31 July 1971 shall be void on the following grounds only, that is to say—

(a) that it is not a valid marriage under the provisions of the Marriage Act 1949 [as amended] (that is to say where—

(i) the parties are within the prohibited degrees of relationship;

(ii) the parties have intermarried in disregard of certain requirements as to the formation of marriage);

(b) that at the time of the marriage either party was already lawfully married;

(c) that the parties are not respectively male and female; [problems have arisen here concerning transexuals see e.g. Corbett v. Corbett (1970)];

(d) in the case of a polygamous marriage entered into outside England and Wales, that either party was at the time of the marriage domiciled in England and Wales.

We have examined these points already in this chapter.

A voidable marriage, on the other hand, is valid. It will remain so until it is annulled by a court at the request of one (or both) of the parties. Such a request must be based on one (or more) particular grounds. It is not a divorce. It is a request for annulment. The 1973 Act lists these grounds as well in s.12. A marriage celebrated after 31 July 1971 shall be voidable on the following grounds only, that is to say—

(a) that the marriage has not been consummated owing to the incapacity of either party to consummate it;

(b) that the marriage has not been consummated owing to the wilful refusal of the respondent to consummate it;

(c) that either party to the marriage did not validly consent to it, whether in consequence of duress, mistake, unsoundness of mind or otherwise;

(d) that at the time of the marriage either party, though capable of giving a valid consent, was suffering (whether continuously or intermittently) from mental disorder within the meaning of the Mental Health Act 1983 of such a kind or to such an extent as to be unfitted for marriage;

(e) that at the time of the marriage the respondent was suffering from venereal disease in a communicable form;

(*f*) that at the time of the marriage the respondent was pregnant by some person other than the petitioner.

These grounds are fairly self-explanatory. Cases (*a*) and (*b*) mean that sexual intercourse has not taken place because one or other party cannot or will not participate. Case (*c*) involves duress of some kind that amounts to fear for your life, your limbs or your liberty; any mistake relied on must be fundamental (e.g. about the nature of the ceremony or its implications) not just about a person's bank balance or job prospects, and unsoundness of mind might be illness or incapacity through drink or drugs. In connection with case (*d*) it will be recalled that we considered marriage and the mentally disordered in Chapter 9. Cases (*e*) and (*f*) speak for themselves.

Applications for decrees of nullity are heard by the courts which deal with divorce petitions. The procedure is similar, and the powers with regard to ordering for financial provision are the same.

MARRIED COUPLES: DUTIES TOWARDS EACH OTHER

Cohabitation

Married couples vary, of course, but broadly getting married gives both people the 'right' to each other's company. This includes a sexual aspect to their relationship, but there is no way of enforcing the rights involved in cohabitation—which are referred to as 'consortium'. The loss of consortium might amount to desertion, and therefore trigger off other rights. We will consider them later in this chapter. Since *R. v. R.* [1991] it is clear that a wife does not give her permanent consent to sex when she agrees to be married.

Maintenance

According to the common law a man is bound to maintain his wife, but she is not bound to maintain him. His duty lapses if she deserts him, or the marriage is dissolved or annulled. Her adultery used to be a bar to maintenance, but (since the Domestic Proceedings and Magistrates' Courts Act 1978) it is now treated as 'conduct to be taken into consideration by the court' if she applies for an order for maintenance. Fortunately for some, legislation has imposed a duty on the wife to maintain her husband where the circumstances require it. The Social Security Act 1986 reflects this duty to maintain both spouse and children. It is used when one spouse claims a welfare benefit like Income Support and there is another person (like a spouse) who is liable to maintain the claimant. A magistrates' court order can reclaim the money from the 'liable relative' under s.24 of the Act.

The magistrates' courts have the jurisdiction to order that maintenance be paid. (We will examine this later in this chapter.) Payments ordered after the couple have formally split up are also called maintenance. Until it was abolished in 1970, the wife had the power to pledge her husband's credit with traders for necessaries—food, clothing, medical and legal expenses etc. There survives still a common household agency presumption—that she can pledge his credit for household necessities—but the husband can revoke this by telling the tradesmen concerned.

Legal relationships It is possible for the couple to enter into legal relationships, e.g. to make a binding contract—although the courts presume against it. Either partner can institute criminal proceedings against the other. They can sue each other in tort but may be stopped from going past the opening stages of the case if the court thinks the action cannot be justified. Rights in succession law will be examined in Chapter 17.

MARRIED COUPLES: DUTIES TOWARDS THE CHILDREN

The duty to educate This extends from the age of five to sixteen. The duty is imposed upon parents, guardians and anyone else 'in possession' of the child. The child must receive sufficient full time education, suitable to his age, ability and aptitude—so schools are not essential provided the duty can be satisfied at home. If the local authority is not satisfied it may apply for an education supervision order. Ignoring it is a crime, and the child may be brought before the local magistrates. Furthermore, there is a duty to ensure regular attendance at school. Prolonged, repeated and unjustified absences show breach of the duty, which is also an offence. If the local authority cannot obtain compliance from the custodians the child will be taken into the authority's care (by use of care proceedings at the magistrates' court), and the parental powers pass to the local authority. (Note also that the local authority has the power to make a resolution vesting all parental rights in itself with regard to a particular child in certain circumstances.)

The duty to maintain This is the duty to provide adequate food, clothing and shelter, if necessary by means of social security benefits. Neglect is a criminal offence, and can also lead to care proceedings. Parents in difficulty can request that the local authority take the child into care. There may be a requirement of financial contribution—but it will not exceed the boarding-out allowance paid to foster parents, no matter what the true costs may be.

Magistrates have the power to order that payments be made to maintain children, regardless of whether they are also considering the question of custody, or of affiliation (naming the father of an illegitimate child).

The duty to protect This varies with the age of the child. The criminal law provides that it is an offence to do the following:

1 leave a child under twelve in a room with an unguarded fire (if death or serious injury results);
2 allow a child under sixteen to train for dangerous performances;
3 give intoxicating liquid to a child under five;
4 be found drunk in a public place while in charge of a child under seven;

5 be involved in the seduction or prostitution of a daughter under 16; or

6 leave a child with a baby-sitter who is too young or with an unregistered child-minder.

There are many others.

As far as the civil (i.e. non-criminal) law is concerned, it is possible for a child to sue his parents for compensation if he is injured through their neglect.

Of course, if the local authority is not satisfied with the treatment of a child, proceedings for care and/or supervision orders (under the Children Act 1989) can be instituted. This might include, for example, cases where medical treatment is denied to a child because of the religious beliefs of the parents. If the treatment is regarded as such as would be provided by or consented to by a 'reasonable parent', then these religious beliefs will probably not be allowed by the local authority social services department to stand in the way of the treatment. Under the Children Act 1989 a court can issue a 'child assessment order' which will last seven days. (We saw this when dealing with magistrates' courts in Chapter 4.) A parent can impose 'reasonable chastisement'. Anything more can result in criminal prosecution for the parent and care proceedings for the child. Social service departments are criticised from time to time for their alleged lack of awareness of the physical conditions under which children are being brought up. Such criticism usually follows a report of some appalling treatment of a child by his parents or those charged with the parental duties towards the child.

The Children Act 1989

This formidable statute was designed to clarify and codify the law relating to children. It repealed and replaced a considerable amount of legislation that had developed piecemeal over many years. There are over 100 sections and 15 schedules. Broadly, the Act covers: orders with respect to children in family proceedings; local authority support for children and families; care and supervision; protection of children; community homes, voluntary homes and voluntary organisations; registered children's' homes; private arrangements for fostering children; child minding and day care for young children and the Secretary of State's supervisory responsibilities and functions. The basic principle underlying the Act is that a child should be brought up within his or her family and that local authority support should be provided where necessary to support and facilitate this.

ENDING THE MARRIAGE: OR NOT

Marriages do not always continue 'till death doth them part'. If the marriage was voidable (seen earlier in this chapter) and the right to avoid has been exercised, it is over. If the couple want to split up but not formally end the marriage, a separation, or maintenance agreement can be made, or a matrimonial order, or a petition can be brought for judicial separation. If the parties are to be freed to remarry, divorce is necessary.

Separation agreements

The couple may agree to live apart so that they are free from the duty to cohabit. The point of a formal agreement is to settle the issues of property ownership, custody of the children, access to them for the other party and some provision for maintenance (*see* pp. 244–6). A maintenance agreement is made where both parties have not agreed to separate but one wishes to leave the other. If a separation agreement is made, then desertion cannot be the ground selected for a later divorce. Often separation agreements are put into a deed—the most formal of legal transactions. This is done to provide concrete evidence of the terms of the agreement. These agreed terms can be varied by a court if the circumstances change.

Matrimonial orders

These are available from the magistrates' courts and many county courts (those which have been designated divorce county courts by the Lord Chancellor).

A matrimonial order can be obtained on one of four grounds specified in the Domestic Proceedings and Magistrates' Courts Act 1978. These are that the party complained of (usually the husband):

1 has failed to provide reasonable maintenance for the applicant; or
2 has failed to provide or make a proper contribution towards reasonable maintenance for any child of the family; or
3 has behaved in such a way that the applicant cannot reasonably be expected to live with him (called the respondent); or
4 has deserted the applicant.

Orders can be made for periodic payments or lump sums.

Judicial separation

This order can be obtained from the Family Division of the High Court, or, in undefended cases, from a divorce county court. These orders are quite rare. There are about 1600 each year, 90 per cent of which are applied for by women. Their main purpose is to provide for parties who do not agree with divorce but who need to separate. A judicial separation order allows them to settle their affairs, to divide the matrimonial property and/or obtain a larger provision for maintenance and settlement of larger (capital) sums than could be obtained from the magistrates. Of course, the marriage survives a judicial separation. The parties cannot remarry without a divorce. Indeed, there may be religious reasons why a divorce cannot be petitioned for, but equally good reasons why the parties should be allowed to split up. Judicial separation can also pave the way for a divorce. Interestingly, although the marriage survives, if one of the parties dies intestate the other cannot claim from the estate as the surviving spouse.

In order to obtain a judicial separation the applicant will need to establish one of the following: adultery, unreasonable behaviour, desertion for at least two years; living apart for at least two years and the other party's consent, or living apart for five years (even if one party refuses consent). These are the same factors which influence the court in granting a divorce, but an important difference is that the court need not be satisfied of the irretrievable breakdown of the marriage, as it must be before a divorce can be granted.

The judicial separation will not be granted until the court is satisfied with the arrangements for the welfare of the children. The same powers exist for financial provision as for divorce. The order can be rescinded if the couple get back together. When the Family Law Act 1996 is in force, such orders will be called 'separation' orders.

Divorce

Divorce is common. The number of divorces has grown steadily since the end of the Second World War, and particularly after reform of the law, such as in the early 1970s. The Policy Studies Institute has predicted that, by 2010 most couples will cohabit before getting married and most marriages will end in divorce followed by re-marriage.

The law is about to be reformed again. The Family Law Act 1996 is in the process of implementation. However, what follows first is the current law, after which the impact of the 1996 Act will be considered. Under the Matrimonial and Family Proceedings Act 1984 there is an absolute ban on the presentation of petitions for divorce within one year of the marriage. There is no ban on petitioning after the year on the basis of what happened during that year. During the first year either spouse can apply for judicial separation, or for a court order relating to domestic violence, or for maintenance.

Divorce: the only ground

Since the Divorce Reform Act 1969 came into force on 1 January 1971, there has been only one ground for divorce: irretrievable breakdown of marriage. There are five facts, 'proof of any of which could satisfy the court that the marriage has broken down irretrievably' (but even if one or more of them can be proved the court, weighing the evidence as a whole, might find that it has not). These five facts are to be found in the consolidating statute, the Matrimonial Causes Act 1973:

The court hearing a petition for divorce shall not hold the marriage to have broken down irretrievably unless the petitioner satisfies the court of one or more of the following facts, that is to say—

(a) that the respondent has committed adultery and the petitioner finds it intolerable to live with the respondent;

(b) that the respondent has behaved in such a way that the petitioner cannot reasonably be expected to live with the respondent;

(c) that the respondent has deserted the petitioner for a continuous period of at least two years immediately preceding the presentation of the petition;

(d) that the parties to the marriage have lived apart for a continuous period of at least two years immediately preceding the presentation of the petition (hereafter in this Act referred to as 'two years' separation') and the respondent consents to a decree being granted;

(*e*) that the parties to the marriage have lived apart for a continuous period of at least five years immediately preceding the presentation of the petition (hereafter in this Act referred to as 'five years' separation').

Before completing this form, read carefully the attached *NOTES FOR GUIDANCE*

IN THE   COUNTY COURT*   * Delete as appropriate

IN THE DIVORCE REGISTRY*   No.

(1) On the   day of   19   the petitioner
                                                        was lawfully married to
                                                        (hereinafter called "the
respondent") at

(2) The petitioner and respondent last lived together at

(3) The petitioner is domiciled in England and Wales, and is by occupation a
                              and resides at
                                                        and the respondent
is by occupation a
                              and resides at

(4) There are no children of the family now living *except*

(5) No other child, now living, has been born to the petitioner/respondent during the marriage (so far as is known to the petitioner) *except*

804378 Dd 8046771 100m 9/87 PP (618)   D.8.

Divorce petition; Crown copyright, reproduced by kind permission of the Her Majesty's Stationery Office

IRRETRIEVABLE BREAKDOWN: THE 'FIVE FACTS'

Adultery

This is voluntary sexual intercourse between someone who is married and someone of the opposite sex other than the marriage partner. A raped woman has not committed adultery, but a man who committed rape has. Curiously, it is not required that the fact of adultery should make it intolerable for the innocent party to carry on living together with the one who has committed adultery. That is, the intolerability does not have to be caused by the adultery. (*Cleary* v. *Cleary* (1974)). If the 'other person' can be named he or she should (normally) be made a party to the proceedings, (the co-respondent).

Unreasonable behaviour

Each case is examined on its merits, but the behaviour must have been such as to cause the marriage to break down. Supporting evidence from friends, doctors, psychiatrists and so on would help establish that the petitioner cannot reasonably be expected to carry on living with the respondent. The matter is considered in two stages. First the behaviour is considered. Then the court will consider whether, in view of that conduct, the petitioner can reasonably be expected to continue to live with the respondent. These elements were described by Dunn J (in *Livingstone-Stallard* v. *Livingstone-Stallard* (1974)):

> would any right-thinking person come to the conclusion that this husband has behaved in such a way that this wife cannot reasonably be expected to live with him, taking into account the whole of the circumstances and the characters and the personalities of the parties?

Desertion

This is one partner leaving against the wishes of the other. The desertion must have lasted at least two years before the petition is filed at the court. The deserted partner can petition without the other partner's consent. The two years must be continuous but, illogically, it can be interrupted by up to six months together although these months do not count towards the twenty-four. (This applies to the 'living apart' rules too.) Furthermore, the parties may continue to live under the same roof, but as two households.

Living apart for two years

Both must agree to the divorce for the petition to be successful; lack of objection is not enough. They could live under the same roof, but separately (e.g. by not sharing meals). Again, a period of six months' interruption can be ignored, but will not count towards the twenty-four.

Living apart for five years

There is no need for both parties to agree, but the respondent could oppose the petition on the basis that the divorce would cause grave financial or other hardship.

In both these 'desertion' 'facts' it is essential that at least one party must feel that the marriage is at an end: *Santos* v. *Santos* (1972).

Associated matters

The court will also wish to consider the issues of custody of and access to the children, the division of matrimonial property and the important question of the provision of maintenance for the spouse and the children.

When the court is satisfied that the marriage has irretrievably broken down a decree *nisi* will usually be awarded. When all the other considerations have been settled, the petitioner can apply for the decree to be made absolute by filling in the appropriate form. This can be done at any time after six weeks from the grant of the decree *nisi*. Of course, the application need not be made. The parties could get back together. The decree *nisi* could be rescinded. It is only when the decree is made absolute that the marriage is dissolved. Only then are the parties free to marry. If they go through a ceremony of marriage before the decree is made absolute it would probably amount to the criminal offence of bigamy, which we have already considered. This gives a period of time for the parties to think about what they are about to do, and perhaps to change their minds before steps are taken which will alter their legal status.

Recognition of foreign decrees

Under the provisions of the Family Law Act 1986 foreign decrees obtained by judicial or other proceedings will be recognised by English law if they are effective under the law of the country in which they were obtained, provided that either party was, at the date when proceedings were started, habitually resident in, or domiciled in, or a national of that country. However, a foreign divorce which was granted otherwise than after judicial proceedings will be recognised only if one of the parties was not habitually resident in the United Kingdom for the year preceding the grant, and if recognition accords with 'public policy'. This reflects the government's rejection of the Law Commission's proposal that foreign non-judicial divorces (such as 'talaq' and consent divorces) should be recognised in the same way as if they were judicial. It is felt that they discriminate against women and can create great financial insecurity.

The Family Law Act 1996

This statute is unlikely to be fully implemented during the twentieth century. However, the one ground for divorce is likely to remain that the marriage has irretrievably broken down. This will be established by the parties having gone through a 'period of reflection and consideration' of the implications and practicalities of divorce for the couple and their children. This will replace the 'five facts'.

The general principles of the new law include support for the institution of marriage, encouragement of reconciliation and, where a marriage has completely broken down, divorce with minimum distress, without unreasonable cost and avoiding the risk of violence to the parties and children.

No divorce order can be applied for unless one year has expired from the marriage date. The formal process will begin with one party making a statement of marital breakdown, but that cannot be made until at least three months after that party has attended an 'information meeting' where details are given of the processes and (perhaps) financial matters and marriage counselling opportunities. Where one party has made a statement, the other must attend a 'meeting' if they wish to make or contest an application to the court relating to a child or financial matters.

The court can direct the parties to mediation on disputes. The 'period of reflection and consideration' gives an opportunity for reconciliation and a consideration about future arrangements. It begins with the fourteenth day after the statement of marital breakdown is received by the court and lasts nine months. These nine months will become eighteen months where there are children of the family under the age of sixteen. They can be further extended (under regulations to be specified) and the clock can be stopped where the parties give notice of an attempted reconciliation. Divorce after a reconciliation interruption of longer than eighteen months or the passage of a year since the 'statement' needs a fresh 'statement'. A divorce order will not be made without a court order dealing with financial arrangements (or a declaration by the parties).

The court must treat the welfare of any children as paramount, taking into account their wishes and feelings in the light of their age and understanding; the conduct of the parties in the upbringing of any child; the maintenance of good continuing relationships between children and parents; and any risk to the children from arrangements for residence, contact, care and upbringing.

There is to be a special defence: that the dissolution of the marriage would result in substantial financial or other hardship, including loss of a future benefit, to the other party or to a child of the family, and that it would be wrong in all the circumstances for the marriage to be dissolved.

MAINTENANCE

This could be applied for by itself, as we have already noted in this chapter or together with proceedings for divorce, nullity or judicial separation.

Totally separately, under the Domestic Proceedings and Magistrates' Courts Act 1978 there is a mutual duty on each party to a marriage to maintain the other and any children of the family.

The court can order periodical payments, secured periodical payments (this is where a capital sum is invested, and can be made available if maintenance payments do not appear). A lump sum can be ordered or it could be paid in instalments. It could be a 'spouse order' or a 'child order' (a 'spouse order' lapses on remarriage). There is no limit to the number of orders the court can make.

In assessing the financial provision that is to be ordered, all the circumstances have to be taken into account. These will include (*see* the Matrimonial Causes Act 1973, s.24): the income, earning capacity and property of each of the marriage partners, and their own needs, obligations and responsibilities, the financial needs of the children (especially education), the standard of living of the family before the provision arose, the income, earning capacity and property of the children, any physical or mental disabilities in either partner or the children, the contribution that was made towards the welfare of the family by each partner, their ages, the duration of the marriage, and so on. Of course, the court must not reduce the means of the respondent below subsistence level. If one partner has agreed to pay a specific amount by way of maintenance, a 'consent order' can be made to seal it. If the partners have been apart for three months or more and regular payments have been made, these could be embodied in a 'consent order', but such an order would lapse if they re-united.

As to the amount that the court will award, there are no fixed rules. However, there are a few guidelines which have developed over time: the starting point is to see to it that the wife gets about one-third of the family assets and in addition to that maintenance, sufficient to give her one-third of the combined incomes of the two partners to the marriage. No two cases are identical. The wife may earn far more than the husband in which case her maintenance would be low. In practice there is rarely enough to go around so that two households can live at the standard enjoyed before the split. Further, there is a trend towards reducing the interdependence after the split. The idea of a 'clean break' is being implemented. This was seen in *S. v. S.* (1986), where periodical payments were terminated with a single capital sum.

However, the 'clean break' principle has been crushed as the Child Support Act 1991 (as amended in 1995) has been implemented. Here a formula is used to calculate the maintenance requirement for each child of the couple (even if they were never married). Much of the legal power of the courts in dealing with child maintenance has been removed by the extensive powers within this Act and given to the Child Support Agency to 'manage' where one of the parents is 'absent' according to the Act—usually where they are separated or divorced. The formula takes into account a maintenance requirement calculated on the number and ages of the qualifying children, the income of both parents, and a limited range of 'allowances' for the parents with a 'safety net' of a protected income for the paying parent.

As the Act came in, there was a hostile reception because of its effects upon the financial arrangements of parents, its approach to maintenance and allegations that the provision was aimed at reducing Treasury expenses and payments from the social security system rather than 'putting children first' by ensuring that those 'absent' parents who did not pay towards their children's upbringing began to do so. There were accusations of 'targeting' absent but easily traceable fathers who were already paying. It was said that the Child Support Agency, established to run the formula system, was slow and inefficient. Indeed, there were large numbers of documented cases of administrative problems. One of the major criticisms was that the system increased maintenance payments for most payers and overturned previous arrangements, many of which involved 'clean break' approaches.

Indicative questions

1 Decide whether the following statements are TRUE or FALSE.

(a) A divorce case is heard in the Magistrates Court.

(b) A case of unfair dismissal is heard by an Industrial Tribunal.

(c) An appeal against refusal of unemployment benefit is heard by a Social Security Tribunal.

(d) The Small Claims Court is a section of the Crown Court.

NEAB

2 (a) Name *two* of the legal requirements necessary for a valid marriage.

(*2 marks*)

(b) How is divorce different from judicial separation?   (*4 marks*)

(c) It is suggested that a will made by a husband in favour of his wife is revoked if the parties subsequently divorce.

Explain whether this statement is true or not.   (*2 marks*)

(d) How would the estate of a testator (a person who makes a will) be divided if the will is revoked by a subsequent marriage and the testator then dies without making a new will?   (*4 marks*)

(e) Explain the legal position which exists under English law, when a person under 18 years of age wishes to marry. How sensible is this present legal position? Give reasons for your answer.   (*8 marks*)

SEG

3 (a) Outline the proposals for divorce reform in the United Kingdom and state how the main proposals are different from the law relating to divorce as it now applies.

(b) To what extent do you consider that proposals for divorce reform will assist in resolving disputes that parents have about the care of their children after separation and the payment of spousal and child maintenance?

NEAB

CHAPTER 17

The Law of Succession

ARE WILLS NECESSARY?

Death is nature's way of telling you to slow down. While you may wander through life largely unaffected by many of the laws discussed in this book, nobody escapes the attention of the law of succession. (None of us gets out of this alive.) There is a very old funeral directors' joke—that they sign their letters 'yours eventually'. The question is, however, whether the law will take care of your affairs automatically after you die, or whether you need to make a will: are wills necessary?

The answer is yes, if you want any direct control over how your property is to be distributed after your death. Only about one in four of those who could make a will actually get around to doing it. If there is no will the property will go to others according to the intestacy rules—which means that your awful aunt might get the stereo. Actually, a will can only direct your property if it is left unchallenged by those who depended upon you. A carefully drawn will can minimise tax liability. A solicitor should be instructed when a will is drawn up. It costs about £50 to make a straightforward will.

The most common errors in home-made wills—perhaps written out on one of the forms available from stationers for about £1—are that not all the property of the person making the will (the testator) is disposed of, and so he dies partly intestate, or gifts are made to witnesses or the spouses of witnesses, who therefore cannot take (although the will remains valid), or the will is altered, and the alterations are not witnessed and are therefore invalid. Further errors include being made without taking into account the effect of a beneficiary dying before the testator, or the testator remarrying, or the testator not taking into account all those who could claim to be dependent upon him, and they later demand that provisions be made from the estate when the will is revealed. A will has no effect until the testator dies.

MAKING A WILL

The testator must be an adult, over eighteen, unless he is in the forces

This is the Last Will AND TESTAMENT of me

of

and I hereby revoke all testamentary dispositions previously made by me

1. I APPOINT   of

of

of

and

Solicitor of

(hereinafter called "my Trustees" which expression shall where the context so admits mean the Trustees hereof for the time being) to be the Executors and Trustees of this my Will

2. I GIVE the following specific legacies free of all tax:-

(a) To   of

my black opal and gold brooch my emerald and diamond ring my double string of pearls my Prince of Wales rope gold necklace my ruby and diamond ring and matching bracelet

(b) To my Trustees all items of personal chattels as set out in any list addressed to my Trustees for them to distribute in accordance with such list

(c) To the said   all the remainder of my jewellery with the exception of any items of jewellery given under the previous sub clauses

3. I GIVE to   and   of

jointly

or if either of them has predeceased me to the survivor of them the sum of

A typical will

free of all tax. This legacy is on condition that they or the survivor of them take and look after any animals excluding fish owned by me at the date of my death but this condition will not apply if I own no animals other than fish at the date of my death

4. I GIVE all my real and personal estate whatsoever and wheresoever not hereby or by any codicil hereto otherwise specifically disposed of to my Trustees Upon Trust to sell call in and convert the same into money with power to postpone such sale calling in and conversion for so long as they in their absolute discretion think fit without being liable for loss and to hold the net proceeds of such sale calling in and conversion and my ready money and any property remaining for the time being unconverted after payment thereout of my just debts funeral and testamentary expenses (hereinafter called "my Residuary Estate") upon the trusts hereinafter declared

5. MY Trustees shall hold my Residuary Estate upon trust to divide the same into equal one hundredth shares and shall distribute such shares as follows:-

(a) To   five shares

(b) To

                                whose Treasurer is currently

            five shares

(c) To   of

                        five shares

(d) To   and   of

                        for them to hold upon

trust   for their son   until he attains the age
of eighteen five shares

(e) To   of

twenty shares or if she shall predecease me
equally between such of her children as shall be living at
the date of my death

(f) To   of

twenty shares or if she shall predecease me
equally between such of her children as shall be living at
the date of my death

(g) To   of

twenty shares or if she
shall predecease me equally between such of her children as
shall be living at the date of my death

(h) To the said   twenty shares or if she
shall predecease me to the said   and

jointly or if either of them shall also predecease
me to the survivor of them

6. I DIRECT that the receipt of the treasurer or other
proper officer for the time being of any charity to whom
monies shall be paid under this my Will shall be   a   full
discharge to my Trustees for the sum hereby given and my
Trustees shall not be bound to see or enquire into   the
application thereof

7. ANY Executor or Trustee being a Solicitor Accountant or
other person engaged in any profession or business may be
so employed or act and shall be entitled to charge and be
paid all professional or other charges for any business or
act done by him or his firm in connection with proving my
Will and the administration of my estate and   the   trusts

hereof including acts which an Executor or Trustee could have done personally

8. IF the trusts of any share of my Residuary Estate shall fail or determine then so much thereof as has not been raised and paid under any power applicable thereto together with any share or part of share which shall have accrued under this provision shall be held by my Trustees as an accretion to the other share or shares (and equally if more than one) the trusts whereof shall not at the date of such accruer have failed as aforesaid and upon the trusts powers and provisions applicable thereto herein contained or such of them as at the date of such accruer shall be capable of taking effect

IN WITNESS whereof I have hereunto set my hand this   day of   One Thousand Nine Hundred and Ninety

SIGNED by the above named   )
)
as her last Will in the   )
presence of us present at   )
the same time who at her   )
request in her presence and)
in the presence of each   )
other have hereunto   )
subscribed our names as   )
witnesses:-   )

and on active service. He must know what he is about, as Cockburn CJ said (in *Banks* v. *Goodfellow* (1870)):

> As to the testator's capacity, he must, in the language of the law, have a sound and disposing mind and memory. In other words, he ought to be capable of making his will with an understanding of the nature of the business in which he is engaged, a recollection of the property he means to dispose of, of the persons who are the objects of his bounty, and the manner in which it is to be distributed between them. It is not necessary that he should view his will with the eye of a lawyer, and comprehend its provisions in their legal form. It is sufficient if he has such a mind and memory as will enable him to understand the elements of which it is composed, and the disposition of his property in its simple forms.

The formalities required and essential for validity were significantly changed by the Administration of Justice Act 1982 which contains a wide variety of unrelated changes all listed in a single statute. Section 17 repealed and replaced the Wills Act 1837, s.9, and set the formalities for making a will. The new version of the section largely repeats them, but it is no longer necessary for a will to be signed 'at the foot or end thereof', but the signature must be written last. This is clear from *Wood* v. *Smith* (1991) where the testator wrote his name first then the will. The court would not accept it.

Now a will is valid if:

1 it is in writing; and
2 it is signed by the testator, or by someone else in his presence and by his direction—so that it appears that the testator intended by his signature to give effect to the will; and
3 this signature is made or acknowledged by the testator in the presence of two or more witnesses present at the same time; and
4 each witness either attests and signs the will or acknowledges his signature in the presence of the testator (but not necessarily in the presence of any other witness).

It must therefore:

1 be written down somewhere, usually as a formal document (although in a case called *In the goods of Barnes* (1926), it was written on an egg shell);
2 be signed; the testator must make a mark, and anything will do as long as it is intended as a signature. The cases include the following examples: a rubber stamp (*Re Jenkins* (1863)), an engraved seal (*In the goods of Emerson* (1882)), and a thumb print (*Re Finn* (1935));
3 be witnessed by two or more witnesses who are present at the same time as the will is signed (or the signature is acknowledged by the testator). The witnesses need to see the signature, not the will. There is no need for them to read it. Anyone who understands what he is doing and can see can be a witness; there is no age qualification. If a beneficiary is a witness the attestation is valid but the gift fails. Furthermore if there is a gift to the spouse of a witness, that gift fails too (Wills Act 1837. s.15); this restriction on taking a benefit is limited, however, to the minimum number of witnesses, namely two. If there are more than two, and if the third and later

witnesses (or their spouses) are beneficiaries then the gifts to them are unaffected (Wills Act 1968, s.1). There must be two witnesses who are not beneficiaries for any further witness who is a beneficiary to keep the gift. This sensible rule was enacted by Parliament in order to reverse the decision (legally accurate, but surely unjust) in *Re Bravda's Estate* (1968) where gifts to two of the deceased's daughters were void because they had witnessed the will—despite the fact that there were two other independent witnesses present;

4 be signed by the witnesses who must sign in the presence of the testator. He need not actually watch. It is enough if he could have watched had he wanted to.

Privileged wills

Some wills can be valid without this formal, strict procedure. They are called privileged wills. They arise usually where the testator is in great danger (and therefore feels he ought to make a will quickly). The Wills Act 1837, s.11, says:

> Provided always . . . that any soldier being in actual military service, or any mariner or seaman being at sea, may dispose of his personal estate as he might have done before the making of this Act.

The privilege was extended to airmen by the Wills (Soldiers and Sailors) Act 1918. A famous example concerned a belligerent airman (*Re Wingham* (1949)), where a RAF trainee pilot put what he referred to as his 'will' onto paper—but it was not witnessed, so it would not be accepted as valid unless, as a trainee, he was on active military service. Denning LJ (as he then was) gave a lucid explanation of the privilege:

> The plain meaning of the statutes is that any soldier, sailor or airman is entitled to the privilege, if he is actually serving with the Armed Forces in connexion with military operations which are or have been taking place or are believed to be imminent. It includes our men serving—or called up for service—in the wars; and women too, for that matter. It includes not only those actively engaged with the enemy but all who are training to fight him. It also includes those members of the Forces who, under stress of war, both work at their jobs and man the defences, such as the Home Guard. It includes not only the fighting men but also those who serve in the forces, doctors, nurses, chaplains, WRNS, ATS, and so forth. It includes them all, whether they are in the field or in barracks, in billets or sleeping at home. It includes them although they may be captured by the enemy or interned by neutrals. It includes them not only in time of war but also when war is imminent. After hostilities are ended, it may still include them, as, for instance, when they garrison the countries which we occupy, or when they are engaged in military operations overseas. In all these cases they are plainly 'in actual military service'.

This privilege has been extended to a soldier serving in Northern Ireland (*Re Jones* (1981)) but denied to an 'indentured apprentice' to a shipping line, who was on leave, without orders to join a ship (*Re Rapley's Estate* (1983)).

So a privileged will can be oral or written; it could lack a signature or witnesses or witnesses' signatures. Provided the testator intended to make a will, it is valid.

CHANGING A WILL

If the will is altered before it is executed (signed and witnessed) then it will be valid in its altered form. Where the alterations are made later, the 1837 Act, s.21, provides that the alteration has no effect unless either 'the words or effect of the will before such alteration shall not be apparent', or the alteration is executed in the same manner as the will itself. As to this point of trying to see what the will said before it was altered, magnifying glasses have been used (*In the goods of Ibbetson* (1839)); the paper has even been held up to the light with a crossing out (obliteration) surrounded with brown paper (*Ffinch* v. *Combe* (1894)). Alterations on the will must be formally executed. They were not in *Re White*, (*dec'd*) (1990) so the unamended will remained valid. A later document which amends a will must be formally executed too; it is called a codicil.

REVOKING A WILL

A will can be revoked by four methods.

Formal method

By a document which is formally executed in the way the will was executed. In fact most wills begin with a revocation clause:

> I hereby revoke all former wills and testamentary instruments made by me and declare this to be my last will.

There is a doctrine with the extraordinary name of dependent relative revocation. It means, broadly, conditional revocation, so that if you revoke your will formally, intending to make another one, or thinking that the rules of intestacy will meet your requirements, and you do not actually make the new will, or the rules do not have that effect (and if there is enough evidence of all this), then the revocation is not effective. The will survives. For example, in *Re Carey* (1977), a man destroyed his will, saying that he had nothing to leave and that it was pointless to have a will. However, he had forgotten that he might inherit under his sister's estate—and he did (£40 000!). The court held that the revocation was dependent on the man having nothing to leave, and as he had inherited from his sister, this condition was not satisfied. In *Re Finnemore* (dec'd) (1991) three successive wills were made, each containing a revocation clause. Substantial gifts were left to the same person in each one, but the second and third were witnessed by the beneficiary's husband. The will was valid, but the gifts to her would fail. Nevertheless, the court accepted the gifts in the first will. Their revocation was held to have been dependent upon the validity of the later wills.

Where a later will is made without a revocation clause then the two are read together, and to the extent (perhaps total) that they conflict the later one prevails.

Informal method   Privileged wills can be made informally, and they can also be revoked informally. They last even if the testator leaves the services (and loses his privileged position to make another one informally—so he could revoke informally but he would have to satisfy the usual requirements to replace it).

By destruction   The Wills Act 1837, s.20, says:

> No will or codicil, or any part thereof, shall be revoked otherwise than as aforesaid, or by another will or codicil, executed in manner herein before required, or by some writing declaring an intention to revoke the same, and executed in the manner in which a will is herein before required to be executed, or by the burning, tearing, or otherwise destroying the same by the testator, or by some person in his presence and by his direction, with the intention of revoking the same.

Here we are concerned with 'burning, tearing or otherwise destroying . . . with the intention of revoking' (called *animus revocandi*). Just writing 'cancelled' is not enough. Tearing off a part of the sheet will usually leave the rest effective. If the testator cannot physically manage to destroy the will, it may be done by someone else, but it must be done in his presence and by his direction. The intention is very important. A mentally disordered testator may make a will during a lucid interval but not revoke it when his illness returns. If the will is lost there is a presumption (rebuttable with appropriate evidence) that it was destroyed *animos revocandi*.

By marriage   This is automatic revocation. A marriage revokes a will unless it was made with that particular marriage in mind, (none other) and the intention that the marriage should not revoke the will. In *Pilot* v. *Gainfort* (1931), for example, the testator named a woman (Diana Featherstone Pilot) and referred to her as his wife, although he did not marry her for three years. The will survived the marriage. The law is now to be found in the Wills Act 1837, s.18 (as substituted by the Administration of Justice Act 1982, s.18).

PROVIDING FOR DEPENDANTS

Relatives are usually provided for in the will, if there is one. If not, they are provided for by the operation of the rules of intestacy (of which, details later).

Where either the will or the intestacy rules do not make 'reasonable financial provision' for dependants, however, they can apply to the court for such provision out of the estate. This right is provided by the Inheritance (Provision for Family and Dependants) Act 1975. Section 1 (1) of the Act says:

> Where after the commencement of this Act a person dies domiciled in England and Wales and is survived by any of the following persons:
> (*a*) the wife or husband of the deceased;
> (*b*) a former wife or former husband of the deceased who has not remarried;
> (*c*) a child of the deceased;

(*d*) any person (not being a child of the deceased) who, in the case of any marriage to which the deceased was at any time a party, was treated by the deceased as a child of the family in relation to that marriage;

(*e*) any person (not being a person included in the foregoing paragraphs of this subsection) who immediately before the death of the deceased was being maintained, either wholly or partly, by the deceased;

that person may apply to the court for an order under section 2 of this Act on the ground that the disposition of the deceased's estate affected by his will or the law relating to intestacy, or the combination of his will and that law, is not such as to make reasonable financial provision for the applicant.

Incidentally, under s.1(1)(c) any child of the deceased can apply. Age, marital status and financial dependence upon the deceased are all irrelevant to the right to apply, but an adult who is quite able to support himself is not likely to sway the sympathy of the court much.

This 'reasonable financial provision' means maintenance—enough to live on, unless the applicant happens to be the surviving spouse, where it means more than just maintenance. The court could, for example, add a lump sum.

The powers of the court are wide and flexible. It may order periodical payments from the estate, lump sums, transfers of property, settlement of property so that the applicant can take the benefit, use of estate property so as to acquire other property for the applicant, and so on. It can make an interim payment too, if the applicant is in sufficient need. It can even order someone else to pay the applicant, if it appears that property was distributed before the death with the aim of avoiding making appropriate provision.

Naturally, the court will take into account all the surrounding circumstances. According to the Inheritance (Provision for Family and Dependants) Act 1975, s.3, these will include: the applicant's financial needs (including education) and his current and potential assets, the needs and resources of other applicants, those of the beneficiaries under the will, the obligations and responsibilities that the deceased owed the applicant, other applicants and the beneficiaries, the size of the net estate, the mental and physical health of the applicants and beneficiaries, and so on. If the applicant is a surviving or former spouse (not remarried) then the age, the length of the marriage and the contribution of the applicant to the deceased's family will be relevant. A rough guide might be the financial provision that would have been ordered had the spouse and deceased been parted by divorce rather than the 'grim reaper'. In *Moody* v. *Stevenson* (1991) the Court of Appeal held that the judge in the court below ought to have asked 'what would a family judge have ordered for the couple if divorce instead of death had divided them?'. Since 1 January 1996, a claim may be made by any person who, during the whole period of two years ending immediately before the date when the deceased died, was living (a) in the same household as the deceased; and (b) as husband or wife of the deceased.

If the applicant falls within s.1(1)(d), the court will consider whether the deceased had taken on the obligation to maintain, on what basis, for how long, whether he knew the child was not his and anyone else's responsibilities towards that child. Similar considerations of assumed responsibility will be taken into account with applicants within s.1(1)(e).

There is a time limit of six months from the date that the estate is made the responsibility of personal representatives within which applications should be made. (There is a power to entertain late applications.)

Using this power the courts have made provision for a variety of dependants: a step-son (*Re Callaghan* (1984)), a step-daughter (*Re Leach* (1985)), a wife after a separation of forty-three years (*Rolands* v. *Rolands* (1984)) and even the subsidiary mistress (*Malone* v. *Harrison* (1979)).

A word about forfeiture. If you murder someone then, fairly logically, you cannot claim under a will left by them, nor under the intestacy rules (considered below), nor can you claim under this 'family provision' legislation. It is a rule of public policy which has been accepted for many years. However, if you are responsible for the death but not a murderer then the court can make an exception in your case, if the circumstances indicate that this would be just. There is a new statute, the Forfeiture Act 1982, under which the court allowed a wife who had pleaded guilty to the manslaughter of her husband to claim from his will. (He had subjected her to violent and unprovoked attacks for many years, and he was killed by a shotgun fired by her during such a quarrel: *Re K. (deceased)* (1985)). It follows that there is now no rule to stop such a claim being made under the 'family provision' legislation. Of course, the court will take into account all the circumstances of the relationship, including the death, when deciding whether or not to make provision.

INTESTACY

If the deceased left no will, he died intestate. If he left a will but failed to dispose of all his property, he died partially intestate. There are intestacy rules which provide for the distribution of property not disposed of by will.

The intestacy rules apply to the distribution of the net estate; that is, the property which is left when the personal representatives (administrators in this case) have paid the funeral, testamentary and administration expenses, together with all the deceased's debts and liabilities.

The rules speak of 'spouses' and 'issue'. A 'spouse' is a husband or wife, not someone with whom the deceased was living (cohabitee, 'common law wife') nor a divorced husband or wife. 'Issue' includes children, grandchildren and subsequent direct descendants. Adopted children and illegitimate children are included, as is a child conceived but not born when the deceased died.

The distribution of the net estate depends upon whom the deceased leaves behind him. There are four main situations:

1 **Surviving spouse and issue** Here the spouse takes all the personal chattels absolutely (furniture, jewellery, books, pictures, etc., but nothing which is used for business purposes), £125 000 (plus interest at 7 per cent from the death to the payment) and a life interest of half of whatever's left. The issue take the other half of the remainder of the net estate (i.e. after the personal chattels and the lump sum have been subtracted), and the spouse's half when he or she dies.

2 **Surviving spouse but no issue** The spouse takes the personal chattels plus £200 000 (with interest as above at 7 per cent) plus half of the balance absolutely. The other half goes to the parents of the deceased (not step-parents or mother/father-in-law). If no parents are alive then any brothers and sisters take the other half of the balance, if they are at least eighteen (or sixteen and seventeen and married). If no brothers or sisters are alive but their issue survive and are eighteen (or sixteen or seventeen and married) then they take the other half.

3 **Surviving spouse but no issue nor any of the relatives mentioned in (2) above** The spouse takes the whole net estate absolutely, although, since 1 January 1996 the spouse must survive the intestate for 28 days to qualify (here, and in cases 1 and 2 above).

4 **No surviving spouse but surviving issue** If the deceased leaves no surviving spouse, then all the residuary estate is held on trust for the issue.

5 **No surviving spouse nor surviving issue** Here the net estate passes entirely to the relatives who survive. This is the order of preference—once a survivor is found nobody lower in the order takes anything. The order is this: first, parents, then brothers and sisters, then brothers and sisters 'of the half-blood', then grandparents, then uncles and aunts, then uncles and aunts 'of the half-blood'. If nobody here survives, the property is called *bona vacantia*—and will go to the Crown.

Where anyone under eighteen receives property upon the operation of the intestacy rules, it is held in trust for them until they reach that age.

PERSONAL REPRESENTATIVES

When someone dies the people who clear up his affairs are called his personal representatives (PRs). Their precise duties depend upon the circumstances they have been left in. There are, broadly, four stages in dealing with the estate: obtaining the right to act as PRs, assessing the value of the estate, obtaining probate and distributing the estate.

Obtaining the right to act

PRs will be either executors or administrators. An executor is named as such in the will. If there is no will, or if there is one but nobody is named (or someone is named but refuses to act) then the PRs will be administrators.

Oath for Executors

IN THE HIGH COURT OF JUSTICE

Extracting Solicitor...

Family Division

Address...

*If necessary to include alias of deceased in grant add "otherwise (alias name)" and state below which is true name and reason for requiring alias

The District Probate Registry at

IN the Estate of*

(^{1})

deceased.

(1) "I" or "We". Insert the full name, place of residence and occupation, or, if none, description of the deponent(s), adding "Mrs", "Miss", as appropriate, for a female deponent

(2) Or "do solemnly and sincerely affirm"

make Oath and say (^{2}): —

that

(3) Each testamentary paper must be marked by each deponent, and by the person administering the oath

(^{1})   believe the paper writing (^{3}) now produced to and marked by (^{3})

to contain the true and original last Will and Testament (^{4})

(4) "with one, two (or more) Codicils", as the case may be

of*

of

formerly of

deceased

(5) If exact age is unknown, give best estimate.

who died on the   day of   19   ,

aged   years (^{5}) domiciled in (^{6})

(6) Where there are separate legal divisions in one country, the state, province, etc., should be specified.

and that to the best of   knowledge, information and belief there was (^{7}) [no]

(7) Delete "no", if there was land vested in deceased which remained settled land notwithstanding his or her death

land vested in the said deceased which was settled previously to h   death (and

not by h   Will (^{4})   ;

(8) Settled land may be included in the scope of the grant provided the executors are also the special executors as to the settled land; in that case the settlement must be identified

and which remained settled land notwithstanding h   death (^{8})

And I/we further make oath and say (^{2})

that notice of this application has been given to

(9) Delete or amend as appropriate. Notice of this application must be served on all executors to whom power is to be reserved unless dispensed with by a Registrar under Rule 27 (3).

the executor(s) to whom power is to be reserved, [save

]. (^{9})

(10) "I am" or "we are". Insert relationship of the executors to the deceased only if necessary to establish title or identification.

And (^{1})   further make Oath and say (^{2})

that (^{10}) (^{11})

(11) "The sole", or "the surviving", or "one of the", or "are the", or "two of the", etc.

named in the said

Execut

Oath for executors

(12) If there was settled land and the grant is to include it, insert "including settled land" but, if the grant is to exclude the settled land, insert "save and except settled land".

and that (^{1})   will (i) collect, get in and administer according to the law the real and personal estate (^{12})   of the said deceased; (ii) when required to do so by the Court, exhibit on oath in the Court a full inventory of the said estate (^{12})

and when so required render an account of the administration of the said estate to the Court; and (iii) when required to do so by the High Court, deliver up the grant of probate to that Court; and that to the best of   knowledge, information and belief

(13) Complete this paragraph only if the deceased died on or after 1 April 1981 and an Inland Revenue Account is not required; the next paragraph should be deleted.

(^{13}) [the gross estate passing under the grant does not exceed (^{14}) £ and the net estate does not exceed (^{15}) £   , and that this is not a case in which an Inland Revenue Account is required to be delivered]

(14) Insert "†25,000" in respect of deaths on or after 1 April 1991, "115,000" in respect of deaths on or after 1 April 1990. "100,000" in respect of deaths on or after 1 April 1989, "70,000" in respect of deaths on or after 1 April 1987, "40,000" in respect of deaths on or after 1 April 1983, or "25,000" in respect of deaths prior to that date.

(^{16}) [the gross estate passing under the grant amounts to £ and the net estate amounts to £   ].
*

(15) Insert currently "10,000" "25,000", "40,000," "70,000", "100,000", or "200,000" as appropriate.

(16) Complete this paragraph only if an Inland Revenue Account is required and delete the previous paragraph.

N.B. The names of all executors to whom power is to be reserved must be included in the Oath.

SWORN by   the above-named
Deponent

at

this   day of   19   ,

Before me,

          A Commissioner for Oaths/Solicitor.

© 1988 **OYEZ** The Solicitors' Law Stationery Society Ltd., Oyez House, 7 Spa Road, London SE16 3QQ

7.93 F25256
5073583
* * *

Probate 4 (DR)

Oath for administrators—surety's guarantee

Executors apply for a grant of probate. Administrators apply for a grant of letters of administration—any will which dealt with only part of the estate is submitted for probate. Sometimes a will fails to mention executors; in this case a grant of letters for administration 'with the will annexed' is sought. An administrator can be anyone who has an interest in the estate. It is usually the next of kin, perhaps with professional help from a solicitor.

A grant of probate or letters of administration is not necessary for a 'small estate'—where the deceased left just cash and personal effects and the relatives are agreed on how they should be shared, and/or the deceased left only a small amount in certain saving schemes (like building societies, or National Savings) where they may get the money out without undue formality. However there is no obligation to pay out in the absence of probate or letters of administration. Any assets which were jointly owned by the deceased and his surviving spouse (house, furniture, video cassette recorder) will pass automatically to the spouse.

If you hear that somebody is applying for probate or letters of administration whom you believe might not be suitable then you can object to the grant by informing the local probate office. You will then be given the chance to voice your objections before any grant will be made. Such an application is called a *caveat*.

An application for probate or letters of administration is made at the Personal Application Department of the local Probate Registry. Forms have to be filled in, details obtained. A death certificate is necessary, and a copy of the will, if there is one.

Assessing the estate

The PRs need to search out details of the deceased's assets in order to fill in the forms supplied by the registry—savings certificates, premium bonds, stocks and shares, unit trusts, accounts at the bank, building society, insurance policies, household and personal goods, money due from an employer, occupational pension, land and other similar property, business interests, unclaimed social security benefits, tax rebates and all the debts owed to the deceased.

As against these assets, the PRs must calculate the deceased's liabilities. These might include: rates owed, rent or mortgage payments, telephone bills, fuel bills, credit card accounts, overdrafts, hire purchase or other credit deals, personal loans, income tax. The PRs should check for other debts by advertising for unknown creditors in the local paper and in the *London Gazette*. Usually two months must be allowed for creditors to come forward. There are other debts which must be taken into account: the funeral expenses (but not a tombstone), probate fees, inheritance tax (if any), any solicitor's bill and other expenses incurred by the PRs (phone calls, travel to the Probate Registry, etc.).

If the debts exceed the assets there is a prescribed order for payment. The funeral testamentary and administration expenses are paid first, then the order of priority is similar to that used when the assets of a bankrupt are divided.

In the High Court of Justice

The Principal Registry of the Family Division

BE IT KNOWN that HENRY ESMOND of 19 Horsa Road Angleton Wessex

S P E C I M E N

died on Wednesday **the** 1st **day of** January 19

domiciled in England and Wales

AND BE IT FURTHER KNOWN that at the date hereunder written the last Will and Testament

(a copy whereof is hereunto annexed) of the said deceased was proved and registered in the Principal Registry of the Family Division of the High Court of Justice and Administration of all the estate which by law devolves to and vests in the personal representative of the said deceased was granted by the aforesaid Court to

JOSEPH ANDREWS Butcher of 25 Sea Road Angleton Wessex and ELIZA DOOLITTLE of 18 Horsa Road Angleton Wessex Widow

It is hereby certified that it appears from information supplied on the application for this grant that the gross value of the said estate in the United Kingdom ~~does not exceed~~/amounts to £ 55,000 and that the net value of such estate ~~does not exceed~~/amounts to £ 50,000

Dated the 1st **day of** February 19 :

Probate Officer

37109 88i9770
25000 4/
LT LTD 867

Probate **Extracted by** MESSRS ROBIN & SWALLOW
ANGLETON WESSEX

PR2

Grant of Probate

Obtaining probate

With all the details to hand the forms can be filled in. These, the death certificate and the will (where there is one) are taken or sent to the local Probate Registry. Naturally, there are fees to pay—for personal application and probate fees. Documents are prepared by the Registry called the Executor's Oath and the Inland Revenue Affidavit. They must be signed by the PRs. They also swear on oath.

The grant of probate is sent on later, with a copy of the will. The original is kept at Somerset House in London.

Distributing the estate

Now that the PRs have the grant they can call in all the deceased's assets. They will open an account into which to pour them. They then drain off enough to pay the deceased's debts and liabilities.

Then the estate can be distributed in accordance with either the will or the intestacy rules, as appropriate. The PRs should then prepare a full account of what was done with the assets of the estate, the deceased's debts, the funeral expenses, the administration expenses, the legacies given out (with signed receipts from the lucky recipients). All the papers should be filed away safely—for twelve years.

Indicative questions

1 Kate has just died and her brother Jeremy has discovered a will made by Kate, without his knowledge, just two weeks before she died. In the last twelve months of her life Kate had suffered from temporary periods of mental illness.

The will had been signed by Kate in the margin on the right-hand side because she did not leave enough space at the bottom. Her signature had been witnessed by three people, two close friends and her doctor, Keith. She has left a small gift of £100 in the will to Keith and everything else, valued at £160 000, to the local animal sanctuary. The £100 gift to Keith was the result of a hand-written change from £1000.

(a) Will Kate's signature in the right-hand margin be effective as a signature to the will? (*2 marks*)

(b) Explain the possible legal difficulties that could arise from:
(i) Kate's periods of temporary illness; (*2 marks*)
(ii) the gift to her doctor; (*3 marks*)
(iii) the change in the gift from £1000 to £100. (*2 marks*)

(c) Kate has made no provision in her will for her husband Michael, who is disabled and living permanently in a nursing home. Kate had paid all the bills for the home during her lifetime. She also has a daughter, Megan, who lives in Australia and whom she has not seen for many years.

Explain to Michael:
(i) what action he must take, so that he may continue to live in the nursing home, assuming that the will is held to be valid; (*5 marks*)
(ii) what the position would be if Kate's will were declared invalid. (*6 marks*)

SEG

2 A valid will must be in writing, signed by the testator and properly witnessed. Even where the will meets these requirements, the distribution of the contents of the will can be challenged by certain specified persons under the provisions of the Inheritance (Provision for Family and Dependants) Act 1975.

Where the testator leaves no will or an invalid will, the deceased's estate will be distributed in accordance with the Intestacy Rules.

The Problem

Lewis and Myfanwy, both in their seventies, had been married for over 50 years. They had three children, Nesta, Owen and Peggy. Nesta and Peggy are married with children of their own. Owen also married Ruth 20 years ago and they had two children, Susan, now aged 19, and Thomas, now aged 16. Owen died in a car accident 10 years ago.

Lewis recently made a will, which he wrote out and signed in the presence of Susan and Thomas, though neither of them signed as witness. Both, however, signed later. The following day, Lewis had the will signed by Una, his next-door neighbour, and the following morning by Victor, his postman.

In his will, Lewis left some money to his sister Winifred, whom he regularly supports. The rest of his estate he left to Peggy because, as he stated in his will, "She is the only daughter who ever comes to visit me." Lewis has since died, leaving an estate valued at £185 000.

(a) Discuss the validity of Lewis' will, taking into account, in particular, the validity of the witnesses. *(8 marks)*

(b) If Lewis' will were to be declared valid, it would almost certainly be contested.

Explain how the relevant legislation would deal with the claims of the following if they were to contest the contents of Lewis' will:
  (i) Myfanwy;
  (ii) Nesta;
  (iii) Ruth. *(6 marks)*

(c) If Lewis' will were to be declared invalid, he would have died intestate.

Explain how the Intestacy Rules would distribute Lewis' estate in these circumstances with respect to the following:
  (i) Myfanwy; *(4 marks)*
  (ii) Lewis' children; *(3 marks)*
  (iii) Lewis' grandchildren; *(3 marks)*
  (iv) Winifred. *(2 marks)*

(d) Comment on how fairly the Intestacy Rules would operate in this situation. *(4 marks)*

SEG

CHAPTER 18

The Worker and the Law

THE CONTRACT OF EMPLOYMENT

This contract provides the basis of the rights, duties and liabilities of the parties to it—the employer and employee. The framework remains that of common law contract rules (as was seen in Chapter 13), but Parliament intervenes increasingly in the labour law field, and there are certain statutes which will require our attention. The contract we are to examine is that for a full time employee rather than an independent contractor (we considered this very important distinction in Chapter 12 when dealing with vicarious liability).

There are no formal requirements for the contract of employment. It could be oral, by conduct, partly written or entirely written. The written contract is to be preferred because its provisions will be readily available for reference. A term that is written in the contract cannot be negatived by evidence of what happens in practice. Furthermore, it will be easier to bring about changes if the contract is written (e.g. reduce overtime, restrict the choice of holiday dates, introduce a shift system). Written contracts of employment are, however, little used today, except for higher management positions.

Whether the contract is written, partly written or just oral, the employee who has a working week of 8 hours or more has a right to receive 'written particulars of employment'. The details required in this written statement are provided by the Employment Rights Act 1996:

1 (1) Not later than two months after the beginning of an employee's employment with an employer, the employer shall give a written statement to the employee which may, subject to s.2 (3), be given in instalments before the end of that period.

(2) The statement shall contain particulars of—

(a) the names of the employer and employee;

(b) the date when the employment began, and

(c) the date on which the employee's period of continuous employment began (taking into account any employment with a previous employer which counts towards that period).

(3) The statement shall also contain particulars, as at a specified date not more than seven days before the statement or instalment of the statement containing them is given, of—

(*a*) the scale or rate of remuneration or the method of calculating remuneration,

(*b*) the intervals at which remuneration is paid (that is, weekly, monthly or other specified intervals),

(*c*) any terms and conditions relating to hours of work (including any terms and conditions relating to normal working hours),

(*d*) any terms and conditions relating to any of the following—

(i) entitlement to holidays, including public holidays, and holiday pay (the particulars given being sufficient to enable the employee's entitlement, including any entitlement to accrued holiday pay on the termination of employment, to be precisely calculated),

(ii) incapacity for work due to sickness or injury, including any provisions for sick pay, and

The Statutory Sick Pay scheme, in operation since 1983, also requires the employer to give details in writing of the 'qualifying days' for calculation of sickness payments, and the rules of notification of absence. In practice these details should be given in this section.

(iii) pensions and pension schemes;

(*e*) the length of notice which the employee is obliged to give and entitled to receive to determine his contract of employment,

(*f*) the title of the job which the employee is employed to do or a brief description of the work for which the employee is employed,

(*g*) where the employment is not intended to be permanent, the period for which it is expected to continue or, if it is for a fixed term, the date when it is to end,

(*h*) either the place of work or, where the employee is required or permitted to work at various places, an indication of that and of the address of the employer,

(*j*) any collective agreements which directly affect the terms and conditions of the employment including, where the employer is not a party, the persons by whom they were made . . .

Section 1 (4) requires that every statement given to an employee under this section shall include a note specifying any disciplinary rules applicable to the employee or referring to a document which is reasonably accessible to the employee and which specifies such rules; and specifying a person to whom the employee can apply and the method of applying if dissatisfied with a disciplinary decision or wishing to seek redress of a grievance.

The idea behind all these requirements, and others which require employers to produce written documents (itemised pay statements, reasons for dismissal, safety policy) is simply to let the employee know where he stands. It must be noted, however, that the written particulars of employment are not the contract of employment; they are only evidence that a contract exists. This very important point was confirmed in the case of *System Floors (UK) Ltd* v. *Daniel* (1981) where the Employment Appeal Tribunal (EAT) stated:

It provides very strong prima facie evidence of what were the terms of the contract between the parties, but does not constitute a written contract between the parties. Nor are the statement of the terms finally conclusive; at most they place a heavy burden on the employer to show that the actual terms of contract are different from those which he has set out in the statutory statement.

All of the details required in the written particulars would be included if the contract were written. Things like lay-offs, guaranteed weeks, pension schemes, holidays, and so on, are not prescribed by law. They are to be agreed. The employer must say what they are, but the law makes no particular demands about time and/or money at times like these. They might well have been settled by negotiation with a trade union—but they should appear in the written contracts made with individuals. Where a statute does make a detailed requirement, such as a minimum period of notice, it can always be varied upwards in the contract, by agreement.

The contract will also contain implied terms. We noted how terms can be implied into contracts in Chapter 13. The courts might imply a term in a particular case if it is needed for the contract to make business sense. In *Stevenson* v. *Teeside Bridge and Engineering* (1971) a construction engineer's contract was held to contain an implied term that he would move his place of work as each job was completed. Alternatively, the term could be implied because of the effect of a particular rule of law, statute or common law. We will examine this effect from each side in turn, as implied duties.

THE DUTIES OF THE EMPLOYER

There are a number of duties required of employers both at common law and under a variety of statutes.

To treat the employee with respect

Until 1875 it was a criminal offence for a servant not to do his work. There were about 10 000 prosecutions brought every year. The courts now regard oppressive conduct as amounting to constructive dismissal. This means that the employer is in breach of the contract. The employee is free to leave and sue for damages (*see* later section on unfair dismissal). In *Cox* v. *Phillips Industries Ltd* (1976), the plaintiff was moved from one job to another. He was not given any precise responsibilities or duties. He became depressed and eventually fell ill. The employers were held to have acted in breach of contract in their neglect of him, and he was awarded £500 damages.

Furthermore, the employer must not unlawfully discriminate among his employees on the grounds of sex or race. The Race Relations Act 1976 and the Sex Discrimination Act 1975 (as amended by the Sex Discrimination (Amendment) Act 1986) are written in the same way: first the idea of discrimination is explained, then that discrimination which is unlawful is stated, then the exceptions, when an employer is able to discriminate.

The definitions of discrimination refer to both 'direct' and 'indirect' discrimination. 'Direct' discrimination is when someone is treated differently because of their sex, race, colour, nationality, ethnic or national origins, for example, in *Grieg* v. *Community Industry and Ahern* (1979) Miss G accepted employment as a painter and decorator but on her first day the personnel officer refused to permit her to commence work as she would have been the only female in the gang.

He offered alternative work which she refused. It was held that she had been treated differently solely because she was a woman and that is unlawful direct discrimination. The questions to be asked are was the woman less favourably treated than a man, and was she less favourably treated because she was a woman.

In another case, *Coleman* v. *Skyrail Oceanic Ltd* (1981), it was said:

> An assumption that men are more likely than women to be the primary supporters of their spouses and children is an assumption based on sex. Therefore the dismissal of a woman based upon an assumption that husbands are breadwinners and wives are not can amount to discrimination.

'Indirect' discrimination is a more difficult concept. It occurs when a condition is applied equally to both sexes, (race, colour, etc.) but it is such a condition that a smaller proportion of one sex (etc.) than the other can comply with it. For example, in *Hussein* v. *Saintes Complete House Furnishers* (1979) the employers had advertised for a sales assistant who must reside more than five miles from the city centre of Liverpool. The condition was applied to both white and coloured applicants, but it was such a condition that a greater proportion of white people than coloured could apply. Five miles from the city centre is the 'stockbroker belt' and predominantly white, whereas the centre of Liverpool has a very high coloured population. The requirement was unlawful indirect discrimination.

In *Price* v. *Civil Service Commission* (1978) it was held that the requirement that applicants had to be aged between seventeen and twenty-eight years was unlawful indirect discrimination as there were more men than women available for work between those ages, due to the fact that women are often unavailable due to child-bearing and bringing up young children. This controversial decision has been followed by *Home Office* v. *Holmes* (1984), where a requirement of 'full-time' working was held to be indirect discrimination; by *Wright* v. *Rugby Borough Council* (1984) where set-hours (i.e. 9 a.m. to 5 p.m.) was held to be indirect discrimination; and *Huppert* v. *University of Cambridge and University Grants Commission* (1986) where a maximum age requirement of thirty-five years was also indirect discrimination.

As far as employment is concerned, both the Sex Discrimination Act and the Race Relations Act make it unlawful to discriminate in job advertisements, short-listing of candidates for interview, the interview itself, terms of employment, opportunities for training, transfer or promotion, access to any benefits, or dismissal. There are a few exceptions, however, including where a person's sex, or colour, etc. is a 'genuine occupational qualification' for that particular job, for example, a photographic model, a counsellor for welfare services to females, or males, or a particular racial group.

Indirect discrimination is unlawful unless it can be justified. The requirement that a VR4 Radial Drill Operator had to be 5'8" tall and fourteen stones in weight was accepted by the tribunal, after medical evidence that it was necessary to be of these proportions to operate this heavy machinery without damage to the operator's health (*Thorn* v. *Meggitt Engineering Ltd* (1976)).

A complainant can take the grievance to an industrial tribunal (*see* Chapter 4). There are other employees who are entitled to 'respect' in specific ways because of statutory additions to the general common law requirement of respect: e.g. the disabled, trade union members, pregnant women, rehabilitated offenders.

However, this duty of respect does not extend to an obligation to provide references. There is no duty to provide a reference; indeed, it may be ill advised to do so in some cases. If it is derogatory a defamation action might follow. If it is full of undeserved praise then the party relying on it could sue (we considered these tortious aspects in Chapter 12). Furthermore, if it recommends an ex-employee who was dismissed as incapable, then an industrial tribunal might well find the dismissal to have been unfair.

To provide work

This is not usually implied into the contract of employment. As Asquith J said in *Collier* v. *Sunday Referee Publishing Co Ltd* (1940):

> Provided I pay my cook her wages regularly she cannot complain if I choose to take all my meals out.

There may, however, be a duty to provide work where not working loses the employee his reputation (e.g. an actor, as in *Clayton* v. *Oliver* (1930)), or, if not working reduces income because the employee is deprived of his commission or piece work rate. It probably also exists in apprenticeship contracts.

To remunerate

This is basic common law duty on the employer. Failure to pay agreed wages amounts to breach of contract. Action can be taken in the courts in the usual way.

The failure also probably amounts to a constructive dismissal of the employee (unless it is very temporary—a brief cash-flow problem, perhaps). The lack of work does not cancel the duty to pay, provided that the employee is ready and willing to work. However, some contracts provide for the lack of work on a guaranteed payments scheme. After having worked for an employer for four weeks, the Employment Rights Act 1996 give the employee a right to guaranteed payments. However, they will not be paid in certain prescribed circumstances; these include where the lack of work is due to a trade dispute, or if he refuses alternative work which is suitable in the circumstances.

There are other statutory rights to payment. They include circumstances where the employee is suspended on certain specified medical grounds, or where the employee is entitled to maternity pay, or is performing duties as a trade union official, or a safety representative, or where the employee has been declared redundant and is seeking work elsewhere, or is pregnant and attending for ante-natal care. Time off is allowed (with pay if the contract provides for it) for public duties such as serving as a school governor or on a jury.

Time off is allowed (without pay unless the contract provides otherwise) for public duties such as serving as a magistrate, an elected councillor, a school governor, etc., or on a jury.

The Wages Act 1986 has repealed the Truck legislation (1831–1940) and other statutes which controlled the method of payment to 'manual workers', and the kinds of, and amounts of deductions from their wages packets. On 1 January 1987 the requirement to pay in 'current coin of the realm' ceased, unless the contract of existing workers at that date contained such a term. This means that employers can now pay both their manual and white collar workers by whatever method they wish, e.g. direct credit transfer, cheque, cash. Deductions from wages can be made by the employer only if sanctioned by statute (e.g. income tax), a term in the contract of employment (e.g. trade union subscription via a 'check-off' arrangement), or if agreed in writing by the worker prior to the deduction being made.

Workers in retail employment are further protected in that there is a duty on the employer not to deduct more than 10 per cent of gross wages for cash or stock shortages. This limit does not apply to the last payment of wages to a worker leaving the employment.

The employer's duty to pay wages is also subject to the Equal Pay Act 1970 and the Equal Pay (Amendment) Regulations 1983.

To indemnify

This includes refunding employees agreed expenses, incurred within the course of employment together with answering to third parties for the authorised activities of employees.

To take reasonable care of the employee

In *Smith* v. *Austin Lifts* (1959), Lord Simmonds stressed that the law should avoid 'any tendency to treat the relationship between employer and skilled workman as equivalent to that of nurse and imbecile child'. However, there is both a common law and a statutory duty upon the employer to take reasonable care. The injured employee would bring his action, not for breach of contract (despite the fact that the courts are quite prepared to regard these duties as part of the contract) but either for the tort of negligence or for breach of statutory duty, or both together.

The Employers' Liability (Compulsory Insurance) Act 1969 requires that employers insure against employees' claims for personal injuries.

There is a general duty at common law upon an employer to take care of his employees. This is a personal duty owed to employees individually. So while a general safety policy may be acceptable generally, if there are individuals at risk because, perhaps, they cannot read warning signs, or they cannot read the language in which the signs are written, or they are disabled, then a greater duty is owed towards these individuals. *Paris* v. *Stepney Borough Council* (1951) (which we considered in Chapter 12) concerned a one-eyed workman who ought to have been particularly carefully looked after.

This general duty of care can be regarded from three aspects:

1 **A duty to provide safe equipment and premises** The case of *Davie* v. *New Merton Board Mills* (1959) involved a workman who was injured by a broken chisel which his employer had provided.

The employer escaped liability because he had used a reputable supplier. This should no longer suffice. The Employers' Liability (Defective Equipment) Act 1969 endeavoured to impose strict liability for the quality of equipment provided. However, the Act has so many hurdles for an applicant to clear before he is entitled to compensation from his employer that there are many who would say it is no longer worth 'the paper it is written on'.

The claimant must prove:

- that he is an employee
- that he suffered personal injury
- that he was in the course of his employment when injured
- that the injury was a consequence of a defect in equipment provided by his employer for the purposes of the business
- that the defect was attributable to a third party (whether identified or not).

2 **A duty to provide competent staff** So, in *Hudson* v. *Ridge* (1957), a persistent practical joker who injured a colleague ought to have been dismissed. The employer was held liable for the injury.

3 **A duty to provide a safe system of work** There have been cases like *Wilsons and Clyde Coal* v. *English* (1938), where the lack of adequate safety precautions in a coal mine was held to amount to a breach of the duty owed by the employer. However, as we saw in Chapter 12, the problem involved in bringing an action in negligence is that the plaintiff must prove fault. Thus, if the nature of the employee's injury was not reasonably foreseeable then this action will fail. Nevertheless, many of the statutory duties are strict; that is, there is no need to prove fault, just failure to meet the statutory requirements. For example, in the Factories Act 1961, s.14(1), it says:

> Every dangerous part of any machinery . . . shall be securely fenced unless it is in such a position or of such construction as to be as safe to every person employed or working on the premises as it would be if securely fenced.

Salmond LJ said, in *Millard* v. *Sierk Tubes* (1969), where an employee's hand was dragged into an inadequately fenced drill:

> Foreseeability of injury is of very considerable importance when the issue is: 'was there a dangerous part of machinery?' Once the two questions: 'is the machine dangerous?' and 'is there a duty to fence it?' have been answered in the affirmative, foreseeability is no longer relevant. If it is then proved that the plaintiff has suffered an injury by some part of his body coming into contact with the machinery and that this would not have occurred if the defendants had complied with their clear statutory duty, the defendants are liable.

We have met the Unfair Contract Terms Act 1977 on several occasions already. We have noted that it provides in s.2(1):

> A person cannot by reference to any contract term or to a notice given to persons generally or to particular persons exclude or restrict his liability for death or personal injury resulting from negligence.

This obviously applies to warning notices in the workplace and exclusion clauses in contracts of employment.

Under the Health and Safety at Work, etc., Act 1974

The 1974 Act creates no civil law liability. Breach of the requirements of the Act and regulations made under it amounts to a criminal offence. The Act contains these provisions in s.2:

> 2 (1) It shall be the duty of every employer to ensure, so far as is reasonably practicable, the health, safety and welfare at work of all his employees.
>
> (2) Without prejudice to the generality of the above, the matters to which that duty extends include in particular:
>
> (*a*) the provision and maintenance of plant and systems of work that are, so far as is reasonably practicable, safe and without risks to health;
>
> (*b*) arrangements for ensuring, so far as is reasonably practicable, safety and absence of risks to health in connection with the use, handling, storage and transport of articles and substances;
>
> (*c*) the provision of such information, instruction, training and supervision as is necessary to ensure, so far as is reasonably practicable, the health and safety at work of his employees;
>
> (*d*) so far as is reasonably practicable as regards any place of work under the employer's control, the maintenance of it in a condition that is safe and without risks to health and the provision and maintenance of means of access to and egress from it that are safe and without such risks;
>
> (*e*) the provision and maintenance of a working environment for his employees that is, so far as is reasonably practicable, safe, without risks to health and adequate as regards facilities and arrangements for their welfare at work.
>
> (3) Except in such cases as may be prescribed, it shall be the duty of every employer to prepare and as often as may be appropriate revise a written statement of this general policy with respect to the health and safety at work of his employees and the organisation and arrangements for the time being in force for carrying out that policy and to bring the statement and any revision of it to the notice of all his employees.

Failure to issue a safety policy statement to employees is a criminal offence which could lead ultimately to a maximum penalty on conviction of £20 000 in the magistrates' court or an unlimited fine and/or up to two years' imprisonment in the Crown Court.

The Act also imposes (s.6) duties on designers, manufacturers, importers and suppliers of articles and substances for use at work, to ensure (1) their product is safe when used properly, and (2) that sufficient information is provided with the product to enable it to be used safely. The combination of s.6 and s.2(2)(c) should mean that all workers know exactly the hazards of working with any particular article or substance, as the employer has a duty to pass on the manufacturer's information, as well as a duty to train his employees in safe working practices.

THE DUTIES OF THE EMPLOYEE

This is the other side of the coin. The law imposes a variety of duties on the employee. They all stem, directly or indirectly, from the nature of the relationship which exists between the employer and employee. It is a relationship of trust. It follows that persistent lateness, theft of the employer's property, go-slows, sit-ins, and similar behaviour are breaches of this trust and consequently breaches of contract. So that in *British Telecommunications* v. *Ticehurst* (1992) a manager who refused to work normally, having returned after strike action, could have his wages docked without ending his contract. It is part of the contract of employment that the employee will work carefully and competently in the interests of his employer. The employee must obey all lawful orders (i.e. those which are within the contract and also within the general law).

The consequence of an employee failing to obey a reasonable and lawful order is clearly illustrated in the case of *A R Dennis & Co Ltd* v. *Campbell* (1978). C was the manager of a betting shop and, against instructions, accepted credit bets of £1000 which were never paid by the customer. The employer successfully sued C, his employee, for breach of contract, i.e. breach of the implied term, and was awarded £1000 in compensation plus costs. This interesting case illustrates the importance of implied terms in the contract of employment, because the actual contract between the customer and the employer could not have been enforced as it was a wager, and therefore unenforceable.

Another obvious breach of duty is the employee taking bribes. He must not allow personal interests to conflict with those of his employer. Any 'secret profit' taken will amount to a breach of contract and can be claimed by the employer. Any activity which might affect the employer's business in a serious way (e.g. setting up in competition) amounts to breach of contract. Any betrayal of trade or company secrets also is breach of contract.

Section 7 of the Health and Safety at Work, etc., Act 1974 imposes duties on the employee to ensure his own health and safety and the health and safety of others as far as reasonably practicable, and to co-operate with his employer as regards safety at work. Thus an employee who refuses to follow safety instructions or use the protective equipment or clothing provided by his employer could be prosecuted under s.7. In addition, if he is injured as a consequence of his actions he may well lose compensation as he will be deemed to have been contributorily negligent.

TERMINATING THE CONTRACT OF EMPLOYMENT

Notice

The contract might be for a fixed term, or it might have been made to achieve a particular task: after the stated time, or on completion of the task the contract ends. Most contracts of employment are open-ended, with provision for termination by notice. The minimum period of notice laid down in the Employment Rights Act 1996, s.86, is as follows:

- after four weeks' continuous service—one week;
- after two years' continuous service—one week per completed year of service;
- after twelve years' continuous service—twelve weeks, which is the maximum entitlement.

After four weeks' continuous employment employees are only required to give seven days' notice to terminate their contract irrespective of length of service.

It is permissible to increase the notice periods, but this must be recorded in writing in the written particulars of employment. If there is no stated period of notice then the common law says 'reasonable notice' must be given, but this cannot be below the statutory minimum requirement, unless it is a dismissal without notice for reasons such as gross misconduct.

Unfair dismissal

A dismissed employee may be able to claim unfair dismissal, even though he has been given the required period of notice, by applying to an industrial tribunal. It is not the same thing as a breach of contract. It is a concept created by statute and based on the idea that an employer must always act reasonably when dismissing employees. So, for example, if the employer had less than the full facts, if the situation did not warrant dismissal, if there were mitigating circumstances, if the disciplinary rules and procedures had not been made clear to the employee, the dismissal may be held to have been unfair.

The right not to be unfairly dismissed applies to all employees who have the required period of service (i.e. currently two years) and are under retirement age. The applicant must also present his/her claim within three months of the notice or the effective date of termination.

The Act places the burden of proof on the applicant to show that they had been dismissed, and there are three ways in which dismissal may take place:

1 where the contract is terminated by the employer, with or without notice;
2 where a fixed term contract has come to an end without being renewed on the same terms;
3 'constructive dismissal', i.e. where the employee terminates the contract, with or without notice, in such circumstances that he or she is entitled to resign without notice by reason of the employers' conduct. This conduct must be such as to amount to a breach of the contract (*Western Excavating (EEC) Ltd* v. *Sharp* (1978)).

Section 98 of the 1996 Act requires that an employer has to justify a dismissal by showing that the reason for dismissal was a valid reason as specified in the Act, and, secondly, the Tribunal has to be satisfied that the employer acted reasonably in all the circumstances surrounding the dismissal. The specified reasons are:

1 related to the capability or qualifications of the employee for performing work of the kind he was employed to do; or
2 related to the conduct of the employee; or
3 that the employee was redundant; or
4 that continued employment of the employee would be contrary to a duty imposed by statute; or
5 there was 'some other substantial reason' of a kind such as to justify the dismissal.

There are certain dismissals which are always unfair, including dismissal for pregnancy, sex and race discrimination and for trade union activities, such as in *Fitzpatrick* v. *British Railways Board* (1992).

Where the industrial tribunal is satisfied that the dismissal was unfair it has the power to order re-instatement (provided there is work to do—*see Cold Drawn Tubes* v. *Middleton* (1992)), re-engagement or compensation as the remedy.

Redundancy

The redundancy payments provisions of the 1996 Act are contained in Part IX. The basic purpose of the scheme is to compensate a long-serving employee for the loss of what amounts to a proprietary right which he has acquired in his job. The Act imposes an obligation on an employer to make his employees a redundancy payment, if, after two years' continuous service the employee is dismissed by 'reason of redundancy'.

'Redundancy' as defined in the Act, arises if:

1 the employer has ceased, or intends to cease carrying on the business at a particular place, or
2 the need for the particular work done by the employee has ceased or diminished, or is about to do so.

Section 163(2) raises a statutory presumption, that if an employee is dismissed, it is presumed to have been for the reason of redundancy unless the employer can prove the contrary. It is therefore for the employer to show that the dismissal was for inefficiency, unsuitability, health reasons, etc., in which case the law relating to unfair dismissal must have been complied with.

An employee who unreasonably refuses an offer of suitable alternative employment when the job ceases will disqualify the employee from receiving a redundancy payment. However, the offer made by the employer must have complied with the requirements of the Act, and whether or not a refusal is unreasonable is a question of fact in every case, with the burden on the employer to show that his offer was unreasonably refused.

In these circumstances the legislation has given employees a right to a four week trial period in the new job, during which time the employee is free to terminate the new contract if he considers it unsuitable, without affecting his right to claim a redundancy payment if the job is in fact unsuitable. The Act does not define what sort of alternative work is suitable in any situation, but employers must have regard to such things as the skills of the employee, the nature of his previous job, the new earnings compared with his previous job, where the new job is in a different location the difficulties this might cause to the employee, and the accepted custom and practice in such situations in that particular job or industry.

The amount of the redundancy payment depends on the employee's age, length of service and wages at the date of redundancy, subject to a specified maximum level of earnings and a maximum of 20 years' service. Employers with less than ten employees are entitled to a rebate of 35 per cent of monies paid under the scheme from the

Redundancy Fund. Larger employers now have to bear the full cost of their redundancies.

Transfer of undertakings

The Transfer of Undertakings (Protection of Employment) Regulations 1981 were passed to give effect to the EC Directive 77/187, the 'Acquired Rights' Directive. These regulations (as amended) preserve the continuity of employment for dismissal and redundancy purposes of employees who are employed immediately before the transfer of a business to a new owner. The new owner will take over the rights, powers, duties and liabilities of the former owner towards those employees.

Indicative questions

1 You are a volunteer worker in the local office of the Citizens Advice Bureau. Claire comes in one day and says, 'My boss has just given me the sack. I can't believe it. I've worked there for months. I've been late for work a few times but I've done my job pretty well and don't deserve the sack.'

(a) What questions would you need to ask Claire to help you to understand the situation as fully as possible? (*8 marks*)

(b) Explain the situation to her to help her to understand the rights and duties involved. (*10 marks*)

(c) What would you advise her to do, and why? (*12 marks*)

NEAB

2 Read the following extracts and use the information in them, and any other information at your disposal, to help you answer the questions which follow.

Extract A
When employees go on strike they will usually, by doing so, be in breach of their contracts of employment. This means that without some special protection, trade unions or trade union officials would face the possibility of being sued for damages every time they called a strike. But the law says that trade unions and individuals can, in certain circumstances, organise industrial action without fear of being sued in the courts. However, recent changes in the law mean that unions now have only limited protection from being sued.
(From *Industrial Action and the Law*, Department of Employment)

Extract B
The Wapping printworkers' dispute has shown that British workers not only have no right to strike without facing the sack, but also that their trade union can do little afterwards to get support from other unions.
(*The Guardian*, June 1986)

Extract C
The right to strike is fundamental for trade unions and their members. It is their ultimate weapon to protect themselves against an employer who tries to force them to work in conditions or at a pay level they are not prepared to accept.
(*Trades Union Congress*)

(a) Look at Extract A.
  (i) What legal steps can an employer take if his employees are in breach of contract because they have gone on strike? (*2 marks*)
  (ii) In what kinds of circumstances can a trade union organise industrial action without fear of being sued? (*2 marks*)

(b) Look at Extract B
  (i) What does the writer mean by making this statement?
  What kinds of industrial action are now unlawful as a result of recent changes in the law? (*4 marks*)
  (ii) What legal steps can be taken against a trade union which gets involved in such kinds of unlawful industrial action? What penalties would the union face? (*4 marks*)

(c) Do you think that the right balance has been struck between the rights of employees to take industrial action and the rights of employers and others to obtain legal remedies against unlawful forms of industrial action? You may use the extracts and your knowledge of any recent events to help you with your answer. (*7 marks*)

NEAB

CHAPTER 19

Social Security

Social security is a system of cash benefits conferred on individuals who satisfy conditions of entitlement. The objectives of a social security system will depend on your point of view. The architect of the system which we have seen for so long in Great Britain was William Henry Beveridge (1879–1963) who was the Director of the London School of Economics from 1919 to 1937. In 1942 he published his famous *Report on Social Insurance and Allied Services* in which he claimed that the aim of social security was the fulfilment of need:

> to abolish want by ensuring that every citizen willing to serve according to his powers has at all times an income sufficient to meet his responsibilities.

On the other hand, others have stressed the redistributive function of social security. Titmuss, for example, in his book *Commitment to Welfare*, wrote:

> to decrease inequalities in the distribution of incomes and command-over-resources-over-life set by the economic system.

Then there is the perspective of social integration. This was stressed by McCarthy in the *Report of the Royal Commission of Inquiry: Social Security in New Zealand* (1972):

> to . . . ensure . . . that everyone is able to enjoy a standard of living much like that of the rest of the community, and thus is able to feel a sense of participation in and belonging to the community.

The Social Security Act of 1986 was publicised as the most important and comprehensive view of the welfare state since Beveridge. Norman Fowler, then Secretary of State for Social Services, wrote in September 1986:

> Our aims are clear. They are to develop a modern social security system which is simpler to understand and to run, and fair in the way that it directs help to those who need it most. We want to create a soundly based system that the country can afford, and one in which people can look forward to independence and security in retirement.

Yet the *Daily Telegraph*, hardly an organ of the hard left, remarked

> There is no comparison between Mr Fowler's exercise and that of Beveridge . . . Beveridge had a grand vision . . . he was aiming at nothing less than the

eradication of poverty . . . if Mr Fowler has a similar sense of vision he has yet to display it.

Before the introduction of this brave new world in 1987, there were about sixty different cash benefits available to those who qualified. Many of them remain, but structural alterations were made. Over the years to 1997 several further changes were made. Possibly the most significant was the replacement of 'unemployment benefit' with the 'jobseeker's allowance' in October 1996. The then Secretary of State, Peter Lilley said:

> Our policies are three-fold. First, to help and encourage people to take jobs. That is why we are introducing the Jobseeker's Allowance. Our Jobseeker's Agreement will be tailored to the needs of individual people, and the efforts each unemployed person needs to make to get back to work. But the right to benefit will be conditional on people genuinely trying to get back to work . . . Second, we need to make work attractive relative to being on benefit. A minimum wage is not the answer. For it would destroy precisely the kind of jobs which give people their first step up the ladder out of dependency. Instead, we want to make it worthwhile for people to accept the kind of jobs which companies can afford to offer them.

With a change of government come new policies and strategies. However, before considering these, we will look briefly at the current system and pattern of benefits.

There are three main types of benefit: National Insurance benefits, means-tested benefits and non-contributory benefits.

1 **National Insurance benefits** These are the benefits where the qualifications are based upon your contribution record into the National Insurance scheme. There is no means test. You do not have to be poor, but your record of contributions must be adequate. The benefits to be gained from an adequate NI contribution record include: invalidity benefit, maternity allowance, retirement pension, sickness benefit, jobseeker's allowance and widows' benefits.

2 **Means-tested benefits** In these cases you do have to be poor, but there is no need for a National Insurance contribution record.

3 **Non-contributory benefits** In these cases special qualifications apply. Your national insurance contribution record is not relevant. You do not need to be poor, they are not means-tested benefits. They include child benefit, attendance allowance, disability living allowance, various exclusions from NHS charges, and so on.

There is a range of means-tested benefits for people on low incomes, whether they are working or not. They include:

1 **Income support**—which, in general terms, is designed to help those who are 18 or over whose income is below a certain level and who are not working 16 hours a week or more. It can be paid to top up other benefits (like jobseeker's allowance) or earnings from part-time work. There are very limited circumstances in which those aged 16 or 17 can claim income support. The amount of benefit takes account of such things as your age, health, number of dependants, income (if any) and savings. The payment will be made

up of three parts: a personal allowance, premiums (for those with special needs) and housing costs.

2 **Family credit**—which is a benefit for working families (at least 16 hours a week) with children. The amount paid will vary with income and the number and age of the children.

3 **Housing benefit**—which is paid by local councils to people who need help to pay their rent. The usual factors are used to calculate the amount payable.

4 **Council tax benefit**—which is designed to offset the council tax for those who cannot afford to pay it. The rules are similar to those for housing benefit.

Under the previous system involving supplementary benefit—claimants had the right to single payments for special or urgent needs. This is not possible under income support. Instead a 'Social Fund' was set up in April 1988 from which single payments or loans can be made. Mostly these payments are discretionary, although there are certain rules which relate to such matters as maternity benefits. The Social Fund has an annual budget. *The Economist* has said 'how a demand determined benefit can be cash limited is still a mystery'. Payments from the fund are divided into four main categories.

1 **Community care needs**—to cover the needs of, for example, those coming out of institutions. The Green Paper which preceded the 1986 Act included here those costs arising from 'a number of family changes which create exceptional short-term pressures such as visits to children in care . . . short-term crises through illness which put particular strain on families'. These payments would not usually be recoverable.

2 **Maternity and funeral expenses**—maternity grants, which were abolished in April 1987, were universal grants of £25 paid to 720 000 women each year at a level which had remained unchanged since 1969. Now a means-tested grant of about £75 is paid from the Social Fund. The death grant (£30, unchanged since 1967, paid for over 600 000 deaths each year) was abolished in April 1987, and replaced with a means-tested recoverable payment.

3 **Budgeting arrangements**—payments are made to cover items such as the provision and replacement of major household items, repairs, large debts, and removal expenses. These are loans, not grants, and they can be recovered by deduction from weekly benefits.

4 **Financial crises**—payments from the Social Fund can be made for such events, whether or not the applicant is on benefit—broadly replacing urgent needs payments, and, as the Green Paper said, they 'will continue to be operated on the basis of a strict test of resources and limited amounts'.

When evaluating policy promises, plans, aims and aspirations, particularly when they emerge from a political party that had been out of power for the best part of two decades, it is as well to have a sense of the sheer scale of the Social Security operation. This is illustrated in figures published in September 1997:

- Total Social Security expenditure in 1996/97 was £92 846m. Of this, £42 337m was spent on contributory benefits and £50 509m on non-contributory benefits. Expenditure on State Retirement Pensions is the largest component at £32 023m.
- The number of families in receipt of Family Credit increased to 725 300 at November 1996, from 648 700 a year before. The average amount awarded rose from £54.80 to £56.92 per week over the same period. The average gross earnings for all families in receipt of Family Credit was £112.81.
- Between May 1995 and May 1996 the number of Income Support recipients decreased by 121 000 to 5.5 million. Over the same period, the average weekly payment increased from £55.56 to £57.04 per week. The number of recipients claiming Income Support for two years or more increased by 46 000 to over 3.3 million at May 1996. The number of one-parent families in receipt of Income Support was 1.14 million.
- In February 1997, the number of Housing Benefit recipients totalled 4.7 million. Of these, 2.8 million were local authority tenants and 1.9 million were private or housing association tenants. Over the year to May 1996, the average payment increased from £39.60 to £41.58 per week.
- In February 1997, the number of Council Tax Benefit recipients was 5.6 million. The average weekly payment in May 1996 was £7.28, compared with £6.71 per week in May 1995.
- The number of retirement pensioners rose to 10.56 million in September 1996, compared with 10.43 million the previous September. In September 1996, the average amount of pension in payment was £70.79 per week for men and £51.82 per week for women.
- The number of recipients of Jobseeker's Allowance (JSA) at November 1996 was 1.8 million. Of these, 1.3 million people were in receipt of Income Based JSA, 0.3 million received Contributory JSA. A further 42 000 received both and 159 000 received neither.

The new Secretary of State, Harriet Harman, outlined her plans for change, first in June 1997, in a letter to her 94 000 staff:

> my ministerial colleagues and I . . . are clear about our goals and want you to know what they are. Our objective is to reduce poverty and welfare dependency and promote work incentives. We want to develop a vibrant system that supports work, savings and honesty. . . . Work is the best form of welfare for people of working age. State expenditure should focus on those who cannot make provision. We must be vigilant in tackling fraud and ensuring value for taxpayers' money. Outdated procedures can discourage people from claiming and frustrate you, the staff, who want to help them . . . We need better, simpler, more efficient services to clients that will result in greater public support for the social security system.

Then, in July 1997, in the House of Commons second reading debate on the Social Security Bill:

> one of the key challenges that we face in reforming welfare is to build a modern, fair and efficient welfare service that commands the support of everyone in our

society . . . The way that social security is delivered at the moment is resented by the public who pay for it, the clients who use it, and the staff who run it . . . For many people, the current system is fragmented, reactive, inflexible and confusing. They are irritated by having to provide the same information over and over again to different parts of the same organisation. They are frustrated that nobody brings together all of the help and advice they need in one place. They are bewildered by the complexity involved in claiming benefit and sorting out child maintenance. And they are exasperated by the length of time that they have to wait for bureaucratic reviews and appeals . . . I am determined to overhaul the service that we have inherited. I want to develop a modern integrated system that is simpler, streamlined and more efficient . . . This Bill lays the foundations for transforming the delivery of welfare in this country. It marks the beginning of the end of the old system that has served to exclude people from the rest of society, writing them off to a life on benefit and ignoring their aspirations and responsibilities. And the beginning of a new modern service that actively helps people to meet their responsibilities to themselves and their families.

The bill received its second reading on 22 July. It contains measures which are designed:

- to improve the way decisions are made;
- to make the system more transparent and accessible;
- to enable improved appeal arrangements;
- to reduce the time taken to hear appeals;
- to change the structure of the appeal body in order to increase accountability for the administration of the appeals process, and to ensure the right expertise is applied to each case. This involves creating a unified 'Appeal Tribunal' and transferring to it the functions of social security appeal tribunals, medical appeal tribunals, disability appeal tribunals, child support appeal tribunals and vaccine damage tribunals;
- to close loopholes which allow people to avoid paying National Insurance contributions and cut red tape to help business through more alignment between the rules on tax and National Insurance contributions.

These are plans on a grand scale. If they are implemented, the lifetime of this Parliament may not be enough to assess their success.

Indicative questions

1 Read the following and then answer the questions, using the extract and any other information at your disposal.

John Brown (35) and Mary Brown (33) have three children aged 13, 11 and 10. John has just lost his job because he refused to consider a move to the new factory on the other side of town. Mary works part-time (15 hours per week) for 'Help the Aged', earning £30 per week. John will now act as a voluntary driver for the 'Help the Aged' Day Centre, three days a week.

(a) What benefits may John be entitled to?   (*2 marks*)

(b) What effect may the following have on John's claim for benefit?

   (i) his refusal to accept a job transfer   (*2 marks*)

       (ii) his decision to do voluntary work three days a week   (*2 marks*)

       (iii) Mary's wage   (*2 marks*)

  (c) (i) Where would John go for help and advice about the way in which he has been assessed for benefit?   (*2 marks*)

      (ii) Briefly outline the changes in the benefit scheme that were made in 1988 which are most likely to affect John.   (*2 marks*)

  (d) 'People who have lost their jobs have earned their right to benefits when they were previously employed.' How do you earn the right to receive benefits when you are unemployed? How far do you think that the present benefit system adequately meets the needs of the unemployed?   (*8 marks*)

NEAB

2 (a) What rights are there to social welfare benefits?

     How might these rights be enforced?   (*10 marks*)

  (b) To what extent does the law provide for those in society who are unable to provide for themselves and their families?

     What changes and improvements would you make to the social welfare provision in this country? Why would you make them?   (*15 marks*)

NEAB

CHAPTER 20

The National Health Service

BACKGROUND

Count the reasons for keeping people healthy. It is not just a matter of sentiment and sympathy. There are essential economic reasons for keeping the workforce at the workplace. It costs money to treat them, and it costs the product of the effort they could be putting in elsewhere. Furthermore, we need that product to pay for the treatment of those who are too young, too old or just too sick to work.

The National Health Service is a huge organisation employing around 1 million people—both full and part time. The range of occupations and professions found within the NHS is probably the widest of any organisation worldwide—over 5000 combinations of grades and areas of work. Every year there are over 8 million hospital in-patients. A total of 485 million prescription items were dispensed in 1996.

Britain's NHS dates back to the National Health Service Act in 1946—but the idea is much older. In the Middle Ages some religious orders made special provision for the sick and needy. The Poor Law Act of 1601 imposed duties to care for them on to the local authorities. Public health became a central concern with the growth of urbanisation in the early 19th century, as shown in the Public Health Act 1848. This statute was particularly concerned with cleaning up the water supply—a matter not far from our minds in the 1990s! Local authority medical officers of health appeared in 1875. There followed a concerted attack on certain infectious diseases such as typhoid and cholera.

However, the move from public health to matters of private care came in the 20th century. Swift advances were made in medical science and education. Medical treatment became more widely available and a school medical service was set up in 1907. Four years later, under the National Insurance Act 1911, a compulsory health insurance scheme was set up. This provided a fee for every doctor for every patient on their lists, and free medical treatment for them all. There were exclusions—dependants of the sick and those above a (low) income limit. Hospital treatment was also outside the scheme. Furthermore, hospital provision was patchy. Poor Law Infirmaries had been taken over (and were often underfunded) by local authorities.

They operated a system parallel to the voluntary sector, which was itself reliant on unreliable charity contributions. Furthermore, there was considerable inconsistency in the coverage of these hospitals across the country.

In 1942 the Beveridge Report started an unstoppable wave towards reform. There was to be a National Health Service. It was to be free at the point of use, and available wherever it was needed. In other words there were to be no economic barriers to health. This was the message of the National Health Service Act 1946.

As a result the local authority and voluntary hospitals were taken over centrally and administered by regional hospital boards, which answered directly to government. Teaching hospitals were treated apart—they were to be run by Boards of Governors, responsible to the government. Family doctors, dentists and opticians were to be administered by local executive councils (containing representation from central and local government as well as the professions) while local authorities retained responsibility for the maternity, child health and immunisation departments.

Considerable re-organisation followed in 1974. Services were integrated under new health authorities. Community services, including the ambulance and school health services, were removed from local authorities, although they retained environmental health, personal social services and hospital social work. Fourteen new regional health authorities were set up. In 1994 these were reduced to eight. Beneath them there were 90 area health authorities. These were replaced in 1982 by 200 or so district health authorities. Family health services were administered by family practitioner committees. These were replaced in 1991 by family health service authorities.

Another overall feature of the 1974 venture was the deliberate introduction of professional management systems. This was done with the aim of proper allocation of resources, very much the underlying pull of the 1990 changes. The trends have been clear: a move towards professionalisation of the operation of the service and more cost-effective use of very scarce resources. We are a long way from the local cottage hospital. This is a new, slick, accountable age.

In 1996 the Health Authorities Act 1995 came into force. Regional health authorities have been abolished. District and family health authorities have been merged into a number of single, all-purpose Health Authorities, each responsible for a geographical area. Their main function is to evaluate the health and healthcare needs of the local population, establish a strategy to meet those needs (together with national priorities) and to implement that strategy by purchasing the necessary services. This is the completion of the 'market' within the NHS, a process begun with the National Health Service and Community Care Act 1990, and, as we will see below, a market that is to be disbanded under the policies of the new Government.

The NHS is currently governed by a set of statutes ranging from the National Health Service Act 1977, to the National Health Service and Community Care Act 1990, and to the Health Authorities Act 1995.

These Acts purport to provide for a comprehensive health service in Great Britain. Subject to certain exceptions, the service is available to everyone without limitation and irrespective of National Insurance contributions. This fundamental principle was echoed in the manifesto upon which the Labour Government was elected in 1997. It says:

> if you are ill or injured there will be a national health service there to help; and access to it will be based on need and need alone—not on your ability to pay, or on who your GP happens to be or on where you live.

This may be important now that reviews have been instituted into central and departmental spending.

Complaints of injustice or hardship in consequence of failure or maladministration in the provision of the service are dealt with by the Health Service Commissioner (more commonly referred to as the 'Ombudsman'). He does not deal with complaints about the exercise of clinical judgement or the provision of general practitioner services. Since January 1997, the Commissioner for England has been Michael Buckley. In his first report he revealed that in 1996–97 the Ombudsman received 2219 complaints about the NHS. This is 24 per cent up on the previous year and an all-time record. During the year, the Ombudsman's office completed 238 investigations—another record.

Public interests are represented by Community Health Councils in England and Wales and by Local Health Councils in Scotland. Half of the membership is appointed by local authorities within the district and the other half by voluntary organisations and other interested bodies. They have the power to obtain information and visit hospitals. Their Reports are published and the relevant health authority's responses are published too. They handle general rather than individual complaints, but they do scrutinise individual complaint-handling procedures.

Under the 1990 Act the Secretary of State has established a number of National Health Service Trusts to take over responsibility for the ownership and management of hospitals and/or other establishments or facilities which were previously managed by Regional, District or Special Health Authorities.

Generally the national health service is free. The cost is met partly from National Insurance contributions but mostly from the Exchequer.

However, there are certain circumstances where charges can be made. These include: hospital or emergency treatment of traffic casualties, hospital accommodation supplied to private patients, extra amenities in hospital for NHS patients (such as private rooms), drugs and a variety of appliances, dental treatment, eyesight tests, and so on. Of course there are exemptions available for many of these charges. They are often means-tested.

Special arrangements have been made with the member states of the European Union to enable UK nationals to obtain free or subsidised medical treatment while abroad. Reciprocal arrangements have been made with a long list of other countries too, such as Australia, Norway and the Caicos Islands!

Patient care

Everyone in Great Britain is entitled to be registered with a doctor. Usually the patient has the choice. GPs in England and Wales have contracts with the Health Authority under which they look after their 'list' of patients—perhaps 2000–3000 people. Both the patient and the doctor have the right to have the patient's name removed from a particular doctor's list. That is, you can change your GP if you like. You do not even have to give a reason.

Under the 1990 Act (and various sets of regulations) it is open to general practitioners to apply for recognition as a 'fund holding' practice. This brings in a lump sum to the practice, along with many obligations concerning the management of the money. There are conditions, of course, one of which is that the patient list must be at least 7000 (only 6000 in Scotland).

The doctor must attend patients at the surgery or at their homes 'if the condition of the patient so requires', as the NHS Regulations put it. Anyone who is not staying for more than three months in a district can remain on their own doctor's list and also apply to be treated as a 'temporary resident' by a local doctor. If they have been around for less than 14 days, such as holidaymakers, then the doctor is expected to give 'immediate necessary treatment'. In emergencies patients tend to go to hospital casualty departments anyway.

There is no right to a 'second opinion'. A patient who is not satisfied should change his doctor. If the doctor fails to obtain better advice when unsure, then this could amount to medical negligence. Often, however, a doctor will agree to have a second doctor examine and make a diagnosis if the patient does not like the news.

Obtaining hospital treatment requires a letter of referral from a GP, unless the treatment is obtained from the casualty department or a 'special' clinic (for sexually transmitted diseases), or a family planning or child health clinic. The patient can leave hospital at any time—although if the doctors do not agree that this is a good idea the patient may be asked to sign an undertaking assuming responsibility for the departure and its possible consequences.

On the other hand, a patient who has been detained under the Mental Health Act 1983, can be kept in if they have a 'notifiable' infectious disease, or if they are incapable of taking care of themselves in their present condition. Here a court order may be required.

It is interesting that it is broadly the same categories of people from whom it is not necessary to obtain consent before medical treatment can be administered. All other patients must agree to what, in other circumstances, could amount to an assault. The consent of parents is usually sought before treating those under 16. Here there sometimes arise extraordinary cases where parents refuse to allow treatment for their children on religious and/or philosophical grounds. It is open to the hospital and the local authority to obtain a court order.

There is a confidentiality between a doctor and a patient, including child patients; and including matters such as contraception. Even where this confidentiality could be broken, say by a court, it very rarely is tested.

As to hospital records, medical records and doctor's notes,

however, there is no general right to see them. This has been marginally affected by the Access to Medical Reports Act 1988, which opens to the patient a medical report requested by an insurer or a former, current or prospective employer. In effect the patient has the right to prevent such a report from seeing the light of day at all because it will require his consent. If it is written, he can have his comment attached.

Plans for the future The Labour Government elected in 1997 has plans for significant changes in the NHS. Frank Dobson, Secretary of State for Health, has set them out:

- transferring at least £100m out of the bureaucracy and into patient care, starting with new intensive care facilities for children and screening for women at risk of breast cancer;
- setting up a major initiative to reduce fraud, which is estimated to cost the NHS over £85m a year;
- launching an action plan to make PFI (Private Finance Initiative) work in the NHS, with work on the first hospitals to start immediately after the PFI Bill is approved;
- bringing in Health Action Zones, to get staff at local level working together to improve the public health;
- getting rid of the waste and inefficiency caused by the internal market.

We have already seen action to recoup in full from insurance companies the cost of treating road traffic accidents and also to improve the organisation of services and enhance the quality of care for patients, including, where approriate, by merging NHS Trusts.

These are laudable goals. There is no shortage of spectators monitoring progress!

Indicative questions

1 Everyone has a right to health care, but how would the right to treatment be secured

(a) when a patient is refused treatment by a doctor for being rude to the receptionist? *(2 marks)*

(b) when a patient wants to see a consultant or a specialist in a hospital? *(2 marks)*

NEAB

2 The average family of four will soon pay the equivalent of some £35 a week for the NHS, compared with about £11 a week in 1978. The reforms will help that money go even further. Doctors will be given more responsibility for the resources they use and managers in the local hospitals will be given more freedom to manage.

A service that puts patients first . . . open to all . . . regardless of income.

(*Source:* Department of Health leaflet, 1989)

(a) What rights to health care does a person have? (*7 marks*)

(b) What recent changes have there been in the provision of health care in this country?

To what extent do you think that a person can exercise his or her rights and duties in relation to health care? (*18 marks*)

CHAPTER 21

Aspects of Housing Law

A CLASSIFICATION OF PROPERTY

Property in English law can be divided up (classified) first into real property (sometimes called realty) and personal property (or personalty). Real property is freehold land. To be in 'freehold possession of land' is an approximation in terminology to owning it in such a way as not to have any hindrances upon you in selling it, or leaving it in your will.

All property that is not realty is personal property. This can be sub-divided into chattels real and chattels personal. Chattels real is the term given to leasehold land; chattels personal comprise all other personal property.

To complete the classification, chattels personal can be subdivided. The subdivision is into choses in action and choses in possession. A chose in action is a proprietary interest which can be protected only by taking legal action. This property has no physical existence and yet it might have considerable value. Copyright, for example, has no physical existence (it is incorporeal property), and the only way a copyright owner can assert his ownership formally is by taking legal action. Such property is, therefore, referred to as a chose (or thing) in action. Any other property (e.g. books, pens, bikes) is a 'chose in possession'. Ownership can be asserted without the need to take legal action. You can go and take it back.

In this chapter we are concerned with the types of property interest in land: freehold and leasehold (real property and chattels real). Freeholders and leaseholders are commonly referred to as 'owners'. The intended meaning may be clear, but the term is technically slightly inaccurate. A freehold estate falls short of the outright ownership possible with choses in possession. A leasehold interest is a temporary thing—a week to 999 years A 99-year lease is quite common on a flat for instance. After it has run its time, and perhaps been assigned (this being loosely referred to as sold) to several people during that time, the interest will revert to the freeholder (or his successor) who granted the lease in the first place.

Now, as the 'owner' of land you may feel that you can do as you please with it. Of course this is not so. Although the owner does have the right to do many things with what he owns, others have rights too. It is important to see the whole package of rights together—those of the owner + those of other individuals + those of the community as a whole (exercised on our behalf by a governmental agency such as a planning authority or an Environmental Health Department).

An owner can, for example, live in or let the property, keep, destroy, sell or otherwise dispose of anything on the property, give the property away or leave it in a will, or sell it to anyone. Further, he may protect his interest in the property by objecting to nuisances and trespasses, use the property as he pleases and build on it if he likes.

He may do these things, however, only insofar as they are consistent with the rights that other individuals may have. Their rights include restrictive covenants which may limit and control development and/or change of use, customary rights to graze cattle, or to cut turf. In addition, tenants under leases will have rights defined in their leases, and under certain statutes e.g. the Housing Act 1996; a building society may have the rights given to a mortgagee, including the right to enter into possession and sell the property. Neighbours may have certain rights to light (but not to a view) which may restrict development, and rights to support for their property, which may restrict earthmoving, and, perhaps, a right to pass over the property. These may be statutory rights, such as those provided by the Access to Neighbouring Land Act 1992 and the Parting Walls Act 1996.

The owner will be further restricted in his rights by those of the community as a whole. Common examples of these rights include the controls over planning and the quality of building works, and over cleanliness and hygiene. There are restrictions on changes in the use to which the property is put, and controls over the nature of fuel burnt, the number of people living on the property, and the amount of water that can be abstracted from the land and from rivers running across it. Claims may also be made on the property: rights to treasure trove found there, rights of entry for gas and electricity and other workmen and officials. Ultimately there is even the right compulsorily to buy the land, even if the owner does not wish to sell it!

AFFORDING TO BE A FREEHOLDER OR LEASEHOLDER: MORTGAGES

A mortgage of land is an arrangement whereby a borrower (called the mortgagor) supplies security for money advanced to him by a lender (called the mortgagee). This mortgage gives the mortgagee rights over the land used as security whereby he can recover his money if the mortgagor fails to repay him. These rights include taking possession, sale of the property, the appointment of a receiver (who may use the land so as to make a profit which can be paid to the mortgagee), and foreclosure (termination of the arrangement).

A prospective purchaser usually approaches a building society for the money. If it is prepared to deal with him he will have a choice of arrangements, usually between a repayment mortgage and an endowment mortgage. The better choice depends upon the applicant's individual circumstances. The difference is, broadly, that the repayment mortgage is paid off over a period of years (perhaps twenty-five) in such a way that each payment comprises an element of interest (which attracts tax relief) and an element of the capital sum lent. On the other hand, an endowment mortgage involves two payments: the one to the building society is just to meet the interest liability; the other is to an insurance company, under a policy which matures when the capital sum falls due (again, perhaps in twenty-five years), and when it matures it yields at least that capital sum. Usually the opportunity to extend the term can be given only to payments on a repayment mortgage.

RENTING A HOUSE

In 1900 85 per cent of homes were rented; in 1980 the figure had fallen to 45 per cent, but it was still a substantial proportion. Of rented homes, about 34 per cent are in the private sector (i.e. involving private landlords), and 67 per cent are in the public sector (mostly local authority landlords, although there is a significant number of housing associations in operation too).

The relationship between a landlord and tenant will be governed by both common law and legislation. Indeed the law of landlord and tenant is a minefield of statute and case law. We can look at only the broadest of outlines here.

RENTING IN THE PRIVATE SECTOR

The statutory protection for tenants is usually referred to, rather loosely, as 'the Rent Acts'. Where the Rent Acts apply the tenant is protected from arbitrary eviction and excessive rent. Most people who rent private residential premises are within the Rent Acts although, since the Housing Act 1988 has been in force, this protection has been reduced.

If the tenancy is of a residential dwelling (i.e. it is a flat, house or bedsit, as opposed to a room in a guest house or hotel or an office or garage), *and* if the tenant has exclusive possession of at least part of those premises, and if the rateable value is not huge, *and* the rent is not very small, *and* the premises are not a holiday let, and the tenant is not provided with 'substantial board' (i.e. full meals), *and* the tenancy is not an essential part of the tenant's job, then the tenant is probably within the protection of the Rent Acts. The extent of that protection will vary, as we will see.

If the above conditions are not satisfied then the tenant is probably outside the Rent Acts, but still the landlord will generally be unable to evict him without a court order, and the tenant will be protected by the laws relating to harassment (which we will consider below).

There used to be a trick used by less scrupulous landlords: they called their tenancy agreements 'licences', and gave the impression

```
(1)  T H I S   L E A S E   made the         day of          19

(2)  BETWEEN  ANDREW UNDERSHAFT  of 123 High Street Greentown

     in the County of Wessex Engineer (hereinafter called the

     Lessor which expression where the context admits includes

     the persons for the time being entitled in reversion

     immediately expectant on the term hereby granted) of the

     one part and  PETER SHIRLEY  of 456 Low Street Blanktown

     in the said County of Wessex Clerk (hereinafter called

     the Lessee which expression where the context admits

     includes the persons deriving title under the Lessee) of

(3)  the other part  WITNESSES  as follows

(4)  1 THE Lessor hereby demises unto the Lessee  ALL THAT

     messuage and premises situate on the west side of Uplands

(5)  Road Greentown in the said County of Wessex and known as

     91 Uplands Road aforesaid hereinafter called the property

(6)  TO HOLD  unto the Lessee for the term of twenty-one years

     from the         day of              19    YIELDING

(7)  AND PAYING  therefor during the said term the yearly rent

     of  ONE THOUSAND THREE HUNDRED POUNDS  (£1300) clear of

     all deductions (except as hereinafter mentioned) by equal

     quarterly payments on the usual quarter days in every

     year the first of such payments to be made on the

     day of              next

     2 THE Lessee hereby covenants with the Lessor as

     follows
```

Clause referred to as	Remarks
(1) Date	Date is left blank at time of typing.
(2) Parties	A description of the two persons involved whose names are given in full (in block capitals).
(3) Testatum	This clause often commences with the word 'WITNESSETH'.
(4) Demise	The lessor grants or leases.
(5) Parcels	Gives a full description of the property which is the subject of the document.
(6) Habendum	States the date when the lease commences and for how long it is to continue. It could commence with the words 'TO HAVE AND TO HOLD'.
(7) Reddendum	States what the rent is and when it is to be paid.

Lease: display, identification and explanation of clauses

that they fell outside the Rent Acts. It is now clear (especially since *Street* v. *Mountford* (1985)) that most of these licensees are tenants and are therefore protected. If you are a lodger you are probably a licensee.

As to the variation in protection for those who are tenants: assuming that the tenancy began after 14 August 1974 (when the distinction between furnished and unfurnished premises ceased to be relevant to the extent of protection) and before mid-January 1989, then if the tenant does not share any living accommodation with his landlord, and does not receive 'attendances' (like cleaning or laundry services) and does not get 'board' (meals) then he has full protection. The Housing Act 1988 deregulated the private rented sector, removing rent control for new lettings by private landlords and housing associations. The Act introduced two distinct types of de-regulated tenancy. An assured tenancy allows the tenant to remain in the property unless a court grants the landlord possession under one of the grounds for possession specified in the Act. An assured shorthold tenancy gives the landlord the automatic right to regain possession of the property after six months. To create an assured shorthold tenancy, the landlord had first to serve a notice on the tenant in a prescribed form.

Over 2 million households rent from a private landlord. An estimated 70 per cent of deregulated tenancies are on assured shorthold terms. A number of landlords who intended to let on assured shorthold terms accidentally created full assured tenancies because they were unaware of the requirement to give prior notice in a prescribed form or because they made a simple administrative error in the procedure. However, life has recently become easier for landlords. Changes introduced by the Housing Act 1996 have removed the requirement to give a notice in the prescribed form. The 1996 Act received Royal Assent on 24 July 1996. The provisions on assured tenancies in Part III, Chapter II, ss. 96–104 and Part V, Chapter II, ss. 148–151 which apply to private landlords and housing associations came into force on 28 February 1997. These changes mean that:

- All new tenancies are automatically assured shorthold tenancies unless the parties agree otherwise.
- Landlords (such as housing associations) who wish to create full assured tenancies either have to serve a notice on the tenant or include a statement in the tenancy agreement saying that the tenancy is not a shorthold tenancy.
- Assured shorthold tenancies no longer have to have an initial fixed term of at least six months. The letting may be on a periodic basis from the outset unless the parties agree a fixed term. The fixed term may be for less than six months if both parties agree. However, the landlord is not able to seek a court order for possession before the end of six months unless one of the grounds in Schedule 2 of the Housing Act 1988 applies.
- New assured shorthold tenants are able to refer their rent to a Rent Assessment Committee for a determination of a reasonable rent only during the first six months of the tenancy rather than during the full initial fixed term of the tenancy.

- The amount of rent which must be owing under the mandatory ground for possession for rent arrears—both when the landllord applies for possession and at the time of the court hearing—has been reduced from thirteen weeks or three months to eight weeks or two months.
- Landlords are required to provide tenants, on request, with a written statement of the main details of the tenancy agreement where there is no existing written agreement or statement.
- It is now quicker and easier to evict anti-social tenants who are causing a nuisance to other people in the locality.

It is never easy to evict a tenant. No one can be evicted without a court order. Sometimes it is easier to get one than at other times. If the tenant is not covered by the Rent Acts an order is quite easy to obtain—but it takes time and it may be suspended for (for example) twenty-eight days. If the tenant is protected by the Rent Acts—fully—then he has a long term security from eviction. There must be serious breach of the agreement, or one of a few special cases must be made. A tenant with less than full Rent Act protection can still expect the court to give him time to find alternative accommodation before giving effect to the order. A landlord can ask for an eviction order where the tenant is in rent arrears or has sublet without consent, or has damaged or altered the premises, or has been a nuisance to neighbours, or has used the premises illegally (and perhaps been convicted of a crime in this connection), or where there has been another serious breach of the tenancy or where the landlord has alternative accommodation for the tenant.

In each case the court must be satisfied that the eviction would be reasonable in all the circumstances of the case. This need not be shown if the landlord is an owner-occupier or a member of the armed forces and wants to come home, or where the premises are a holiday home, or where the tenancy is shorthold.

Of course, before a tenancy can be ended, by either party, whether or not a court order is later required to obtain possession of the premises, a proper notice to quit must be issued by the landlord. If the tenant gives less notice than he should, this gives the landlord the right to rent for the extra period, subject to his obligation to mitigate his loss (i.e. he must try to relet), but landlords do not often pursue such rights. They just refuse to repay deposits.

As to the landlord's notice to quit, it must be given in the correct form or it will be ineffective and any court action will be dismissed until a proper notice has been served, and the necessary period of notice has expired. Some stationers sell standard form notices.

There are also regulations which require the landlord to add such things as reminders that agencies like Citizens' Advice Bureaux exist to help tenants.

Some landlords are unpleasant people. Harassing a tenant is a criminal offence. It carries a maximum penalty of £5000 fine and/or six months' jail from the magistrates, or an unlimited fine and/or two years' jail from the Crown Court. Despite this apparent seriousness such prosecutions are rare and fines are small The police are very reluctant to act, the local authority prefer conciliation, and a private prosecution by a tenant might involve the tenant paying the landlord's costs if he loses.

Nevertheless, the law exists. The Protection from Eviction Act 1977 s.1(3) says:

> If any person with intent to cause the residential occupier of any premises—
>   (a) to give up the occupation of the premises or any part thereof; or
>   (b) to refrain from exercising any right or pursuing any remedy in respect of the premises or part thereof;
> does acts calculated to interfere with the peace or comfort of the residential occupier or members of his household, or persistently withdraws or witholds services reasonably required for the occupation of the premises as a residence, he shall be guilty of an offence.

So harassment would include locking the tenant out, changing the locks, turning off the gas or electricity, removing slates from the roof, blocking a shared lavatory and/or generally bullying or assaulting the tenant or his family. A tenant subjected to this kind of treatment should report his circumstances to the local authority, and maybe to the police.

THE PUBLIC SECTOR: THE CONTENT OF PROTECTION

About 30 per cent of all homes are rented from the public sector (67 per cent of rented homes). Despite an increasing number of local authority tenants who are seeking to exercise their right to buy, the vast majority still choose to pay rent.

Such tenancies fall outside the protection of the Rent Act 1977, but the Housing Act 1985 has provided something very similar for them: they are called secure tenancies. The 1988 Act has had an effect here too. Nevertheless, the local authority will need a possession order before it can evict. Broadly, the same grounds apply as in the private sector (considered above) but there are additional grounds. These include:

- where the tenant lied his way into council accommodation (e.g. by giving false statements about his circumstances);
- where the tenant was housed in a particular unit as a temporary measure (e.g. pending repairs elsewhere);
- where the house is overcrowded or underpopulated (the council must achieve a proper use of its property);
- where the unit is 'specialised' (e.g. for the elderly or handicapped) and the tenant is not qualified; or
- where the local authority proposes to demolish the site, and has found a suitable alternative.

In every case the court must be satisfied that the grant of the possession order would be reasonable in the circumstances.

An important difference between public and private sector housing is that the rent officer has no power to decide the level of local authority rents. It is a matter of politics and economics.

The Housing Act 1996 provides for local authorities and housing associations the opportunity to create 'introductory' tenancies. They are not compulsory. Their creation will be a matter of local need and politics. They were first seen in the London Borough of Wandsworth and the city of Manchester in February 1997. The idea here is that the tenants are 'on probation' for a year before gaining the full protection given to secure tenants. So the landlord can obtain eviction orders with the right procedure rather than the right 'grounds'. The 1996 Act also helps with existing secure tenants. It:

- strengthens grounds for possession based on nuisance and annoyance, to cover behaviour within the locality of the tenant's property and also the behaviour of visitors to the property;
- makes it possible for a landlord to use professional witnesses in court instead of calling the victim of anti-social behaviour to give evidence;
- makes it possible for a landlord to evict nuisance tenants, lodgers or visitors who have been convicted of an arrestable offence in the locality of the dwelling;
- speeds up the repossession process by allowing proceedings against a tenant to begin as soon as a notice for possession has been issued, rather than waiting 28 days (in case of local authorities) or two weeks (for other social and private sector landlords);
- allows the landlord to dispense with the issuing of the notice of possession where the court thinks it just and equitable;
- provides a new ground for eviction where a partner has fled the home because of violence or threatened violence.

Indicative questions

1 Ahmed is looking for a flat and has found one which the landlord is prepared to let on a shorthold tenancy.

(a) Explain what right Ahmed would have under this type of tenancy

    (i) with regard to the rent he pays, *(1 mark)*

    (ii) to protection from eviction. *(1 mark)*

(b) What would be the disadvantages of Ahmed's position? *(2 marks)*

NEAB

2 Read the following extracts from the housing booklet 'Regulated Tenancies' and answer the questions which follow.

A

Most lettings by non-resident private landlords will create a regulated tenancy.

A regulated tenant has important rights concerning the amount of rent that can be charged and security of tenure.

B

A fair rent is assessed by a rent officer and recorded in the local rent register which is maintained by the rent officer and is available for public inspection.

C

Security of tenure: the landlord must obtain a possession order from the courts before the tenant can be made to leave.

(a) Briefly explain the following from the above extracts.

    (i) 'regulated tenancy' (Extract A)   *(1 mark)*

    (ii) 'rent register' (Extract B)   *(1 mark)*

(b) If you were a regulated tenant and thought you were paying too much rent, how would you go about having a fair rent fixed?

    What is taken into account in making the decision?   *(8 marks)*

(c) If you were a landlord of a regulated tenancy and wanted to re-possess your property, what legal steps would you have to take to have the tenants moved out?   *(6 marks)*

(d) How far do you think the balance of rights and duties between landlords and tenants is fair? What changes, if any, would you make to improve the situation?   *(8 marks)*

NEAB

3 Study this extract and then answer questions (a) to (e) which follow.

Sweeping reforms are needed in landlord and tenant legislation because existing laws are unduly complicated leaving tenants unaware of their legal rights, the Law Commission said yesterday. Although the report is regarded by the Commission as preliminary it suggests that some forms of leases for houses and flats should be banned.

(Adapted from *The Guardian*, 29 May 1987)

(a) What is a tenant?   *(2 marks)*

(b) What is the definition of a lease?   *(4 marks)*

(c) Explain the rights which a landlord has over property which has been leased to another.   *(4 marks)*

(d) What obligations are owed by a tenant of property as regards visitors?   *(5 marks)*

4 Read the following extracts on **HOUSING** and answer the questions that follow using the information in the extracts and any other information you may have to help you.

Extract A

Protection from eviction

If you have your own room, or share a house or flat with others, and your landlord lives at a completely different address, you may be fully protected by the Housing Acts.

If you are a tenant, your landlord cannot get you out unless a County Court is satisfied that one of the grounds for possession applies in your case.

Before the landlord can go to court, the tenant has to be given a written notice to quit.

You do not have to leave when it ends. The County Court decides, NOT the landlord. You will have the right to attend the court hearing and put your side of the case.

You may qualify for legal aid to pay some or all of a solicitor's bill.

So, if you are asked to leave your home, STAY PUT and GET ADVICE right away.

(*Source:* extract from a Housing leaflet)

Extract B

Harassment

If your landlord harasses you in any way or tries to force you to leave your home, you can do something about it.

Harassment and illegal eviction are criminal offences and your local council can take action on your behalf.

Extract C

Andrew is renting a one-bedroom flat in the centre of town. Recently he complained to his landlord about the house being in a poor state of repair. Today he returned home from work to find his belongings stacked in the garden and the locks changed.

Pinned to the front door was a note from his landlord. It said, "You no longer have any right to occupy these premises."

(a) Read Extracts A and B.

    What do you understand by the following?
    (i) Notice to quit
    (ii) Grounds for possession
    (iii) Harassment

Look at all Extracts.

(b) What steps should the landlord have taken to make his actions legal?

(c) What action can Andrew take?

(d) It is said that recent changes in the law have given landlords too many rights and tenants not enough.

    How far do you think this is the case?

NEAB

CHAPTER 22

The Motorist and the Law

BEFORE YOU DRIVE AWAY

Having scraped together the money for your 'set of wheels', be it a moped, a motorbike or a car, you cannot just hit the road. The vehicle must be registered and licensed. Your name, as the 'keeper', must be entered onto the 'log book' (vehicle registration document), you must have a valid driving licence of one sort or another, you must have at least third party insurance cover and, if the vehicle is three years old or more, you must have an MOT certificate for it (it is still a Ministry of Transport certificate, even though the Ministry was replaced by the Department of Transport years ago).

The registration and licensing of vehicles is handled by the Driver and Vehicle Licensing Agency (DVLA) Swansea. Your vehicle needs both before you can drive it on a public road. If you bought it secondhand then you need to send the change of 'registered keeper' to DVLA. The 'log book' will be rewritten to include you and the details of the 'previous recorded keeper', the date of the last change, and the number of previous keepers—along with all the details about the vehicle. There will be a plate (moped or motorbike) or set of two plates (car) which carry the registration number allocated to the vehicle by the DVLA. These must be displayed. They can be matched to you by police computers. An excise licence must also be paid for and displayed. Without a 'tax disc' you cannot even park on a public road and there is no escape in saying that you do not drive the vehicle. Furthermore, in August 1997, a new scheme was launched to encourage those who might have felt reluctant to buy tax disks. It seems that during 1996/97 the loss of revenue from Vehicle Excise Duty (VED) was around £175 million. So your vehicle could now be wheel-clamped and impounded. This scheme started in the 33 London boroughs and will roll out across the country. Contract clamping teams will patrol the streets looking for vehicles that are not properly taxed.

Motorists will have to pay a fee of £68 to release the wheel clamp, or a £135 impounding fee plus £12 per day storage if the vehicle remains unclaimed for more than 24 hours. In addition, offenders must produce a current tax disc or a surety payment against obtaining one. The surety is forfeit if no licence is produced within fourteen days. Vehicles left unclaimed after five weeks will be crushed or sold by auction. Evaders will also face prosecution, with a maximum fine of £1000 for a car or motorcycle, and up to £25 000 for a heavy goods vehicle.

The Minister for Roads, Baroness Hayman, said:

> being caught in this clamp-down will certainly hit the pockets of road tax dodgers much harder than the cost of a vehicle excise licence. Honest motorists are fed up with seeing the hard core who continually evade paying their road tax . . . We are out to deter the evader with the threat of inconvenience, large fines and prosecution. We will not be penalising those whose tax disc has fallen off the windscreen or are a few days late renewing their tax. Law abiding motorists have nothing to fear.

As the driver, you need to be licensed too. You can obtain a driving licence for a moped at sixteen, but you need to be seventeen for a motorbike or a car. You will start with a provisional licence. This lasts until you pass your test and apply for a full licence and that will normally last until you are 70. This does not apply to a motorbike provisional licence which lasts for only two years. If you have not passed a 'test of competence' (after a course of training) and then passed the two-part driving test for a motorbike licence then you cannot have another provisional licence for a year (i.e. you have two years on and one year off). These changes were brought about because of the large number of deaths and serious injuries amongst young motorbikers. At the same time the maximum size of machine you can drive on a provisional licence was reduced from 250 cc to 125 cc. Of course, all provisional licence holders are 'learner' drivers and must display 'L' plates. You must sign your licence and carry it with you when you drive, or be prepared to produce it in person at a police station within seven days of being asked by a policeman.

Having passed your driving test you now step into the light cast by the Road Traffic (New Drivers) Act 1995 which came into force in June 1997. This means that drivers who tot up six or more penalty points on their licence within two years of passing their driving test will be forced to become learners again. The two-year 'probationary period' will begin on the day the first driving test is passed.

Should they 'score six' they will have to display 'L' plates once more and be accompanied by an experienced driver until they re-pass both the theory test and practical driving test. It seems that road accidents among learner drivers are rare but, once having passed the test, new drivers are among the highest risk groups. In a large-scale survey by the Transport Research Laboratory, 42 per cent of drivers who had received a fixed penalty notice or summons, for an offence in the first year after passing the test, had been involved in an accident, compared with 18 per cent of those who had not offended. In the second and third year the proportion of 'offenders' involved in accidents remained about twice that of the other group. So, as Baroness Hayman, the Road Safety Minister, said:

> six points on a new driving licence will be the road back to 'L'. The first months of a person's driving career are by far the most dangerous. Those who ignore their

training and drive irresponsibly will now risk losing their full driving licences far more quickly. I hope that the possibility of losing a licence that they have worked hard for will persuade new drivers to act more responsibly behind the wheel, reducing the risk to themselves and other road users.

You must also be insured. It is the use of the vehicle which must be covered. Another driver may be covered to drive your vehicle, and you may be covered to drive his. In each case the very least the law requires is that any 'third party' be insured; you and your insurer are the first and second parties, so this basic cover only extends to the car or the person you hit. You are not covered. A better, but more expensive, alternative is to have 'comprehensive' cover. (In fact the very least that the law requires is that third party personal injuries be covered—not necessarily property—although most basic policies include third party property damage.)

When injuries are sustained to a person or property and the driver was uninsured or was one of those so-called 'hit and run' people, the injured party is left to sue for compensation someone who, probably, could not afford to insure or who did not stop to give his name. While these are criminal offences that does not compensate the victim. The insurers have together set up an organisation called the Motor Insurers' Bureau which, in defined circumstances, will see to it that the basic minimum cover is paid and a restricted amount of property cover is given.

The vehicle, on its third birthday (from first registration—not tax), needs an MOT certificate. The test is more extensive than it was but cannot be regarded as any real form of consumer protection for those who buy secondhand. It just shows that the tests were satisfied when applied. It is no guarantee of quality. (No more is the name of the 'registered keeper' on the log book necessarily the name of the true owner.)

Apart from the need to subject the vehicle to the prescribed MOT test, it must also conform to the Construction and Use Regulations. It is a crime to use a vehicle which does not meet these requirements, or to cause or permit such use. They are very complicated.

ON THE ROAD

There is an enormous range of offences that can be committed by motorists. There is also a wide range of penalties that the courts can impose. At the one end the driver can plead guilty by post (e.g. for exceeding the speed limit for the first time), and at the other end of the range there is an automatic disqualification for at least a year (e.g. for drunken driving).

Most motoring offences result in your licence being endorsed. Exceptions to this include parking and lack of a tax disc (vehicles excise licence). Where the court sees no special reason for not endorsing your licence it will usually go on to awarding points for the offence. As a general rule, once you have collected twelve points in a three-year period you are liable to be disqualified for at least six months. The number of points each offence attracts varies. For instance, speeding carries three points and dangerous driving between three and eleven. If you have already been disqualified for six months in the last three years the minimum is increased to a year; if you have been disqualified more than once in the past three years then the minimum disqualification is two years. This system is often called 'totting-up'.

This idea of stepping up the penalties in line with the seriousness of a course of behaviour is seen again in the extension of the 'fixed penalty' scheme which used to apply only to stationary offences. The levels of the penalties increase if the recipient of the fixed penalty notice does not pay up. The idea behind the scheme is to save time. The courts are clogged enough already, and any change in procedure which can relieve that backlog of work is to be welcomed.

There are over six million 'less serious' motoring offences dealt with by the police each year. If a motorist receives a fixed penalty notice—and they may be given for a wide range of offences (well over 200), then he has the choice of either paying up or contesting the case in court, and he has twenty-eight days to make up his mind. If he does nothing then the penalty will increase by half as much again and this amount will be enforced as an unpaid fine. The police have the choice of giving a warning, giving a fixed penalty notice, or prosecuting in the normal way. Only the police have the choice to issue this range of notices. Where the offence is endorsable the penalty ticket is yellow. Otherwise the ticket is white, and can also be issued by a traffic warden. Once the police officer has decided to issue a yellow notice he will ask to see the motorist's driving licence. This is to check whether there are already penalty points on it. If there are, and with those for the current offence, they add up to twelve or more then the offence is reported for prosecution. The motorist will have to attend at the court because nobody is disqualified in his absence. If there are not enough points to warrant this action, then the ticket will be issued, and the driver will be asked to hand over his licence (or to present it at a police station within seven days).

A driver can therefore be disqualified by the 'totting up' process (mentioned above). He can also lose his licence for a single offence if it is serious enough. Drunken driving and causing death by dangerous driving are the most famous examples. Both carry an automatic ban (except in the rarest of cases, such as the 'laced drinks' example).

'Drunken driving' means driving or attempting to drive a motor vehicle on a road or other public place with a proportion of alcohol in the blood which, as ascertained by a laboratory test, exceeds the prescribed limit at the time the laboratory specimen was produced. There are several ways of measuring the alcohol level: the limits are 80 milligrams of alcohol in 100 millilitres of blood, or 107 milligrams of alcohol in 100 millilitres of urine, or 35 micrograms of alcohol in 100 millilitres of breath. This last one is the usual one used, in connection with the use of a machine called an intoximeter. It has been described as a little like blowing into a transistor radio.

Under the Road Traffic Act 1991 there is an offence of causing death by dangerous driving when under the influence of drink or drugs. It provides that an offence is committed where a person causes the death of another person by driving a mechanically propelled vehicle on a road or other public place without due care and attention, or without reasonable consideration for other persons using the road or place—and he is, at the time when he is driving, unfit to drive through drink or drugs, or he has consumed so much alcohol that the proportion of it in his breath, blood or urine exceeds the prescribed limit, or if he fails to provide a properly-requested sample of breath or urine. This offence carries obligatory disqualification for at least a year.

The 1991 Act followed upon an extensive review of the law in this area.

CYCLISTS

Cyclists are road users, and subject to the same laws, except that they cannot be imprisoned or disqualified. They can, however, be fined. There is a set of 'Construction and Use' Regulations which apply specifically to pedal cycles.

It is an offence to ride a cycle on a road (including a bridleway) dangerously or without due care and attention, or without reasonable consideration for others who are using the road.

It is an offence for more people to be carried than the machine was designed for. It is also an offence to promote or participate in unauthorised cycle road racing or speed trials.

Furthermore, there are some laws that apply only to cyclists: for example, those who dismount and walk through red traffic lights are still 'riders', but when crossing at a pedestrian crossing they are 'walking'! There are special rules about parking. Cyclists can ignore yellow line restrictions, but it is an offence to leave a pushbike in a dangerous place, on a footpath or on a traffic clearway. Cyclists can be convicted of being drunk in charge of their bikes and fined for it, but they are not subjected to the breathaliser procedures.

The scale of cycle usage is often underestimated. In the summer of 1996 a statistical report on cycling in Britain was published. It draws together statistics from a range of sources. They were intended to inform debate and enable local authorities to compare cycling in their area with the national picture. Here are a few highlights:

- From 1994 to 1995, there was a slight increase in annual on-road cycle traffic, from 4.4 to 4.5 billion km.
- Cycle traffic fell substantially from 24 billion km in 1949, although there was some revival from the mid 1970s to the mid 1980s. In terms of all road traffic, cycling declined from 37 per cent in 1949 to just 1 per cent in 1995.
- 38 per cent of households in 1993/95 owned a bicycle.
- On average, men do more than three times the annual cycle mileage of women.
- cycle mileage by children fell by more than 40 per cent from 1975/76 to 1993/95.

- In 1993/95, commuting accounted for 47 per cent of cycle mileage for those of working age.
- Cycling is in the top five sporting activities for each age and sex.
- In 1991, 3.4 per cent of males in Great Britain usually cycled to work, compared with 2.4 per cent of females. The three areas with the greatest proportions cycling to work were Cambridge, York and Oxford. In Cambridge, a quarter of men and nearly a third of women cycled to work.
- Of the 117 highway authorities in England and Wales, 48 had no purpose-built cycle ways in 1995. Shropshire had the greatest length of cycle way (130 km), followed by Durham (88 km) and Berkshire (80 km).
- Information and figures on thefts of bicycles are available from the British Crime Survey. In 1993, it is estimated that there were over six bicycle thefts per 100 bicycle owners. This amounted to a total of nearly 600 000 thefts, nearly three times more than were recorded by the police.
- About a third of bicycles stolen had been postcoded. Of these, 17 per cent were returned, compared with 13 per cent of those without coding.

APPENDIX 1

Bibliography

This is a list of more specialised books on the areas we have considered. The publishers are listed too, but not the editions. You should **always** ensure that the law book you are reading is the latest edition. The law changes quickly.

How to Study Law – Bradney et al (Sweet & Maxwell)

Studying Law – Kenny (Butterworths)

Learning the Law – Glanville Williams (Sweet & Maxwell)

How To Use A Law Library – Thomas & Cope (Sweet & Maxwell)

Introduction to Law – Harris (Butterworths)

James' Introduction to English Law – Shears & Stephenson (Butterworths)

General Principles of English Law – Redmond & Shears (Pitman)

The Modern English Legal System – Smith & Bailey (Sweet & Maxwell)

The English Legal System – Walker and Walker (Butterworths)

Smith and Keenan's English Law – Keenan (Pitman)

Introduction to Legal Method – Farrar & Dugdale (Sweet & Maxwell)

The Politics of the Judiciary – Griffiths (Fontana)

Civil & Criminal Procedure – Williams (Sweet & Maxwell)

The New Civil Court in Action – Barnard & Houghton (Butterworths)

Company Law – Farrar (Butterworths)

Partnership Law – Morse (Blackstone)

Freedom, the Individual and the Law – Robertson (Penguin)

Cases and Materials on Civil Liberties – Bailey, Harris & Jones (Butterworths)

Commercial Law – Furmston & Shears (Cavendish)

Commercial Law – Goode (Penguin)

Tort – C D Baker (Sweet & Maxwell)

Tort – Winfield and Jolowicz (Sweet & Maxwell)

The Law of Torts – Street (Butterworths)

Atiyah's Accidents, Compensation and the Law – (Butterworths)

The Law of Contract – Treitel (Sweet & Maxwell)

The Law of Contract – Cheshire, Fifoot and Furmston (Butterworths)

Contract Law in Perspective – Tillotson (Cavendish)

Consumer Law – Leder & Shears (Pitman)

The Consumer, Society and the Law – Borrie and Diamond (Penguin)

Consumer Law and Practice – Lowe and Woodroffe (Sweet & Maxwell)

Criminal Law – Smith and Hogan (Butterworths)

Family Law – Cretney (Sweet & Maxwell)

What to do when Somebody Dies – (Consumers' Association)

Textbook on Succession – Borkowski (Blackstone)

Employment Law – Jefferson (Cavendish)

Bowers on Employment Law – John Bowers (Blackstone)

Modern Employment Law – Whincup (Heinemann)

The Law of Social Security – Ogus, Barendt & Wikeley (Butterworths)

Introduction to Housing Law – Burnett (Cavendish)

Road Traffic Law – McMahon (Blackstone)

APPENDIX 2

Examination Technique

The aim of this chapter is to point out some of the common mistakes made by examination candidates and to try to provide some useful hints on how to approach the examination day and the examination paper itself. All too often candidates' efforts are spoilt by paying insufficient attention to considering how to tackle the examination paper. They have obviously spent considerable time learning the material outlined in the syllabus but then let themselves down by not presenting the information in the correct manner. It is hoped that this chapter will help to avoid such disappointment.

Common mistakes made by examination candidates

1 Failing to answer the right number of questions, either because they answer too few or too many questions. They do not check the rubric and so, for example, fail to complete the required number of questions from different sections of the examination paper.

2 Writing the conclusion to an answer before the main part of the answer has been completed. Or writing too short an answer so that no part or particular point is properly developed.

3 Answering the question they hoped would be set rather than the question the examiner has actually set. It may be the right topic but the answer bears little relation to the required approach for the particular question.

4 Running out of time so that the paper is not completed or the last answer is very short and incomplete.

5 Too much time spent on the first answer; sometimes over half the examination time has obviously been spent on this answer to the detriment of the other answers.

6 Writing the question out which is a complete waste of time and earns no marks.

7 Writing social or general answers rather than answers that have a mainly legal content. The social or general context in which the law operates can be dealt with but should not dominate the answer.

8 Poor handwriting so the examiner cannot even read the answers.

The examination itself

1 Make sure you arrive in good time for the examination. If you arrive late and hot and bothered you have got to waste time settling yourself down.

2 Make sure you have everything you need, pens, pencils, rulers, etc. If you need a lucky mascot take it with you

3 Make sure the desk is comfortable, i.e. not too close to a radiator or in hot sun. If it isn't level do something about it before the examination begins.

4 Make sure you have the correct answer book and that you have filled in your name, examination number and centre number correctly.

5 Read through the examination paper carefully and slowly at least twice before you decide which questions you are going to answer. Check the number of questions you need to answer.

6 Select the questions you are going to answer and tick them on the examination paper. If you don't think you can do the required number at first, don't panic, just choose as your last question one you at least recognise and can attempt to answer.

7 Use the first few minutes of the examination to make brief notes on each of the questions you are going to answer. This will be helpful to you if you are running short of time at the end of the examination and trying to write and think quickly. It should help you to get at least the main points of an answer down in a reasonable order.

8 Plan how much time you can spend on each answer and try to keep to your time schedule. If the examination paper is in sections make sure you answer questions from the sections you have been taught. It is easy to become confused in the heat of the moment and think you do not recognise the questions because they relate to parts of the syllabus on which you have received no instruction.

9 Write the answer to the question you know best first to calm your nerves and give yourself confidence. Make sure you answer the right number of questions

by ticking them again on the paper as you complete them. If you are short of time write your last answer in a coherent note form making sure you bring out the important points relevant to the question.

10 If possible leave yourself enough time at the end of the examination to check your answers quickly. If you have made notes and jottings that you don't want marked, cross them out neatly.

11 If you have used any supplementary answer sheets make sure your name is on them, number them and tie them into the main answer book.

Answering examination questions

1 The most important principle is to read the question carefully; each word is important. This should set you off on the right track.

2 Note the plaintiff and defendant, who is to be advised about what? Identify the areas of law involved and pick out the main facts. Make a note of any likely defences and remedies.

3 Try to write a short introductory paragraph. For example, a short history of the law in that area or something that sets the law in context.

4 Structure your answer so that you work through in a logical way. State the principle of law involved at each step and try to support it either by reference to a decided case or an example. Make sure, e.g. that you have stated and explained all the elements of a tort or defined the appropriate area of contract or criminal law.

5 Try to use accurate legal phrases and expressions, e.g.: discharge of duty: rescission of contract: void and voidable contracts.

6 Use cases to illustrate your points of legal principle whenever possible. Try to put the name of the case, but if you cannot remember it don't worry. Indicate the case you mean by a brief reference to the facts. Concentrate on the legal principle involved in the case.

7 The argument of the legal points involved is more important than the answer itself. Don't worry if you don't know the answer but make sure you have argued the point from both the plaintiff's and the defendant's point of view.

8 Try to write a short concluding paragraph in which you sum up the main points and attempt to answer the question which you were being asked.

9 Practise trying to write answers in the allotted time under examination conditions prior to the examination itself. Timing answers is vitally important and will help to improve your confidence as well as your technique. Try and obtain past examination papers to help you become familiar with the type of questions you are likely to face in the real examination.

10 Try to be as up to date as possible in the law you include in your answers, e.g. watch the newspapers for new and relevant statutes and cases.

Answering problem questions

1 The aim of a problem question is to encourage the candidate to explain the law and then apply it to a set of hypothetical facts to provide a legal answer.

2 All too often candidates do not use the problem questions to display their knowledge, leave too much unsaid or do not expand a point. You should assume the examiner knows nothing of the topic.

3 Method and reasoning are more important than the answer or conclusion reached. It is therefore very important to explain fully the steps by which the answer was arrived at.

4 It is necessary to identify the relevant areas of law involved and the plaintiff and defendant. If the rubric states you are to advise a particular party then you will need to advise 'for' and 'against'. Or the rubric may say 'discuss' when you will need to be certain you have identified all potential plaintiffs and defendants and possible areas of law involved.

5 Make sure you explain all legal points fully, e.g. the elements of a tort or what constitutes acceptance in contract. Definitions are useful starting points. Try to support each element or legal point with authority, i.e. an appropriate case that illustrates the point involved.

6 When quoting a case make sure it is identified either by names or facts and then concentrate on explaining the principle on which the decision is based.

7 The most important part of an answer to a problem question is the application of the law to the hypothetical facts. Do not leave this until the end of the answer; try to apply the law to the appropriate facts as each stage of the answer is completed. For example if the problem is to do with negligence use the facts to illustrate: (i) why a duty of care is owed; (ii) what constitutes the breach; and (iii) what constitutes the damage that results.

8 Work your way systematically and logically through the facts. For example don't refer to defences until you have established the appropriate tort or breach of contract. Make sure you are not advising someone to sue who has suffered no damage.

9 If possible, try to round off your answer by drawing a conclusion.

Answering essay questions

1 Read the essay question very carefully and make sure you know what you are being asked to discuss.

2 Use an opening paragraph or introduction to set the scene for the approach you are going to take in the answer. It may be useful at this stage to identify the areas of law you will be referring to.

3 Try to develop your answer logically. If possible deal with a point completely before moving on to the next; it always looks 'bitty' if you have to come back to a point later in the answer.

4 Use appropriate case law to illustrate the legal points you are making in your answer in exactly the same way as with the answers to problem questions.

5 Try to include a quotation or comment from reading you have done which relates to the answer. If possible include your own comments and thoughts on the matter under discussion. Try to give as balanced a view as possible of any arguments which may be relevant. If there have been recent developments or new statutory provisions which may not be in the text books but which you know about, include a reference to them.

6 Keep checking that your answer is relevant, that you are not straying off the point. Try not to lapse into 'social' answers or too much generality; remember it is a law examination paper and requires legal answers.

7 Before you write the conclusion read the question again. Use the last paragraph to bring together your main arguments and to emphasise the points which you feel answer the question most satisfactorily. Make sure you finish the answer in such a way that the examiner is in no doubt that you understand the question and have really tried to discuss the issues and come to an appropriate conclusion.

8 If it is an essay question that requires a large amount of factual information make sure that you include as much explanation and detail as possible on each of the areas that you discuss. If you can remember most of the areas that you feel are relevant then try to state them in the introduction to the answer so that you create a check-list or structure for the rest of the answer. Cases, examples or section numbers of statutes will again be very important and should be used whenever possible.

Answering short answer questions

1 Check how many parts you have to answer in each question. The number of marks given for each part will indicate how much time you should spend on each part. Questions carrying only a small number of marks will require only brief answers; perhaps one word or one sentence.

2 If you cannot do part of a question after thinking about it then move on to answer the parts you do know. Do not waste time worrying about parts of answers you cannot complete.

3 Where an answer has higher marks make sure you write in clear accurate sentences explaining the principles or terms used and supporting your answers with reference to cases or statutes. Keep checking that the answer you are giving is relevant and really is answering the question. If you cannot remember any relevant authority at least give a good explanation using examples or other relevant items of topical interest. At the end of the answer it might be acceptable to include your own views or opinions on the subject.

Answering 'stimulus' questions

1 Read the stimulus material carefully and identify the part of the syllabus to which it relates.

2 The number of marks given for each part of the question will indicate how much time you should spend on each part.

3 In your answer be certain to identify and explain the relevant areas of law and explain how it applies with cases, statutes or examples.

4 It may be appropriate at the end of the answer to include your own comments and ideas but make sure they are always relevant to the question and relate to the legal material you have included in your answer.

Grammar, punctuation and spelling

Whatever type of question you are answering, correct grammar, punctuation and spelling are always important.

APPENDIX 3

Course Work

Nearly all GCSE examination boards require candidates to complete course work as part of the examination. With most boards it counts for 20 per cent of the final mark.

When approaching course work it is important to follow some basic rules:

1 Make sure you know what you are required to do to complete the course work satisfactorily. For example, how long should the work be? There are no extra marks for exceeding the stated length. When must it be submitted and in what form?

2 Choose a topic that interests you and discuss it with your teacher.

3 Write a plan of how you propose to approach the topic. What are you trying to find out and why? Your plan should set out your aims and objectives and where you propose to look for your material.

4 Try to be original in your approach, look for a different angle or slant on the facts.

5 Think about the best way to gather the information. There is a whole variety of sources. For example, interviews, surveys, samples, newspaper articles, television and radio programmes, leaflets and fact sheets, books and magazines. For some methods of data collection you may need to obtain prior permission or approval. For example, for interviews or surveys.

6 Never just copy information from another source. Try to put it into your own words. If you use material from books or magazines make sure you give the source in an appendix at the end of your work.

7 Think about the best way of presenting your information. Sometimes, graphs, bar charts and pie charts say things more clearly than words. If you do use diagrams or charts, make sure you label them and comment on their meaning in the text. If you take photographs, make sure you have permission to use them.

8 Course work is designed to test your understanding of material as well as encouraging you to comment on it and draw conclusions. You start your work by summarising the background to your chosen topic. This may involve stating and explaining the law

summarising the facts or setting out the answer. However, most of the marks are awarded for your evaluation of the material you have collected. Make sure your comments are related to the aims and objectives you have set yourself at the start of the work.

9 The most important part of any course work is the conclusions you reach. Make sure you set these out clearly and concisely. It is often helpful if someone else reads your work and asks you questions on it. In that way you will be certain that anyone reading your work understands it in the way you intend.

10 Make sure you present your work in the form required by the examination board and that any necessary forms have been completed. Your work should be clear, tidy and well-presented. Include an indication of the content at the front and at the back include as appendices any extra material or sources of information that you have referred to in the text.

11 Always use correct grammar, punctuation and spelling.

Examples of course work with some suggested sources of information

1 The work of the Magistrates' Court.
(a) Textbooks.
(b) Visits to your local court.
(c) Interviews with the clerk and a magistrate.
(d) Data on the number and type of cases dealt with.
(e) Cuttings from newspapers on types of sentence awarded for crimes committed by adults and juveniles.

2 The importance of insurance.
(a) Definition and meaning of insurance and why people pay for it.
(b) Leaflets showing types of insurance, their cost and conditions.
(c) Comparison of policies on, for example, house insurance from two companies.
(d) Interview with an insurance broker.
(e) An insurance policy and the information required to complete it.

3 Legal capacity.

(a) What the law says about the ages when, for example, young people may marry, vote etc.

(b) Survey of views of young people on the legal limitations on their capacity.

(c) Survey of views of parents on the limitations.

(d) What changes you would make and why.

(e) Draft a short piece of legislation making such a change.

INDEX